ETHNIC POLITICS AFTER COMMUNISM

Ethnic Politics after Communism

Edited by

Zoltan Barany and Robert G. Moser

Cornell University Press
Ithaca and London

Cornell University Press gratefully acknowledges receipt of a University Cooperative Society Subvention Grant awarded by the University of Texas at Austin, which aided in the publication of this book.

First published 2005 by Cornell University Press
First printing, Cornell Paperbacks, 2005

Printed in the United States of America

Library of Congress Cataloging-in-Publication Data
Ethnic politics after communism/edited by Zoltan Barany and Robert G. Moser.
   v. cm.
   Papers originally presented at a conference held at the University of Texas at Austin in Apr. 2003.
   Includes bibliographical references and index.
   ISBN-13: 978-0-8014-4377-0 (cloth : alk. paper)
   ISBN-10: 0-8014-4377-6 (cloth : alk. paper)
   ISBN-13: 978-0-8014-7276-3 (pbk. : alk. paper)
   ISBN-10: 0-8014-7276-8 (pbk. : alk. paper)
   1. Europe, Eastern—Ethnic relations—Political aspects—Congresses. 2. Former Soviet republics—Ethnic relations–Political aspects—Congresses. 3. Ethnic conflict—Europe, Eastern—Congresses. 4. Ethnic conflict—Former Soviet republics—Congresses. 5. Postcommunism—Europe, Eastern—Congresses. 6. Postcommunism—Former Soviet republics—Congresses. I. Barany, Zoltan D. II. Moser, Robert G., 1966–
   DJK26.E84 2005
   305.8'00947—dc22

2005012285

To our uncles:
William B. Barany
János Horváth
the memory of Horváth Zénó

And to
Kenny Moser
Al Grebenick
the memory of Walter Moser

CONTENTS

PREFACE AND ACKNOWLEDGMENTS

Ethnicity is one of the primary political forces in the world. The political predilections of diverse ethnic groups are instrumental to the stability or instability of governments, the vitality of democratic freedoms, and the peacefulness of interstate relations. Two distinct and contradictory perspectives regarding the role of ethnicity and nationalism emerged at the end of the Cold War, one optimistic and one pessimistic. The former drew on ideas of liberal internationalism in predicting an era of international peace (and presumably domestic tranquility) as a by-product of the spread of liberal democracy, whereas the latter envisioned worldwide cultural conflict surrounding insurmountable divisions between antagonistic civilizations. It might be too early to judge which of these perspectives captures the role of nationalism and ethnicity more accurately in the early twenty-first century. Nevertheless, this book is an attempt to take stock of the power of ethnicity in the region—postcommunist Europe and Eurasia—that sparked this debate in the first place.

To make the book coherent and consistent, we decided that we needed to identify key concepts pertinent to ethnic politics on which individual chapters would be based. Our hope was that taken together, the theoretical and empirical explorations of these conceptual areas would yield a more or less comprehensive survey and broad understanding of ethnic politics in the postcommunist world. By definition, then, we were interested in how various aspects of ethnic politics develop and change after communism. We agreed that the following issues were crucial to address: (1) the fall of the Soviet empire and its impact on nationalities and ethnic groups, (2) ethnic identity and culture, (3) ethnic mobilization, (4) ethnic parties and voting, (5) ethnic conflict, (6) ethnic migration, and (7) the impact of normative standards and external institutional actors on national minorities.

Our approach treats ethnicity as both cause and effect within the transitional politics of postcommunist states. We asked the contributors to consider how ethnic forces influenced political outcomes ranging from voting to violence and protest mobilization to language acquisition. Conversely, each chapter demonstrates that political behavior itself has an impact on the forms and strength of ethnic identity. Thus, ethnicity is deemed to be a contested, malleable, and constructed force rather than a static characteristic inherent in the attributes of groups and individuals with a common religion, race, or national origin. The nature of the transition away from communist rule in Eastern Europe and Eurasia brings into focus issues that are germane to ethnic politics around the world. The study of ethnicity in the postcommunist region provides a unique opportunity to examine its pivotal force in the context of the most dramatic changes of the past quarter century.

The sequencing of the chapters is deliberate and follows inductive reasoning. The massive changes in ethnic politics discussed in this book were, to a large extent, set in motion by the fall of the Soviet empire, which in itself was partially caused by ethnic factors. Changes in and the relationship between culture and ethnic identity are critical issues without which the ethnic phenomenon cannot be understood. Ethnic mobilization is the vehicle that allows ethnic groups to enter the political arena to express their interests, register their demands, and gain representation. In the newly democratic societies of Eastern Europe and Eurasia, much of ethnic politics has been played out in the institutional framework of the party system. Voting seldom settles political debates conclusively between ethnic groups: at times differences are expressed in ethnic conflict that may turn violent. One of the fundamental responses of ethnic groups intent on escaping persecution, discrimination, and violence is to move to more hospitable areas. Finally, given the ongoing process of European integration, it is important to understand the norms and the institutions that attempt to uphold and promote them and their impact on minorities residing in postcommunist regions. The individual chapters in this volume correspond to these themes. The conclusions reached regarding the power of ethnicity over these processes and the propensity for violent conflict and extremism are eclectic, containing as many optimistic scenarios as pessimistic ones.

This book is somewhat unusual in that its editors wrote neither the introduction nor the conclusion. After weighing the pros and cons of drafting these sections ourselves, we concurred that asking two prominent scholars to contribute the introduction and the conclusion would benefit the book for two important reasons. First and foremost, the insights of two senior experts on ethnopolitics could not but add fresh perspectives to the volume as a whole. Second, both introductory and concluding sections customarily include assessments of or references to the chapters that make up the bulk of the book. We thought that our long and close "relationship" to the chapters (including to our own, of course) might have inadvertently sown the seeds of partiality. Therefore, obtaining contributions with more objective views appeared to be a superior alternative. Although we did offer Ron Suny and Roger Petersen—who graciously agreed to write these portions of the book—general guidelines of what we were looking for from them, we naturally gave them *carte blanche* regarding their commentary on the chapters.

This book originated in a symposium held at the University of Texas at Austin in April 2003. When we began to think about this endeavor, our principal objective was to entice the leading scholars in the field of ethnic politics to work with us. We were extremely fortunate to secure the participation of our entire "first-choice lineup"—an exceptional group of contributors. They revised papers originally written for the symposium twice: first to respond to the thoughtful and provocative comments and criticisms offered at the meeting by Rogers Brubaker and the other participants; and a second time to take into account the helpful suggestions of anonymous reviewers.

Obviously an enterprise like this needs substantial financial support. We are lucky to work at the University of Texas at Austin, where funding for worthwhile scholarly projects has been attainable with relative ease. Thomas Garza, director of the Center for Russian, East European, and Eurasian Studies; Richard Lariviere, the dean of the College of Liberal Arts; and John Higley, the chairman of the Department of Government, wished us well and provided the resources that made the symposium possible. Numerous UT graduate students, most notably Julie George, donated their time to help us run the meeting. Roger Haydon of Cornell University Press was the only editor we approached with this project; fortunately for us he was interested in it and once again confirmed his reputation as a wise and sure-handed guide of manuscripts.

Thank you all!

ZOLTAN BARANY
ROBERT G. MOSER

Austin, Texas

ETHNIC POLITICS AFTER COMMUNISM

INTRODUCTION

Nation-making among the Ruins of Empire

RONALD GRIGOR SUNY

Because of the weakening of the centralized Soviet state and the ensuing collapse of the Union itself, the study of nation formation, nationalism, ethnic conflict, and, paradoxically, empire, has emerged from the shadows of Sovietology into the bright light of historical and social scientific inquiry. East Central European scholars had long devoted much attention to nation and nationalism, but one can almost precisely date the turn of public and scholarly interest of their "Russianist" colleagues toward the non-Russian peripheries of the USSR to the late 1980s, when overt popular resistance to policies of the Gorbachev government first manifested itself in Kazakhstan (December 1986), Estonia and Lithuania (1987–1988), Azerbaijan and Armenia (February 1988). Even when earlier Moscow-centered scholarship on elite politics and political history had given way in the 1970s to social history and regional politics, the study of the Soviet Union had tended to be almost exclusively about Russians, with Russia standing in for the entire multinational federation. There were always a few hearty scholars, usually émigrés of various nationalities, who insisted on the importance of "the national question," but their contribution seldom received the recognition enjoyed by those who wrote about "Russia proper." The explosion of mass protests in the Caucasus and the Baltic region ended that marginalization, and a new generation of graduate students took advantage of the opportunities to travel to the "borderlands," learn esoteric languages, and work in formerly forbidden archives. Universities now sought historians and political scientists, anthropologists and sociologists able to add the second string of nation-alities or Central Asia or Ukraine to their Russian/Soviet bow.

Shortly before these new investigations (and investments) in non-Russian studies took off, the academic understanding of nations and nationalism had begun a paradigm shift from a positivist, reified idea of the nation as the natural, perennial division of humankind to a more his-toricized, constructivist notion of the nation as a product of human action and imagination—a historical product of the efforts of activists and intel-lectuals, artists and poets, warriors and statesmen. Constructivists argued that the nation as a form of community and the nation-state as a partic-ular kind of polity were products of the modern era, which uniquely brought together groups of people who believed that by virtue of shared cultural characteristics—be it a language, religion, history, or ancestry—they had the right to political self-determination, a piece of the world's real estate, and perhaps a state of their own. The international discourse of the nation, which arose in the early modern period and became nearly universal through the nineteenth and twentieth centuries, legitimized state power as the representative of a purported nation. Culture and pol-itics were merged in a powerful synthesis that linked the affective con-nections to a cultural community with the rational benefits thought to derive from subordination to legitimate authority. The modernist or con-structivist idea of the nation contrasted sharply with the more familiar notion of nationalists (and of many journalists and scholars) that nations were the ancient, primordial, and natural form of human community that existed through time only to emerge in modernity as ubiquitous and uni-versally recognized as legitimate. Ernest Gellner originally invoked the term "sleeping-beauty nations" in a discussion of the primordialist view in which nations are "awakened" by modernity, and I later contrasted the "sleeping beauty view" with the modernist, constructivist "Bride of Frankenstein view" of the nation.[1]

Although the constructivist perspective on what makes a nation grad-ually became dominant in the Western academy, many of the subjects of research, particularly the nationalists who were themselves actively con-structing new nations and states, deeply resented and actively resisted the challenge to their primordial, naturalized conception of their own national existence. Both official policy and Soviet scholarship had pro-moted a primordialized idea of continuous and bounded nations for several generations, since the heyday of Stalinism, and the thought that the nation might be a kind of fabrication was anathema to beleaguered nation-builders. The inescapable irony is that the very people most consciously and deliberately constructing the new national narratives told themselves that they were merely uncovering what had always been there.

More recently, walls between scholars from east and west have steadily been crumbling, and recognition of the centrality of cultural diversity in considerations of state security, national unity, and democratic development has increased intellectual and political engagement in the larger problem of how to manage multiple ethnicities in a single state. Empires long provided one example, but built as they were on principles of distinction and discrimination and on hierarchies of power and disempowerment, they appeared inappropriate, even archaic, in an age of equality and democratic participation. Nation-states faced another dilemma. Built as they are on legal equality and on the principle that peoples who share a culture have a right to self-determination, statehood, and territory, nation-states confronted the reality that defining who makes up the nation and who is left out becomes paramount. The nation can be defined territorially to include all of its citizens regardless of origin, ethnicity, or religion, or the nation can be defined in ethnocultural terms as belonging only to the people who share the ethnic culture however defined. Most states, notably in Eastern Europe and Eurasia, approach neither of these ideal types but appropriate hybrid forms of ethnonational and civic nationalism. Often constitutions speak in civic nationalist terms, whereas cultural and educational policies tend toward nationalizing practices. By excluding or marginalizing some people on their territory, ethnocultural or ethnoreligious states compromise their democratic credentials, even while claiming to be representative of the nation as a whole. But minorities within the state easily pick up the universal discourse of the nation, and their demands resonate beyond the boundaries of the state—either with co-nationals in other states or with powerful players on the international scene. No nation, even in an age that celebrates sovereignty, is any longer an island to itself.

This volume brings together the problems associated with ethnic politics generally with the specific context of postcommunist transformation. Leninist-style party states had a particular set of effects on the ethnic landscape of Eastern Europe and Eurasia. First, they took ethnicity seriously, despite their antinationalist ideology and internationalist program for class revolution. From their first days in power—and even in earlier discussions and polemics—the Bolsheviks were obsessed with the "national question": how to maintain a great state in the territory of the former Russian empire and to recognize the right to national self-determination for the dozens of peoples who now lived under their rule. Their eventual solution was a federal system that recognized territorialized ethnic cultures and granted them a degree of autonomous power but all under the ultimate authority of the unified Russian Communist Party. The inherent tension between centralized power of a unitary state and the national cultural units of what became a pseudo-federation was contained for several decades by the figure of Stalin, who gave formal recognition to national differences and cultural expression (within strict limits) while building a single Soviet state with a single Soviet people and a shared Soviet culture.

Second, over time class distinctions, which had been fundamental to the original Bolshevik project of building socialism, gave way to a leveling or proletarianization of the whole population, until the principal lines of difference were ethnonational. These differences grew harder and more primordial from the 1930s on, so that in many areas of Soviet life the major indicator of what a person or group was, what opportunities or disadvantages a citizen or a people might have, stemmed from ethnicity rather than from social origin, profession, or even ideological origin. Eventually, the line in Soviet internal passports that identified one's class origins disappeared, while the nationality line remained to the end.

Third, in the Soviet Union ethnicity was tied to territory and to the political structure that governed that territory. The triple connection that bound a specific people to a specific territorial unit created a sense not only of belonging to a particular space but also to ownership of that space. The powerful legacy of possession of a republic or region by the nationality whose name it bore (Armenia for Armenians, Tuva for the Tuvans) became the basis for new independent states in 1991 and the continuity of ethnic republics in the Russian federation.

Over the seventy years of one-party power in the USSR, and the half-century of Communist rule in East Central Europe, politics were deeply ethnicized. As de facto nations developed in the Soviet space with all the trappings of nationhood except sovereignty, Communist states, paradoxically, became among the most nationalist in Europe. But since as in most parts of the world, the boundaries of national cultural community and the official boundaries of the state seldom fully coincided, once the imperial hold of the Soviet Union loosened, ethnic conflicts broke out in several parts of the old empire. Where it was possible to fight against one's people's enemies, where there were mountains (in the Balkans or Caucasus) or help from co-nationals (as in Transnistria), bloody battles were fought. Some countries (Georgia, Azerbaijan, Moldova, Tajikistan, and Yugoslavia) divided or even dissolved in ethnic civil wars. Other states (Czechoslovakia, Hungary, and Romania) peacefully resolved their differences through "velvet divorces" or conciliatory treaties. Still others (Estonia and Latvia) avoided violence despite deep-seated hostilities between majority and minority and gradually moved from hard-line policies toward minorities to more tolerant measures in response to outside pressure.

Postcommunist Eurasia, from East Germany to the Pacific, is a veritable laboratory of experiments, some failed, others successful, of dealing with the seemingly intractable problems of ethnicity. In this volume not only are the dilemmas and failures explored, not only are the successes explained, but projections of future scenarios and suggestions for possible resolutions are also put forth. Haunting the various essays are the important questions of how ethnic diversity and potential conflict can be managed by states still in the transition from state socialism to wherever they might be going. How can justice for minorities be affected in states that intimately identify with a single dominant ethnic nation? How can minorities be effectively included in a democratizing process? Is the future of the region a system of sovereign, democratic states mutually respectful of one another or some form of neo-imperialism in which the former hegemon intervenes under the banner of security? Are the new players in the region, the United States and the European Union, about to replace older forms of intervention with new, ostensibly more benign ones, in the name of international norms of civility and human rights?

The appropriate place to begin answering these questions is in an historical investigation of the older forms of dominance, namely empire. In the opening essay Mark Beissinger takes a hard look at how the experience of the Soviet Union alters our understanding of the concept of empire. Fundamental to any theory of empire is a practice of "nonconsensual control over culturally distinct populations," but the more interesting question is how that nonconsensual control changed over time. Contemporary states are not simply either empires or not empires but "are subject to a politics of becoming empires," which for Beissinger comes down to claims that a state is violating norms of self-determination and state sovereignty that are basic to the contemporary nation-state system. Challenging the most prevalent theories of empire, he argues that an empire is not a particular state structure but a claim about a state's practices and an outcome—that is, a widespread recognition of the truth of that claim. Empire is now recognized as illegitimate rule, and therefore the very labeling of a state as empire in the age of nation-states begins to undermine its legitimacy. Here empire is a subjective valuation of a state: once the Soviet Union was widely seen as an empire, its days were (at least more) numbered (than they had been).

Empires and nations in the modern age mutually constitute each other, and their meanings refer back to discourses of legitimation. Whereas in

earlier ages conquest or dynastic claims or divine will were adequate
sources for ruling diverse peoples over vast spaces, once the discourse of
the nation became dominant in the nineteenth century, legitimacy turned
from top down to bottom up. It was now the people constituted as the
nation that provided the source of legitimate power to the state officials.
Empires that failed to reconstitute themselves as nations suddenly became
archaic political forms, violators of sovereignty. Beissinger continues with
the "Soviet state played a pivotal role in the history of empires precisely
in fuzzing the boundary between [nation-]state and empire and pioneering new forms of nonconsensual control by which culturally distinct
populations within a state and beyond the borders of a state could be
ruled." The USSR skillfully disguised nonconsensual rule in a language
of national self-determination and sovereignty, blurring "the line between
domination and consent." Like the United States, the Soviet Union used
international norms of self-determination and sovereignty as a new form
of imperial rule, while anticolonialist movements employed the charge of
empire against the hegemonic power of powerful states.

Although Beissinger's heaviest emphasis falls on the importance of the
moment when states are recognized as empires, he does not completely
dismiss structural factors. Even if one distinguishes multinational states
that attempt to promote equality and participation among dominant and
minority peoples from empires that rule through distinction, discrimination, and subordination of the periphery, the fundamental difference
between these two kinds of state is less about "the presence or absence of
objective structures of control or even policies of inequality and discrimination, but rather whether politics and policies are accepted as 'ours' or
rejected as 'theirs.' Practices of nonconsensual control and objective
inequalities play central roles in what makes grievance likely. But grievance is a collective claim, not an objective condition." In my own schema
(which seems to me to be consistent with Beissinger's view) multinational
states, difficult to maintain as they may be, are an alternative to empire
or a homogenous nation-state, but they are delicately balanced on the
fragile fulcrum of tolerance, equality, and effective participation in the
polity of all citizens while recognizing the diversity of the constituent
peoples. The question of whither contemporary Russia—toward empire
domestically (consider Chechnya) and neo-imperialism in the Near
Abroad (consider its policies toward Georgia) or toward a multinational
state (think of Tatarstan) and respect for the sovereignty of its neighbors
(think of its evolving policies toward the Baltic states)—remains a question for future investigators. Beissinger notes recent trends away from rec-

ognizing post-Soviet Russia as an empire, but whether that will continue to be the case with Putin's state remains a question.[2]

In his essay David Laitin shows how the Soviet cultural equilibrium in language use—Russians able to remain monolingual, while non-Russians had to choose between monolingualism in their native language or bilingualism with its advantages for social mobility—broke down in Estonia after the collapse of the Soviet Union. In the period of transition Estonians attempted to eliminate Russian-language use and to pressure Russians to leave Estonia. Russians reacted, however, not by emigrating in large numbers but by accepting the Estonian cultural hegemony and attempting to learn Estonian. These findings, published in Laitin's prize-winning book *Identity in Formation*, emphasized choice. Here Laitin refines his earlier conclusions to take into account the shift in Estonian government policy in 2000. Instead of inducing out-migration, the Estonians opted for an integration program both to deflect pressures from the European Union, which was critical of Estonia's citizenship policies, and to co-opt some Russian politicians into supporting one or another domestic political party. In the early twenty-first century social processes have resulted in a "dual integration model"—Russians are acquiring Estonian cultural forms (and Estonians are exposed to some Russian cultural forms!), while both Estonians and Russians are acquiring European cultural practices. Here choice is less evident than in the early 1990s; nevertheless, the advantages of adapting to the new world of Estonian cultural dominance and integration into Europe lead Russians to integrate into both Estonia and Europe.

Laitin's Estonia presents a model of ethnic cooperation superseding a conflictual one, as the comparative advantages of integration and exclusion are weighed. One might add that the sense of threat to a small nation that felt deeply that its very existence was at stake in the 1980s and 1990s has dissipated in the post-1991 international context in which a weakened Russia faces a dynamic and attractive European Union open to the Estonians.

Zoltan Barany contrasts the postcommunist fate of two East Central European ethnic groups, the Albanians of Macedonia and the Roma (Gypsies). Although Albanians have managed through ethnic mobilization to win recognition of their ethnic group and to participate in Macedonian politics, the Roma have remained marginalized throughout the region. To explain the variation in outcomes for these two ethnicities, Barany proposes a simple model of "mobilizational prerequisites." The greater the political opportunity afforded a minority, the stronger its ethnic identity, the more united and effective its leadership, and the greater the group's organizational capacity, the more likely an ethnicity is to realize its political goals through mobilization. Other factors also play a role, such as the political program of the group, its financial resources, its effectiveness in communicating to the larger community, and the efficacy and power of its collective symbols. The Roma are particularly disadvantaged, according to the model, for they are scattered and divided, not well organized, with a small and impotent intelligentsia and a weak ethnic identity. Macedonia's Albanians, on the other hand, enjoy a strong ethnic identity, an articulate leadership, effective political parties, clear political objectives, abundant financial resources, powerful symbols, and effective communication through their large family networks.

One form of ethnic mobilization, through political parties and elections, is explored by Robert G. Moser, who looks at the contrasting cases of Russia and Lithuania. Some observers have posited ethnic diversity as disruptive or even destructive of democracy, but Moser considers the complex ways in which ethnicity has been integrated into representative politics in the postcommunist political landscape in which decades of Leninist party rule had leveled class distinctions. The variety of cases in Eastern Europe is impressive: strong ethnic parties in Romania, Bulgaria, and Slovakia; weak ones in Ukraine; ideology still more salient in voters' political choices than ethnicity in Russia, yet even in that country, where no minority rises to more than 4 percent of the population and ethnic parties are largely absent, minority representation is significant. In countries where ethnicities are polarized (Estonia, Latvia, Lithuania, Slovakia, Romania, Bulgaria, and Moldova), minorities have either been excluded from politics or have formed important ethnic parties; in countries where there is little ethnic polarization (the Czech Republic, Poland, Hungary, Russia, and Ukraine), elections have been structured around nonethnic parties.

Russia and Lithuania have roughly the same proportion of minority ethnics (20 percent), yet the degree of effective participation in electoral politics is significantly different. In Russia minorities are too small and too dispersed to form effective ethnic parties, yet despite the lack of ethnic mobilization, they have been able to take advantage of the ethnofederal system both to control or to have great influence in more than two dozen regions and republics and to be elected to the central legislature. The advantage that federalism provides most positively affects the smaller nationalities, while the largest minority, the Tatars, is the most underrepresented, in part because of their great dispersion, in part because of Russian fears of Tatar nationalism. In many cases minorities have benefited from the quasi-democratic nature of Russia's political system, in which ethnic elites basically control the outcome of elections in their regions. In Lithuania, on the other hand, the two principal minorities (Russians and Poles) are either internally divided or, in the case of the Russians, relatively prone to partial assimilation. The smallness of the non-Lithuanian ethnicities and their internal divisiveness have worked against formation of ethnic political parties.

Questioning the usual suspicion of ethnicity undermining democracy, Moser's fascinating investigation leads him to optimistic conclusions. Under certain conditions ethnically divided societies are able to maintain competitive democratic systems. Ethnic minorities can be effective, particularly in proportionally representative electoral systems, if they are large enough to overcome the legal threshold for parliamentary seats and if they can hold together an ethnic voting bloc. Concentration of a minority in a specific geographic area aids in single member districts, even in the absence of specifically ethnic parties. Ethnic federalism not only tends to ethnicize politics but also can substitute for a lack of ethnic geographic concentration. Relative assimilation into the majority population (Russians in Lithuania, Russians in Ukraine, Ukrainians in Russia) can lead to effective alliances between minorities and majority parties. Finally, in contrast to the findings of many observers that ethnic diversity increases party fragmentation, Moser finds that in certain circumstances, ethnic diversity can actually constrain the number of parties. In non-Russian regions in Russia, ethnicity is the marker of identity that in highly fluid elections gives voters cues that can lead to more cohesive voting blocs. In these regions, which are usually highly controlled by elites, there is little electoral competition. Ethnic leaders have been exceptionally loyal to central leaders (from whom they receive a variety of benefits). Here instead of divisive ethnic politics one finds ethnic minorities acting as a cohesive voting bloc, supporting major parties, and consequentially lessening party proliferation. There is no inevitability leading from ethnic diversity to democratic failure or to violent conflict.

Daniel Chirot takes a very different view. In his comparison of ethnic civil war in Côte d'Ivoire in the years after the death of its moderate leader, Félix Houphouët-Boigny, and the relative ethnic peace in Romania and Bulgaria after the collapse of state socialism, he proposes a dual explanation. On the one hand, the creation and evolution of effective nation-states is a long historical process that appears to be universal; on the other, timing, the international context in which the nation-making occurs, and the kinds of leaders who emerge to manage it are key to peaceful nation formation. Historically, nations took hundreds of years to become stable, coherent collectivities, defended by an international system that "pretends that all states are nations." Although France underwent the kinds of turmoil and conflict that gave birth to nations in the sixteenth century and afterward, Romania and Bulgaria entered that stage in the mid- and late nineteenth century, a period marked by conflict, expansion, anti-Semitism, and the ethnic cleansing of minority peoples. Côte d'Ivoire is now engaged in the difficult process of nation-building, and in the absence of liberal and moderate leaders the country has degenerated into the kind of mass violence that characterized another unfortunate state, Yugoslavia. Chirot argues that political actors are key to successful nation-formation, but in the case of Africa it will be necessary for Europe or the United States to intervene. Though the impression is certainly not intentional, Chirot's pessimistic vision of the near inevitability of conflict and the need for outside intervention remind this reader of the recent film *Tears of the Sun*, starring Bruce Willis as the gun-toting savior of misguided natives, more than of the pre-9/11 *Black Hawk Down*, which warned the West not to muck around in other people's fights.

Charles King looks at the relationship of ethnicity, states, and migration and seeks to go beyond microeconomic or simple structuralist or ethnocultural explanations of the phenomenon of migration. In the late 1980s migration soared in postcommunist Europe and Eurasia, peaking in the early 1990s and then falling off for the rest of the decade. As a result of warfare and ethnic conflict, particularly in the Balkans and Caucasus, hundreds of thousands of people became "internally displaced," dislocated but remaining in their home countries rather than becoming refugees abroad. But no easy explanations exist for the patterns of migration and movement. King looks at two cases for some answers: the policies of "kin-states" toward their co-nationals in the diaspora, and the traffic in women. Citizenship requirements and diaspora laws (statutes applying to ethnic co-nationals abroad), like the Hungarian Status Law of 2001, codify the relationship between states and dispersed ethnicities. Diaspora laws give certain privileges to individual immigrants that share the ethnicity of the dominant nationality of the receiving state, but they are actually a measure to regulate migration, rather than an effort to intervene in the life of the diaspora.

Turning to the traffic in sex workers, King emphasizes that researchers have focused on economics in this "industry" while neglecting the important role of states. In Eastern Europe the weakness of postcommunist states, the particularities of geography, and the loose visa regime are all factors that facilitate the movement of roughly half a million people a year through the region. Trafficked women make up a significant portion of that number. The strength of ethnic networks, often involving women recruiters, accounts for the variation in which countries do the most trafficking—not the local culture (or the beauty of the women!). For King, ethnicity is "both less and more than it might appear. It is less in the sense that it rarely functions as an inscrutable form of 'identity,' working itself out in the lives and behaviors of individuals, much like the mysterious *Geist* of German Idealist philosophers. It is more in the sense that it masks a variety of social networks of trust and mechanisms of sanction, all of which need to be investigated on their own terms."

In the final essay political theorist Will Kymlicka raises the essential question of how the international community might best act to protect minorities in modern nation-states. Although there is no overall, undisputed international (or even European) norm of minority rights, through the 1990s Western countries in fact worked to guarantee the rights of minorities for a variety of humanitarian and security reasons. Various provisions of the United Nations and the Organization for Security and Cooperation in Europe have affirmed a right to self-determination for all peoples and a right to enjoy one's own culture in community with other co-ethnics. No right to autonomy or statehood, however, has been unconditionally supported, and Kymlicka seeks an intermediate position between the right to self-determination and simple cultural protection. In fact, the international community supported territorial autonomy for ethnic minorities (e.g., the Swedish speakers of the Åland Islands in Finland, German speakers in South Tyrol in Italy, Puerto Rico, Catalonia, the Basque Country, Flanders in Belgium, and Scotland and Wales) until it became essentially universal for groups of more than 250,000 individuals. Only Corsicans (who number about 175,000) among Western European groups that have demanded autonomy have not yet received it. Autonomy and official bilingualism has become the dominant practice in the West, though not in Eastern Europe.

By the second half of the 1990s the enthusiasm for territorial autonomy had dissipated, largely as a result of resistance from postcommunist states, which thought of themselves as unitary ethnonational states and possessed the short-term memory of the recent dissolutions of the Soviet Union, Czechoslovakia, Georgia, Azerbaijan, and Yugoslavia. Autonomy, it might be added, had a sour smell from the long years of pseudo-federalism and phony autonomy that had been practiced by the USSR and other state socialist regimes. At the same time security concerns had become the prime motivation for intervention in support of minorities. When ethnic violence occurred, as in Moldova, Georgia, Azerbaijan, Bosnia, Kosovo, or Macedonia, Western organizations rushed in and pushed for some form of autonomy to resolve the crisis. Where there was no violence, and states were resistant to recognize minority rights, the international community held back and urged restraint and calm. Ironically, the security approach rewarded violence on the part of minorities and intransigence on the part of states. Although Kymlicka remains skeptical of the possibility of working out or enforcing an international norm, European organizations have generally adopted the idea of "effective participation" of minorities in public affairs, especially in matters affecting them, as a standard. As vague and contested as they are, international norms, like effective participation, nevertheless, offer "a starting point for democratic debate, not the end-point."

In the first decade of the twenty-first century, conflict, violence, and mass killing have been more closely connected with ethnic and internal civil wars than with interstate wars. Hundreds of thousands of people have been killed, maimed, or forced from their homes since the collapse of the Communist regimes. Although struggling democracies have been built in some postcommunist states (most notably in the northwestern states), authoritarian states remain in power through much of the southern tier of Eurasia. Several states have fallen apart along ethnic lines, yet others have instituted tolerant systems that recognize cultural diversity. The picture is varied, in many ways not as bleak as might appear in daily readings of the press.

The study of ethnic and civil conflict has become a growth industry since the heady days of the Soviet decline. The easy turn toward explanations derived from "ancient tribal hatreds" or embedded deep-seated historical animosities gradually gave way to a variety of analyses coming out of rational choice and international relations theory. Ethnic conflict was then pictured as having little to do with ethnicity and much to do with the instrumentalist aims of state actors and nationalist elites. The breakdown of states and empires led to anarchic situations in which each side, however defined, saw the other as a potential threat and acted preemptively to gain the upper hand before it was too late. The structural impasse of the security dilemma, in which one side's ambition to become more secure only makes the other less so and gives it an incentive to build itself up, along with the resultant security spiral, fit well the escalations of violence in the Balkans and the Caucasus. But rationalist explanations based on cognitive strategic choices by actors who know what they want failed to explain convincingly why masses of people respond to the calls of nationalist leaders or act often against their own apparent interests. To amplify the rational approach, scholars added myths, symbols, and collective narratives that shaped the worlds in which ethnic actors formed their beliefs, preferences, and behaviors. Eventually, some theorists turned to the emotions that lay behind both strategic choices and the symbols, myths, and stories that people told about themselves and the "others." And the search for understanding goes on.[3]

The essays in this volume range from optimistic to pessimistic, but overall the impression they give is of no inevitable slide from difference to discrimination to conflict. Genocide is not our inevitable future. Rather, even politicians for their own strategic reasons work to reconstruct the discourses, reshape the identities, and alter the rhetoric that divides peoples. They may not be borrowing directly the insights offered by the academy, but life itself seems to demonstrate that there are few fixed essences in human experience, few indelible markers that separate one people from another. Culture certainly matters, but "civilizations," whatever they may be, are less likely to clash than to blend into one another, to borrow and to share what is best about them. At the end of the day a globalizing world, with people on the move all the time, forces us all to choose between an impossible nostalgic isolation or a dynamic celebration of difference.

1

RETHINKING EMPIRE IN THE WAKE OF SOVIET COLLAPSE

MARK R. BEISSINGER

How does the collapse of the Soviet Union alter or confirm existing theories about empires? Perhaps the most important element of the Soviet collapse for theories of empires was the very fact that the Soviet Union was labeled an empire in the first place. After all, the Soviet Union was founded, as Terry Martin has put it, as "the world's first postimperial state,"[1] to the European imperial system. Moreover, according to the formal, legal underpinnings of the contemporary state system, empires are not supposed to exist anymore. They are part of history, supposedly eliminated during the first six decades of the twentieth century and universally replaced by "empire's nemesis"[2]—the modern nation-state, a form of polity whose most conspicuous characteristics are its claims to represent a distinct and legitimate political community, its claim to the exclusive right to rule over a bounded territory, and the recognition of these claims by other polities making the same claims. As Dominic Lieven has observed, "In the second half of the twentieth century the notion of 'empire' disappeared from the contemporary political debate and became the property of historians."[3] By the 1970s and early 1980s little scholarly interest in general was exhibited toward empires and imperialism, with most of the attention arising out of Marxist scholarship and directed toward the study of "dependency" and "neo-imperialism"—the postimperial legacies of a then extinct European imperialism.

This consignment of empires to history seemed based on good reason. Only a few formal remnants of the overseas empires that once encompassed the globe still remained (most of these, islands constituting global strategic outposts for European or American power), and as one study of these territories concluded, for most "the trend has been, with the approval of the local population, towards greater integration than to a severing of ties,"[4] so that what once was regarded as colony became a legitimate part of the controlling state. Moreover, unlike the situation fifty or a hundred years ago, no political entity today describes itself as an empire or claims to be pursuing imperial ends. Indeed, for many the very idea that there are contemporary empires seems on the surface absurd. Rather, the principles of territorial sovereignty and of *uti possidetis* (literally, "as you now possess"—the norm once applied to wartime conquests, but now reserved for postcolonial boundaries) encourage acceptance of existing state configurations.

The collapse of the Soviet Union and the end of Soviet control over Eastern Europe challenged these assumptions at their very core, which is why they are potentially such fertile ground for a serious rethinking of empires. The Soviet collapse not only was accompanied by an explosion of nationalism and anti-imperial mobilization; it also gave rise to an explosion of scholarly literature on empires, as the fundamental issues of empire—what empires are, how they emerge, why they collapse, and what follows after them—have once again come to the fore. The vast majority of scholars have approached these issues transhistorically—by which I mean that they assert the fundamental similarity between the Soviet Union and traditional empires, treating the Soviet Union as "the last empire" and the analytical equivalent of the ancient Roman or Hittite Empires, or, at the very least, the British, Tsarist, Ottoman, and Habsburg variants.[5] The problem with this kind of transhistorical thinking is not that one cannot find parallels across the centuries and millennia and across these political units at a high level of abstraction. Empires have cores and peripheries. But then again, so do contemporary states. Empires exercise sovereign control over peoples who consider themselves distinct political societies. But again, this is true of many modern multinational states as well. Empires have been likened to a rimless wheel in which peripheries interact on all significant issues mainly with the center.[6] Yet, were capital flows, communication systems, movements of people, or systems of governmental regulation to be mapped in most modern states, one would likely find much the same spoke-like pattern. Thomas Barfield has suggested that there is good reason that many of the characteristics we commonly associate with empires can be applied as well to most large, modern-day multinational states. As he notes, these similarities should not be surprising because "empires were the templates for large states."

> Historically, empires were the crucibles in which the possibility of large
> states was realized. Indeed, it is difficult to find examples of large states
> in areas that were not first united by an empire. . . . It was the experi-
> ence of empire that changed the political and social environment and
> created the capacity to rule large areas and populations in the states
> that followed. . . . Thus large states were most common in areas where
> empires broke up and the imperial pieces became large states.[7]

Transhistorical theorizing about empires commits what William Sewell
has aptly called the fallacy of "experimental time." It fractures history and
assumes that one can discover generalizations by comparing instances
commonly placed under the same label across different societies widely
separated by time, despite the very different assumptions and meanings
that agents hold about these phenomena and despite the fact that these
phenomena are not entirely unrelated—that is, the example of earlier
instances exercises a direct causal influence on subsequent manifestations
across time.[8] The meaning of empire shifted enormously over the nineteenth century, shifted still further when applied to the Soviet Union,
and may be shifting yet again when applied to systems of authority within
the context of a globalizing, unipolar world.[9] Moreover, what we label as
empires are not the independent observations that transhistorical interpretations pretend they are, but are rather interdependent phenomena
across time in which rulers have learned from previous successes and failures concerning how to institutionalize control over multicultural populations. Soviet leaders, for instance, learned considerable lessons from the
collapse of prior multinational empires, and these lessons altered fundamentally the ways in which they (and other rulers) established control
over their own population and populations beyond their borders.

In what follows, I examine the ways in which contemporary empires
differ from empires of the past. I show that the boundaries between multinational states and multinational empires and between regional or global
hegemons and informal empires are more fluid and contested than most
theories of empire admit, that claims to nationhood and national self-
assertion are central to the process by which contemporary states become
empires, and that the structure of nonconsensual control that theories of
empire have traditionally emphasized is not a given but rather emerges
through interaction between political practice and oppositional politics.
I illustrate this with the examples of the Soviet Union and post-Soviet
Russia, drawing as well on other cases. Like its predecessor state, contemporary Russia remains variably subject to labeling as empire in both
its internal and external relationships. These claims have fluctuated over

time, and in some respects Russia has been moving away from widespread recognition as empire in recent years. But contention over whether post-Soviet Russia is an empire remains central to the politics of the Eurasian region, and may in fact never fully disappear.

The transhistorical approach to the study of empires leaves us with the false comfort that the Soviet Union was the "last empire," somehow unique among contemporary states in this quality, and that despite the sudden recognition of the Soviet Union *qua* empire, empires are now—finally and truly—an extinct political breed.[10] I argue quite the contrary. Rather than "the last empire," the Soviet Union should be understood instead as one of the first of a new form of empire whose crucial contributions were its denial of its imperial quality and its use of the very cornerstones of the modern nation-state system—the norms of state sovereignty and national self-determination—as instruments of nonconsensual control over culturally distinct populations, thereby blurring the line between state and empire. In this sense, there is no such thing as "the last empire." Rather, some states in the world today, like the Soviet Union, remain vulnerable to widespread labeling as empire. When ultimately denuded as "imperial," such states are subject to disintegration, reconfiguration, or retrenchment, so that the politics of empire remains central to the ways in which aspects of our contemporary state system are challenged, maintained, and transformed.

Empire as Claim and as Outcome

Because the key concepts that emerge from transhistorical analysis of empire remain highly abstract,[11] some scholars have argued that the term "empire" adds nothing to our conceptual vocabulary and should be exorcized from political analysis.[12] This is one possible approach to dealing with the problems associated with a concept that has been stretched to cover an excessive variety of objects and whose meaning has undergone fundamental shifts.

At the same time, the root issue raised by most theories of empire—that of nonconsensual control over culturally distinct populations—is real and abiding. Despite formal decolonization, the issue has hardly disappeared from our world. Rather, in a certain subset of cases, empires have seemingly reemerged, despite formal decolonization. The Soviet Union and a number of other contemporary states (for example, post-Soviet Russia, the United States, Ethiopia, China, India, Indonesia, Great Britain, Spain, France, Turkey, and Iran) have been variably labeled (and in some cases, widely labeled) as empires by minorities inhabiting them, by populations abroad resisting their control, or by large portions of the international community. This act of labeling is itself a critically important political phenomenon, as empires in the contemporary world are widely understood to be illegitimate, representing violations of the norms of self-determination and state sovereignty that lie at the basis of the contemporary state system.

Rather than argue that the Soviet Union is mislabeled as an empire and that the term is entirely irrelevant for analysis of its collapse or for political analysis more generally, I argue instead that the Soviet experience begs us to contemplate how those polities we call empires have transformed over time. Such examination reveals how the exercise of nonconsensual control over culturally distinct populations within or beyond a state's borders has altered the increasingly porous boundaries between multinational states and multinational empires and between global or regional hegemons and informal empires, the fundamental identity processes underlying modern conceptions of empire, and the ways in which accusations of empire become a potent category for nationalist resistance against certain states but not others.

In today's world large multinational states and global or regional hegemons are not intrinsically empires in the same way in which ancient empires, European overseas colonial empires, or European overland empires of the nineteenth or early twentieth centuries are usually contemplated. Indeed, most states described as empires today are postimperial in that they emerged in the wake of the collapse of empires, do not claim to be empires, and do not claim to be heirs of previous empires (though some forces within these societies often view them in this fashion). In the nineteenth century it was frequently quipped that Britain had an empire but that Russia was an empire, illustrating the difference between overseas and overland empires. As Ronald Suny has rightfully argued, however, the Soviet Union did not begin as an empire; rather, it became one.[13] Rather than being or having empires in some intrinsic sense, contemporary states are subject to a politics of becoming empires, and it is to that politics which most theories of empire have typically failed to devote attention. If we are to have a concept of empire that is relevant to contemporary phenomena like the Soviet Union, we need to shift away from essentialist conceptions of what empires are to an understanding in which the label of empire itself lies at the center of contention.

This shift from a purely structural and transhistorical understanding of empire to one which places claims-making and identity at the core of what empire is parallels trends within the study of nationhood, in which nation is no longer taken as a timeless community or substantive reality, but rather, in Rogers Brubaker's words, as "institutionalized form, practical category, and contingent event."[14] Indeed, the parallels between the study of nationalism and the study of imperialism run much deeper than is usually recognized. Much as nations constitute claims to self-determination and sovereignty, empires in the contemporary world are widely understood to represent violations of the norms of self-determination and state sovereignty that lie at the basis of the contemporary nation-state system. Moreover, in today's world use of the term "empire" to describe a state's relationship with a culturally distinct population or with another state is usually a statement that advocates and anticipates that this relationship should and will fall apart, much as the term "nation" implies a certain stance and anticipation of outcome.

But such a shift in perspective also raises questions about whether empire, like nation, is better thought of, as Brubaker puts it, as a "category of practice" rather than a "category of analysis."[15] My answer is that we cannot entirely dispense with thinking about empire (like nation) as a category of analysis. If we were interested in empire only as a claim, there would be no sense in considering empire as anything more than a category of practice. Yet, we are interested in empire not merely as claim, but also as outcome (that is, as a situation in which such claims grow widespread, "stick" with regularity, gain hegemonic use, or become a potent frame for large numbers of people). That the Soviet Union today is routinely labeled as an empire throughout much of the world (even by many Russians)—something that was not true prior to the late 1980s—is a social fact, not merely a category of practice. Like nation or class,[16] empire in today's world is a conceptual variable that emerges out of political and social practice and whose widespread presence or seeming absence merits social scientific explanation. Moreover, contention over the existence of empire (like nation) lies implicit within the use of the concept itself. We lack—at least in English—words like "empirehood" and "empire-ness"— the equivalent of "nationhood" and "nationness" (meaning "the quality of being regarded as a nation") that would allow us speak about empire as a variable attribute rather than as a timeless, reified thing.[17] Much as Brubaker recognized that "To argue against the realist and substantialist way of thinking about nations is not to dispute the reality of nationhood,"[18] understanding empires as claims rather than as things does not undermine the factualness of empire as a political outcome or of "empire-ness" as a variable quality of states. Rather, it begs from us explanations of why certain states are or are not labeled as empires and of how contemporary empires come into being—the latter, of course, being one of the classic questions which theories of empire have traditionally addressed, but for which they are ill-equipped to tackle in a world in which the label of empire is itself at the center of contention.

Thus, empire today is not a transhistorical form of polity. Rather, empire is better understood as a claim and an outcome, and "empire-ness" as the degree to which a polity gains recognition as empire. Empire today is a claim specific to a particular historical era—an era of national-ism. And it is primarily a subversive vocabulary that seeks to challenge the power of the large multinational state from within on the basis of its violation of norms of self-determination, or the power of the global or regional hegemon from without by invoking norms of state sovereignty. This claim has power in part because of the ways in which the interna-tional community goes about recognizing claims to self-determination and sovereignty; in international law, the right to independent statehood is largely restricted to collectivities under colonial, alien, or racial subju-gation, whereas sovereignty is primarily contemplated in formal, legalis-tic terms rather than as empirical control. As an outcome, empire is a situation in which claims to being subject to imperial control grow wide-spread, gather weight, and become increasingly hegemonic.[19] Although this resonance and recognition of empire as a claim, like claims to nation-hood, vary considerably over time and space, there are also cases in which relatively stable outcomes are evident—in which a polity (like the Soviet Union) comes to be routinely referred to as empire, without much reflec-tion concerning how this label came about. Such stable outcomes occur only in the aftermath of successful anti-imperial mobilization and major contraction of state power. But the widespread presence of the discourse is itself a sign that such a contraction is likely imminent.

The Rise of Nationalism and the Structuration of Modern Empires

Any analysis of empires must address what, in most scholarly analyses, is seen as the central feature of all empires: imperial structure. The specifics of scholarly definitions of empire may differ. But at the center of almost all definitions is a claim about empire as a structured relationship of dom-ination. This is true of the classical Marxist literature on the subject as it is of more recent non-Marxist scholarly contributions.[20] Michael Doyle has developed what is probably the most widely cited definition of empire. As Doyle puts it, empire "is a system of interaction between two political enti-ties, one of which, the dominant metropole, exerts political control over the internal and external policy—the effective sovereignty—of the other, the subordinate periphery." For Doyle, an empire is a relationship in which the sovereignty of one political society is "controlled either formally or informally by a foreign state." In Doyle's analysis, the major issue in defining empire is its relational dimension—and in particular, the question of the identifying the effective control by one political society over another. As Doyle says, his definition implies that "to explain the existence of empire, or a particular empire, one must first demonstrate the existence of control; second, explain why one party expands and establishes such control; and third, explain why the other party submits or fails to resist effectively."[21]

Like most theorists of empire, Doyle focuses excessively on demonstrating the existence and nature of control and insufficiently on the issues of the illegitimate and nonconsensual character of control and the nature of the political societies being controlled. Both omissions are closely bound up with the politics of claims-making that underlies imperial structure. Doyle concentrates on the issue of "effective control" of a subordinated society largely because, drawing on Dahl's understanding of power, he assumes a behavioral approach to empire, thereby allowing him to analyze both formal and informal empires by examining actual control over policy outcomes, irrespective of whether such control is recognized by those subject to it. And though he acknowledges that resistance is one of two key signs by which to judge the presence or absence of "effective control," Doyle does not capture the sense of illegitimate and nonconsensual rule that the contemporary usage of empire most clearly implies. Here, I blame the transhistorical approach assumed by Doyle and most theorists of empire, for throughout most of history empire did not imply illegitimate or nonconsensual rule, though it does so today unambiguously.

Perhaps as serious a problem in Doyle's definition is the fact that center and periphery as political societies are taken as ontologically prior—that is, they are assumed to exist as centers of primary allegiance prior to the establishment of the controlled relationship. This becomes particularly problematic when the political societies that are controlled are assumed to be national in character; this was, of course, the case for the Soviet Union—and has been the case for most empires since the early twentieth century. The failure to address the nature and emergence of the political societies constituting empire is a serious lacuna within most theories of empire when we contemplate that, prior to the last two hundred years, most people throughout the globe thought of themselves in religious, local, class, tribal, and clan terms, not as members of national communities. For ancient empires this is perhaps not a significant analytical problem, for religious, local, class, tribal, and clan communities in most instances existed prior to the establishment of imperial control, though imperial control often played a significant role in reconfiguring these allegiances. Most ancient empires consisted of control by one elite over another elite, with the primary goal being the establishment of an effective and accepted center of authority over narrower territorial, kinship, tribal, and city-state affiliations.

But when theories of empire are applied to the last two centuries, it is usually assumed that the political societies that are dominated are not religious communities, localities, classes, tribes, or clans, but rather nations or nationalities.[22] Indeed, today we are unlikely to regard a polity that consists of a multitude of religious communities, localities, classes, tribes, or clans as an empire at all—even if such a polity were large, repressive, and created on the basis of conquest.[23] Rather, such a state is likely to be viewed as simply a culturally plural state. This difference between the nature of the political communities said to constitute imperial peripheries in modern and ancient empires is critical, for nationhood is not an inherent quality of human consciousness, but a phenomenon constructed by states and national movements—in fact, movements that frequently define themselves in opposition to empire. Moreover, often a widespread sense of nationness within populations emerges only in or after the process of imperial collapse itself.[24] When addressing the phenomenon of modern empires, most theories of empire leave unaddressed the issue of where national political societies come from, and in many cases, in primordialist fashion, simply assume their longstanding status prior to the establishment of imperial control.

A closer inspection shows that our modern conception of empire is itself a product of the rise of nationalism. The term "empire" (*imperium*) in ancient Rome originally referred to the legal power to issue laws—close in many respects to our modern notion of sovereignty. The concept entered European political discourse to refer to any supreme and extensive political dominion,[25] which, in the premodern world, contrasted with more diffuse or contractual systems of authority. In this sense *imperium* did not necessarily imply sharp differentiation between core and periphery or an illegitimate rule, though it did imply a sovereign power over multiple and diffuse political societies, and it was the sovereign dimension of power rather than its exploitative or dominating role that was empire's most conspicuous feature in the premodern world. When Henry VIII proclaimed England an "empire" in the 1530s, his main intention was to assert his sovereignty vis-à-vis the pope and to declare that he would not tolerate interference in the affairs of his realm from Rome.[26] As one inquiry into the changing usage of the term concluded:

> If an imaginary reporter had approached some politically-minded men of letters in the late 1830s or early 1840s [in England] with the request to define the terms *Empire* and *imperialism*, clear answers would not have been readily obtained. Some might have come forward with the startling reply that Empire was just another name for the British Isles or, perhaps, a more fanciful name for England.[27]

As late as 1885 Edward A. Freeman, a British historian whose life spanned most of the nineteenth century, observed that "It is only in quite late times within my own memory, that the word 'empire' has come into common use as a set term for something beyond the kingdom."[28]

It is ironic that a term that was essentially a signifier for sovereignty through the early nineteenth century had become, by the late nineteenth and early twentieth centuries, a signifier for the violation of sovereignty. Yet, this transformation provides the vital clue concerning the identity politics and the politics of claims-making embedded within empire's contemporary usage. Concern about the consequences of empire in the eighteenth century revolved largely around the implications of unit size for individual liberty, with English and French political philosophers (such as Montesquieu, Rousseau, and Burke) arguing, based on their interpretation of the Roman experience, that large and extensive states were more likely to suppress individual freedoms. Still, the essence of their critiques was an attack on the institutions of absolute monarchy, not an attack on colonialism. A discourse of national self-determination was not introduced into the meaning of empire until the last quarter of the nineteenth century. Several factors converged to bring about this massive transformation in meaning: (1) the growth of ethnically based nationalist movements oriented against European overland empires, particularly in Ireland, the Balkans, and East Central Europe, and the politicization of the issue of self-determination within Europe itself; (2) the "high" imperialism of the 1870s and 1880s, when European empires carved up Africa and expanded their presence in Asia in a rush for colonies, with a number of new participants (such as Germany and Belgium) entering the fray, creating a truly global system of European empires that left few corners of the world unclaimed; and (3) the growth of anti-imperial sentiment within the core cultural groups of European empires, fueled in particular by the Boer and Spanish-American wars, and politicized specifically by socialist oppositions within Europe. Within the overland empires of East

Central Europe and the Balkans, as ideas of democracy and nationhood spread eastward, nationalist entrepreneurs contrasted the self-determination of the nation with alien rule by the Habsburg, Ottoman, or Romanov Empires.

Thus, even before the creation of the first systematic theories of empire, a subtle transformation had already occurred in the nature and meaning of the term. Would-be nations were coming to constitute the basic units over which empires ruled, empires had come to signify the violation of sovereignty rather than sovereignty, and national self-determination had become the main mode by which empire was to be transcended. The rise of the word "imperialism" as a term of abuse in the late nineteenth century and the appearance of the first theories of imperialism in the early twentieth century further transformed the meaning of empire by mobilizing anti-imperial sentiment within imperial metropoles, connecting war and exploitation with mechanics of European industrial capitalism, and providing indigenous elites within European colonies with a powerful rationale for claiming national status for their territories. With the end of World War I, the principle of national self-determination was applied as the basis for postwar settlement in those overland European empires that had lost the war; meanwhile, African and Asian possessions of the German and Ottoman Empires were transformed temporarily into French and British colonial mandates for, as the League of Nations Covenant put it, "peoples not yet able to stand by themselves under the strenuous conditions of the modern world."[29] It was here that would-be nations were confirmed as the fundamental structures constituting empires, and empire was transformed into an unambiguous pejorative signaling the violation of sovereignty rather than sovereignty. As Koebner and Schmidt note, this meaning of the term became prevalent in the twentieth century, enabling "peoples in distant regions of the earth, living without any traditions in common, to feel united in fighting a joint enemy."[30]

In short, since at least the end of World War I, contemporary empires have been assumed to be based on nonconsensual rule and to consist of would-be or dominated nations, whose legitimate claims to self-determination and sovereignty have been violated. In this sense, imperial structure is not a given; rather, the very notions of center and periphery as applied to modern empires are in significant part the product of the rise of nationalism. And as most scholars of nationalism would recognize, nations are not simply matters of objective inequalities, flows of resources, patterns of interaction, or facts of military conquest. They are claims to a certain status. Indeed, in the case of the decolonization of European overseas empires, little more than the struggle against imperialism formed the basis for the claim to nationhood.[31] What is so obviously missing in most discussions of imperial structure is the issue of the emergence of a separate and dominated *national* political community. Doyle, for example, argues at one point that "imperial government is a sovereignty that lacks a community"[32]—a statement that parallels closely Gellner's definition of nationalism as "a political principle, which holds that the political and national unit should be congruent."[33] Yet, Doyle fails to address the issue of where a sense of community comes from. Structural theories of empire beg the question of how actual practices of control and the resistance to control (that is, state policies such as segregation, integration, discrimination, extermination, autonomization, and assimilation, as well as opposition practices of identity construction and mobilization) play themselves out in the emergence of a sense of dominated national political community or, conversely, in a sense of legitimate civic authority.

The point is that the structure that we ascribe to modern empires cannot be separated from the practices engaged in by authority that fail to produce a sense of legitimate rule and the politics of national identity that generates successful resistance. Most theories of empire do not recognize the claims and identity processes embedded within empire, since they do not problematize how the sense of structural differentiation they posit comes about. But recognizing this assumption moves us still further: if nonconsensual control and claims to nationhood are central to what makes an empire (at least since the early twentieth century), then it is not difficult to imagine that rulers might eventually recognize this as well and adjust, presenting control as consensual when it is not and problematizing the boundary between states and empires. In fact, the Soviet state played a pivotal role in the history of empires precisely in fuzzing the boundary between state and empire and in pioneering forms of nonconsensual control by which culturally distinct populations within a state and beyond the borders of a state could be ruled.

Self-Determination, Sovereignty, and Nonconsensual Control

Various factors explain why the fluid boundary between states and empires was not a central concern of scholarly inquiry into empire until recently. For one thing, the demise of European overseas empires did not raise the issue boldly. European overseas empires rested on a much clearer dualism between citizen and subject than was true of overland empires, though recent scholarship has realized that the divide between core and periphery was never as crisp and impermeable in European overseas empires as was typically described in most theories of imperialism. As recent studies have argued, the colonies of early modern Europe are better understood not as integrated with and highly controlled from an imperial core, but rather as "reflections or logical extensions of the states to which they were symbolically attached," with colonies often possessing a great deal of autonomy and independent authority.[34] Moreover, as Frederick Cooper and Ann Stoler tell us, "The otherness of colonized persons was neither inherent nor stable," that "difference had to be defined and maintained," and that European overseas empires "were imagined in relation to contiguous as well as noncontiguous territory," so that "'nation-building' and 'empire-building' were mutually constitutive projects."[35]

The fluid boundary between multinational state and multinational empire was also not raised starkly by the collapse of European overland empires (Tsarist, Habsburg, and Ottoman) at the end of World War I. Again, this was not because core and periphery were precisely delineated in these empires. They were not. Many scholars have noted that prior to the nineteenth century it would have been difficult even to identify clear cores and peripheries in most overland empires, at least in any ethnic or national sense. The Ottoman Empire, for instance, was never dominated by a Turkish ethnie; many of its leading personnel were recruited from among the Greeks and Slavs of the Balkans. The Habsburg and Russian Empires were aristocratic empires. Both incorporated aristocratic elites from disparate cultures (in the case of the Habsburgs, an actual "Dual Monarchy" with Hungary). Neither empire defined itself in ethnic terms, but rather territorially, seeking to foster loyalty to the imperial enterprise irrespective of the cultural and religious backgrounds of its subjects.

The failure to problematize the fluid boundary between multinational state and multinational empire in these cases was due primarily to the fact that these entities were empires precisely because they claimed to be empires. They saw nothing wrong with the imperial label, understood it in the older sense as a claim to sovereign control, sought to build legitimacy around the figures of their emperors, and saw the greatness of their imperial enterprises as the primary foundation for political loyalty. Alex Motyl has argued that whether a polity calls itself an empire is irrelevant; rather, "state" and "empire" are conceptual entities that we as scholars create, and what matters instead are the criteria by which we choose to call them—that is, the imperialism of the scholar.[36] But Motyl's reasoning is faulty, for in this instance Type II errors (failing to reject a false null hypothesis) are much more likely than Type I errors (rejecting a true null hypothesis). It is much easier to develop criteria (such as size, power, or cultural makeup) that would enable us to decide that a polity does not qualify to be an empire despite its rulers' claims to be one than it is to develop criteria that would allow us to reject a polity's claim not to be an empire, particularly in a postimperial world of states in which the label of empire is associated with illegitimacy and the expectation that the polity will disintegrate. Precisely because we no longer live in a world of naked force but in a world of mass politics in which legitimation and image matter tremendously, it makes an enormous difference how polities present themselves to their populations and to the world. Today, no state that cares about its legitimacy would dare label itself an empire, and this fact tells much about how the nature of control—as Doyle noted, the central issue of empire—has transformed. Today, in a world of mass politics, domination can certainly continue to exist, but it can no longer understand itself or project itself as domination.[37]

It was precisely their inability to adjust to the new conditions created by the rise of mass politics that proved the undoing of the Habsburg, Tsarist, and Ottoman Empires. These three self-styled empires took radically different approaches to their national problems in the face of relatively similar pressures of modernization and international competition. Yet, none could be preserved in the face of rising demands for mass inclusion from the intelligentsia, mobilization for national self-determination among a number of minorities, and the obsolescence of imperial formulas for mass legitimation. State-building and modernization imperatives, imposed in part because of rivalries with other European empires, necessitated simultaneously the education of subject populations and attempts to foster their greater integration—a contradictory mix that led toward heightened cultural awareness (and, often, cultural grievance) among newly created national intelligentsias. Most important, in all three empires old formulas for legitimating imperial rule held declining sway within populations in a world whose vocabulary was increasingly national, mass-based, and rooted in notions of popular sovereignty.

In the Soviet case, however, we are dealing with a fundamentally different phenomenon from self-avowed European empires. As Dominic Lieven has observed, "A Russianist by definition comes to the study of empire from a strange angle."[38] This strange angle is forced on us because of the ways in which Bolshevik leaders (in contrast to previous empires, and indeed, in direct response to their collapse) consciously utilized the principles of national self-determination and state sovereignty as modes of structuring nonconsensual control, thereby obfuscating the boundaries between coercion and consent, empire and state. Terry Martin has aptly pointed to how the failed examples of the Habsburg, Tsarist, and Ottoman Empires strongly affected the way in which the Bolsheviks fashioned their nationality policies.

> Lenin and Stalin understood very well the danger of being labeled an empire in the age of nationalism. In fact, here lies the real connection between the Soviet Union's national constitution and the collapse of the Habsburg and Ottoman empires. The nationalities crisis and final collapse of the Habsburg empire made an enormous impression on Lenin and Stalin, who viewed it as an object lesson in the danger of being perceived by their population as an empire. As a result, the Soviet Union became the first multiethnic state in world history to define itself as an anti-imperial state. They were not indifferent to the word "empire." They rejected it explicitly.[39]

Instead, after having established control over much of the territory of the Tsarist Empire by force, Bolshevik leaders constructed a specifically state form of ethnofederalism based on principles of sovereignty and self-determination. The Bolsheviks, of course, originally had rejected a federal solution to the Russian Empire's "nationality question." But nation-state forms crept into Marxism-Leninism as a way of disarming non-Russian nationalism after numerous nationalist movements during the Civil War had attempted to construct their own national states—which, in most cases, were overrun by the Red Army. Thus, the Soviet state, in sharp distinction from all European powers at the time and even the United States, would not have formal colonies and would not constitute itself as an openly imperial enterprise, but would rather project itself as a post-imperial form of power, a civic state that aimed to transcend national oppression in the name of class solidarity. What Martin calls the Soviet "Affirmative Action Empire" specifically attacked "Great Russian chauvinism" and instead sought to disarm nationalism by granting diminished forms of nationhood—national territories, cultural autonomy, and indigenous leaderships—to minority populations. The rationale was that by granting elements of self-determination, formal sovereignty, and cultural autonomy, the Soviet state could avoid the sense of grievance that had fueled the collapse of the Habsburg, Tsarist, and Ottoman Empires, and as socialism gained hold and class relationships were transformed, the basis for national discord would dissolve. The republics constituting the new Soviet state were legally sovereign entities that mimicked nation-state form, even though in substance they were thickly controlled from Moscow. According to the Soviet constitution, the USSR was a voluntary federation, with union republics supposedly retaining the right to secede—a legal fiction that eventually came back to haunt Soviet leaders.

In this respect, the Soviet Union's internal organization represented a radically different form of politics from nineteenth-century European empires. It cloaked nonconsensual control in the language of self-determination and utilized norms of self-determination and sovereignty to blur the line between domination and consent. The Soviet Union was in this respect a direct response to the new world of mass politics that had undermined the Habsburg, Tsarist, and Ottoman Empires—a world in which form and appearance had come to matter equally in shaping public perceptions as substance. Despite the widespread practice of violence and coercion against society in the Stalinist era, the extent to which Soviet control over its non-Russian territories was nonconsensual varied over space and time. Although revolts against Stalinist rule did take place (particularly during and after World War II in the Northern Caucasus and among groups incorporated as a result of the Molotov-Ribbentrop Pact), the Soviet state also at times enjoyed significant support among segments of its minority populations—injecting further uncertainty concerning whether the Soviet state rested on domination or consent, was empire or state. By the late 1950s and early 1960s, even most Balts had reconciled themselves to Soviet rule and its seeming immutability. On the eve of perestroika it was widely argued that Soviet institutions had achieved a degree of broad-based legitimacy within the Soviet population and that persuasive methods of rule had replaced state-sponsored intimidation. Indeed, this was one of the assumptions underlying the introduction of glasnost in the first place. But whatever legitimacy the Soviet regime had accumulated dissipated under the influence of glasnost, its revelations of Stalinist crimes, and the tide of anti-imperial nationalism that it precipitated, so that opposition movements from all groups, Russians included, eventually came to claim victimization at the hands of a Soviet "empire."

The international dimension of Soviet control also differed sharply from previous empires in the use of nominally independent nation-state units that Moscow covertly penetrated and monitored as a means for holding sway over territories and populations beyond Soviet state borders. Traditional overseas and overland empires had distinct practices for controlling political units that they did not intend to incorporate. Suzerainty originated in feudal law to describe the mutual obligations between lord and vassal and, with the rise of the modern state, came to refer to a limited sovereignty exercised by a dominant state over a dependent state. The notion of protectorate, which developed out of Roman imperial practice and is still used today in international law to recognize the legitimacy of remaining overseas colonial possessions, similarly denotes an ill-defined sovereignty of one state over another, especially in the area of defense and foreign relations. Protectorates imply a paternalistic and potentially temporary authority exercised in the interest of a population, whereas suzerainty implies a much more personalistic and patrimonial relationship of obligation between rulers. Even though scholars of imperialism refer to these as practices of "informal empire" (generally because they involved the exercise of control outside an empire's formal boundaries), in most cases suzerainty and protectorate were formal, legal, and overt relationships. Both practices were intimately associated with imperialism and colonialism and therefore inappropriate for the exercise of large-scale control in a postimperial world in which form and appearance mattered.

By contrast, Soviet rulers perfected the use of the modern nation-state form for constructing a covert form of informal control (informal in the sense of being outside the state's formal boundaries), thereby again blurring the line between voluntary and involuntary rule. Analogous phenomena had occurred earlier; the Athenian Empire, for instance, had exercised control over a series of independent Greek city-states by manipulating them through threats and maintaining hegemony over their internal politics. But what distinguished the Soviet practice of informal empire in Eastern Europe from the Athenian Empire was the way in which it utilized modern norms of state sovereignty to solidify control beyond its borders. This was not an entirely unique Russian invention. The United States in 1903 had utilized similar methods for gaining control over the Panama Canal, engineering the secession of Panama from Colombia, and then utilizing the new Panamanian state to keep foreign powers out and to grant exclusive control over the canal.[40] But no polity ever was as effective or as systematic in doing this as the Soviet state.

The practice first emerged in Russia at the time of the Russian Civil War, when it was unclear whether to incorporate territories of the former Tsarist Empire directly into the Russian Soviet Socialist Republic or simply to bind them by international treaty and party controls to Moscow. Ukraine, Belorussia, and the Transcaucasus at first were treated by the early Soviet leaders as legally independent states bound only by treaty to Soviet Russia, though eventually these republics formed the basis for the USSR. As an alternative to integration, in the early 1920s the concept of "people's republics" was invented to deal with territories that had previously had a suzerainty relationship with the Tsarist Empire (Bukhara and Khiva) or where it was believed that formal independence might help ward off interventions by foreign powers when Bolshevik ability to back up control with force was weak (such as against the Japanese in the Far East and the Chinese in Tuva and Mongolia). Here, the norms of state sovereignty were used to extend control further than Bolshevik resources would have otherwise permitted and to prevent outside powers or diaspora populations from interfering with Bolshevik influence. Eventually, the Far Eastern People's Republic was abolished and was directly incorporated into the Russian republic when the threat of Japanese occupation receded, whereas the Khivan and Bukharan people's republics were transformed in 1924 into the republics of Uzbekistan and Turkmenistan. Mongolia and Tuva, however, remained formally independent during these years, though their affairs were tightly controlled from Moscow.[41]

Some East European Communists, upon coming to power, sought to integrate their states directly into the USSR as union republics. But for the most part integration was not the solution pursued after World War II. Instead, Stalin opted to create people's republics, which in theory were supposed to be a halfway stage between a bourgeois and a Soviet republic (though the goal of integration as a Soviet republic was never seriously pursued).[42] Again, the rationale for using sovereign state forms to extend power beyond one's borders was tactical, reflecting the inability to integrate the vast territories conquered after the war and the desire to exclude external powers and diasporas from interfering with Soviet control. This rationale is exemplified by the starkly different fates that befell the Baltic states and Poland: incorporation of the former directly into the USSR, but continuation of Poland as an independent state after World War II. Both Poland and the Baltics had been territories of the Tsarist Empire lost at the time of the Russian Revolution. Both were hotbeds of national resistance to Soviet control. Their different fates had more to do with the political contexts in which these regions came under Soviet domination. The Balts were initially incorporated as part of the Molotov-Ribbentrop lands in 1939–40, when Nazi complicity to incorporation meant that international restraints against incorporation were few, and the capabilities to exercise control were in place. Even so, the charade was choreographed to appear as voluntaristic acts of self-determination. Those portions of Poland that were occupied by the Soviets at the time were incorporated directly into Ukraine, Belorussia, and Lithuania. By contrast, control over those territories of Poland not incorporated into the USSR in 1939 took place during the early Cold War, when, as Adam Ulam noted, contrary to Western perceptions at the time, the Soviet Union was weak and overextended.[43] By utilizing norms of state sovereignty while penetrating and monitoring local governments, the Soviets created a buffer zone between the USSR and Western Europe, excluded the influence of external powers and diaspora populations from the region, and mobilized the power of numbers to demonstrate to the Soviet population the correctness of the socialist path by creating socialist state units akin to the USSR. This system of control enjoyed some degree of complicity by the Western powers, which at Yalta initially accepted Soviet control over Eastern Europe and which later, by the detente era, accepted it as a normal fact of geopolitics. But Soviet domination in Eastern Europe differed in quite significant ways from the forms of informal control used by European colonial powers. Soviet domination was instead a masked form of control—a system of states (and eventually, a formal alliance of states) which were recognized juridically by the international community of states as sovereign entities, but whose politics were controlled from abroad through multiple covert channels. In this sense, the Soviet system was an informal empire well adapted to a world of states; it is indeed now viewed by international relations experts as "the most striking modern example of an informal empire."[44]

In a context in which the line between states and empires has become blurred, empires are no longer simply about control. They are also about claims to nationhood and about the illegitimate and nonconsensual nature of control. But one of the crucial consequences of this is that, although hidden transcripts of resistance may well function beneath the surface of politics, overt resistance becomes the main criteria used by most observers to judge whether a relationship is "imperial." With respect to hegemonic structures in general, John Ikenberry and Charles Kupchan have observed that "the outcomes we would expect to see if coercion were at work may not differ substantially from those associated with socialization," making it "difficult to determine the extent to which a specific outcome follows from either the manipulation of material incentives or the alteration of substantive beliefs."[45] Effective control in this sense is not a sufficient indicator of empire if empire is understood as based in lack of consent. David Lake has elaborated on this problem further with respect to identifying an informal imperial relationship:

> The problem with recognizing any informal [imperial] relationship is that the exercise of residual rights of control is evident only in out-of-equilibrium behavior. In the case of an informal empire, for instance, when the limited rights of the client are understood by both parties, no resistance occurs, no overt coercion is necessary, and the local government complies with the wishes of the dominant state *as if* in an alliance. Only if the client tests its constraints or the patron's patience will the informal imperial controls become manifest.[46]

In the case of Eastern Europe, the frequent and extensive resistance offered by populations in East Germany, Poland, Hungary, and Czechoslovakia against Soviet domination made Soviet repression and nonconsensual control transparent, causing widespread identification of this situation as one of informal empire (despite significant pockets of support for Soviet control in East Europe—most notably, in Bulgaria). By contrast, internal recognition of the Soviet Union as an empire occurred relatively suddenly—in the course of weeks, months, or a few years, and only in interaction with the nationalist mobilization of other groups. On the eve of the collapse of the USSR, few observers treated the USSR internally as an empire. Rather, widespread recognition of the Soviet Union as an empire—both among its own citizens and abroad—came as part of a massive upsurge of nationalist contention within a short time that affected multiple groups and ultimately destroyed the Soviet state. Moreover, it was a process that was differential across these groups, with particular structural conditions—urbanization, assimilation, group size, and ethnofederal status—playing large roles in whether potential target audiences responded to anti-imperial frames.[47] Eventually, as the future of the Soviet state grew bleak, even nomenklatura elites jumped onto the anti-imperial bandwagon, seeing in it a path to the maintenance and consolidation of their power. In short, in the contemporary world resistance is central to the making of empires. Highly centralized control over a multinational population, even if it resembles the spoke-like rimless wheel that many see as a hallmark of empire, is unlikely to be recognized as empire unless it is accompanied by significant resistance.

How Contemporary States Become Empires

Let me summarize and elaborate on the argument up to this point. First, although nonconsensual control over culturally distinct populations within or beyond a state's borders has been the core idea of what empires are about since the term altered meaning in the nineteenth century, scholars have failed to devote sufficient attention to the nature of the entities being controlled and how the structure that scholars have traditionally identified as central to empire comes about. Empires in the contemporary world are not just relationships of control of one political society over another; they are, rather, *illegitimate* relationships of control specifically by one *national* political society over another. Thus, embedded within our contemporary understanding of empires are a politics of *national* identity and a politics of *claims-making* that were not part of the

politics of empire prior to the nineteenth century. This renders transhistorical, structural arguments about empire problematic.

Second, in the contemporary world the difference between large multinational states and empires has grown fuzzy, in part because most large
multinational states are built on the templates of former empires, in
part because the nature of control over culturally distinct populations has
altered, with norms of state sovereignty and self-determination coming to
be harnessed by states toward purposes of control. Ian Clark has observed
that although much of the discourse of the post-Cold War order has "been
avowedly about self-determination, there comes a point where the 'soli-
darist' dimensions of an international society might also be regarded as
a veiled form of hegemony or empire." As Clark argues, the question that
needs to be addressed today "is the extent to which it is these very principles of international legitimacy that define the nature of the contemporary imperial project. Imperial rule . . . may have lost its legitimacy, but
might legitimacy be the new form of imperial rule?"[48] The Soviet Union's
practice of using international norms of self-determination and sovereignty as ways of structuring control was in large part responsible for this
transformation.[49] Within a world in which sovereignty and self-determination are established norms, empire has become a part of the oppositional politics used by those challenging the large multinational states or
hegemonic power beyond state borders.

Third, scholars need to pay greater attention to how specific state practices translate into a sense of dominated national community within those
states that come to be widely labeled as empires. In addition to coercion
and repression, specific state policies of inequality, segregation, discrimination, assimilation, or integration are likely to be implicated in the production of an oppositional consciousness. By focusing on such policies,
scholars can engage the counterfactuals of empire. Was, for instance, post-
Franco Spain headed toward widespread accusations of representing
the Castillian Empire before it gave significant autonomy to Basques and
Catalans in 1978? Could the Soviet Union have avoided becoming an
empire if it had continued with the more open version of ethnofederalism it practiced in the mid-1920s, if it had not incorporated the Balts in
1940, or if it had avoided the practice of ethnofederalism altogether? Ultimately, the fundamental difference between a large multinational state
and a multinational empire is not the presence or absence of objective
structures of control or even policies of inequality and discrimination, but
rather whether politics and policies are accepted as "ours" or rejected as
"theirs." Practices of nonconsensual control and objective inequalities
play central roles in what makes grievance likely. But grievance is a collective claim, not an objective condition.

Fourth, the central problem of analysis posed by empires in a post-imperial world is again not whether a state is an empire in some timeless or essential manner, but rather how the porous boundary between state and empire is traversed through a contentious politics of claims-making—that is, the process by which a multinational state comes to be recognized as an empire or an empire comes to be recognized as a state. How do we recognize empire not merely as a claim, but also as an outcome? There is some truth in the assertion that empires in today's world are merely another name for failed states, and an empire can be unambiguously recognized only after a multinational state has collapsed, particularly if we think of empire as a stable and irrevocable quality. But in cases like the Soviet Union or Ethiopia, a widespread recognition of empire emerged prior to state collapse and was part of the process that brought about state collapse, not merely a reflection of the outcome of state failure. The main indicator by which most people judge whether a polity is or is not an empire today is the extent to which resistance to control is widespread and successful, so that resistance to a large extent makes empires. Thus, any explanation of the structuration of contemporary empires must deal with the ways in which empires emerge out of a politics of resistance, whether this be in part as an expression of mass resistance against non-consensual rule or in part as the use of anti-imperial language by political entrepreneurs seeking to establish or to consolidate their power.

Fifth, the past makes a difference. Actually, in the vast majority of cases of failed states over the last fifty years, the failed state was rarely if ever referred to as an empire, even if failure occurred within a multinational context.[50] Thus, not all large multinational states are subject to widespread charges of empire, even in the context of state failure. Rather, it is almost exclusively those large multinational states built out of the fragments of former imperial cores—a fact that points to the important role of history as both a frame and a resource for those challenging multinational states. Dominic Lieven has commented that India and Indonesia, like the Soviet Union, were also vast multiethnic countries, but have managed to survive because they do not bear "the historical stigma of empire" in the same way that the Soviet Union did.[51] Terry Martin has recently elaborated on this idea with respect to the Soviet Union, arguing that Lenin and Stalin were responding precisely to the danger posed by the historical stigma of empire when they fashioned Soviet ethnofederalism. As Martin notes, "India and Indonesia had the benefit of the doubt; they would have to prove to their subjects and the world that they were empires; the Soviet Union would have to prove the opposite."[52] Although it would be difficult to argue that Indonesian or Nigerian policies toward minorities were significantly less exploitative than those of the Soviet state, in general discourses of empire in these cases have been muted. Why have these regimes, even though they are built on the templates of empires in place prior to European colonization, been successful in eluding the "historical stigma of empire" while the Soviet Union was not? The reason seems related to the difference between a postcolonial and a postimperial state. Occupation and reconfiguration by an outside power and the moral cleansing effect of gaining independence through struggle against European colonialism make it more difficult for accusations of empire to stick, irrespective of the objective nature of the policies pursued.[53]

Finally, recognition of a polity as an empire is likely to be more widespread not only in the wake of state collapse, but also when new regimes are attempting to extend or consolidate their control over a culturally distinct population or when states attempt to project their power abroad in new and intrusive ways.[54] Thus, America's war against Iraq beginning in 2003 evoked widespread accusations of American empire, as the United States moved to exert its power in new and unexpected ways within the world system. Actions that extend state power but do so in self-defense are less likely to gain the imperial label, which is why most acts of state expansion in the contemporary world are portrayed as acts of self-defense rather than territorial aggrandizement—a reflection of the power of international norms to shape the ways in which we understand events. By contrast, claims that a polity is an empire are likely to recede in periods of domestic and international stability or when a territory or group has been subject to longstanding control. The number of years in which a territory is controlled by a state often has a powerful effect on whether a population or the international community labels that state's rule as imperial.

A number of postimperial states built around former imperial cores (Austria, Germany, Sweden, Portugal, Belgium, and Japan, for example) now are rarely subject to accusations of empire. In these cases, defeat in war, revolution, foreign occupation, and/or radical downsizing decreased the prevalence of labeling as empire—at least as long as active mobilization by territorially concentrated minorities and attempts to project power abroad remained limited. By contrast, Russia, Ethiopia, China, Britain, France, Spain, Turkey, the United States, and Iran are all, to varying degrees, still subjected to labeling as empires—in large part because they were never subjected to extensive foreign occupation, still contain territorially concentrated minorities who, in significant numbers, reject the dominance of these states over them, and in some cases (such as the United States and France) are active in projecting their power abroad in violent and often controversial ways.[55]

Thus, the politics of becoming an empire in the contemporary world can be understood as a form of tipping game in which perceptions of a polity as an empire vary over time, depending on a series of factors: (1) the economic, social, cultural, and political policies of the state that structure nonconsensual control and foster a sense of national identity; (2) the degree of nationalist resistance to state efforts to project control; (3) the historical background of the state and whether a "stigma" of historical empire exists; (4) the bandwagon effects produced by state strength or weakness; (5) whether a state attempts to consolidate or extend control over populations (either within or outside the state) in new ways; and (6) whether an action is legitimated as self-defense. Indeed, several empire games are being played simultaneously: between states and nationalist oppositions to states (either internally or abroad) over support within subordinate populations; between states and nationalist oppositions to states over support within the international community (also an important community of "observers"); and between states and nationalist oppositions to states over support within politically dominant populations (the loss of legitimacy within dominant populations often being a critical element in the recognition of a relationship as "imperial" and in bringing about change in state control).

Post-Soviet Russia and the Politics of Empire

A case study of one postimperial state—post-Soviet Russia—illustrates some of the ways in which postimperial states can continue to be subject to widespread labeling as empire. Since its birth in 1991, post-Soviet Russia has remained variably subject to labeling as empire in both its internal and external relationships. These claims have varied over time and space and remain widespread within some contexts, though in many respects post-Soviet Russia has been gradually moving away from widespread recognition as empire, in spite of its bloody war in Chechnya. Contention over whether post-Soviet Russia is an empire has remained a central aspect of politics in the Eurasian region. The ebb and flow of such accusations illustrate how states negotiate the porous boundary between empire and multinational state and the factors that help give rise to contemporary empires.

Despite the collapse of the Soviet Union, the historical stigma of empire continues to hang over post-Soviet Russia, just as it did over the Soviet state. As Vladimir Putin noted shortly after becoming Russian president in March 2000, "In our experience, Russia is still perceived as a remnant of the former Soviet Union." Putin contended that this view is wrong, as the new Russia "is not an empire," but rather "a self-confident power with a great future."[56] This statement, of course, was made only months after Putin had initiated the Second Chechen War, which produced a massive and devastating assault on the city of Grozny (the second in five years), tens of thousands of civilian deaths, and hundreds of thousands of refugees. Today, Russia remains subject to labeling as empire, both by observers abroad and within its own borders. As Charles King recently wrote in the pages of *Foreign Affairs*:

> Russia is still something close to an empire—an electoral one, perhaps, but a political system whose essential attributes are simply not those of a modern state. Central power, where it exists, is exercised through subalterns who function as effective tax- and ballot-farmers: they surrender up a portion of local revenue and deliver the votes for the center's designated candidates in national elections in exchange for the center's letting them run their own fiefdoms. Viceroys sent from the capital keep tabs on local potentates but generally leave them to their own devices. State monopolies or privileged private companies secure strategic resources and keep open the conduits that provide money to the metropole. The conscript military, weak and in crisis, is given the task of policing the restless frontier—fighting a hot war in Chechnya and patrolling the ceasefire lines of cold ones in the borderland emirates of Moldova, Georgia, and Tajikistan. Such arrangements do make for federalism of a sort, but in an older sense of the word. The concept comes, after all, from Rome's practice of accommodating threatening peoples by settling them inside the empire and paying them to be foederati, or self-governing border guards. It is federalism as an imperial survival strategy, not as a way of bringing government closer to the governed.[57]

Yet, despite King's suspicion that empire may be masquerading as federalism once again, and despite the brutality of the Chechen wars, charges of empire by some of Russia's minorities have grown less frequent in recent years, as Russian control over its non-Russian territories has stabilized, mobilization has diminished, and opportunities to contest state boundaries have dissipated.

Accusations of post-Soviet empire were widespread among non-Russian nationalist activists in the immediate aftermath of the Soviet collapse. Russia's minorities were among the last groups to mobilize within the tide of nationalism that brought about the collapse of the Soviet state. This lateness within the tide was shaped to a large extent by their position within the ethnofederal system. Whereas nationalist movements among groups with union republics were strongly influenced by the anticolonial frame developed by Baltic nationalist movements, nationalist movements among minorities within the Russian Federation focused instead in the late 1980s on raising their status from autonomous to union republics, often seeing the USSR government as an ally in this struggle against the Russian republic.[58] The parade of sovereignties in the second half of 1990, in which federal subunit after federal subunit (including Russia) went about declaring sovereignty, exercised a strong effect on the non-Russian republics of Russia. But it was only in 1991, as the collapse of the Soviet Union became imminent, that nationalist movements within a few of Russia's non-Russian republics—most conspicuously, Chechnya and Tatarstan—began to agitate for full-scale independence, treating both Soviet and Russian republican rule as forms of Russian colonial power. Mobilization in Chechnya and Tatarstan against Russian imperialism reached its peak in the aftermath of the August 1991 coup, when the Soviet government collapsed, union republics declared their independence, and effective authority fell into the hands of Boris Yeltsin's government.

Inspired by these events, an anticolonial revolution was carried out in Chechnya in the fall of 1991 that brought General Dzhokhar Dudaev to power, leading to the declaration of Chechen independence from Moscow. Moscow refused to recognize this act, instead insisting that Chechnya remained an integral part of the Russian Federation. The failure of Russia's repeated attempts to overthrow the Dudaev regime and to reestablish control over Chechnya eventually led to the First Chechen War, from 1994 to 1996. As Yeltsin said in his address justifying what he referred to as the "police action" in Chechnya, Russian soldiers were merely "protecting the unity of Russia," an "indispensable condition for the existence of the Russian state."[59] However, the Russian involvement in Chechnya was widely viewed, both within Russia and outside, as an act of resurgent Russian imperialism (not to mention how most Chechens understood these events—as merely the continuation of a 150-year armed resistance to Russian imperial power).[60] These perceptions were compounded by the incompetence of the Russian military effort, which, despite its brutality, not only failed to extinguish Chechen resistance, but in the end also saw the city of Grozny recaptured by the insurgents.

By contrast, the Second Chechen War (1999–), which emerged in response to a series of terrorist acts carried out by Chechen Islamic radicals in Russia and the attempt by these groups to export Islamic revolution to neighboring Daghestan, has been more readily accepted by the international community and by Russia's own population. Rising global fears of Islamic radicalism fostered a very different international climate. And though the Second Chechen War has been as brutal (perhaps more brutal) than the first, the more successful effort by the Russian military to marginalize Chechen rebels and the continuing spate of terrorist acts carried out by Chechen fighters within Russia have helped to undermine accusations of empire against Russia—at least within the international community and among Russia's other minorities. Devastated and exhausted by two successive wars, much of Chechen society itself has been forced by circumstances to accept Muscovite control begrudgingly. Putin has argued that the Chechens "are not a defeated people. They are a liberated people."[61] Russia's continued use of norms of self-determination and sovereignty as modes of control is well illustrated by the March 2003 referendum held in Chechnya, under severe conditions of war and widespread violations of human rights, over a new constitution for the territory that proclaimed Chechnya "an inalienable part of the territory of the Russian Federation." (Not surprisingly, the referendum won overwhelmingly.)[62]

With the collapse of the Soviet state, Tatarstan was similarly affected by a major wave of anticolonial mobilization in 1991. Public opinion polls in Tatarstan in fall 1991 showed that 86 percent of Tatars favored the complete independence of Tatarstan,[63] and a referendum held in March 1992 produced a 61 percent majority in favor of recognizing Tatarstan as "a sovereign state and a subject of international law." But in contrast to Chechnya, the issue was co-opted by the local nomenklatura, who utilized the opportunity to assert an ambiguous status for the republic within Russia that included far-reaching autonomy. Eventually, the influence of separatist nationalist movements waned. By the mid-1990s the secessionist sentiment that had once been significant in Tatarstan had dissipated, separatist movements had grown marginalized within the political process, and Tatarstan's membership within the Russian Federation had come to be accepted by the overwhelming majority of Tatars. The threat of the breakup of Russia (seemingly imminent in 1992–93, evoking a series of books and articles by Western experts on the subject)[64] now seems to have receded, as Russian boundaries have grown normalized and accepted by the vast majority of Russia's minorities.

But Tatarstan's ambiguous relationship with the Russian Federation—as constituent republic or former colony—continues to color much of the politics of the region. Accusations of Russia as empire persist, proliferating at moments when Russia attempts to renegotiate elements of Tatarstan's autonomy, and occurring largely in response to Tatar fears that Moscow seeks to extinguish Tatarstani sovereignty and to assimilate Tatars to the dominant Russian culture. The adoption of the two-headed eagle as the official symbol of the new Russian state, for instance, was widely portrayed by many Tatars (as well as members of Russia's other minorities) as a symbolic reaffirmation of the continuity of Russian imperial projects. (By contrast, Yeltsin and his advisors portrayed this as an attempt to associate the new Russian state with a pre-Soviet history of statehood.) In the late 1990s the introduction of new Russian passports, which omitted the nationality category previously utilized in Soviet passports, was seen by many within the Tatar elite as an attempt to undermine minority efforts to promote local cultures and the indigenization of local governments. More recently, anti-imperial discourse among Tatars mounted in connection with the emotion-laden disagreements over the categories to be used in the 2002 Russian census. (Many Tatars saw an attempt to divide and conquer in the Russian government's efforts to allow the choice of Tatar subethnic identities to be counted as one's ethnic group.) Anti-imperial discourse among Tatars also increased as a result of Russian opposition to the use of the Latin alphabet in Tatarstan.[65] As Rafael Khakimov, one of the chief advisors to the Tatarstan government, described Tatar fears of resuscitated empire, "There's an imperial spirit arising again in Moscow. It's very popular there right now to believe that empire is right, that we must put an end to the republics like Tatarstan."[66]

Post-Soviet Russia also suffers from a stigma of empire in its relations with other post-Soviet states.[67] Shortly after becoming prime minister in 1999, Vladimir Putin said that Russia is not nourishing "imperial plans" with regard to the CIS countries, though it intends to pursue its interests with regard to what it refers to euphemistically as its "near abroad."[68] But the boundary between "regional power" and "imperial power" has been a contested one. In the Baltic, for instance, Soviet-era settlers are frequently referred to as a potential fifth column for a renewed Russian imperialism. Russia's continuing denial that Soviet incorporation of the Baltic ever amounted to an occupation (due largely to fears that Russia could be held legally responsible for the consequences of Soviet rule) only has added to such suspicions. Russia's attempts to influence Georgian politics, its role in the Abkhaz rebellion, its continuing presence at its military base in Javekheti, and its threats to invade Georgia in pursuit of Chechen fighters have brought about recurrent accusations that Russia is continuing an "imperial policy" toward the Transcaucasus region. As one source notes, "The Georgian press is stuffed with anti-Russian publications, and 'imperialists' is the softest expression in them."[69] Belarusian nationalists have criticized the Belarusian-Russian Union as a plan to "recapture Belarus in order to plunder it and use our people's labor."

Aleksandr Lukashenka's efforts at reintegrating Belarus with Russia force Belarusians to choose "between living in a free and independent European state, and poverty on the outskirts of the Russian empire." Support for Lukashenka, they argue, "means to approve the restoration of the Russian empire."[70] In Ukraine, when Russia took an uncompromising position on Ukraine's $3.7 billion energy debt and demanded that Ukraine pay for it by turning over some of its enterprises in the fuel, metallurgical, and machine-building industries to Russia, accusations that Russia was harboring "imperial ambitions" grew widespread.[71] Similar accusations can be heard in Armenia in relation to Russia's increasing control over Armenian energy production and distribution as part of deals intended to cover Armenian energy debts. To Putin's chagrin, the creation of an economic community within the CIS consisting of Russia, Ukraine, Belarus, and Kazakhstan in 2003 brought about immediate accusations from nationalists in these states that Russia was seeking to restore the Soviet Union.[72]

The point is that not only has Russia has not overcome its "stigma of empire," either within Russia or in its relations with its former Communist domain, but also that accusations of empire rise and fall in connection with specific events, driven by the ways in which Russian policies and practices inspire opposition to themselves. So far, post-Soviet Russia has avoided empire as outcome. Indeed, the general trend seems to be toward gradually fewer accusations of empire, particularly as Russian politicians have committed to stable borders, Russia's attempts to manipulate its diaspora and open threats against its neighbors have diminished, Russian stateness has gradually consolidated, and national resistance to Russia's current territorial configuration has grown marginalized. Yet, the possibility that an imperial outcome could be part of post-Soviet Russia's future remains.

Pro-Imperial Discourses as Longing for Lost Order

As a concluding note on the evolving nature of empires, I turn to consider briefly a counter-discourse about empire that finds reflection in certain elite circles within both contemporary Russia and the United States—a positive discourse about empire as a way of reestablishing order in a disorderly world, a longing for control in a world out of control. Empire in this view represents a simpler world in which order reigned, powerful states could exercise their will with little constraint, and the civilizing missions of these states could be fulfilled. This too is a subversive discourse within today's context, particularly with respect to international norms of self-determination and state sovereignty, and exists primarily as a discourse among policy analysts or opposition politicians. Leaders in both Russia and the United States have refused to associate publicly with this view, which contradicts public transcripts of the exercise of power. That this discourse of empire as a longing for order appears within both the United States and Russia is itself intriguing. Russia and the United States were repeatedly subject to accusations of empire throughout the twentieth century and have repeatedly denied the imperial character of their policies. Yet, for quite different reasons a sense of uncontrolled disorder has been felt among both the winners and the losers of the now transcended Cold War international order.

In the Russian case, open calls for empire have emerged among those mourning the collapse of the Soviet order and the civilizational values for which it stood. In Russia this is specifically an opposition discourse, a nationalist critique of Russian foreign policy that began in the mid-1990s in the aftermath of the waves of nationalist mobilization that unraveled the USSR and of the violent disorder that followed.[73] Open proponents of a renewal of empire have called for more assertive efforts to defend the interests of Russians in the "near abroad" and to create a new state, centered on Russia, that would encompass the peoples of the former USSR and would reflect Russia's civilizational mission within Eurasia. Vladimir Bochkarev, the governor of Penza province, for example, has argued that Russia suffers from an inadequate geopolitical structure that does not correspond to its ambitions to be a great state. To defend Russia's strategic interests properly, "the creation of a new federation empire is a sort of super-task, the solution of which opens the way to the construction of a unique coalition of states, in which each will live in their national reality—not only the Chechens and Tatars and Armenians, but even the people of the Eurasian near and far abroad."[74] A book published in Moscow in 1996 entitled *Neizbezhnost' imperii* ("The Inevitability of Empire") aimed, according to its preface, to provide "a historical, political, and philosophical argument for Empire as the brightest and most progressive phenomenon in the development of world civilization, and especially in the development of Russia." As one author in the volume wrote, "The attempt to create 'national states' in place of Empire consigns the peoples living within them to a semi-feudal, Middle-Ages existence, deforms state structures, and kills ethnic communities through a false liberalism."[75] As another nationalist author has put it:

When they say that a Russian empire is bad and that Russia has ceased being an empire, this is said by our enemies, our opponents, who do not agree with our civilizational ideal, do not agree with our historical path, and in principle would like to see us turn into some kind of dependent, regional, small state-nation with the loss of our strategic and civilizational orientations and, as they say, messianism.[76]

This pro-imperial discourse within Russia largely remains confined to the nationalist opposition and runs boldly counter to the Russian government's announced policies of respecting post-Soviet boundaries and accepting the results of 1991. Post-Soviet Russia may seek to extend its sphere of influence across the post-Soviet states. But much like its Soviet predecessor, it cannot openly accept the label of empire. As Putin observed shortly after his election as president, "Whoever doesn't regret the collapse of the USSR has no heart, and whoever wants to restore the USSR has no head."[77]

By contrast, in the United States a pro-imperial discourse emerged in the wake of the 9/11 events and the Bush administration's attempts to extend American control to Afghanistan and Iraq. As Michael Ignatieff has noted, "If Americans have an empire, they have acquired it in a state of deep denial."[78] Yet, America's forceful assertion of power after the September 11 attacks brought about the first open references to the need for American empire since the late nineteenth century. Rather than an oppositional critique of foreign policy, as in Russia, in the United States a positive discourse of empire emerged almost entirely among foreign policy experts—as a justification for sustained American efforts to shape forcefully an increasingly disorderly world to its own liking. At the same time, some experts warned against the potentially disastrous consequences of imperial "over-extension." As one source summed up the rationale for American empire:

[O]rderly societies now refuse to impose their own institutions on disorderly ones. This anti-imperialist restraint is becoming harder to sustain, however, as the disorder in poor countries grows more threatening. Experience has shown that nonimperialist options—notably foreign aid and various nation-building efforts—are not altogether reliable. The logic of neoimperialism is too compelling for the Bush administration to resist.[79]

Indeed, some Bush administration advisors wear the imperial badge unabashedly; as neoconservative guru William Kristol put it, "We need to err on the side of being strong, and if people want to say we're an imperial power, fine."[80] Similarly, for Max Boot the greatest danger for American foreign policy is "that we won't use all of our power for fear of the 'i' word—imperialism." Yet, the vast majority of Americans continue to feel uncomfortable speaking of the United States as an empire, and the Bush administration, in its public face, has been careful to steer away from any such language, consistently denying imperial intent. As Boot concludes, "Given the historical baggage that 'imperialism' carries, there's no need for the U.S. government to embrace the term. But it should definitely embrace the practice."[81]

In this respect, the transformations pioneered in part by the Soviet state in the nature of political control remain very much in force. Nonconsensual control for both post-Soviet Russia and the post-Cold War United States continues to be cloaked in the language of self-determination and sovereignty, blurring the line between domination and consent. And if the experience of the Soviet Union is any guide to contemporary politics of empire, widespread recognition of the imperial quality of contemporary Russia and America is likely to be associated with the degree of successful resistance offered in the deserts of Mesopotamia and the mountains of the Northern Caucasus.

2

CULTURE SHIFT IN A POSTCOMMUNIST STATE

DAVID D. LAITIN

This chapter examines cultural shift and interethnic relations in post-communist Estonia. The data presented herein do not demonstrate the inevitability of ethnic polarization that many analysts feared.[1] At least in Estonia, processes of cultural assimilation from Russian to Estonian miti-gate the oft-repeated image of solidary ethnic groups in conflict with one another. However, although many have portrayed ethnic polarization as especially dangerous, the processes of Russian assimilation into Estonian culture (and its variants) are hardly benign.[2]

There is no doubt, no matter how one evaluates the changes in the past decade, that a massive cultural revolution has occurred in the post-Soviet world. From a linguistic point of view, the Soviet Union had a well-established cultural equilibrium in its final decades of existence.[3] Russians were assured of their historic right to remain monolingual, no matter where they lived in the union. Titulars (those after whom the republics were named) could remain monolingual in their ancestral languages for a wide variety of occupations if they remained in their republics, but the full world of opportunity would not open to them unless they developed facility in Russian. The non-Russian minorities in the republics also had strong incentives to become bilingual, but in their ancestral languages and Russian. Compared with the titulars, however, these minorities had fewer institutional supports for their ancestral languages and over a few generations became monolingual in Russian.

This equilibrium can be described as demanding of individuals a 2 – 1 language repertoire. For a full range of mobility prospects, titulars needed to know two languages. Russians needed to know only one (2 – 1). Minorities were often bilingual but for most functions needed only a single language (2 – 1), Russian.[4] By the 1980s these rules had become so deeply internalized that no one demonstrated what might be called "choice" behavior; most Soviet citizens merely walked blithely down the equilibrium path.

The collapse of the Soviet Union undermined this equilibrium. From the late 1980s, leaders of the republics passed legislation that challenged the right of Russians to remain monolingual; a range of services in these republics, including public education, would demand facility in the titular language. When the union disintegrated in 1991, these laws became awesomely real. Moreover, as the new republics created markets and sought international contacts, the value of English increased rapidly. Suddenly, people saw language repertoires as a choice, not as a social given. Russian-speaking titulars had to decide whether to enroll their children in titular-medium schools; this was an investment in the futures market for languages. Meanwhile, Russians living in non-Russian republics had to decide whether to immigrate to Russia, where their language repertoires would be sufficient for nearly all social interactions, or to remain in their republics. And if they were to remain, they needed to figure out whether it would pay off to equip their children in the titular language. This was the issue millions of Russian-speakers were posing to themselves and their families.[5]

Over the course of the 1990s, as a result of historical paths and strategic choices, distinct equilibria began to stabilize in the separate republics. In Kazakhstan and elsewhere in central Asia, Russian-speakers looked for good opportunities to emigrate, and grabbed those opportunities when they appeared. In the long term, Russian-speaker emigration would lead to rationalization of the Central Asian republics in the titular languages. In Ukraine, Russian-speakers in the east and south organized themselves locally to assure the long-term dominance of Russian in their oblasts. Russian-language speakers' organizational efforts gave hope that some form of federal or consociational protection for a binational state would be negotiated. And in Estonia and Latvia, Russian-speakers began, but only in a trickle, to reverse the assimilationist tide. Instead of the titulars slowly becoming bilingual in their ancestral language and Russian, it would be the Russians who would slowly become bilingual in their ancestral language and the official language of their new state. In this period, ethnographic research in several republics revealed a day-to-day reality faced by Russians seeking to condition their linguistic (and migrational) behavior on the expected choices of co-ethnics. Strategies of linguistic coordination were palpable.[6]

For the Estonian case, several critical moments of choice led to its equilibrium. Estonian nationalists in the late 1980s mooted the notion—either through inducements or coercion—to make the Russian-speaking minority disappear from within the boundaries of their about-to-be independent state. But despite a cacophonous political transition, both the Estonians and the Russians developed coordinated expectations about the future. Estonians were certain that the era of Russian hegemony was over, and that they could condition their future on being citizens of an Estonian-language state looking westward toward the European Union (EU). Although 26 percent of Estonian nationals claimed fluency in Russian (the actual figure was probably much higher, but there was strategic underreporting in surveys), in 1991 Estonians chose to abjure Russian and not to pass that facility on to their children.

The Russians were put in a bind, forcing a response. The Estonian choice to eliminate Russian from their repertoire would make it impossible for Russians in the future to communicate with state authority in Russian. They also recognized the heavy costs of any return to Russia, where economic opportunity was paltry. Most important, they lacked the networks and resources to coordinate as Russians in demanding a binational state. In consequence, some Russian parents moved to get their children educated in Estonian-language schools. Once some parents made this move, others saw their own children potentially weakened in future labor market competition with Russians fluent in Estonian, and sought to get their children fluent in Estonian. Even in Russian nationalist cities such as Narva, a flood of Russian families applied to matriculate their children in Estonian medium schools. Given this political reality, and constrained by international oversight and their own liberal instincts, the Estonians' utopian dream of an ethnic cleansing was inexorably abandoned.

The Russian response—in its basic acceptance of Estonian cultural hegemony—compelled the Estonian government to face a new reality, and to make new choices. The notion that the Russian-speaking population could not be ignored became a new common sense. No longer could a policy of induced out-migration be supported. In 2000, a political compromise of "integration"—welcomed by EU observers, agreeable to a coalition of Estonians, and acceptable to the Russian leadership—became the state's new, though ambiguous, choice.

Integrationist trends were quite surprising to many scholars of Estonia. Sensitive to the colonization of Estonia by Russians, the centuries of

Russian domination over Estonian society, and the courageous resistance of Estonian patriots to Soviet rule, these scholars portrayed Estonians and Russians as separate societies with impermeable boundaries separating them. Integration of Estonians into Russian/Soviet culture was evaluated either as a form of insincere co-optation or as a sign of cultural pollution. To be sure, these scholars acknowledged that some Estonians, those born in Russia, were avatars of Soviet rule. But most of these Russian Estonians, after returning to Estonia to rule on behalf of the Communist Party, discovered their nationalist roots and became born-again Estonians. With the fall of Communism, in this literature, the idea that Russians might assimilate into Estonian culture was not considered seriously among Estonian experts.[7]

These experts ignored sociological theory. In the theoretical literature in sociology, assimilation and integration are hardly unusual processes.[8] In the study of nationalism, Gellner blazed a trail demonstrating that if mobility opportunities existed for national minorities in industrial centers controlled by a national majority, members of the minority group would seek to learn the language of the dominant group and adopt its cultural practices.[9] Subsequent research showed that even if a minority population would prefer nonassimilation, the incentives for individuals to assimilate—to get the best jobs before their neighbors assimilate, or to avoid paying for translation services—would over time and across generations lead to an assimilationist cascade, such that the minority culture would virtually disappear.[10] A revisionist national history of France confirms this assimilationist perspective. France until the second third of the nineteenth century was a polyglot (and some might say multinational) state, but through conscription, education, and the economic pull of Paris, potential minority nationalities became French.[11]

In this chapter, sensitive to the integrationist literature in sociology, I dissect the multifaceted processes of cultural change in Estonia. I start by differentiating three integrationist processes, all of which are consistent with the assimilationist model presented in *Identity in Formation* that predicted a cultural "tip" for the descendents of the present Russian-speakers toward a common Estonian national culture. The data show elements of all three of these newly collected processes but to different degrees of importance. Yet the story is more complex still. These three processes are clouded by a congeries of contradictory trends. Despite these trends, the slow but inexorable move toward an assimilationist cascade is largely confirmed.

But Estonia is not near its tipping point. There is instead a slow adjustment to cultural realities rather than an immediate pressure to choose, characteristic of cascades. Off the central political stage, where the drama of Estonian/Russian relations is still vibrant, calculation for coordination is no longer all that observable; young Russians and Estonians are responding to incentives that were the result of earlier coordination behavior. A tip may be a generation away. Meanwhile, the actual behavior of calculation about one's cultural future plays a lesser role. Such choice behavior involving careful calculation and self-conscious coordination can be observed only when the future equilibrium is not known. At least in Estonia, the transition is over, and a new cultural equilibrium has already been internalized, to which even the nationalist state has accommodated itself. The frenetic exercise of coordinating with one's ethnic brethren, so characteristic of the early 1990s, is over. It seems, then, that the distinct equilibria that were the result of active coordination mechanisms in the early 1990s are in a stable way conditioning people's expectations. Choice remains relevant because all options are not foreclosed; but for many Russians in Estonia, who are following trails blazed by an earlier generation, choice is less observable.

Taking off from where *Identity in Formation* left off, this chapter examines how the Estonian government reacted to the Russian cultural strategies. It then moves to the underlying social dynamics—leading to a 2 + 1 model of integration—that occur beneath the eyes of the law. With the 2 + 1 model in mind, the chapter assesses the implications of the integration reality for the possibility of social conflict.[12] Finally, with so much emphasis given here to a deterministic equilibrium path, the chapter concludes by assessing the issue of strategy and agency in post-Soviet cultural change.

Three Models of Integration

There are three possible models of Russian integration in Estonia that are all consistent with the data presented in *Identity in Formation* (see figure 2.1).

Standard Integration

This is a two-way process. The minority adopts a large range of cultural practices associated with the dominant culture; meanwhile, because of the contact that is part of integration, members of the dominant culture begin to adopt, unevenly and selectively—and often as fads and fashions—some of the cultural practices of the minority.

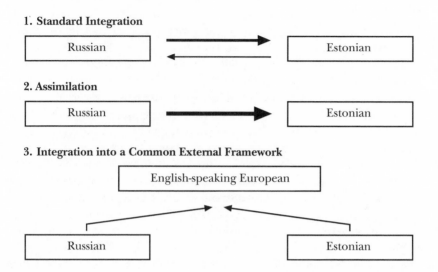

Figure 2.1 **Three Models of Integration**

Assimilation

This is a form of integration in which the minority adopts virtually all cultural practices of the dominant group in society, and in which adoptions of cultural practices of the minority by members of the dominant group are barely discernible.

Integration into a Common External Framework

This third model of integration is often associated with postcolonial culture. In this model the dominant group as well as the minority both condition their cultural behavior on some external model, and integrate through a common exposure to this external model.

The sociological data collected for this project support a fourth model, which combines all three of the preceding models. Yet, the data also support the view that among the congeries of processes, the incentives for assimilation of the Russian-speaking populations into Estonian culture remain quite powerful, thereby revealing that despite evidence of standard integration in Estonia, the cultural cross-breeding is so asymmetric as to look far more like assimilation.

The Elite Political Game

The Estonian Political Class

Estonian policy initially reflected an unrealistic goal of cleansing the society through politically induced out-migration. Yet by 2000, a variety of factors had led the Estonian political class to reconcile itself to an integration program with goals that bordered on the assimilationist ideal, in which Russians would adopt in public forums the Estonian language and way of life, though they were not expected to give up entirely their home language, their religion, or their sense of being of Russian heritage. Meanwhile, Estonians would be immune to Russian cultural practices.

Several political motives induced the Estonian leadership to sponsor an integration program. First was the domestic political reality of party competition.[13] Pro Patria—the most nationalist among Estonian parties—ruled Estonia from 1992 to 1995, years in which Russians were derisively called "aliens" in legislation, and policy was oriented toward remigration to Russia. The party's fall from grace was due more to the harshness of its economic reform package than to its nationalist policies. When Pro Patria resurrected itself in 1999, however, the nationalist fervor of the mid-1990s had dissipated, and the party had to reinvent itself.

In order to bring a more practical administration to the city of Tallinn, Pro Patria Mayor Yuri Mois had constructed a Quadruple Alliance in the City Council. For it, he co-opted the leading Russian politicians, who were satisfied with control over the Department of Integration and Public Safety, which allowed them to distribute program funds to their supporters. Although this strategy infuriated many party members (and eventually collapsed in scandal), Pro Patria leaders recognized that one cost of governing was the strategic advantage of building coalitions with Russians, or at least making strategic concessions on its nationality agenda.

After the 1999 national elections, Pro Patria had the chance of returning to power but required coalition partners. (Noncitizens cannot vote in national elections, so Russian-favored parties play a lesser role in parliamentary coalitions.) The prime minister designate, Mart Laar of Pro Patria, built a Triple Alliance with the Moderates and the Reform Party. The Moderates had gained many seats in this election and were a force to be reckoned with. Marju Lauristin, a prominent parliamentarian, became the chairman of the Moderate parliamentary caucus. Lauristin had been in academic exile in Tartu, where she led a team of researchers studying the problems of integration. After the elections, she got the Moderates (and the Reform leaders were in accord) to demand a more enlightened policy, based on sociological research, in regard to the Russians. Pro Patria accepted this, with the hope that they could manipulate the terms of the agreement and impose an assimilationist orientation to integration that would not compromise their vision of Estonia as having a single nationality. What is noteworthy is that the decision to take the integrationist course had little to do with Russian input, as the Reform and Moderate Parties' social bases are intellectual Estonians and not Russians. Meanwhile, the Centrists, the nonethnic party that has garnered Russian-speaking votes, played virtually no role in the development of the integration program.

The alliance compromise by Pro Patria evoked ire in its own ranks, and even greater ire among spokespersons for the Russian-speaking population who saw their ideological clarity blurred by partisan practicality. For example, S. Smirnov criticized "national radicals" who "betray their principles and begin to flirt with some representatives of the Russian-speaking population."[14] He was especially appalled when former Prime Minister Andres Tarand revealed that if the Triple Alliance needed a few extra votes, its partners would seek them even from among the Russian parties. So, Smirnov deduced, "right wing national-radicals are ready to bring Russian politicians for filling holes, but they are not ready to share power with them."[15]

A second motivation for the program was to satisfy "Europe." Pressure from the Organization for Security and Cooperation in Europe (OSCE), from the EU, and from the Open Society Institute (OSI) put Estonian nationality policy (however legal) in a dark light. But in the wake of the integration program, these organizations have toned down considerably their criticisms. The Baltic News Service reported that the OSCE high commissioner on ethnic minority affairs, Rolf Ekeus, praised the integration program in Tallinn while insisting "that integration is a mutual process, where both language communities of Estonia should participate."[16] And the 2001 OSI report on "Minority Protection in Estonia" was only mildly critical that the government did not rein in its own national radicals; but it had no brief against the legal framework as outlined in the integration program.[17] Also, as a reward for Estonia's integration program, OSI gave greater editorial control to Estonians for its revised edition published in 2002. This edition contained hardly any criticism. The integration program has induced Europe to drop its guard in regard to the treatment of minorities in Estonia.

A third motivation for the integration program was that of social, political, and economic reality hitting the nationalist coalition between the eyes. By 1998, the hoped-for out-migration of Russians to Russia had dried up, and even the most utopian nationalists came to terms with the social fact of a permanent Russian-heritage minority. Russia's post-1998 economic recovery also changed calculations. In the early years of independence, many Estonian politicians thought that there could be no future value in trade to the east. But even this view confronted new realities. For example, former Prime Minister (and once Estonian state plenipotentiary in Ida-Virumaa) Tiit Vahi, now of a leading investment group, is seeking to reduce customs barriers in Ida-Virumaa to enhance his company's trade, now only 3 percent with Russia.[18]

A fourth motivation has been the desire of the Estonian political class to provide a public good. Katrin Saks, then minister of ethnic affairs, gave the official version: "Linguistic-communicative integration means first the improvement of the knowledge of the state language among the non-Estonians. The inadequate language skills decrease their competitiveness on the labor market; it also limits their possibility for acquiring the higher education and diminishes their participation in political and cultural life."[19] To be sure, lack of Estonian diminishes their chances in the labor market largely because the Estonian rulers fashioned the labor market in order to discriminate against monolingual Russian speakers. But it is nonetheless logical that a common language lowers transaction costs. In this sense, linguistic hegemony is a public good.

The collapse of the Triple Alliance in January 2002 brought the Reform Party and the Center Party into a temporary governing coalition, with few policy initiatives, none affecting the integration program. The March 2003 elections brought into prominence a newly formed party, Res Publica, which leads an alliance with the Reform and People's Union parties. Res Publica had no clear policy on integration; media reports suggested that it would scrap the integration program and do away with the Ethnic Affairs portfolio, whose minister serves as the chairman of the Integration Foundation. But Res Publica's Reform Party ally did not want to arouse suspicion in Europe and persuaded Res Publica leaders to maintain the portfolio. Nonetheless, without a powerful Estonian alliance in support of it, the future of the integration program is not assured.

The Russian Political Class

Spokespersons for the Russian-speaking population have adopted an ideal that is more integrationist than assimilationist. In fact, they have been openly critical of the orientation of the government program. For example, Viktor Andreev of the United People's Party of Estonia portrays it as a "one-sided process."[20] Maxim Rogalski writes in *Estoniya*, "[Y]ou cannot remain silent when the elimination of Russian language schools is discussed. If we keep silent, we agree that in the near future our children will come across a question: to be totally assimilated is to belong to the lower layers of the society."[21] Indeed, criticisms were so loud that being co-opted into the program was costly for Russians. In fact, two moderate Russians—Mikhail Stalnukhin and Vladimir Velman (both of the Center Party)—quit the Integration Foundation to show their displeasure over its mode of operation.[22]

The tone of Russian response in the media is often that of bitter irony. Aleksandr Erek in *Molodezh Estonii* portrays integration as a commercial enterprise in which the Estonian government pursues a set of policies that are paid for by interested Europeans.[23] In *Õhtuleht*, Sergei Stadnikov writes that the language program is designed not by those who brought a democratic Estonian republic, but by national radicals who came later. These radicals, he says, received their higher education in their mother tongue (although of Soviet character). It is thus implied that Estonia is doing dastardly deeds that were not even practiced in the Soviet Union. In *Molodezh Estonii* Svetlana Loginova writes about the so-called "monkey's labor" of policemen and other important officials wasting time going to Estonian language classes, getting certificates, and then forgetting the language and not doing their work. The only profit, she reckons, goes to the state language examiners.[24] This is echoed by Yevgeny Kapov in *Estoniya*, writing about police after a raid on the Ida-Virumaa and Narva police prefectures: the police "who are not afraid to go under bullets or bandit's knife turned to be helpless before a language inspector. . . . This is really the union of state and criminal structures!" So the police, he says, who do not take bribes from citizens, pay bribe-like penalties to the inspectorate. Kapov writes ironically that the police can tell robbed Estonians "*vabandage* ["sorry," in Estonian] that we can't catch your thief "—if Marge Mägi [language inspector for Ida-Virumaa] were robbed—"because the police were in language class."[25]

And irony gets to the heart of the (Soviet-sounding) propaganda of the integration campaign itself. A correspondent with the initials T.A. in *Molodezh Estonii* writes on the fostering of integration through penal sanctions: "The question on the role of penal sanctions," he insists, "should be addressed to those who started the ad campaign of integration under the motto 'Friendship begins with a smile.' "[26]

But irony sometimes turns into bitter farce. On May Day 2002 in Narva, the Unity of Russian Citizens, led by Yuri Mishin, was pushing for a Macedonian model for Ida-Virumaa's incorporation into Estonia. Followers moved toward the central square in an "empty pot march" singing the *Internationale*! In the story on the same event in *Eesti Päevaleht*, Ants Liimets (a town administrator and chairman of the Narva Estonian Society) reported that the anthems of Russia and the USSR were played at the beginning of the meeting, and that there was no Estonian flag to compete with the Soviet flag as well as the defunct flag of the Estonian Soviet Socialist Republic.[27] (The march wasn't as anti-Estonian as Liimets's image suggests. The former vice-mayor of Narva, Gennady Afanasyev, reportedly congratulated the participants in Estonian.)[28]

Despite the harsh tone and antics of the critics, the Estonian political reality—as was the case for Estonian politicians—brings strong incentives to compromise. First, the policy is not as harsh as it is often portrayed. Despite a tone in the OSI report "Minority Protection in Estonia" that reflects some of the deeply hostile opinions about minorities that crop up in Estonian discourse, the current laws—on citizenship, for example— are "technically consistent with international standards."[29] This is not entirely true of the language policies—regarding street signs, public advertisements, and pubic services—but these are less central to Russian complaints than issues that *are* troubling (such as the education require- ments). Although problems do exist, Estonian laws on minorities are humane and well within the European liberal tradition.[30]

Second, the Russians in Estonia are divided politically. Veronika Maandi writes that attempts to create a Republican Union of Russian Compatriots, with the support of the Russian Embassy, or even a Coordi- nation Council for Russian organizations, have faced difficulties.[31] This is so for any sort of organizational structure for Russians in Estonia. There- fore, elements of the Russian-speaking population are always ready to bolt from a proposed unified Russian position to extract concessions from Estonians ready to bargain with them.

Third, many Russian leaders recognize that co-optation is the only route to influence. The Russian Federation (RF) created a Division on the Work with Compatriots Abroad (UORCE), with the goal of preserva- tion of the Russian language. But the Russian president, it was reported, urged compatriots to get citizenship, to vote, and to protect their rights. "Therefore, in spite of specific *wiliness* in the policy of integration, from the first days of its existence in Estonia," it was reported in the Russian- language press, "UORCE spoke in favor of this course." The Russian lead- ership in RF has advised compatriots to leave if they are unhappy, but if they stay, UORCE reportedly advised Estonian Russians that "they should integrate into the society and actively participate in the life of these coun- tries."[32] In a similar vein, Dmitry Rogozin, a member of the international affairs committee of the RF State Duma, advised accepting the integra- tion invitation. In Tallinn, he urged Russian compatriots to get "political power. . . . If you will gain the option to elect deputies into the European parliament and into the Estonian one, only then will they take you into their consideration." And with that, Russians should organize into some form of "Baltic Assembly of Russian Compatriots." And so, "The Russian youth should know Estonian. They should be more ambitious than Estonians. They should cut their way into the European institutions through Estonia. Estonia should be represented in NATO by Russian generals. . . ."[33] And Viktor Andreev, a deputy in the Riigikogu (the Estonian parliament), from Kohtla-Järve, tells Galina Smolina of *Molodezh Estonii*, "Growing up, our children should become competitive on the labor market. This will be an integration into the real life with maintaining a Russian mentality."[34] Sergei Ivanov, writing as a Riigikogu member and president of the now-defunct Russian-Baltic Party of Estonia, cites the flexibility "necessary to search for allies and partners, make coalition agreements, join with power. . . . The ten year history of Russian political movements in Estonia has shown pretty convincingly that the most efficient strategy for real defense of electoral interests becomes collaboration, involvement and representation in a wider than only our Russian spectrum. . . . [V]oters just refuse to vote for isolated Russian political life. . . . From those Russian electors who come to vote, almost a half give their votes to Estonian parties; less than a third vote for Russian parties. The UPPE [United People's Party of Estonia, a Russian party that had presented a common list for national elections from a set of smaller Russian parties] has recently made its choice, and officially went over to the Center party camp. . . . Apparently the stage of ethnic parties is coming to an end."[35] In light of this analysis, Ivanov took a faction of his party and got official status for it as a corporate group within the Reform Party, and the rump Russian-Baltic Party shortly dissipated.

To be sure, Russians can bet on the wrong horse in seeking allies. Evgeni Kapov, writing of the situation in Kohtla-Järve, says integration generated only trifles from the "master's table" in the sphere of culture.[36] But it turns out that this is because his city is governed by the Center Party, which he contends was hated by the then-governing coalition at Toompea (home to the Estonian parliament). Political coalitions pay, the Russians have learned. Too divided among themselves, and too weak with a small percentage of the national electorate, Russians face the political reality that they must join coalitions with useful Estonian partners to help influence the course of integration.

Integration Policy

Between Estonian and Russian political maneuverings, a policy had to be implemented. Although a full review of implementation is not possible here, it is worth noting that there have been many local successes. Yana

Mayevskaya reported on the Integration Foundation's 56 projects in summer/farm camps. Most of the incidents in her report are of Russian children integrating and having a good experience. Although the camps lack a critical mass of Estonian children, she writes, "each day they [the Russian children) do hear Estonian speech."[37] In another of her reports, she interviews the principal of the Mustamäe General Education Gymnasium, who chronicles a week his students spent in Pärnu and Sauga. In Tallinn, he says, we would invite Estonians to be our guests, but we were never invited back. But once the Integration and Security Department brought our children to the countryside, it changed. Meanwhile, the principal of the Estonian school in Sauga saw integration in a positive light as his students started to study Russian beginning in the sixth grade, and this program gave them practice.[38]

To be sure, not all are happy about these encounters. An article in a May 2000 issue of *Õhtuleht* uses the Russian *Integratsiya* as its headline. Its correspondent complains ironically about the funds spent by the Ministry of Agriculture to support the summer language program of noncitizens living in farmhouses. "The chickens in those houses will be counted in the autumn and then we can see whether the boarder has developed himself in Estonian or rather, as a result of the training program, the farm families have started to use the language of internationality communication [that is, the Soviet term for Russian]."[39] This implies correctly, however, that integration in real life has come to mean a mutuality of learning, though the dominant trend is that of Russians acquiring Estonian.

According to one European monitoring official, although each element of the integration program is politically innocuous and has few detractors, the overall integration policy has a coercive edge.[40] First, the language examinations are getting increasingly less forgiving. In *Eesti Päevaleht*, Anneli Ammas reports on the failed grades of Ida-Virumaa principals taking the language exam, and language inspector Marge Mägi is quoted as saying, "If I were the mayor, I would release those school principals, who have not managed or wanted to learn the state language at least on the advanced level."[41] An ironic article by Rein Sikk in *Eesti Päevaleht* reveals how hard the expert Estonian exam is—even for Estonians. He provides a good description of what one needs to do to pass, adding that failure means having to immigrate "to Latvia with shame." He ends with: "On the whole, there are thousands of non-Estonian experts, who have to go through the same thing. In the box of the integration theoreticians there is a long applause" for anyone who could pass such an exam.[42]

Second, the mode of enforcement of integration reeks of vigilante justice. Not only state officials, but citizens as well, police the program. Õhtuleht reported that an Estonian woman, Anne, reported to authorities that her census enumerator, Natalja, spoke weak Estonian: "I would have given her the mark '5+' for her assiduity, but a '3−' for the knowledge of language. I think that the census officer should have spoken Estonian better."[43] Natalja was called to the office of the Head of the Service of the Census, and he reported to the newspaper that she had a higher education and a C-level (moderately high) certificate in Estonian, and must have been in "a flurry" on her first day on the job. Just as the Swiss have reported to police on undocumented neighbors, the Estonians' own committed (and often nosy) citizens provide free policing for the inspectorate.

How then to assess the program? Jüri Kõre, a member of Tartu municipal council writing an opinion column in Eesti Päevaleht, noted that even the Danes and Swedes admit that their own integration models do not work. "But it is not right to say that we do not have integration. We have the integration but it works according to this earlier voluntary and individually cognized way, not always according to the writings in the book with blue covers, 'Integration in the Estonian Society 2002–2007'. . . . The people with higher education but without the knowledge of Estonian are in the labor market in much worse conditions compared with the non-Estonians who have lower education but who know Estonian. . . . The clever Russians will make the choice themselves."[44] I agree. For this reason, I now examine a level below that of policy implementation: the underlying social dynamics of integration.

The Underlying Social Dynamics

The underlying social reality is undoubtedly far more complex than the three ideal-type models initially presented. In fact, in varying strength, there are six trends that involve elements of integration: (1) Estonian Russians integrating into Estonian culture; (2) Estonians integrating into Russian culture; (3) Russians integrating into an English-speaking European culture; (4) Estonians integrating into an English-speaking European culture; (5) Estonian Russians integrating into a post-Soviet Russia, Commonwealth of Independent States (CIS) culture; and (6) Estonians integrating into a Finnish/Baltic culture. (See figure 2.2, "The Actual Model of Integration.") The result will be a slightly modified form of the 2 + 1 cultural repertoire I envisaged for Estonia in an earlier work.[45] In

Figure 2.2 **The Actual Model of Integration**

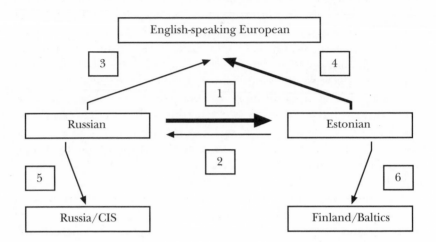

the 2 + 1 model, Estonians who seek a wide range of mobility opportunities need only Estonian + English (2). Meanwhile, Russians seeking similar opportunities need Russian + Estonian + English (2 + 1). To the extent that Estonians would need Russian, there would be a simple three-language model for all. The separate elements of the 2 + 1 model are analyzed in the subsequent subsections.[46]

Russian → Estonian—Arrow 1

It is now well-known that Estonian and Russian opinion has converged through the 1990s for most issues such as evaluation of democracy, independence of Estonia, and joining the EU. To be sure, areas of considerable difference still exist—for example, on NATO and foreign relations with Russia—but these are the exceptions.[47] In addition, a cultural convergence has occurred, going mostly in the direction of what is depicted in arrow 1, reflecting Estonian-Russians integrating into Estonian culture. Whatever the rhetoric on both sides of this divide, the social reality of Estonian-Russians adopting the cultural practices of Estonians is quite significant.

Estonian expectations about this process have been cautionary at best and downright negative at worst. Ambassador Mart Helme in an opinion piece in *Eesti Päevaleht* writes, "The opinion of the Estonian media about the integration is not different from the attitude of the Estonians themselves who believe it is hopeless."[48] Lauri Vahtre, a member of the Riigikogu, representing the Pro Patria Party, has criticized the concessions involved in the integration program. "Doors have been opened for a new wave of immigrants," he writes. "Language skill certificates have been turned into a farce and, to top it all off, the plans to begin the transition to a mainly Estonian language secondary education system have been abandoned. To put it more simply: the fully Russian secondary education system of today will remain. . . . I'm not saying that we are doomed to sink [as the Titanic did]. . . . [B]y no means do I wish to say that the breach in our hull is as irreparable as was the case with the 'Titanic'. Yet, I do wish to say that by signaling the persistence of the Russian language secondary education the coalition of the Center and Reform Parties has significantly breached the hull of the nation state. This breach needs to be closed at all costs."[49]

Not all Estonian-language opinion is that negative. See, for example, *Eesti Päevaleht* of October 2, 2000, in which Andrei Hvostov accuses national radical Estonians of being like the totalitarian states in "which the public enemy is genetically determined."[50] But he points out that stereotyping breaks down in the world of sports. A certain Nikitin is the darling of Estonians because of his wrestling prowess and because he wears Estonia's blue-black-white flag; for Russians because his name is Valeri Nikitin. Few know, Hvostov reports, that his home language is Estonian. The evidence shows that Nikitin is not that unusual in that Estonian practices are seeping into Russian culture.[51]

Indeed, Estonian ways of speech are infecting the Russian language as spoken in Estonia. I had recorded a half hour of talk show on Tallinn radio in both languages. Linguistic experts looking at the transcripts of those shows and of the newspaper reports used for this chapter pointed to several areas in which Estonian ways of speech had worked their way into local Russian. For example, one reporter for *Molodezh Estonii* wrote that Narva residents would be interested in getting some articles from his newspaper.[52] He used the Estonian-style passive voice for "were interested" (*zaintersovany*), quite unusual in Russian. In Estonian there are no short adjectives. And consistent with Estonian form, Russians in everyday speech (Radio 4) sometimes use long adjectives (*delikaatne*) rather than the typical shortened version (*delikaten*). And Estonian words replace Russian ones. For example, on Radio 4 call-in show, a woman spoke of *Paldiski-mante* (Paldiski road, in its Estonian form, rather than *na Paldiskom shosse*, the Russian alternative), but this change, my linguist informant reports, goes back to Soviet times. In the Estonian press and radio, in contrast, there are no "Russianisms" to report.

More impressive than the nonreciprocal corruption of Russian with Estonian speech is evidence that suggests a shift from the expectation that all Russians would retain Russian as the primary language of education to a new expectation that it would one day be Estonian.[53] The new evidence in support of this position is impressive. Valery Novikov, director of the Läänemere Gymnasium, reports that there were two applicants for every place in his school's language immersion program.[54] In response to an article by Mart Nutt in *Eesti Päevaleht* arguing that concessions on language will lower the motivation to learn Estonian, V. Andreev writes in *Molodezh Estonii*: "The author is mistaken. Practically there are no people among non-Estonians now who don't realize the necessity of learning Estonian. On the contrary, the interest and the knowledge level of Estonian constantly grow, especially among the non-Estonian youth."[55] The Estonian Open Society Institute found that although only about 6 percent of Russian-speaking children who were enrolled in Estonian-medium programs agree with the choice of their parents, about 25 percent of Russian families want their children to attend an Estonian school.[56] In recognition of the growing influence of Estonian speech, a new expression in Estonian, "positive Russian," refers to those "who have successfully overcome the distance on the integration marathon."[57]

My 2002 survey, in collaboration with Mikk Titma, of Estonian-Russian ninth graders and their parents paints a similar picture of the expectation of a "tip" toward Estonian. Here are some highlights from tables presented in the appendix.[58]

> They (on a 4-point scale, with 4 meaning very little) feel almost as much in common with Estonians (2.58) as they do with Russians from Russia (2.32) [table 2.1].
>
> Their intention to learn Estonian is greater than for any other foreign language, including English [table 2.4].
>
> Only 2.93 percent want their children to be educated only in Russian; nearly three-fourths want their children to be educated at least in part in Estonian [table 2.7].

It is often observed, contrary to the trend of assimilation, that Russians do not expose themselves to Estonian media. It is said that they have better entertainment on Russian television, and that Estonian media lacks coverage of Russian affairs.[59] But the data suggest [table 2.11] that Russian youths expose themselves to the Estonian radio station Sky Plus even more so than their Estonian counterparts. Table 2.11 shows furthermore that the three Russian stations hold little allure for the Russian students, though their parents on average listen a bit to Radio 4, which provides local commentary in Russian on public affairs. In general, the rather surprising results from this survey reflect a common exposure to radio broadcasts that are European in music and Estonian in language.

To be sure, a cultural "tip" is not moving equally in all cultural realms. The one place that would promote a more general intergenerational cultural tip is the elementary school, for it is here that minorities—at an age when they are presumably most adaptable—get absorbed into a new network of relations, and into a social world as defined by majority cultural practices. Any "tip" of enrollment in Estonian medium schools is not, however, on the horizon. Although some 25 percent of Russian-speaking parents had expressed the desire to send their first-form children to Estonian schools, by 1997 less than 10 percent were doing so.[60] The administrative problems to accommodate parental demands for Estonian-language instruction are formidable, as is the recruitment of qualified teachers. But even in schools where Estonian-medium instruction is implemented, problems remain. Studies of these children show that the transition even for first-form Russians is not an easy one, as "teachers and students are unable to successfully resolve communication problems arising from inter-cultural differences."[61] In light of this, one report concludes, "Having Russians in the Estonian school within the integration process is one of the possibilities, the significance of which will decrease through the gradual renewal of the Russian school [in which Russian would be the medium of instruction but within an Estonian curriculum, and for which Estonian would be a required subject]."[62]

One other area of cultural difference concerns religion. The survey data show the well-known Lutheran/Orthodox religious divide. Although it had been assumed that religion played little role in both communities' social life, the data show that Russians are less secular, pray more often, and report having gone to church more regularly [table 2.8]. These differences are not great but they are statistically significant ($X^2 = .01$ for importance of religion).

In a challenging diachronic study from 1993 through 1995 of ethnic relations in Estonia, Geoffrey Evans emphasizes continued polarization. Yet these data show the beginnings of a reversal of the tides. Seven times as many Russians report being more similar to Estonians than Estonians who report being similar to Russians. Four times as many Russians report discussing politics with Estonians than Estonians who report discussing politics with Russians. Two-and-a-half times as many Russians report marrying outside their nationality than Estonians. Although polarization does exist, as Evans concludes, the data indicate that it is Russians who are now emphasizing their similarities with Estonians (the first move toward assimilation) rather than the reverse.

Estonian → Russian—Arrow 2

I wrote in *Identity in Formation*[63] that Estonians had made a credible threat to lose Russian facility; and in fact this has become a popular wisdom. The following report provides a recent confirmation of this view. The account, written in an ironic tone by *Molodezh* Estonii reporter Aleksandr Erek, states: Urve Läänemets, a representative of the Ministry of Education, "has stated one more seditious idea" on pedagogy, "that it is unreasonable to be guided by only Western pedagogical science . . . that there is a lot of useful and necessary material in the East, from which we persistently keep turning away. It appears that today it is difficult to find a fresh issue of the Russian magazine *Pedagogy*."[64] It is indeed seditious to say that Estonians have borrowed a worthwhile cultural product from Russia.

But my survey data show that arrow 2 is not a mirage. Here are some important factors showing why the arrow, though thin, makes for a social reality not of pure assimilation, but of weak integration.

> Estonians feel a far greater sense of commonality with Estonian-Russians than they do with Russians from Russia, Finns, or Germans [table 2.1].
> Estonians intend to learn Russian more than German or Finnish [table 2.4].

This attraction to the Russian language, which I did not expect, has two sources. First, young Estonians are curious about the pervasive culture that surrounds them, and they want to understand the advertisements, the newspaper headlines, and the street talk that is in Russian. Second, the national school curriculum requires two foreign languages. Most schools compete for teachers of English (in the mid-1990s, many were supplied by the American Peace Corps program) but can get teachers of Russian at low cost and high availability. Therefore, to fulfill the national curriculum, Estonian students are in most cases *de facto* required to study Russian.

> 48.68 percent of Estonians want to have Russian as one of the languages of instruction for their children [table 2.7].
> Estonian schoolchildren feel closer culturally to Russians from Estonia than did their parents, and even feel closer to Russian-

Estonians than Russian-Estonian schoolchildren feel toward Estonians [table 2.9].

These trends support a weak integration model over a pure assimilation model, whatever the true intentions of the policy makers.

Estonians and Russian-Estonians → Europe—Arrows 3 & 4

The standard integration model, however, is only partly accurate, for both Estonians and Russians have been adopting the cultural practices of an external model, an English-speaking Europe. To be part of Europe has clearly been a quest for many Estonians, and for some leading figures such as former President Lennart Meri, it seemed more important than consolidating the national project in Estonia itself.

Even nationalist Estonians know that they are conditioning their behavior on a new European standard. Airi Selgmäe, a student at Tallinn Pedagogical University, wrote a letter to *Eesti Päevaleht*, saying that Estonian parents get worried when their kindergartners come home with a word of Russian (due to the integration program, mixing kindergarten children), "but [they are] stroking hairs and feeling proud, when their offspring is using some English words at the age of three or four."[65]

And Alexander Shegedin in *Estoniya* nicely captures a similar social dynamic when he writes of Estonia's future: "Strictly speaking, not 'Estonization' but rather 'Westernization' of language and culture, and only half-joking, it is not impossible that soon we will have a situation when all residents of Estonia start together and without difficulty communicate in a strange mixture of Estonian and Silicon Valley/Hollywood jargon, spiced with a great deal of Russian slang."[66]

The survey data show a strong connection to Europe for both Russian and Estonian schoolchildren.

The sense of being a representative of European culture is moderately low, but slightly stronger for the Estonians [table 2.2].

More than half of the students correctly knew the exchange rate of the euro (in kroons), again slightly better for the Estonians than the Russians [table 2.3].

From an intergenerational standpoint, the trend toward a European orientation is faster for the Russians than for the Estonians, however. For students whose parents were also interviewed, there was virtually no intergenerational difference among the Estonians, but a rather rapid one among the Russians [table 2.10]. It seems that Estonian independence opened up Europe for Russians, while it opened up Estonia for Estonians.

But it is English-speaking Europe, not the heartland of Europe (Germany), that students are attracted to. There is little sense of commonality with Germans, and Estonians feel more in common with Russians from Russia than they do with Germans [table 2.1]. They also want to learn Russian much more than German. But learning English is the greatest cultural product to acquire for all young Estonians [table 2.4].

Estonia ← → Other Foreign—Arrows 5 & 6

The surveys show a moderate attraction for Russian-Estonians to Russia/CIS (arrow 5).

> Of all groups of others, Estonian-Russians report that they have most in common with Russians from Russia [table 2.1].
>
> When students were surveyed about their knowledge of foreign countries, the highest-scoring item for the Russian-Estonian students was knowledge of the colors of the Russian flag—far greater than was the case for the Estonian students [table 2.3].
>
> But when asked to identify an ideal place to do advanced study or work, Russian Estonians vastly (by nearly a factor of four) preferred Europe over Russia, indicating that ties to Russia are more to the past than to the future [table 2.5].

The attraction of a common Baltic identity for Estonians, however, is thinnest of all, and perhaps arrow 6 should be imperceptible.

> Estonian students, to be sure, know a good deal about Finland. Their knowledge of the colors of the Finnish flag got the highest grade of the five questions asked about foreign countries, and considerably more Estonian students than Russian students answered the question correctly [table 2.3].
>
> But Estonians feel more in common with Russian Estonians than they do with Finns [table 2.1].
>
> And when asked about studying five foreign languages, Estonians indicate that they study Finnish the least of all [table 2.4].

Summary and Extensions

Figure 2.2, "The Actual Model of Integration," sums up the underlying social reality illustrated by the survey material as well as by newspaper reports and radio transcripts. The actual model is one in which all residents of Estonia are moving toward a common 2 + 1 cultural framework— *they are adding rather than substituting cultural repertoires.* Russians, to the extent that they will be responsive to a wide range of social mobility options, will equip themselves with Russian, Estonian, and English (2 + 1); Estonians will get by with Estonian and English (2), but many continue to learn Russian (2 + 1). Knowledge of German, Finnish, and other languages will be for other purposes than participation in society and social mobility. *This is a model that supports two integrations: one into an Estonian dominant culture in Estonia, and a second into an English dominant culture in Europe.*

Two questions remain unanswered in the skeletal version of figure 2.2, and will require future research to develop. First, what might happen to processes of Russian assimilation (arrow 1), given the attraction of Europe (arrows 3 and 4)? Indeed, this worries Estonian nationalists a good deal, and helps explain why Estonian public opinion was for a long period so skeptical of EU membership.[67] Indeed, the data suggest that Russians will be quicker to take advantage of the European option to reduce the pressures on them for Estonian assimilation while Estonians try to keep the European project separate from their nationalist one. The separation of these two levels of integration supports the notion of the accumulation of cultural repertoires rather than a choice among them.

Second, how robust are the trends reported here? Suppose that a resurgent Russia would attract professional labor from Estonia. This could change the assimilationist calculus of Russian-speakers. Suppose an alliance in Estonia between newly enfranchised Russians and a non-nationalist social democratic party (close to what the Center Party represents) captured the median Estonian voter. Would this reduce the pressure for assimilation and make possible a Swiss-like cultural confederation? Although exogenous change is always a possibility, my conjecture is that the assimilationist and the Europeanist projects are sufficiently institutionalized as to be able to withstand fairly high degrees of shock. I therefore expect a deepening rather than an abandonment of these trends. In conjecturing about the robustness of two-tiered cultural equilibrium, I contend that it is not only self-enforcing, but self-reinforcing as well—that is, that over time this equilibrium will hold in the face of a wider range of external shocks.[68]

Social and Political Impact and Implications for Violence

Despite the social reality of a two-tiered integration that is in equilibrium, in the sense that no one has an interest in undermining it through his or her own strategic behavior, the cultural scene in Estonia cannot be described as harmonious.

For one, epithets fly through Estonian political space. Russians use the term *muulasy*, from the Estonian *muulased* ("non-Estonian," or literally "the others"), with a made-up Russian declension (*muulased*). Here they are intimating that they think that all Estonians think that they are all "soviets"; the Russians use the Estonian term in a bitter way to show how insulting it is to them.[69] A *Postimes* editorial reported, "It will be sad and shameful, if a non-Estonian becomes the mayor of the capital of the Estonian state."[70] And the sobriquet "colonizer" continues to be used. In a letter to *Õhtuleht*, Eero Laidre sees the United States and England both guilty of giving "silent consent" to "the crimes against humanity of the communists." They sent "[OSCE official Max van der] Stoel here to immortalize the results of the massive migration of colonizers."[71]

Insults often fly inadvertently. Katrin Saks, former minister of ethnic affairs, ordinarily used a highly Estonized Russian in explaining the integration program to Russians. "The integration of Estonian society," she was reported to have said, "presupposes two processes—social unification on the basis of possessing [*na osnove vladeniya*—this is a direct translation from Estonian, and not colloquial Russian] Estonian language and acquiring [*obreteniya*—this is not colloquial, as *polucheniye* is normally used in this context, and is more forgiving than *obreteniya*] Estonian citizenship on one side, and preservation of ethnic differences on the basis of recognition [*na osnove priznaniya*—not colloquial Russian] of cultural rights of ethnic minorities."[72] Despite the substance of the message, the semantics have a stilted feel and in consequence an imperialist lilt to the ears of the Russian-speaking readers of *Molodezh Estonii*.[73] Saks was also reported in *Molodezh Estonii* to have used *Estonifikatsia* for integration (implying that Russians were to be Estonified), which is presented as a mirror of what the Estonians bitterly complained of in *Russifikatsia* in the Soviet period.[74]

The insults go both ways. For example, in *Molodezh Estonii* M. Petrov reports that the integration program is an analog to Heinrich Himmler's eastern policy, in seeking to lead a NATO spearhead to destroy Russia.[75]

But the conflict is not only in words; a specter of violence exists as well. In *Molodezh Estonii* S. Smirnov raises the specter of "Kosovo-type metastases."[76] In another issue of *Molodezh Estonii* M. Petrov mentions Martin

Luther King and many Algerians in France as "hardly the last in the chain of mutual violence" that is linked to the best-intentioned programs of integration.[77] And in *Estoniya*, Alexander Shegedin writes that the "persecution of the Russian language . . . in no way promotes the stability level in the new national states."[78]

Several violent incidents in Paldiski in early January 2001 involved Russian gangs, Estonian military police, and bystanders; insults and drunkenness led to the ugly brawls. According to victims, they were asked if they knew the Estonian language; when they answered no, they got beaten.[79] There have also been reports of fights between Russian and Estonian youngsters in the Tallinn district of Õismäe.[80]

These incidents may not be new to the integration era. Priit Hõbemägi, editor of *Eesti Päevaleht*, writes of his childhood in Tallinn in the 1960s, that "a fight with stones was not a rare incident. . . . These happened, because the Russian boys who were living in the bog boarding school extorted money from the Estonians alone on the street. . . . Information about the 'war' spread fast from mouth to mouth. . . . The 'nationally' dangerous places were usually known. For example, in the streets near the moor, known also as the 'Russian village,' it was not so safe for the Estonian boys to hang around. . . . One could get a punch in the teeth from the Russians. . . . Why am I talking about all this? Because the conflicts between the Russian and Estonian young people is nothing new in Tallinn. . . . And remember that even earlier the German boys came to fight in our backyards."[81]

How should one interpret the current wave of youth violence with an ethnic/national flavor? Tarmo Leinatamm has a theory on recurrent ethnic fights in Lasnamäe (a mixed neighborhood in Tallinn), which surprised him, having lived in a mixed environment there for years while Russians and Estonians intermingled calmly in the vestibules. He surmised that the violent incidents were provoked by Estonian interests in giving work to an "integration authority."[82] This speculation is far-fetched, but it does reflect a more widespread incredulity that the national issue in Estonia would really involve violence.[83]

Katrin Saks is equally incredulous. She is reported to have said that "there is no ethnic hostility" in Estonia. Her evidence is "testified . . . by how painfully we react to these single incidents. If it happened every day, we would not react like this."[84] Here I think Saks is right. The key (from a comparative perspective) is that these melees, especially the one in Paldiski, did not set off a chain reaction across the country, as similar communal violent acts have a way of doing in northern India and elsewhere in the world.

It is therefore fair to report that although violence has erupted in mixed ethnic/national zones, these incidents have not spilled over into chain reactions of bloodletting. In fact, incidents like the ones in Paldiski are similar to ones in all zones of integration in modern industrial societies. Gangs recruited through ethnic attachments thrive under conditions of increasing contact among ethnic groups, and violence is often the result of incidents provoked by mixed couples (the highest form of integration) and exacerbated through alcohol. *The reported incidents appear to me to be a by-product of integration rather than evidence of its failure.* The specter of Kosovo is far more rhetoric than reality.

Conclusion

In 2000, the Estonian political class changed direction in regard to its Russian-speaking minority. In the first decade of the restored republic, the orientation of the government had been to reduce to manageable levels the size of the Russian-speaking population. By 2000, the orientation was to the peaceful integration of Russian-speakers into Estonian social and cultural life. By 2003, the political support for the new program had weakened. Nonetheless, many of the goals of the integration program were being fulfilled not necessarily by government action, but rather by underlying processes that gave incentives to Russian-speakers to adopt Estonian cultural practices. Government policy should then be seen as at most reinforcing trends rather than directing them.

The underlying processes in Estonia today reflect a dual integration model. One of those two processes (that of Russians acquiring Estonian cultural forms, and of Estonians getting a little exposure to Russian cultural forms in exchange) has been reinforced by a complex policy program of integration. But much of the success of that program is due to the underlying social reality that the Russian-speaking population faces in Estonia—namely, that social mobility requires accommodation with the integration program, and in fact Russians use the program's facilities to imbibe even more Estonian culture than the program could have done without Russian practical consent. Russians' adoption of Estonian cultural practices, with long-term implications for assimilation, is clearly the dominant trend in this first integration process.

A second integration process—a common adoption of the cultural forms of an English-speaking Europe—is proceeding simultaneously with the Russian/Estonian integration process. Although the Estonians had been more assiduous than the Russians in acquiring European cultural credentials, the Russians do not fall far behind and are Europeanizing from an intergenerational standpoint faster than their Estonian counterparts. Indeed, many Estonians fear that rapid Europeanization will undermine their national project. The Estonian political class will therefore work assiduously to keep the two integration processes (arrow 1 and arrows 3 and 4 in figure 2.2) separate.

Two other integration processes can be detected as well, but in a minor key. Estonian-Russians are maintaining cultural contact with Russia/CIS in a sustained way, mostly through exposure to the media. Meanwhile, Estonians are retaining capability in Russian, and feel far closer culturally to Russians in Russia than they do to Balts, or Germans or other national models from the West. (This trend does not merit an arrow in figure 2.2, but it is a trend worth following.) In sum, a dual integration process marks the Estonian cultural scene. Russian-Estonians assimilate into Estonian cultural practices and Russian-Estonians as well as Estonians jointly assimilate into English-speaking European cultural practices.

The outcome of these processes has marked a vast cultural change within a decade in Estonia. In the mid-1980s, a 2 − 1 language equilibrium was well-established, with Russian as the only lingua franca. By the early 2000s, a 2 + 1 equilibrium had evolved, in which Estonian and English had become the languages of internationality contact. The Estonians revel in this change; meanwhile, Russian-speakers have adapted to its reality.

The processes described in this chapter have a deterministic quality to them. In contrast, in *Identity in Formation* I emphasized the role of choice in the selection of one's own culture. The cultural identity of any group, I argued, is endogenous to the political processes in which ethnic groups are participants. To the extent that Estonians provided a high-status model to the Russian minority, and to the extent that Russian-speakers had no easy exit option, I argued, Russians would begin to explore the possibility and payoffs for assimilation. Does this change in emphasis imply that strategic action is less important in culture than my earlier models highlighted?

My use of the term "cultural equilibrium" should be a clue as to an answer. In games of repeated interaction, the standard meaning of an equilibrium is a strategy set in which no actors have an incentive to change their strategy in the next interaction. Hence, in equilibrium, most players do not think about their future strategies, and certainly do not compute the payoffs of all possible alternative strategies. Born in Nice and now living in Paris, a Frenchman does not wake up each morning and calculate the expected payoffs for opening conversation with his spouse in

Swedish (as opposed to French, in which he has always conversed with his wife). In equilibrium, habit dominates calculation.

But the ubiquity of habitual behavior in equilibrium does not make choice models irrelevant. For one, as more and more Russian-Estonians grapple with learning Estonian, there will surely appear linguistic revivalists who will seek to restore Russian to its past glories in Estonia. These entrepreneurs will seek to demonstrate that if all people of Russian ancestry in Estonia returned to Russian, all of them would be better off. A choice model keeps open the possibility of entrepreneurial activity in articulating a new equilibrium.[85] Second, environmental conditions could change such that the old equilibrium no longer is optimum. For example, if trading opportunities with Russia were suddenly to become more lucrative than those with the EU, the cultivation of "Russianness," especially among Estonians who have Russian ancestry, might be attractive enough to induce cultural calculation. The equilibrium described in this chapter, working toward a 2 + 1 language outcome, is self-reinforcing. But even so, the post-Soviet world is sufficiently unstable that we must not ignore the possibility of reversal and strategic action to establish a new equilibrium.[86]

However fragile and open to strategic undermining, the evidence at hand suggests that the trends portrayed in figure 2.2 reflect the present Estonian reality. The Estonian political class has facilitated these processes through its integration program, but social and economic realities have played a larger roll in sustaining them. The Russian-Estonian political class has complained about these policies, but it has been co-opted sufficiently such that its objections are mostly rhetorical. Everyday ethnic violence cannot be ruled out; but such violence appears more a by-product of the integration process and less an example of an unbridgeable ethnic divide. In sum, young Russian-speakers will have little choice but to accept the challenge of a dual integration process—into Estonia and into Europe.

APPENDIX TO CHAPTER 2

Tables

All the tables are derived from data collected from September through December 2002, with a sample size of 600 ninth-grade students, 400 from Ida-Virumaa (the heavily Russian-speaking region in the northeast) and 200 from Harjumaa (the region around the capital city with a slight Estonian majority). About half the students from each region are Estonians; the other half are Russians.* Of the 600 students interviewed, complementary interviews were conducted with 195 of their parents (randomly chosen); 99 were parents of Estonian students, 91 were parents of Russian students, and 5 were parents of students from other nationalities. The data file from which the following tables were constructed is available to the research community on request from the author.

* In Ida-Virumaa 45.5% were Estonians, 50.5% were Russians, and 4.0% were other nationalities. In Harjumaa, 53.4% were Estonians, 43.6% Russians, and 3.0% other nationalities.

TABLE 2.1
Sense of Commonality

Respondent feels in common with:	Estonians	Russian-Estonians
Estonians	*	2.58
Russian-Estonians	2.51	*
Russians from Russia	3.46	2.32
Finns	3.23	3.41
Germans	3.58	3.43

Comparative means by nationality of respondent:
Lower number = More in common*
1 = very much; 2 = much; 3 = relatively little; 4 = very little

TABLE 2.2
Do You See Yourself as a Representative of a Certain Culture?

Respondent as a representative of:	Estonians	Russian-Estonians
Estonian culture	2.10	3.10
Russian culture	3.42	1.85
European culture	2.84	2.96
English-speaking culture	3.29	3.44
Soviet culture	3.79	3.52

Comparative means by nationality of respondent:
Lower number = More representative
1 = very much; 2 = somewhat much; 3 = not much; 4 = not at all

TABLE 2.3
Knowledge about Foreign Countries

[Percentage of Correct Answers]

	Estonians	Russian-Estonians
Value of ruble	24.01	51.27
Colors of Russian flag	76.64	95.27
Value of euro	57.24	53.09
Colors of German flag	79.28	76.00
Colors of Finnish flag	88.16	72.36

TABLE 2.4
Intention to Learn Foreign Languages

[How Often Do Young People Like Yourself Study This Language?]

	Estonians	Russian-Estonians
Estonian	1.08	1.15
Russian	1.58	1.49
German	2.12	2.15
English	1.21	1.28
Finnish	2.76	3.04

Comparative means: Lower number = More frequently
1 = regularly; 2 = sometimes; 3 = rarely; 4 = most do not learn it

TABLE 2.5
Dream Place to Do Advanced Study and Work

[Percentage of Respondents Who Chose Each Area]

	Estonians		Russian-Estonians	
Country	Study	Work	Study	Work
Estonia	54.0	51.5	28.9	25.9
Russia	2.0	.7	15.4	7.7
EU: Germany, UK or France	18.7	16.5	28.1	27.4
Finland	.7	3.0	4.8	5.5
USA	19.7	21.1	11.4	24.5

TABLE 2.6
Family Willingness to Move If Opportunity Exists

Destination	Estonians	Russian-Estonians
Another city in R's region in Estonia	2.49	3.09
Another region in Estonia	2.46	3.07
Russia or CIS	3.52	3.32
Europe	2.96	3.07

Comparative means: Lower number = Greater willingness
1 = We are ready to go; 2 = In general, we are ready to go; 3 = We are not fully ready to go; 4 = We're completely not prepared to go

TABLE 2.7
In What Language(s) Would You Want Your Child to be Educated?

Language	Estonians	Russian-Estonians
Only Estonian	21.38	4.03
Only Russian	0	2.93
Estonian + Russian	8.22	22.34
Estonian + Russian + English	40.46	50.18
Mother tongue + English	24.34	9.89

TABLE 2.8
Religious Orientation

Characteristic	Estonians	Russian-Estonians
Percentage of Lutheran	11.88	2.91
Percentage of Orthodox	11.55	56.36
Importance of religion to you (mean value)	3.06	2.88
How often do you pray? (mean value)*	3.68	3.50
Church attendance (mean value)**	3.86	3.80

Comparative means: Lower number = Greater religiosity
1 = very important; 2 = somewhat important; 3 = relatively unimportant; 4 = absolutely unimportant
* 1 = more than once per day; 2 = once per day; 3 = less than once per day; 4 = never
** 1 = more than 5 times per month; 2 = 3–4 times; 3 = 1–2 times; 4 = In general I haven't been to church

TABLE 2.9
Intergenerational Cultural Proximity: Estonians and Russians from Estonia

Nationality	Closeness of "other" for students	Closeness of "other" for parents	Difference
Russian-Estonians (toward Estonians)	2.58	2.57	+.01 (less close in next generation)
Estonians (toward Russians from Estonia)	2.51	2.61	−.10 (closer in next generation)

Comparative means: Lower number = Greater perceived closeness
1 = very much; 2 = much; 3 = relatively little; 4 = very little

TABLE 2.10

Intergenerational Cultural Proximity: Estonians and Russians toward European Culture

Nationality	Students	Parents	Difference
Estonians	2.97	2.96	.01 (less close in next generation)
Russian-Estonians	2.52	2.94	−.42 (closer in next generation)

Comparative means: Lower score = More representative
1 = very much; 2 = much; 3 = relatively little; 4 = very little

TABLE 2.11

Favorite Radio Stations

Nationality	Sky Plus (European music with Estonian DJ)	Europe Plus (European music with Russian DJ)	Radio 4 (Russian commentary)	For Russian-Estonians: Maximum (Russian information); for Estonians Radio Uuno (Estonian commentary and music)
	Student mean (Parent mean)			
Estonians	2.29 (2.67)	3.67 (3.79)	3.78 (3.65)	2.50 (3.11)
Russians	2.12 (2.47)	3.41 (3.37)	3.74 (2.69)	3.32 (3.91)

Mean scores: 1 = very often; 2 = somewhat often; 3 = somewhat rarely; 4 = never

3

ETHNIC MOBILIZATION IN THE POSTCOMMUNIST CONTEXT

Albanians in Macedonia and the East European Roma

ZOLTAN BARANY

Ethnic mobilization has been the most important development that has led to improvements in the conditions of most ethnic minorities in postcommunist states. The minority policies of new governments may not have helped them. Social attitudes toward them may have actually deteriorated. Their economic situation may have worsened. But, if the newly democratizing states afforded them the opportunity to organize themselves—as most did—chances are that their political marginalization has noticeably diminished.

Ethnic mobilization resulted not only in reduced marginalization and institutional discrimination. Through their mobilization efforts ethnic groups called the attention of their fellow citizens, their local and national governments, as well as international governmental and nongovernmental organizations to their predicament. Without mobilizing themselves many ethnic groups in the postcommunist world might have remained the vulnerable subjects of their states and societies. The direct and indirect benefits of ethnic mobilization have included thousands of social and economic programs that yielded enormous material dividends financed locally and from abroad. Other fruits of mobilization have been constitutional amendments, a host of new or modified laws that reverse discrimination, and, perhaps most important, better access to and enhanced opportunities in all areas from health care to the media. Clearly, ethnic mobilization is a potent weapon with which to right historical wrongs. Explaining it and placing it in the postcommunist framework are the objectives of this chapter.

I begin by discussing the concept of ethnic mobilization and its implications to the postcommunist context. Then I move on to a systematic assessment of what I consider the prerequisites of successful ethnic mobilization. In the balance of the chapter I examine two examples of recent ethnic mobilization in Eastern Europe. My selection of the cases—Albanians in the Republic of Macedonia and Roma/Gypsies across Eastern Europe—was prompted by three factors. First, the Albanian minority in Macedonia has followed an unorthodox path, running the gamut of mobilizational projects from party formation to violent ethnic conflict. Second, a comparative analysis of the Roma's mobilization experiences in several rather than just one or two East European states might better illuminate the reasons for their modest achievements. Third, the mobilizational performance of the Gypsies has been far inferior to that of "Macedonian" Albanians even though state policies toward the Roma have been more favorable. I suggest that the mobilizational prerequisites model I outline in the first part might help explain the disparities between these cases.

Ethnic Mobilization and Postcommunism

Ethnic Mobilization

Ethnic mobilization may best be conceived as the process "by which groups organize around some feature of ethnic identity (for example, skin color, language, customs) in pursuit of collective ends."[1] Political mobilization is "the process by which a group goes from being a passive collection of individuals to an active participant in public life."[2] It denotes the deliberate activity of a group of individuals for the realization of political objectives. Mobilization is attitudinal insofar as there is a firm commitment to action and requires "means of translating this commitment into action or observed behavior."[3] The goals generally encompass enhanced interest representation; cessation of political, social, and economic discrimination; and improvement of the collective's conditions and social standing. Mobilization needs to produce and maximize political resources that will amplify the group's influence: these typically include attracting votes, activating sympathetic third parties, and building coalitions. Such resources may also entail political goods like disruptions, protests, and violence, all of which may be used as bargaining chips.[4]

Mobilization can be measured by the active membership of the organizations created, the amount of resources accumulated, the number of programs established, and the number and size of demonstrations and protests organized.

A variety of causes may bring about ethnic mobilization but conditions of relative deprivation—whether social, economic, or political—are nearly always at its root. Ethnic mobilization may occur even in the absence of such exclusion or marginalization in cases where the mobilizing community intends to improve its circumstances vis-à-vis other ethnic groups in society. Ethnic mobilization may be triggered or stimulated by the complete or partial removal of obstacles in the way of ethnic activism, the emergence of charismatic leader(s), and/or instances of distress or injustice suffered by the ethnic group. The nature of ethnic mobilization may depend on the identity of those blocking it (whether it is the state, a political actor, or another ethnic group), the circumstances of the injury suffered by the ethnic group (for example, violent or nonviolent), as well as prevailing political, social, and cultural rules, norms, and values affecting political activity. In sum, ethnic mobilization is fueled by people's grievances about their relative deprivation and their determination to pursue their political interests.[5]

There is little evidence to support the contention that those experiencing the most deprivation, or those at the lowest level of a class hierarchy, will be the most likely to take part in mobilization activities.[6] In fact, ethnic mobilization is usually led by the middle class, and ordinarily individuals of middle-class background predominate its base of active participants. There are two reasons for this. First, mobilization requires resources which the most deprived usually do not possess. Second, those on the lowest rungs of the socioeconomic ladder often do not have the motivation and the initiative necessary to participate in organized activities.[7]

Clearly, the chances of marginal populations to acquire political and economic power are increased if they manage to organize themselves in a cohesive way.[8] Ethnopolitics may be thought of as the final stage of a process that begins with ethnic mobilization.[9] This process may be divided into three distinct phases. The first is the formation and strengthening of ethnic identity, the sharpening of the ethnic group's boundaries vis-à-vis other groups. The second is the securing of the prerequisites for political action, such as financial resources, leaders, media outlets, and enhancement of the group's unique identity through the sharing of symbols and participation in social activities. The third stage is the actual political action taken to promote the interests of the ethnic group. At this stage ethnic groups actually make demands on governments in a variety of ways whether peaceful (for example, petition drives, electoral campaigns) or violent (for example, rioting, armed conflict). The objective of ethnic mobilization may be relatively modest, such as increasing access to education in the minority's language. Other mobilizing groups may identify more ambitious goals, such as the reunification of an often mythical but still politically salient ethnic homeland.[10]

In the enormous and quickly growing literature on ethnic politics, ethnic mobilization per se has received relatively scant attention. Three perspectives emerged in the early (1960s and 1970s) theoretical work on ethnic mobilization.[11] Developmental theories of ethnic mobilization tended to view it as a phenomenon that was inextricably linked to the early phases of state-building and generally occurred in less developed societies.[12] In contrast, the structural differentiationist approach held that modern states may, in fact, enhance impulses for ethnic mobilization rather than thwart it as developmentalists argued.[13] Finally, the ethnic competition perspective contended that ethnic mobilization was, foremost, the result of rivalry and contention between different ethnic groups, and that the state played only a secondary role in stimulating mobilization.[14]

Recent studies have focused on more specific dimensions of ethnic mobilization. Rasma Karklins's work on the final years of the Soviet Union showed how the delegitimization of the *ancien régime* went hand in hand with the delegitimization of old ethnic policies and that democratization was tied to ethnic power sharing.[15] The mobilization efforts of noncitizen immigrant minorities who reside in Western Europe but nevertheless are not entitled to the international mobility encouraged by the European Union (EU) have been the focus of innovative work in Europe.[16] Other recent work integrates class-based factors with racial and ethnic factors to examine what motivates African-Americans, Latinos, and others to mobilize and become active in politics.[17]

Ethnic Mobilization and (Postcommunist) Regime Change

Systemic transition from one regime type to another is usually rooted in interrelated sources such as massive societal change, economic development, and redistribution of political power that may culminate in revolution, civil war, or a negotiated replacement of one elite with another. Perhaps the most important factor capable of stimulating ethnic mobilization is this sort of political change (and particularly the transition from authoritarian to democratic regimes). Transition periods tend to go hand in hand with a decline in the effectiveness of state power and flagging state attention to concerns that are not directly related its survival. As such, these transitions generally create opportunities for mobilization by disenfranchised or marginal groups. Organizations and informal groups that do not directly aim to defeat the weakening regime usually find that the fluid political situation stimulates a higher degree of state tolerance toward them and thus increased elbow room to pursue their objectives. Not surprisingly, regime transitions also tend to boost the capacity of ethnic minorities and other marginalized populations to gain political recognition through mobilization.

At the same time, regime transition also tends to amplify nationalist and extremist social attitudes and thus denotes special difficulties for ethnic minorities. Changes in the economic system often mean deteriorating living standards for various social strata whose growing insecurity creates a need to find community with others similarly affected. Regime change might evoke nationalist sentiments in the disenchanted masses of the majority group particularly if those who seem to benefit from economic changes are members of ethnic minorities. This, in turn, provides an auspicious opportunity for "ethnic entrepreneurs" to forge new social alliances and loyalties and to manipulate nationalist and anti-minority themes. In postcommunist lands political liberalization and the newly gained freedom of expression for a time removed prior limitations on the dissemination of extremist views and contributed to interethnic tensions and, in some cases, violence.

The end of state-socialist rule in Eastern Europe and Eurasia permitted the political organization of virtually all marginal populations. In addition, postcommunist ethnic mobilization was facilitated by the collapse of Marxist-Leninist ideology that allowed the forging of alternative nationalist ideologies. The objectives of specific ethnic mobilization processes show wide disparities in the postcommunist region. Some ethnic minorities (for example, Hungarians in Romania and Slovakia, Turks in Bulgaria) wanted to achieve levels of political representation commensurate with the size of their populations. These and many other previously marginalized ethnic minorities quickly realized this goal if there was no substantial state opposition to their mobilization. Other ethnic minorities (such as Albanians in Kosovo, Armenians in the Nagorno-Karabakh region of Azerbaijan, Chechens in Russia) designated independence as their goal. But the violent outcomes in these cases reflect the fact that even during regime transition, when state control typically weakens, governments—especially federal states—are likely to do their utmost to block the mobilization efforts of ethnic minorities perceived as threatening to the state's territorial integrity.

Thus, in order to answer the question "Why are some states more likely to permit ethnic mobilization than others?" one must look at the state and the ethnic minority under consideration. First, state response to mobilization is conditioned by the state's political and socioeconomic development, especially its level of democratization and the strength of its political institutions.[18] And second, assuming that states are rational actors—which requires a leap of faith—their decision to impede or encourage ethnic minority mobilization will also depend on the minority's political goals, organizational capacity, its relations to the majority population and other minority groups, economic power, demographic characteristics, and domestic and international support. Ultimately, it is difficult to make generalizations about the tremendously diverse state responses to ethnic mobilization because, to a large extent, they are contextually determined.

Mobilizational Prerequisites

After 1989 East European states created the political opportunity for ethnic minorities to mobilize and to secure representation in state, regional, and local legislatures through electoral competition. A number of large ethnic communities—for example, Hungarians in Romania, Turks in Bulgaria—across the region were able to do just that. Virtually all of their candidates ran on their own ethnic parties' tickets, and nearly all those who voted for them were their co-nationals.

Nonetheless, there are some notable exceptions, most conspicuously the Roma. Given that in several East European states they comprise a substantial percentage of the overall population (Bulgaria 8.5, Hungary 4.7, Romania 6.6, and Slovakia 9.5), one would expect that they, too, would have gained a more or less proportionate political presence once they were granted the opportunity to mobilize. This did not happen. In fact, in 2001 the Roma held just six seats in East European national legislatures, and only one of them acquired his mandate as a representative of a Gypsy party. The low political efficacy of the region's Roma is all the more surprising because they, unlike other ethnic minorities, have received considerable financial assistance and advice on mobilization from Western NGOs, governments, and international organizations. At the same time, these and other actors have brought intense political pressure to bear on East European states to improve their treatment of Gypsy minorities. Although the age-old and widespread societal discrimination against the Roma persists, state policies toward them have become more progressive in the past decade. Nor can discrimination alone account for the relative failure of their political mobilization, given that suppressed marginal groups all over the world manage to mobilize in spite of discrimination.

To explain this puzzle, I turn to my "mobilizational prerequisites" model that helps to evaluate ethnic and other groups' preparedness for political mobilization.[19] I argue that successful ethnic mobilization requires a well-specified, functional bundle of mobilizational prerequisites. I discuss them here in descending order of importance.

Political Opportunity

If the authorities representing the dominant group do not grant marginal groups the chance to pursue political mobilization, even an ethnic group possessing all other mobilizational criteria will fail. Doug McAdam, Herbert Kitschelt, Sidney Tarrow, and others associated with the political opportunity structure approach have called attention to the critical importance of the external environment (broadly speaking, the state and the political system) to social movements.[20] Nonetheless, as Tarrow cautions, political opportunity is not a single variable but a cluster of several, such as the presence or absence of influential allies and realignments in the party system.[21] Political opportunity is the only mobilizational prerequisite exogenous to the mobilizing group.

Ethnic Identity and Its Formation

The second fundamental requirement of political mobilization is a clearly formulated identity that members of the ethnic group share, accept, and uphold. Ethnicity, like all identities, is relational; it attests to an awareness of collective identity comprised of attributes like shared history, traditions, culture, and language. Though the importance of ethnicity among the other factors that comprise identity is contextually determined, for most people ethnic belonging tends to be one of the most important—if, indeed, not *the* most momentous—marker of identity. In Joseph Rothschild's words, the great advantage of ethnicity over other emblems of personal identity is "its capacity to arouse and to engage the most intense, deep, and private emotional sentiments."[22]

Ethnicity is one of several identity options whose value is enhanced in some circumstances and diminished in others. Throughout history, many ethnic groups have vanished as they gradually lost their identity and were absorbed by other ethnic groups. The preservation of spatial, social, and cultural distance from other ethnic groups, the refusal of assimilation and integration may, in favorable circumstances, ensure the survival of an ethnic group's identity. Ethnic identity "is developed, displayed, manipulated, or ignored in accordance with the demands of particular situations."[23]

The common presumption that an ethnic group would by definition possess a well-formed identity is erroneous, particularly in the cases of populations marked by cultural, social, and linguistic diversity. In order to flourish, ethnic identity must be consciously preserved, sustained, and strengthened. Ethnic identity may be formed and enhanced through a number of methods. These may include the celebration of a historical personality, the commemoration of pivotal past events whether fortunate (a victorious battle) or cataclysmic (the Holocaust), and the organization of festivals to conserve the ethnic group's traditions and culture. The chief objective of these endeavors is to add substance and depth to individuals' ethnic identity, as opposed to any "other" identity, such as identity based on geography, occupation, or gender.

The purpose of identity formation, preservation, confirmation, and articulation is to make members of the ethnic group cognizant of their common identity—in other words, to make them appreciate their collective past. "Wherever the memory of the origin of a community . . . remains for some reason alive," wrote Max Weber, "there undoubtedly exists a very specific and often extremely powerful sense of ethnic identity."[24] For Weber, shared political memories constitute a vital component of ethnic identity and thus are extremely important for ethnic group membership. Although the political mobilization of an ethnic group is made difficult by the lack of a well-rounded collective identity, the mobilization process itself enriches and energizes ethnic identity and contributes to the formation of the ethnic group's political identity.[25] Ultimately, ethnic mobilization is the politicization of ethnic identity.

An ethnic community's experience in political activism bolsters its ethnic identity and, ultimately, its chances of mobilization, because the community can draw on, learn from, and critically examine its mobilizational history. Memories of independence or autonomy may also propel the ethnic group toward political activism. (Think only of the Albanian community in Kosovo in the late 1990s.) Ethnic solidarity is another important aspect of ethnic identity. This ethnic fellowship may develop as the result of numerous factors: for instance, prejudicial state policies in housing, welfare, education, or taxation often promote mobilization processes.

Leadership

Another indispensable component of the "standard equipment" ethnic groups need to make credible political claims is a pool of potential leaders who enjoy authority in their community and are capable of giving organizational form to the group. Ordinarily individuals who are qualified for leadership come from the ranks of the intelligentsia; therefore, it is helpful if the overall educational level of the ethnic community allows the formation of a critical mass of educated individuals.

The quality of leadership may determine the success of the organization or movement. Those heading the ethnic movement might be natural leaders whose academic qualifications, economic position, social standing, and political background predestine them for leadership. Alternatively, leaders may emerge by way of a deliberate selection mechanism which might adopt criteria such as the capacity to interact with the ethnic group as well as with other (particularly the dominant) ethnic group(s), politicians, or business leaders.

If the group is divided, leaders need to negotiate compromises and achieve a consensus on at least the elemental goals and tactics of the mobilization process. Rifts within ethnic elites generally impede, whereas cooperation fosters, the ethnic group's chances for mobilization.[26] One of the key tasks of leaders is to forge links with the population hitherto uninvolved in politics.[27] The leader's success in enlisting the participation of the population depends to a large extent on the level of support he receives and the number of rivals who challenge him.

Organizational Capacity

The institutional form through which mobilization itself is expressed is one of the most significant aspects of ethnic mobilization. Once ethnic activists decide to create an organization, a number of issues need to be deliberated. Would an exclusive, elite-type organization serve the group's objectives better, or do circumstances require a mass party or movement? Should the main profile of the organization be political, economic, or cultural? A principal condition of any ethnic organization's political effectiveness is raising the communal consciousness of its members.[28] Mobilizing groups must also identify the people (for instance, businessmen, intellectuals, women) whom the group wants to attract to the organization and the method of their recruitment.

Ethnic parties do not exist in all multiethnic political systems. Nonetheless, as Donald Horowitz notes, in many ethnically divided societies parties tend to organize along ethnic lines.[29] The number of institutions involved in an ethnic group's political representation is also a decisive organizational issue. It would appear logical that a single organization that acts as the sole representative of the ethnic group would increase cohesion in the community. In fact, Paul Brass has argued that it is critically important "that one political organization be dominant in representing the demands of the ethnic group against its rivals."[30] Still, some ethnic communities, like the Roma, are so deeply split along occupational, tribal, or other lines that one organization could not possibly articulate their interests. Conversely, a relatively homogeneous ethnic population might create a large number of organizations because of rivalries within its leadership or dissimilar political views among its members. Under what conditions is a single organization able to assert itself, and what circumstances foster organizational fraction? The answers may depend on numerous related variables such as leadership competition, generational disputes, interfamilial and clan tensions, ideological cleavages, and class differences.

If more than one party represents an ethnic group, these parties will benefit by cooperating, particularly come election time. The establishment of an umbrella organization or electoral coalition aiming to represent the entire ethnic community can be very effective in increasing the ethnic group's political voice. Alternatively, an ethnic party may need the political and organizational assistance of mainstream parties. Alliance structures are often governed by the political conditions of the moment, but can nevertheless yield increased political representation, stability, support, and strength for the ethnic party.[31]

Program

As Milton Esman notes, "[E]thnic mobilization is facilitated by and indeed usually requires an ideology, a coherent set of articulated beliefs" about collective identity, interests, and aspirations—the reasons that justify collective action.[32] Although such a group credo is useful in shaping the movement and encourages cohesiveness, ethnic mobilization can occur in its absence. More important is the decision a mobilizing ethnic group must make about the *profile* of its activities. It might choose to concern itself primarily with cultural, economic, political, or other issues. Mobilization also requires the identification of the collectivity's shared objective. Such aims might be general (such as improvement of the group's economic conditions) and/or specific (such as the halting of discriminatory practices against members of the group in a given school district). Consensus about certain goals can be expected to increase an ethnic group's ability to take joint action.[33]

Ordinarily, gauging the effectiveness of the movement's activities increases with the generality of the goal. Identifying realistic goals is crucial for the success of ethnic mobilization *and* for the accomplishment of these aims. The reasonableness of an objective is primarily determined by situational factors. In exceptional cases, setting unrealistic goals or exploiting the appeal of an archaic, mythical past can be essential to mobilization, and can even be more effective than identification of a more practical goal.[34]

Financial Resources

Ethnic groups that are mobilizing are rarely rich in resources; in many cases the reason for their mobilization is to reverse their economic deprivation. Publicizing activities, printing newspapers and campaign materials, maintaining offices and lines of communication, and paying employees takes money. No active organization can exist without financial support, and determining where the required funds will come from (state or foundation patronage, private donations, membership fees, or external resources (such as an emigré community) is a dilemma that is better tackled early on.

Communications

Clearly, the mobilizing group must get its message out to the community. This requirement presupposes a number of factors. In order to be receptive, the population in question should have high literacy rates and share a common language. Given that the dominant group usually supervises a media typically prejudiced against ethnic minorities, it is particularly important that the group control (and, preferably, own) media outlets (newspapers, radio and television stations), or at the very least maintain connections to sympathetic media agencies. Ideally, the group should also enjoy a certain minimum living standards that would permit access to radios, television sets, books, and newspapers.

Symbols

Shared symbols that are widely recognized and surrounded by the affection and loyalty of the community assist the mobilizing group.[35] The flag, monuments, and public spaces endowed with historical meaning, poems, anthems, and anniversaries of historical events can all be meaningful tokens of the community's commitment to collective action and can be additional means of its cohesion. When no such symbol or tradition is readily available to the ethnic group (because, for instance, such symbols have not been preserved in popular memory or in written or pictorial form), it must be "invented"; that is, it has to be created afresh.[36]

The precise weight of mobilizational prerequisites is impossible to ascertain because they are, to a considerable degree, contextually determined. Nonetheless, it is possible to make broad generalizations about their relative weight. I contend that the first four prerequisites (political opportunity, ethnic identity, leadership, and organizations) are critical; without them ethnic groups will not mobilize. Of these four, political opportunity is both the only factor exogenous to the mobilizing community and the most indispensable one. Strong ethnic identity, effective leadership, and an organizational profile are the endogenous prerequisites for mobilization. A program, financial resources, communications, and symbols can be extremely useful for mobilization, but positive mobilizational outcomes can be realized in their absence. In other words, though shared symbols and/or a coherent plan of action will indisputably facilitate the ethnic group's political mobilization, they are rarely critical to its success. Yet it bears reiterating that the setting is crucial in determining the weight of individual prerequisites. For instance, in an area densely populated by members of the ethnic group, access to the media may not be as crucial to successful mobilization as in regions where the group's concentration is low.

Albanian Political Mobilization in Macedonia

Background

Albanians have been present in the western Balkans for millennia but succeeded in establishing their internationally recognized independent state—which included a mere 60 percent of Albanians in the region—only in 1912. For most of the twentieth century the vast majority of the rest lived in Yugoslavia, particularly in Kosovo (Serbia) and western Macedonia. In the interwar period and in the aftermath of World War II widespread state-sponsored discrimination and numerous atrocities made their conditions exceedingly difficult. In state-socialist Yugoslavia the situation of Albanians residing in Macedonia was the worst among all the constituent republics: their access to political, social, and economic resources was severely limited.[37] In the 1980s Macedonian policies tried to limit the traditionally large Albanian families to two children and prohibited giving them "nationalist" Albanian names, denied their rights to display their symbols, and increased discriminatory policies in education, employment, and culture. The independent Republic of Macedonia quickly became a textbook case of what Brubaker has called a "nationalizing state,"

> of and for a particular ethnocultural "core nation" whose language, culture, demographic position, economic welfare, and political hegemony must be protected and promoted by the state.[38]

Still, Albanians in Macedonia—who comprised, 22.9 percent (442,914) of the country's population, according to the 1994 census, and 25.17 percent (509,075), according to the 2002 census[39]—have been able to significantly improve their lot through political mobilization.

Political Opportunity

Although the 1991 Macedonian Constitution proclaimed "the national state of the Macedonian people" albeit with "full equality and permanent coexistence provided for" others, the main body of the document was far more democratic.[40] In fact, state authorities not only allowed the political mobilization of all ethnic minorities but even provided financial support for some mobilization projects (for example, minority television and radio programs).

Ethnic Identity

Albanian ethnic identity is strong. Although most Albanians are Sunni Muslims, their primary identification has been ethnonational, not religious.[41] Although large numbers of Albanians live in three separate states (about three million in Albania proper, two million in Serbia and Montenegro [especially in Kosovo], and more than five hundred thousand in Macedonia), they consider themselves members of the same nation, use the same literary language, and share a common history.

Throughout most of their history Albanians were marginalized by a succession of foreign powers (for example, Romans, Ottomans, Serbs). Although the occupying forces used a variety of methods aimed at subjugating Albanians—from selective discrimination and half-hearted integration to forced assimilation and attempted annihilation—Albanian identity, if anything, has been reinforced in the process. Furthermore, until at least the early twentieth century, the territory of the contemporary Macedonian state was almost exclusively referred to as a geographic region. In other words, "Macedonians" were not considered a nationality separate from the Albanians, Bulgarians, Greeks, and Serbs who inhabited the area.[42] The ethnic diversity of the region's people actually inspired the French term for fruit salad, macédoine.

In Yugoslav times, ethnic solidarity between Kosovars and Macedonian Albanians was already very strong.[43] The vast majority of college-educated Macedonian Albanians attended the Albanian-language university in Kosovo's capital, Prishtina. During the Communist period Albanians in Yugoslavia had limited opportunities to maintain contacts with their brethren in Albania proper, in large measure because of the isolationist policies of the Albanian state. Starting in the mid-1980s, however, as a result of the gradual disintegration of Yugoslavia and the opening up of Albania itself, cross-border relations among Albanians increased exponentially. Political developments since the mid-1990s have further enhanced the pan-Albanian identity in Macedonia's Albanian community.

The strength of Albanian identity is also evidenced by the fact that intermarriage between ethnic Albanians and others is almost nonexistent in Macedonia. According to a 1974 study, 95 percent of Albanian parents would not let their sons marry a girl of a different nationality; for daughters the figure was even higher.[44] In addition, ethnic Albanian leaders in Macedonia aimed to eradicate some of the ancient Albanian traditions damaging to their community. For instance, in the early 1990s they conducted a more or less successful campaign to end the traditional blood feuds between ethnic Albanian families.[45]

In short, Albanians in Macedonia and elsewhere in the Balkans tend to live in close-knit families, actively follow their age-old traditions, are aware of their long and tumultuous history, and use the Albanian language as their mother tongue. Albanian culture is rich in ancient myths, many of them depicting a heroic past, others imparting the lesson that norms and rules of conduct set by tradition are far more important than official laws and regulations.[46] The vast majority of Albanian children learn these legends in their families; official socialization processes have little chance of contesting their psychological and cultural impact. Moreover, even ordinary Albanians tend to be quite familiar with the greats of Albanian culture and the major outlines of Albanian history. Virtually all ethnic Albanians are familiar with the fifteenth-century struggles of Gjergj Kastrioti Skënderbeu (Scanderbeg) against the Ottoman invaders, the Albanian "national awakening" around the turn of the twentieth century that led to independence, and the large-scale atrocities committed against Albanians in Yugoslavia in 1944–1948 and in the 1980s and 1990s.[47]

Leadership

By the late 1980s the Albanian intelligentsia had emerged as "the real defender" of its community, sharply denouncing Kosovo's loss of political and cultural autonomy and increasing discrimination against Albanians, especially in Macedonia.[48] With the proclamation of independent Macedonia in 1991, institutional obstacles to mobilization disappeared and a number of talented Albanian leaders took the initiative to organize their communities. Nearly all of them were respected intellectuals educated at the University of Prishtina.

From the beginning, the leaders of ethnic Albanians in Macedonia have fallen into two broad categories: political moderates, like Nevat

Halili and Abdurahman Aliti, who were careful not to scare the majority Macedonians with extremist demands, and radical leaders, like Arben Xhaferi and Menduh Thaçi, who did not shy away from threatening the country's territorial integrity in their rhetoric. Until the late 1990s moderates dominated the Albanian side in interethnic negotiations (particularly in the multiethnic government). After the 1998 general elections, however, the more radical forces came to the fore. Perhaps the most well-liked Albanian politician in contemporary Macedonia is Ali Ahmeti, the leader of the Democratic Union for Integration (DUI) and the former political director of the National Liberation Army (NLA) that engaged the Macedonian Army in the "mini-war" of February–August 2001. Ahmeti's popularity is rooted in the NLA's success in obtaining more rights for Albanians and in his remaining untainted by corruption (unlike most other politicians in Macedonia, regardless of ethnicity).

Organizations
Albanians in Macedonia succeeded in establishing political parties that have effectively represented their interests. Founded in 1990, the moderate Party for Democratic Prosperity (PDP) did surprisingly well in Macedonia's first ever democratic elections (also in 1990), garnering 18.3 percent of the vote and sending twenty-three deputies to the 120-seat legislature (*Sobranie*). The larger of the two ethnic Albanian parties, the PDP was an important participant in Macedonia's coalition government in 1992–1998. To discredit its rivals, the PDP occasionally accused them of being a mere appendage of Ibrahim Rugova's Albanian Democratic Alliance of Kosovo.[49]

The PDP's more radical wing split from the party in 1996 and established, under Xhaferi's leadership, the Democratic Party of Albanians (DPA). The DPA adopted far less compromising positions than the PDP, particularly with respect to the flag, language rights, and education.[50] According to one expert, the DPA is an articulate champion of liberal values rather than the militant saber rattler portrayed by the Western press.[51] In any event, the DPA joined the Internal Macedonian Revolutionary Organization-Macedonian National Unity (VMRO-DPMNE), a nationalist party established in 1893, in the coalition cabinet of 1998–2002.

While in government, both parties managed to pursue their fundamental aim—to transform Macedonia into a two-part federation of Slav Macedonians and Albanians through an overhaul of the constitution and legal order—through the existing political institutions, and were rewarded with governmental and diplomatic posts.[52] Both parties, however, called into question the very legitimacy of the same institutions they participated in while in opposition.

The Democratic Union for Integration (DUI), the third important Albanian party in Macedonia, grew out of the NLA. The terms of the August 2001 Ohrid Agreement—negotiated between the NLA and the Macedonian government—resulted in numerous tangible improvements in the conditions of Albanians. (The NLA was a guerilla army, the structure and financing of which benefited from the participation of its larger sister organization, the Kosovo Liberation Army.)[53] Not surprisingly, the DUI was the clear winner of the ethnic Albanian vote in the September 2002 general elections, gaining sixteen mandates (in contrast to the DPA's seven and the PDP's two). The DUI became a member of the new coalition government, led by the multiparty formation "Together for Macedonia." Xhaferi's DPA pledged to cooperate with the DUI "to work for the Albanian cause."[54]

Although smaller ethnic Albanian political parties—such as the People's Democratic Party, Democratic Alliance of Albanians-Liberal Party, and the Party of Democratic Action—have not been able to challenge the dominance of the PDP, DPA, and DUI, occasionally they, too, have been able to send a representative to the legislature. The three larger ethnic parties are relatively well organized, with offices in most cities and towns with sizable ethnic Albanian communities (Tetovo, Gostivar, Skopje). They—like other Macedonian parties—tend to be hierarchical, with the leadership serving as the only official information channel.[55]

Program

From the beginning, clear objectives have promoted Albanian political mobilization. Albanian leaders argued for constitutional changes guaranteeing Albanians full equality from the first day of independent Macedonia. They wanted collective status in the state and would not be reconciled to mere integration held out by majority Macedonians. More specifically, they demanded the naming of Albanians as one of the two constitutive nations of Macedonia, recognition of Albanian as an official language in areas where at least 20 percent of the population was Albanian, governmental and diplomatic appointments corresponding to the actual size of their parties in ruling coalitions, an autonomous state-supported university with Albanian as the language of instruction, and civil service employment commensurate with the size of the Albanian population.

Their leaders also knew what they did not want. The notion of a Greater Albania which would incorporate all Albanians (from Kosovo, Macedonia, and Montenegro) has been seldom raised because few

Albanians in the former Yugoslavia find that alternative attractive; they cite inferior economic conditions and, to a lesser extent, limited opportunities to practice their religion in present-day Albania. Moreover, Albanian leaders seem to be aware of the aversion of the United States and European powers to further border changes in the western Balkans. Even during the 2001 armed clashes Ahmeti repeatedly insisted that the NLA was interested neither in Greater Albania nor in a Greater Kosovo but in fully equal status for Albanians in Macedonia.[56] By publicly distancing themselves from threatening Macedonia's territorial status, Albanians improved the chances of negotiated settlements.

Financial Resources
Although Albanians were economically marginalized in the former Yugoslavia, many of them have successfully exploited the expanding business opportunities in the last decade. As a result, some predominantly ethnic Albanian towns, like Gostivar, have become quite prosperous. Moreover, the traditionally close kinship ties in the Albanian community have served as an economic buffer for the less fortunate.

Albanian mobilization has been financed by several sources. First, local Albanians contributed to the cost of mobilization by way of party membership fees and donations. The relatively large Albanian diaspora (particularly in Italy, Switzerland, and the United States) has also been an important source of financial contributions. Throughout the hostilities in 2001, for instance, Albanians in Switzerland held regular weekend fundraisers, netting tens of thousands of dollars for their cousins in Macedonia.[57] A large portion of the NLA's weapons and equipment was smuggled across the border from Kosovo. Moreover, Albanian organizations—particularly the NLA—received a substantial share of their funds from ethnic Albanian criminal networks specializing in drug trafficking and arms smuggling.[58]

Communications
The traditionally large and tight-knit families and the dense residential patterns of the Albanian community in Macedonia have aided their mobilization efforts. A further advantage is that virtually all ethnic Albanians are native speakers of the Albanian language. These factors have ensured that information flow among Albanian leaders and activists has been smooth and relatively secure.[59] Numerous television and radio stations (both state-supported and private), daily newspapers, and weekly magazines cater to the Albanian community. In most areas heavily populated by Albanians (northwestern Macedonia) radio and television broadcasts

as well as newspapers originating in Albania and Kosovo are widely accessible. Finally, many ethnic Albanian civic and political organizations maintain their own Web sites.

Symbols

Knowledge of their shared history, culture, symbols, and mother tongue has bolstered the ethnic identity of Albanians in Macedonia (and elsewhere). Their national symbols, especially the flag, which bears the emblem of Skënderbeu (a two-headed eagle), have further promoted Albanian identity, particularly as their public display has met with staunch Macedonian opposition both before and after 1991. The draft peace proposal prepared by local and international experts during the 2001 ethnic conflict contained an entire chapter on national symbols which was later included in the Ohrid Agreement. It permits local authorities to display the emblems (flag and crest) of the majority community next to the Macedonian ones on or in front of local public buildings.[60]

Results of Mobilization

Albanian ethnic mobilization has been successful by any measure. A large proportion of the Albanian community was mobilized as early as 1991. For instance, in the January 1992 referendum over 90 percent of eligible Albanians voted, 74 percent of them for cultural and political autonomy.[61] Even prior to the 2001 "mini-war," ethnic Albanians benefited from their political mobilization in several ways. Their political parties have been included in all coalition governments since 1992, they received important ministerial portfolios (at times as many as five) in all of them, and an increasing number of civil service jobs on all levels have been earmarked for Albanians. The state also made efforts to increase opportunities for Albanians in higher education (albeit at Macedonian-language institutions).

The 2001 hostilities resulted in major gains for ethnic Albanians, codified in the Ohrid Agreement. These included a new constitution in which references to the ethnic background of Macedonian citizens would be removed; the recognition of Albanian as an official language (along with Macedonian); the right of Albanians to bilingual documents and identity cards; the use of Albanian language in the legislature; the transfer of some powers from the central government to local authorities; raising the Albanian component of the state police force from 5 percent to 25 percent; legalization and state financing for the previously illegal University of Tetovo and the establishment, with Council of Europe funds, of the multilingual Southeastern European University in the same city; and amnesty to rebel fighters.[62] In September 2001 the Sobranie ratified the agreement, with 91 votes in favor, 19 opposed, and 2 abstentions. Two months later, it formed a Committee on Relations between Ethnic Communities, which includes seven ethnic Macedonian and seven Albanian legislators in addition to one member each from the Serbian, Vlach, Turkish, Romani, and Bosnian minorities.[63]

Gypsy/Romani Political Mobilization in Eastern Europe

Background

The Roma are the only transborder, non-territorial people in contemporary Europe. Originally from the Indian subcontinent, they have been a part of East European societies since their arrival in the region some seven centuries ago. From that point on, they have been consistently and comprehensively marginal and marginalized politically, economically, and socially regardless of country or regime type. Their objective socioeconomic conditions, which actually had improved during four decades of state-socialist rule, have rapidly and markedly deteriorated in the competitive economic environment of the postcommunist era. Concomitantly, interethnic relations have worsened as long-standing anti-Gypsy prejudices have frequently found expression in overt discrimination while the Roma's deepening social problems and reliance on modest state resources have continued to fuel tensions.

Political Opportunity

The one significant gain East European Gypsies made from the post-communist transition was the opportunity to freely organize. As a rule, after 1989 the state no longer restrained Romani mobilization although in some cases it divided and played off Gypsy organizations against one another. Moreover, particularly in the early 1990s and in some of the region's states (for example, Slovakia and Bulgaria) state authorities and some contending parties attempted to scare Roma into voting for their side. Nonetheless, these efforts were limited to a few areas, and their impact was not sufficient to negate the political opportunity available to Roma.

Ethnic Identity

Gypsy ethnic identity is weak and it is hard to define because of the diversity of Romani communities. Fundamentally, Roma do share the same origins, culture, and traumatic history in Europe. These experiences include centuries of nomadism, an incredibly wide variety of institutionalized persecution (from nearly five hundred years of slavery [from about 1348 to 1864] in the Romanian principalities through slaughter under the Nazis to forced sterilization by Communist authorities in Czechoslovakia), and the fact that the Roma have not had a "home state" to provide haven or extend protection to them. East European Gypsy communities are geographically diffuse and socioeconomically diverse, attributes that impede mobilization. Through the centuries the Roma have accumulated a rich collection of customs, folklore, and skills. Changes in social and economic conditions have nonetheless allowed an ever smaller number of Gypsies to adhere to the exacting standards of ancient Romani culture and traditions which are, therefore, not part of the identity of the vast majority of the contemporary Gypsy population.

An even more important problem is that many Roma do not consider themselves part of a cohesive ethnic group, but primarily identify instead with a tribe or other subgroup to which they belong. Some Gypsies refuse to identify themselves with their ethnic background altogether, in large part because of fear of discrimination or because of a perceived sense of ethnic inferiority. For instance, in the March 2001 Czech census only 11,716 Roma chose to declare themselves as such; in the May 2001 Slovak census only 92,000 did so. Most experts agree, however, that their real numbers are at least 200,000 and 500,000, respectively.[64] (In this context, the denial of ethnic identity actually harms one's community, given that state policies tie financial support for ethnic groups to their size according to census figures.) Many educated Roma try to marry *gadje* (non-Roma), and hide their identity from the children resulting from these mixed marriages. The next generation is usually assimilated.[65]

There is an enormous cultural distance between the tiny Romani intelligentsia and the masses of undereducated and often apathetic ordinary Gypsies, which contributes to the poor political communication in the Romani community. The strengthening of a Gypsy national identity necessarily would involve the invention of tradition because the Roma—who lack their own written historical tradition—have little to draw on.[66] The tremendous diversity of Gypsy communities has made the unfolding of the Romani movement all the more difficult. Intra-community cleavages further split an already small potential constituency and impede mobilization efforts.

The fact that there is little ethnic solidarity between the Roma constitutes a further hindrance to their political mobilization. Most Gypsies do not share an "imagined community" or the personal and cultural pride of belonging to a nation. They comprise a most diverse ethnic group that can be differentiated according to lifestyle (peripatetic or sedentary), tribal affiliation, occupation, language, religion, and the time of arrival in a given country. In several East European states, such as Bulgaria and Romania, tribal identity—primarily rooted in the traditional economic activity of a group—remains a significant bond. Marrying across tribes is highly unusual; many Gypsies intermarry with other Romani groups more rarely than with *gadje*. The Gypsy population is vertically rather than horizontally differentiated and is becoming increasingly hierarchical because of expanding economic opportunities; groups that do better tend to distance themselves from those they leave behind.[67] Romani mobilization is still in its infancy; it is little more than a decade old. Therefore, in terms of mobilizational experience, the Gypsies have little to draw on that could bolster their identity. In imperial and authoritarian states a few Roma managed to organize several short-lived Gypsy associations that were, in nearly every case, fragmented by infighting. Few Roma, however, are aware of these mobilizational attempts. In the socialist period the state succeeded in keeping ethnic activism down, but a handful of Gypsy activists did emerge from the state-controlled Romani organizations. They have become the backbone of the postcommunist mobilization efforts.

Leadership

Romani organizations are elite-driven and paternalistic. The minuscule Gypsy intelligentsia and middle class have not generated a large pool of leaders. Romani politics has become the bailiwick of a small group of intellectuals and activists who have not been successful in drawing the Romani masses into politics.

Romani elites have been plagued by a number of problems that have cost the East European Gypsies dearly. The most important leadership problem Roma have encountered has been what one Gypsy activist calls "our national disease, *hamishagos* (to meddle or to disturb)" that "makes us want to hinder, instead of help, our own who are getting ahead."[68] Ironically, substantive differences between feuding Romani activists are often negligible, and the source of contention is mainly their ambition to supplant one another. Few Romani politicians allow that there could be legitimate approaches and views other than their own. Those who do not accept the position of the leader are often ostracized. One of the most important shortcomings of many Romani activists and leaders is their inability to work well with state authorities. To be sure, state officials, particularly in the early 1990s, at times succeeded in manipulating and dividing Romani leaders. Still, Gypsy activists tend to dismiss the genuinely good intentions of government officials, insist that a state agency or ministry deal exclusively with them and not with other Romani leaders, or let personal innuendo dominate their dealings with authorities. As some Gypsy leaders admit, their own inability to harness the goodwill of the government has been a major impediment to their mobilization.[69]

In addition, Romani elites are split along two major axes. The most important division is between traditional and modern leaders. Typically, the former tend to be rooted in and possess a keen understanding of their communities and have little formal education, but have been successful in business or some other respected endeavor. New-style activists, on the other hand, tend to be younger, more dynamic, well educated, and more clearly focused on practical objectives. They are also more at home in *gadje* society and can communicate with state officials with much greater ease than traditional leaders. Not surprisingly, government bureaucrats and foundation officials tend to prefer dealing with the "modern" activists.

The other important split is between those who are best described as "radical" or "extremist" versus those who are more moderate. Both types have advanced the Roma's cause in different ways. Radical activists have been instrumental in keeping the Roma on the government's agenda and in public focus. They often wildly exaggerate their points and unfairly accuse state organizations and others of ignoring the Gypsies' conditions. Moderates are more prepared to seek compromise and to view their own communities in a critical if compassionate manner. They have tended to be more effective in accomplishing pragmatic goals and completing tangible projects, but those who finance their programs might well have been motivated to give by extremist leaders.

Organizations

Gypsy organizations receive a poor grade when evaluated by Huntington's criteria of institutionalization:[70] they tend to be rigid and unadaptable; have simple structure and few, often ill-defined, objectives; and are marked by disunity. The most conspicuous attribute of Romani mobilization is the relatively large number of organizations (of all kinds, including self-help, cultural, and political) created throughout the last decade; in 1999, there were approximately 75 in the Czech Republic, 250 in Hungary, 35 in Macedonia, 58 in Romania, and 92 in Slovakia.[71] Why are there so many Romani groups? First, after decades of prohibition, the chance to start independent organizations was tempting for Gypsy and non-Gypsy activists alike. Second, new association laws made it relatively easy to register formal groups. Third, the increasing availability of public and private financial support for Gypsy-related organizations motivated their formation. Finally, like others, many Roma activists indulged their desire to be in leadership positions by establishing their own organizations. With the maturation of Romani activism and the increasingly rigorous fiscal monitoring of funding agencies, the number of new organizations has begun to taper off and more of them have become successful in pursuing projects useful for the Roma.

Are there too many Gypsy organizations in Eastern Europe, as many observers and Romani activists claim? Not necessarily. An increasing proportion of organizations are effective and have served as practical training grounds for thousands of Gypsies across the region, thereby directly contributing to Romani mobilization. Most of the Romani organizations are local but there are more and more regional and national ones with branches in communities. For instance, *Partida Romilor* (Roma Party, PR), the most important Romanian Gypsy political organization, has established active branch offices in nearly every county of the country, and *Lungo Drom*, a Hungarian sociopolitical organization, claims to have as many as six hundred local groups. The fact that the majority of East European settlements with substantial Romani communities are home to some sort of Gypsy organization (whether a political party, dance club, soccer team, or self-help group) is an important accomplishment of Romani activism.

Romani mobilization should be viewed in evolutionary terms. With the passing of time, the number of Gypsy organizations that have positively affected the Roma has grown, many of their projects now are actually making a difference in the lives of ordinary Roma, and a growing number of activists have gained experience and focused on practical, worthwhile endeavors.

Program

The general aims of Romani organizations are similar across the region and are much like those of other marginalized ethnic minorities. They include full recognition and effective enforcement of minority and civil rights, promulgation of strong antidiscrimination laws, implementation of affirmative action programs in education, housing, employment, and social welfare, and broadcast time in the state-owned media proportionate to the size of the Romani population and its fair portrayal therein. One of the most important and divisive demands of Gypsy mobilization has been education in Romani language. Some leaders support this objective because they believe that it would strengthen the ethnic identity of their communities. Others are opposed to classes in Romani because of their conviction that it would further increase the social distance between

Gypsies and *gadje* and that it would diminish the Roma's chances on the labor market.[72]

The programs and demands of Gypsy groups have been frequently unreasonable—either unattainable, not warranted, or both—and the inevitable failures have increased the political apathy of many Roma and have eroded support for their organizations. For instance, Gypsy parties routinely promise their supporters to place a specific number of their politicians in the local, regional, and state legislatures and nearly always fall short of their pledges. More sensible objectives have been crowned with some successes, such as the translating of schoolbooks to the Romani language in Romania, and securing of state financial support for privately organized Romani-language schools in Poland.

What makes goals "reasonable" to a large extent depends on local conditions: the strength of the Romani organization as well as the priorities and possibilities of local, regional, or state authorities. For instance, in the mid-1990s increasing Romani-language radio and television time for Macedonian and Romanian Gypsy parties was a realistic goal; for their Bulgarian counterparts it was not, even though the objective conditions existed in all three states.

Financial Resources

For the most part, Romani mobilization has been paid for by non-Roma because the Gypsies' own contributions remain, on the whole, minimal. This can be explained by the modest income of most Roma and the reluctance of most wealthy Gypsies to support Romani causes. To be sure, a handful of activists have committed considerable personal resources to Roma-related events, activities, and programs. A few prosperous businessmen with political aspirations—among them Amdi Bajram (Macedonia), Florin Cioaba (Romania), and Kyril Rashkov (Bulgaria)—bankroll not only their own parties but also a number of Gypsy-related causes.

Across the region, the bulk of financial support for Gypsy groups and activities has come from the state. Governments in Hungary, the Czech Republic, Poland, Romania, and Slovenia have fully or partially financed hundreds of Romani organizations and NGOs. In some cases the state provides support in proportion to the membership of the organization, in others only if the group can raise a certain percentage of the requested funding from other sources. Frequently, however, the state has not been an impartial grantor of its favors, and its political preferences rather than the comparative merits of Gypsy organizations have determined the amount of disbursed funds.

Domestic and international foundations and in some cases foreign governments and international organizations are another major source of
financial support for Romani NGOs. In a few instances Gypsy political
organizations have received funding from mainstream parties in
exchange for campaigning for them in Romani communities or for entering into political alliances. Notwithstanding the various sources of financial support, most Romani organizations are poorly funded. There are
simply too many groups competing for the finite amount of available
funds.

Communications

Romani leaders have long recognized the persisting biases of the mainstream media and have tried to build access to them. Since 1989 Romani
leaders also have campaigned for the creation of independent Gypsy
media outlets. Many have regarded independent radio stations and television channels especially desirable because they would have allowed the
Roma to control programming and to enjoy freer access to broadcast
time. Their task has been all the more challenging given that in many
areas only a small minority of Gypsies speak or understand the Romani
language.

Gypsy activists have established and sustained dozens of periodicals in
the region. This is no mean feat, considering the obstacles Romani publications constantly face. First, funding is scarce and there is vigorous competition between applicants. Moreover, revenues from advertisements are
low because potential advertisers are put off by the small circulation of
Gypsy magazines and the low purchasing power of most Roma. Second,
Gypsy periodicals appeal to a limited readership, given that many Roma
are illiterate or read little.[73] Third, typically the distribution of Romani
magazines and newspapers is a difficult task. Subscribers are few (primarily relevant NGOs and government agencies, prisons, and the like, but
few ordinary Roma), and street vendors, because of their prejudices or
the anticipation of low sales, are in most cases unwilling to carry Romani
papers. Fourth, editors have encountered problems in recruiting and
retaining qualified journalists. Finally, in many areas only a minority of
Gypsies can read Romani, so it is not useful as a language of publication.
This is another drawback because it robs Gypsy communities of the inti-
macy, exclusivity, and pride only Romani language publications could
provide.

Radio and television broadcasts for and about the Roma can have a
much larger impact because the proportion of Gypsies who use these
media outlets is much higher. Since 1989 most East European state radio

and television companies (and a few Romani businessmen, notably in Macedonia) have introduced programs for the Gypsies or kept on the air those that originated in the socialist period. Romani activists often complain that political and socioeconomic issues comprise an all too small share of program content.

Symbols

The absence of a written Romani tradition means that Gypsies have few symbols that could have inspired their mobilization processes. Gypsy culture and history is preserved mostly in the Roma's rich oral tradition; there are no monuments, memoirs, or other symbols around which Romani activists could rally their people. History has been an alien concept in Romani culture, where the dead are rarely mentioned and seldom become the subjects of commemoration.[74] In recent years international Gypsy groups, in order to create enduring symbols that could buttress Gypsy identity, have chosen a Romani flag and anthem. Unfortunately, the majority of ordinary Gypsies are not aware of them.

Results of Mobilization

The weakness of Romani mobilization is all the more noteworthy because the Roma, unlike other minorities, have received substantial financial and other assistance from international organizations and NGOs. The discrepancy is particularly notable when considering the collective political action and strength of other East European ethnic minorities, including the Albanians in Macedonia and the Turks in Bulgaria. Although some East European states made occasional efforts to contain Romani mobilization by intimidating would-be Gypsy voters, these incidents did not constitute a major reason for the lackluster success of Romani mobilization. These attempts occurred almost exclusively in the early 1990s, when Romani activists were inexperienced and ordinary Gypsies were easily deceived, and the incidents were largely isolated.

The fact that Gypsy political organizations routinely divide the Romani vote between themselves, however, has been far more important in reducing their parliamentary representation. For instance, thirteen Gypsy parties registered prior to the 1998 Slovak national elections, but eventually none could run candidates for parliament on its own. Four years later, for similar reasons, the Roma failed to place a single member of parliament (MP) in the Bratislava legislature, even though they constituted nearly one-tenth of Slovakia's population. In order to combine their strength, Romani groups in every East European state have repeatedly formed or tried to form electoral coalitions and umbrella organizations with other Gypsy organizations. The majority of these bodies have come up against the same problems as individual Gypsy associations: mutual disdain, infighting, and a marked inability to reach compromises.

Given their failures to gain political representation on their own, several East European Gypsy organizations have tried to build relations with mainstream political parties. Such parties, however, have seldom entered into electoral coalitions with Gypsy parties, for two reasons. First, the proportion of the Roma in the general population is relatively small and their voting participation has been typically far below that of the majority. Second, putting a Gypsy on a party's list has been widely recognized as a liability because of widespread societal biases against Roma. In general, mainstream parties seek to co-opt the Roma through short-term political calculations rather than a prospective electoral program. The average politician's view is that he or she cannot rely on Gypsy votes because the Roma are unreliable and easily manipulated. For instance, prior to the 1998 national and the 1999 presidential elections, campaign workers of two leading parties distributed food in the Romani suburb Shuto Orizari in Macedonia, but the Gypsies voted for another party which ignored them in their campaigns.[75]

Since 1989 several incidents of political parties' attempts to purchase the Romani vote with cash or through the staging of festivities for a Gypsy community have been reported throughout the region. A recent example is the Hungarian Socialist Party's courting of the Romani population in the town of Jászapáti prior to the June 2004 national election of Hungary's representatives to the European Union. Party activists promised the town's Roma 5,000 forints (about $25) each and a free "beerfest" in exchange for their vote.[76]

The first serious electoral agreement between a major party and a prominent Romani organization was the "protocol" between the Party of Democratic Socialism in Romania (PDSR) and the Partida Romilor, regarding the December 200 national elections. The agreement was struck at the PR's October 1999 national congress.[77] According to the PDSR-PR concord, the PR would support the PDSR's campaign and encourage Roma to vote for Ion Iliescu's party. In return, the PDSR offered to extend social help to the Roma and to involve the PR in policy making. The pact was beneficial for the Roma for three reasons. First, for the first time in their history, a major political party was willing to sign a policy agreement with them. Second, the PDSR committed itself to solve the Roma's social problems through a national strategy to be elaborated by the PR. Finally, the PDSR agreed to co-opt the PR into the governing process and promised them several influential places in the government.[78] Within weeks after its December 2000 electoral victory PDSR delivered on its promise.

Traditionally the Roma have kept their distance from politics that many conceive of as a *gadje* concern and endeavor. A large percentage of ordinary Gypsies (90 percent in 1994 in Hungary) have been unaware of their organizations.[79] Also, many Roma simply do not know how to cast ballots. Activists have documented numerous cases in Romania when the local Gypsy leader went to vote for the entire Romani community or when Romani votes were invalid because they voted for all of the Gypsy organizations on the ballot.[80]

Several patterns of Romani voting behavior can be identified. First, the majority of Gypsies tend to vote for the party in power or for the party that is expected to win.[81] Second, a disproportionately large number of Roma have voted for the successors of former Communist parties, which is a logical manifestation of many Gypsies' nostalgia for the relative security and prosperity they associate with the socialist era. Third, though other large ethnic minorities in the region tend to vote along ethnic lines, Gypsies often do not because they have little confidence in their own. According to a recent analysis, "a Romani candidate is likely to receive only about a third of the votes of Romani voters and is unlikely to gain many votes at all from the majority population."[82] Finally, the voting participation rate of Gypsies—according to reliable estimates, less than 15 percent—is far below that of the rest of the population.[83]

Considering their proportion in the general population, there should be dozens of Romani MPs across the region. Instead, in 2001 there were six, and of the six, only one (Amdi Bajram of Macedonia) represented a Gypsy party. An often overlooked yet important point is that there might actually be quite a few more Roma in East European legislatures who do not openly identify themselves with their ethnic heritage.

Progress *has* occurred in Gypsy mobilization, however, and this progress is most clearly measurable in the growing number of Romani elected local officials. On the local level—especially in areas where Gypsies make up a substantial proportion of voters—Romani activists have improved their electoral record with each successive local election. In Romania, for instance, voters elected 106 Gypsies as local council members in 1992, 136 in 1996, and 160 (and four county councilpersons) in 2000.[84] In Bulgaria relatively few Romani local officials were elected until the October 1999 local elections. For the first time, two Gypsy parties (*Svobodna Bulgariya* and the Democratic Congress Party)— though not registered as ethnic parties—managed to get ninety-two of their candidates elected.[85] Again, in addition to these Roma, dozens of others have succeeded in local elections representing mainstream parties and, quite likely, dozens more who do not openly identify themselves as Gypsies. In sum, there are now hundreds of Gypsy local councilpersons and perhaps a dozen municipal mayors and deputy mayors across Eastern Europe.

Generally speaking, Gypsy political activism tends to be most effective in countries (Hungary and Romania) where the Romani community is substantial in both absolute terms and as a percentage of the overall population, *and* where state policies have been at least somewhat supportive both politically and financially regardless of the government in power. In countries where the Romani population is relatively small and/or widely dispersed (Czech Republic, Macedonia, Poland) or where state policies have impeded Gypsy political activism (Bulgaria, Czech Republic, Slovakia until 1998) Romani mobilization is less likely to succeed.

Conclusion

The postcommunist regime change afforded ethnic and other minorities the opportunity to alleviate their political marginality. Nonetheless, their preparation for collective political action varies widely. After more than a decade of mobilization, Albanians have not only attained political representation commensurate with their numbers but also gained a number of important concessions which promise to improve their long-term conditions in Macedonia. Gypsies, on the other hand, remain woefully underrepresented in Eastern Europe's polities. The reasons for this disparity are primarily explained by the fact that the preparations of these two ethnic minorities for political mobilization could not be more different. Ethnic mobilization is a continuous process, however, and as Gypsy associations and their leaders mature by virtue of their protracted participation in political processes, they are likely to become more effective.

One of the fundamental objectives of ethnic political mobilization is to exert pressure on the state to formulate and implement policies favorable to the ethnic group. Since the fall of the *ancien régime*, the East European states' policies toward ethnic minorities have become more progressive. These policy shifts have been due in part to ethnic mobilization and, especially in the cases of minorities that have been less effective in their mobilization efforts, to the relentless pressure of international organizations like the Council of Europe, the Organization for Security and Cooperation in Europe, and especially, the EU.[86] These and other international organizations possess strong leverage vis-à-vis the East European states, the primary foreign policy objective of which is to obtain membership from them.

The model of mobilizational prerequisites detailed here and illustrated through the Albanian and Romani experiences is broadly applicable not only to cases of ethnic mobilization but also to social and political movements in a variety of contexts. This model should be especially useful for comparative studies of social and political movements. Looking at cases of ethnic and other types of mobilization through the lens of mobilizational prerequisites should facilitate the rigorous evaluation of these movements and their chances for success. To be sure, although some prerequisites—political opportunity, strong ethnic identity, effective leadership, and a clear organizational profile—are critical to mobilizational success, the weight of other variables will depend to a degree on the particulars of each case. Not all prerequisites need be positive in order to produce desired mobilizational outcomes; but clearly, a group's chances of success increase with the number of prerequisites attained.

4

ETHNICITY, ELECTIONS, AND PARTY SYSTEMS IN POSTCOMMUNIST STATES

ROBERT G. MOSER

Ethnically diverse societies produce unique and often dire dilemmas for democratization. Scholars have long noted that states with significant ethnic cleavages face inordinate obstacles to the maintenance of competitive politics, leading many scholars to cite some degree of ethnic harmony or analogous developments such as "stateness" or agreement on state borders as preconditions to successful transitions to democracy.[1] Naturally, a countervailing literature has also developed examining the factors (typically institutional or elite-driven) that can overcome these obstacles and successfully implant democracy in ethnically divided societies.[2]

Electoral politics lie at the heart of the problems of combining democracy with ethnic diversity. The supposedly deleterious effects of ethnic division and electoral politics run in both directions. Deep ethnic divisions tend to undermine democracy by introducing exclusion and polarization into electoral politics. If ethnic divisions are translated into ethnically based parties, politics tend to polarize around ascriptive identities; majorities feel threatened, whereas minorities feel excluded, rendering the maintenance of competitive elections and democratic decision making arduous at best.[3] Conversely, competitive elections spur ethnic mobilization in divided societies. Snyder has argued that the introduction of competitive elections in countries with weak democratic institutions actually amplifies the incentives and opportunities of elites to resort to nationalist appeals, thus increasing the likelihood of ethnic conflict.[4]

Postcommunist states of Eastern Europe and the former Soviet Union provide an intriguing laboratory for studying the interaction between ethnicity and electoral politics for a variety of reasons. First, and most obviously, the region is quite ethnically diverse, with relatively homogenous nation-states like Poland or the Czech Republic being the exception rather than the norm. Secondly, ethnic minorities in the region are usually geographically concentrated (and sometimes reside in ethnically defined federal subunits), both of which produce additional potential for ethnic mobilization and electoral clout at the regional and national levels. Thirdly, the repeated establishment and subsequent breakdown of multinational empires in the region have further politicized ethnicity. Nationalist movements emerged to push for independence during imperial breakdown. Subsequently, postimperial politics have been complicated by the confluence of nationalizing states, old minorities, and new minorities comprising previously hegemonic peoples.[5] Finally, some have argued that Communist rule left relatively flat civil societies largely devoid of well developed class cleavages, making ethnicity the most likely cleavage defining politics.[6]

In this chapter, I examine the role ethnicity plays in electoral politics, concentrating on the intersection between ethnic divisions, party development, and legislative representation of minorities. After an extensive examination of the relevant literature on these issues, I offer two case studies on Russia and Lithuania. These two cases were chosen for several reasons. First, they both employ a mixed electoral system, which allows voters to cast two ballots, one in a proportional representation (PR) contest and one in a single-member district (SMD) election. This allows one to examine the impact of different electoral rules on ethnic representation, while holding social conditions constant.[7] Second, although the two countries employ similar electoral systems, their ethnic composition and ethnic relations are quite different, which allows for an effective comparison of the impact of social context on the electoral mobilization of minorities. Finally, both cases offer the most complete data for analysis of minority representation and the impact of ethnic composition on party development at the subnational level.

This chapter is broken down into four parts. I begin with a discussion of the wide-ranging literature on ethnic electoral politics, concentrating on three interrelated aspects of the phenomenon—ethnic parties, legislative representation of minorities, and the impact of ethnicity on party system fragmentation. Next, I discuss the growing literature on ethnicity and electoral politics in postcommunist states and develop a framework for examining the factors that influence ethnic electoral politics in the region. Thirdly, I take a more in-depth look at my two case studies—Russia and Lithuania—to further explicate the degree to which the postcommunist experience reinforces and challenges our understanding of these phenomena. I end with some tentative conclusions and implications.

Ethnicity and Electoral Politics

The literature on ethnic politics has been dominated by issues of identity and identity formation while the mobilization of such identity in the electoral realm has received less attention.[8] Ethnic divisions can be manifested in a variety of ways in the electoral arena. When given full voting rights, ethnic minorities can be incorporated into democratic electoral processes as one of several components within a large catchall party/coalition or as the core element of a more narrowly defined ethnic party. A single ethnic party can vie for the votes of co-ethnics, or a multitude of such parties can compete with one another for the support of a single ethnic group. An ethnic group can vote as a cohesive voting bloc or be internally split by divisions of class, region, or culture. Parties claiming to represent particular ethnic groups (whether of the majority or minorities) can put forth moderate proposals or extremist positions.

In turn, these outcomes are influenced by other factors relating to demography, socioeconomic conditions, institutions, and elite interactions. Such factors as the electoral system, the relative size and geographic concentration of minority ethnic groups, the degree of social distance between ethnic groups, and the historical incorporation of groups within the polity all help to determine how ethnic divisions affect electoral outcomes. With such a wide range of potential outcomes and causal factors, the question of the impacts of ethnicity on electoral outcomes quickly becomes a very broad and complex one.

Much scholarship examines ethnicity as one of many factors influencing preferences of individual voters. Where available, survey research can tell us whether members of different ethnic groups have distinct partisan attachments and policy preferences. Once ethnicity is established as a significant cleavage, however, its impact on electoral outcomes and the party system requires additional investigation. Such research often (but not exclusively) addresses three main issues: the role of ethnic parties, legislative representation of (minority) ethnic groups, and the relationship between ethnic diversity and party fragmentation.

Ethnic Parties

Donald Horowitz states that an ethnically based party "derives its support overwhelmingly from an identifiable ethnic group . . . and serves the interests of that group."[9] Thus, an ethnic party is defined by its monoethnic constituency even if its target group does not faithfully give all or even most of its support to the party claiming to represent it. The impact that ethnic parties have on electoral politics depends on their relative strength within the party system and their interactions with other parties.[10]

In ethnic party systems electoral outcomes become fixed and certain groups can be forever assured of being in power because of their majority status while other minority groups are permanently excluded from governing coalitions. Such circumstances transform elections from uncertain enterprises that produce shifting majorities to exercises with very predictable outcomes. In Horowitz's language, an election contested by an ethnic party system often ceases to be an election at all and degenerates into a census.[11]

The rise of ethnic party systems directly threatens democratic stability in a variety of ways. The party or parties representing the majority population may establish a single-party government and end the democratic experiment in reaction to the threat (real or perceived) of minority electoral mobilization. Ethnic parties of both the majority and minority often resort to extremist positions, further polarizing politics and undermining cooperative ethnic relations. Finally, permanently excluded minorities may take violent action ranging from secession if territorially concentrated to riots and other civil disturbances if territorially dispersed. Even if not resorting to violence, excluded minorities tend to see the regime as less legitimate, which could hurt the long-term viability of democracy.[12]

A related body of work has examined the interrelationship between electoral systems, ethnic parties, and interethnic conflict. Scholars led by Lijphart have recommended proportional representation as a method of inclusive representation within a broader system of consociationalism. PR is presumed to favor the representation of minorities by allowing smaller parties (that is, minority ethnic parties) a reasonable chance to achieve representation.[13] A rival school of thought headed by Horowitz has countered that consociational systems lock in ethnic divisions and that electoral systems in divided societies need to provide incentives for voters to pool their votes behind moderate, multiethnic coalitions. Reilly has argued that preference voting systems, such as the alternative vote (AV) and single transferable vote (STV), provide the centripetal incentives necessary to push voters and elites into coalitions that reach across ethnic divides.[14]

The literature on ethnic parties tends to presume their existence in ethnically divided societies.[15] Both sides of the debate over electoral system effects on interethnic conflict seem to expect the rise of ethnically defined parties. Advocates of PR argue that electoral engineers should work to accommodate and to co-opt ethnic parties into the political system; centripetalists argue for electoral arrangements that force elites to resist this "natural" urge and push them to form multiethnic coalitions.

Minority Representation

The representation of minorities in national legislatures is another important aspect of ethnic electoral politics. Domestic political actors and international forces regard ethnic diversity of legislatures as a standard indicator of the ethnic inclusiveness of the regime. Legislative representation carries powerful symbolic power for ethnic minorities and often becomes an end in itself even when minorities have little or no chance of participating in the governing coalition.[16]

The ability of ethnic minorities to win legislative seats is usually seen as a consequence of electoral systems and of the size and geographic concentration of minority populations. When minorities are geographically concentrated, single-member district elections may provide certain advantages by enabling an ethnic party to become one of the two major parties in its "home districts" or by pushing major parties to run minority candidates in these districts to attract the ethnic vote. Barkan argues that in Africa, this geographically polarized voting pattern enables plurality systems to produce legislative representation for minorities that is as proportional to their share of the population as PR systems would be.[17] Under an SMD system, the ethnic character of electoral districts becomes the major factor influencing the likelihood of minority representation. In the United States in 1990, African-American congresspersons were almost exclusively elected from districts with majority-minority populations in which African-Americans made up a plurality.[18] A similar situation existed for Hispanic congresspersons, leading some scholars to argue that a combined minority population above 50 percent is a virtual precondition for minority candidate success in the United States.[19]

Despite the advantages of SMD elections for concentrated minority populations, multimember PR systems are usually seen as preferable to single-member district systems for the representation of ethnic minorities because PR allows smaller parties—some of which could cater to minority groups—to successfully contest elections. Furthermore, PR with high district magnitudes (meaning many representatives elected from each PR district) provides greater incentives for parties to field more diverse sets of candidates to capture ethnic voting blocs, whereas minority candidates in SMD elections are usually relegated to majority-minority districts.[20] Taagepera argues that ethnoracial minority parties are counterproductive in single-member districts. Although minority parties may win the few seats where their ethnic group is concentrated, these parties will win too few seats to play a meaningful role in a governing coalition or as an opposition party in the two-party systems that usually emerge out of single-member district systems. Such parties are much more viable under PR rules that produce lower effective thresholds to representation and multiparty coalitions that could better incorporate smaller parties representing minority interests in decision-making structures.[21]

Ethnic Diversity and Party Fragmentation

The study of ethnic parties and legislative representation of minorities views the interrelationship between ethnicity and electoral politics through the prism of ethnic relations. But ethnic diversity also has broader effects on the party system. The most important of these general effects is party system fragmentation. Scholars have frequently used ethnic diversity as a proxy for social heterogeneity. Such studies have shown a strong and positive relationship between the number of ethnic groups and the degree of party system fractionalization.[22] The social-cleavage theory of party origins assumes that ethnic diversity promotes party proliferation by producing discrete electoral constituencies that will support different political parties.[23]

Cross-national studies have tended to focus on the interactive effect of ethnic heterogeneity and electoral structure on the number of parties. Both Cox and Ordeshook and Shvetsova argue that the effective number of parties is a product of the interaction of these two forces rather than the individual or cumulative effect of each.[24]

This area of research presents a great opportunity for further research, given the paucity of studies done at the subnational level. The one district-level examination of ethnic diversity and party fragmentation produced findings in line with cross-national studies. Jones found that ethnic heterogeneity was positively correlated with party system fragmentation in Louisiana state elections.[25] Other studies are necessary, however, to see whether this relationship holds outside the American context.

Ethnicity and Electoral Politics in Postcommunist States

Like the literature on ethnic politics in general, scholarship on ethnic mobilization in postcommunist states has tended to focus on identity and

mass attitudes. Writing at the beginning of postcommunist democratization in the early 1990s, Evans and Whitefield predicted that Eastern
European states with significant minority populations would have party
systems dominated by ethnic cleavages and "stateness" issues.[26] Subsequent scholarship has largely reinforced the idea that ethnicity remains
a dominant cleavage in many postcommunist states and plays a significant
role in political attitudes and vote choices in a wide variety of postcommunist states, including Ukraine, Slovakia, Bulgaria, and the Baltics.[27]
Other scholarship, however, has questioned the salience of ethnicity in
party preferences in Russia and has suggested that ideology (socialist
values) outweighs ethnic identity as an influence on preferences for
socialist parties in Ukraine.[28]

Although ethnicity has been a consistently strong cleavage in ethnically
diverse postcommunist states, the manner in which ethnic cleavages have
influenced the viability of ethnic parties, legislative representation of
minorities, and party fragmentation has varied considerably.

Ethnic parties are certainly common phenomena in postcommunist
elections, but they are not prevalent in all ethnically diverse states of the
region. Romania, Bulgaria, and Slovakia have significant ethnic parties;
but Ukraine, which has one of the largest minority populations in the
region and an electorate clearly influenced by ethnic divisions, lacks
strong parties explicitly devoted to the representation of Ukraine's
Russian minority. Rather, ethnic, regional, socioeconomic, and ideological cleavages culminate in a party system in which Russian-speakers have
become an important but not the sole constituency of the Communist
Party of Ukraine.[29]

The various roles that ethnic parties play in the political system of postcommunist states have also received scholarly attention. Although much
of the literature on ethnic parties has emphasized a spiraling dynamic of
confrontation between extremist ethnic minority parties and nationalist
parties of the majority, the experience in Eastern Europe generally has
not showcased this most detrimental aspect of ethnic party politics.
Rather, parties representing ethnic minorities, such as the Turkish party
in Bulgaria, the Movement for Rights and Freedom (MRF), and the
Democratic Union of Hungarians (UDMR) in Romania, have been able
to carve out a niche as mainstream actors within emerging party systems.[30]
The UDMR in Romania and a coalition of Hungarian parties in Slovakia
have even taken part in government coalitions.[31]

On the other hand, the danger that ethnic divisions would give rise to
ultranationalist parties of the majority has also not materialized for most
countries of the region. Radical nationalist parties of the titular majority

remain a lingering but marginal threat to democratic consolidation in the region, averaging less than 5 percent of the vote in countries that have held three postcommunist elections.[32] Survey research has also suggested that support for such parties is as much a protest vote driven by opposition sentiment as it is an expression of nationalism.[33] In short, peaceful coexistence and even periodic cooperation seem more prevalent than extreme polarization in postcommunist states with significant ethnic parties.

Few studies of legislative representation of minorities have been undertaken because data on the ethnic identity of candidates and legislators are hard to find. But clearly postcommunist states vary widely in the ability of their ethnic minorities to achieve legislative representation and the means by which minorities gain election. Alionescu notes the widespread representation of ethnic minorities in Romania, ascribing minorities' electoral success (particularly that of smaller groups rather than the larger Hungarian minority) primarily to an electoral system that provides "positive discrimination" to ethnic parties. In Romania, ethnic parties can win a seat in the lower house if their national vote total is greater than 5 percent of the average number of votes needed to elect a single deputy. In the three postcommunist elections this threshold was equal to less than 1,500 votes.[34]

Finally, ethnic minorities have influenced the general contours of postcommunist party systems in a variety of ways. Ethnic diversity has not always promoted party fragmentation in postcommunist states.[35] Birnir has challenged the conventional wisdom regarding ethnicity and party systems by emphasizing the stabilizing effects that ethnic minorities can have on party systems in new democracies. Using a comparative case study of Eastern European and Latin American countries, she argues that the existence of ethnic minorities tends to reduce electoral volatility between elections and thus bolster party system stability by supplying relatively unstable electorates with a group of ethnic voters who tend to have more concentrated and stable preferences.[36]

Determinants of Ethnic Electoral Politics

What accounts for different patterns of interaction between ethnicity and electoral politics in postcommunist states? Of course, some variables are unique to each context, indeed to individual ethnic groups within countries, yet certain factors can be expected to frame the nexus between ethnic divisions and electoral mobilization. Four interrelated factors appear to be most important in determining whether and how ethnicity affects electoral dynamics.

Demographic Factors

First, demographic factors surely play a dominant role in how ethnic identity is translated into electoral preferences and outcomes. This is foremost a matter of resource mobilization. Democratic elections are all about mobilizing and coordinating the actions of large numbers of people. A common identity, such as ethnicity, that can prompt particular preferences and behaviors and penalize others is a decisive tool in such a process.

Three aspects of the ethnic composition of states should be highlighted—size of the minority population, relative diversity of the minority population, and geographic concentration. Size matters because larger ethnic minorities offer the potential for larger voting blocs. Thus, one would expect countries with larger minority populations to have relatively higher numbers of minority representatives, greater viability of ethnic parties, and more significant effects on the party system. Secondly, the relative diversity within the minority population affects potential for mobilization. For example, although Russia has a relatively large minority population, it is quite diverse, with no one group comprising more than 4 percent of the general population. This, of course, severely hampers mobilization around ethnic identity. Thirdly, the geographic concentration of minority groups influences electoral mobilization. Geographically concentrated minorities can more easily mobilize than dispersed populations and, more important, can become majority populations within individual electoral districts or in elections to regional and local bodies.

Institutional Factors

A host of institutional factors affect the relationship between ethnicity and electoral politics. Citizenship laws determine who can vote and can exclude whole minority groups from the electoral process, as seen in Latvia and Estonia.[37] Various aspects of electoral laws impact how ethnic groups are incorporated into the electoral process. Proportional representation and SMD elections provide very different incentives for ethnic mobilization as do open versus closed lists within PR systems. Some countries make special allowances for ethnic representation in the form of reserved seats for minority groups (Croatia) or "positive discrimination" for minority ethnic parties (Romania); such allowances enable minorities to attain legislative seats while achieving levels of electoral support far below the legal threshold for representation.[38] The presence or absence of such institutional provisions for minority representation not only influences the number of minority representatives in the legislature but also affects the way ethnic populations mobilize in elections.[39] Other institutions such as ethnic federalism also have dramatic direct and indirect effects on the electoral mobilization of minorities.

Ethnic Relations
The nature of ethnic relations also surely plays a role in the ability of ethnic minorities to win legislative representation and the manner through which they mobilize to contest elections. But the influence of hostile or conciliatory relations on electoral mobilization of ethnic groups is complex. Minority groups that historically have suffered discrimination under previous regimes may be more inclined to mobilize in an ethnic party to protect their rights in a new democracy. If these ethnic parties prove electorally successful, such minorities may have more representation than more assimilated, less antagonistic minorities. Of course, ethnic polarization can also lead to majority backlash, resulting in either exclusion of minorities from full political participation if the majority feels sufficiently threatened (for example, in Estonia and Latvia) or the prevalence of nationalist rhetoric in parties of the majority (as seen in Slovakia and Bulgaria). Thus, it is hardly surprising that in a ranking of ethnic polarization by Evans and Need, countries with more ethnic polarization (Estonia, Latvia, Slovakia, Romania, Lithuania, Moldova, and Bulgaria) have tended to either exclude minorities or have prominent ethnic parties; the countries in the bottom half of the list (Czech Republic, Hungary, Russia, Poland, Ukraine) tend to either have very small minority populations or have had elections structured by nonethnic parties.[40]

On the other hand, one cannot say that positive ethnic relations always leave the subject minority groups at an electoral disadvantage in mobilizing co-ethnics or in achieving legislative representation. Accommodative relations offer their own avenues for representation and political influence. Romania's Hungarian party (UDMR) and Bulgaria's Turkish party (MRF) have benefited substantially by demonstrating their ability to act as responsible parties within their systems and to cooperate with other parties. Such behavior has won these parties central roles in government formation while sustaining support among their core constituency.[41] Moreover, more assimilated minorities have greater opportunities for representation through nonethnic parties and as individual candidates in majority-dominated single-member districts.

Elite Interactions and Politics
Overlaying (and interacting with) the impact of demography, institutions, and ethnic relations is the influence of elite interactions. Numerous studies have pointed out that the trajectory of ethnic politics in the

electoral realm has been conditioned by decisions made by elites at crucial junctures. Csergo argues that in both Romania and Slovakia, ethnic politics were polarized in the initial stages of postcommunist state-building because of intractable differences between majority nationalists who pursued a "nation-state" strategy of political development and minority elites who preferred a pluralist state model. But subsequent elections brought on more consensual politics through an alliance between moderate parties of the majority and Hungarian minority parties willing to moderate their demands for autonomy.[42] The conscious effort on the part of Bulgaria's Turkish MRF party to serve as a centrist force balancing the two larger parties on the right and left played a crucial role in the development of its niche in Bulgarian politics.[43] In Russia, ethnic elites delivered votes from their regions to Yeltsin and Putin in presidential elections as bargaining chips in the continuing battle over power between the center and the regions.[44]

Two Cases of Ethnic Electoral Politics under Postcommunism

To better clarify the varying experiences of ethnic electoral politics in postcommunist states and the myriad of demographic, institutional, and political factors that help to determine different outcomes, the following section examines more closely the relationship between ethnic diversity and electoral politics in two cases—Russia and Lithuania.

Russia

Russia is unique among postcommunist states in terms of its ethnic composition. It has a significant minority population—close to 20 percent—similar to many countries of the region, such as Bulgaria, Romania, and Slovakia. Unlike these states, however, Russia lacks a single major minority group. Instead, the non-Russian population is composed of literally dozens of very small ethnic groups.

No single ethnic minority accounts for even 4 percent of the population in the Russian Federation, and only three groups (Tatars, Ukrainians, and Chuvash) make up over 1 percent. A pan-national identity uniting non-Russians around a religious identity such as Islam is complicated by the religious diversity of non-Russians. Although radical Islam has been perceived as the major threat to Russian territorial integrity in the wake of the war in Chechnya, large groups among non-Russian minorities are Christian, including Ukrainians, Belorussians, Mordva, and

TABLE 4.1
Ethnic Composition of Russia and Lithuania

	Russia		Lithuania
Nationality	Percentage of total population	Nationality	Percentage of total population
Russians	81.5	Lithuanians	83.5
Tatars	3.8	Poles	6.7
Ukrainians	3.0	Russians	6.3
Chuvash	1.2	Belorussians	1.2
Bashkir	0.9	Ukrainians	0.7
Others	9.6	Others	1.6

Sources: Harris, 1993; NUPI website on ethnicity in Russia, www.nupi,no/cgi-win/Russland/etnisk.exe/ total; Statistics Lithuania, 2002.

Karelians.[45] Language also provides little chance to unify the diverse non-Russian ethnic groups. Moreover, because of the state's Russification efforts and effects of modernization, 7.5 million non-Russians (about a quarter of the minority population) have shifted from their native tongue to Russian as their first language.[46]

The composition of Russia's ethnic population cannot be understood without acknowledgement of its institutionalization within an ethnofederal structure. The Russian Federation has continued the Soviet practice of defining some of its federal units along ethnic lines.[47] Russia is composed of eighty-nine regions that are divided into twenty-one republics, forty-nine oblasts, six krais, two cities (Moscow and St. Petersburg), ten autonomous okrugs, and one autonomous oblast (the Jewish Autonomous Oblast). Republics, autonomous okrugs, and the Jewish Autonomous Oblast make up the thirty-two regions based on ethnic homelands.

Russia's ethnofederal structure has produced two categories of ethnic groups. One category includes groups without an "ethnic homeland"—that is, a federal subunit named after an ethnic minority group. These groups (for example, Ukrainians, Belorussians, and Germans) tend to be geographically dispersed and relatively assimilated into the Russian population. The other category is made up of groups with an ethnic homeland (for example, Tatars, Bashkirs, and Chechens) that tend to be geographically concentrated and relatively unassimilated. On average 66 percent of titular nationalities live in their designated federal units. But there are several important exceptions. The largest non-Russian minority, the Tatars, is also one of the more dispersed groups with an ethnic homeland, with only 32 percent of Tatars living in Tatarstan. Only 2 percent of Jews live in the Jewish Autonomous Oblast, and only 29 percent of the over one million Mordva live in Mordovia.[48]

As Harris has demonstrated, Russia's ethnic federalism has had a huge influence on ethnic identity among non-Russians. Those groups provided with ethnic homelands managed to retain their native languages and resist assimilation efforts to a much greater extent than (often larger) minority groups that were not similarly institutionalized in the federal structure.[49] Moreover, regional governments in ethnic homelands have cultivated ethnic mobilization in center-periphery relations. The very designation of ethnic federal units has produced incentives and resources for the cultivation of an ethnic cadre of elites and mass mobilization tied to ethnicity.[50] The titular nationality constitutes a majority in a small number of the ethnic federal units and in very few single-member electoral districts, which makes the symbolic power of an ethnic homeland one of the most important factors in the representation of minorities in the Russian legislature.

Ethnic Parties

Russia has been largely devoid of parties with appeals to specific minority ethnic groups. Only in 1995, when forty-three parties ran in the PR half of the election, did ethnically defined parties contest election. NUR (a Muslim party) and the Interethnic Union contested the PR half of that election, each receiving less than 1 percent of the vote. Other parties (such as PRES in 1993, Edward Rossel's Transformation of the Fatherland in 1995, and Fatherland-All Russia in 1999) attempted to craft an appeal to protect regional interests vis-à-vis the center, which held some appeal to ethnic republics that were at the forefront of regional demands for greater autonomy. Indeed, Tatarstan's president, Mintimer Shamiev, played a leadership role in the most successful of these parties, Fatherland-All Russia. But these parties were multiethnic coalitions dominated by Russians that played down ethnic appeals to court support from wealthy Russian regions that also had economic incentives to pursue autonomy from Moscow.[51]

The lack of ethnic parties in Russia is best understood through the prism of demography and resource mobilization. The minority population is too dispersed across different ethnic groups to support viable ethnic parties. The absence of a single dominant ethnic minority like the Turks in Bulgaria or Hungarians in Romania or Slovakia has severely hampered attempts to mobilize ethnically based parties. But institutions have played a secondary role. Ethnic federalism has produced minority elites geared toward regional politics in their ethnic homeland and political strategies emphasizing bilateral relations between the center and the regions rather than representation in the national legislature. Moreover, until recent changes made by Putin, regional leaders were automatically appointed to the upper house of the legislature (Federation Council), which provided representation of minority elites in a national legislative body without the burden of electoral competition.

Minority Representation

What is surprising in the Russian case is the extent to which ethnic minorities managed to achieve legislative representation despite the lack of mobilization through ethnic parties.[52] Russia's mixed electoral system gives voters a chance to cast two ballots—one for a party list in a proportional representation (PR) contest and one for a candidate in a single-member district plurality election. Each tier of the system elects half of the 450 members of the lower house, the State Duma.

Given the ethnic makeup of Russia, one would expect both the PR and plurality tiers of Russia's mixed electoral system to underrepresent non-Russian ethnic groups. No single ethnic minority constitutes a large enough share of the population to plausibly field an ethnic party capable of overcoming the 5-percent legal threshold or to compel a nonethnic party to include minority candidates on its PR lists to capture the "ethnic" vote. One could imagine minorities faring better in plurality elections, given the geographic concentration of those minorities within federal subunits. But there are only twenty-four majority-minority districts out of a total of 225 and, of these, only fifteen had a Russian population under 40 percent.[53] Yet, despite these demographic obstacles, both tiers elected a relatively large percentage of non-Russians to the State Duma. Politicization of ethnic minorities in ethnic homelands and assimilation of certain non-Russian groups, most notably Ukrainians, seem to have circumvented demographic and institutional constraints to minority representation and elected surprisingly high numbers of non-Russians. Table 4.2 shows the ethnic representation of deputies elected in the PR and single-member district tiers of the 1993 and 1995 parliamentary elections, along with the representation/population ratio in each election for every ethnic group with at least one deputy in 1993 or 1995.[54]

Several striking patterns persist in the two elections. Neither the PR nor the single-member district tier overrepresented the majority ethnic group despite the advantages Russians possessed under both systems. Russians were elected to the legislature in almost identical numbers in both tiers and in nearly equal proportion to their population. By comparison, Anglo men and women make up approximately 80 percent of the population of the United States but over 91 percent of the U.S. Congress.[55]

Although non-Russians in general benefited in both PR and SMD elections in equal measure, the type of non-Russian ethnic group enjoying representation differed substantially depending on the electoral system.

TABLE 4.2
Ethnic Representation in Russian PR and SMD Elections, 1993–1995

Ethnicity	# (%) of deputies in 1993 PR election	# (%) of deputies in 1993 SMD election	Rep./Pop. ratio in 1993 elections	# (%) of deputies in 1995 PR election	# (%) of deputies in 1995 SMD election	Rep./Pop. ratio in 1995 elections
Russian	191 (84.5)	182 (81.3)	1.02	186 (84.2)	182 (81.3)	1.01
Tatar	2 (0.9)	2 (0.9)	0.24	5 (2.3)	4 (1.8)	0.54
Ukrainian	13 (5.8)	9 (4.0)	1.65	13 (5.9)	12 (5.4)	1.89
Jewish	5 (2.2)	2 (0.9)	4.32	2 (0.9)	1 (0.4)	1.81
Armenian	2 (0.9)	1 (0.4)	1.94	1 (0.5)	2 (0.9)	1.86
Chuvash	0 (0)	0 (0)	0	1 (0.5)	0 (0)	0.18
Bashkir	1 (0.4)	3 (1.3)	0.98	0 (0)	2 (0.9)	0.49
Belorussian	5 (2.2)	2 (0.9)	1.95	3 (1.4)	3 (1.3)	1.65
Mordvin	0 (0)	0 (0)	0	1 (0.5)	2 (0.9)	0.92
German	0 (0)	3 (1.3)	1.43	0 (0)	1 (0.4)	0.39
Buryat	0 (0)	2 (0.9)	1.43	1 (0.5)	2 (0.9)	2.39
Darghin	0 (0)	1 (0.4)	0.83	0 (0)	1 (0.4)	0.92
Ingush	0 (0)	0 (0)	0	1 (0.5)	1 (0.4)	3.00
Ossetian	0 (0)	2 (0.9)	1.48	3 (1.4)	1 (0.4)	3.33
Karbar	0 (0)	1 (0.4)	0.77	0 (0)	1 (0.4)	0.85
Mari	0 (0)	1 (0.4)	0.45	0 (0)	1 (0.4)	0.50
Yakut	0 (0)	1 (0.4)	0.77	0 (0)	1 (0.4)	0.85
Avarets	1 (0.4)	1 (0.4)	1.08	0 (0)	1 (0.4)	0.59
Korean	0 (0)	1 (0.4)	2.86	0 (0)	2 (0.9)	6.43
Komi-Permayak	0 (0)	1 (0.4)	2.00	0 (0)	1 (0.4)	2.20
Evenk	0 (0)	1 (0.4)	20.0	0 (0)	1 (0.4)	22.0
Lakets	0 (0)	0 (0)	0	1 (0.5)	0 (0)	3.14
Kumyk	0 (0)	0 (0)	0	1 (0.5)	0 (0)	1.16
Balkar	0 (0)	0 (0)	0	1 (0.5)	0 (0)	4.4
Adigets	1 (0.4)	0 (0)	2.50	1 (0.5)	0 (0)	2.75
Karachai	0 (0)	1 (0.4)	2.0	0 (0)	0 (0)	0
Komi	1 (0.4)	1 (0.4)	1.74	0 (0)	0 (0)	0
Tuvin	0 (0)	1 (0.4)	1.43	0 (0)	1 (0.4)	0.92
Cherkes	1 (0.4)	0 (0)	6.67	0 (0)	0 (0)	0
Lacassian	1 (0.4)	0 (0)	2.86	0 (0)	0 (0)	0
Georgian	1 (0.4)	0 (0)	2.22	0 (0)	0 (0)	0
Udmurt	0 (0)	1 (0.4)	0.41	0 (0)	0 (0)	0
Kalmyk	0 (0)	1 (0.4)	1.82	0 (0)	0 (0)	0
Latvian	0 (0)	1 (0.4)	6.67	0 (0)	0 (0)	0
Koryak	0 (0)	1 (0.4)	20.0	0 (0)	1 (0.4)	22.0
Khanti	0 (0)	1 (0.4)	10.0	0 (0)	0 (0)	0
Greek	1 (0.4)	0 (0)	3.33	0 (0)	0 (0)	0

Sources: Moser, 2001; Pyataya Rossiiskaya Gosudarstvennaya Duma (Moscow: Izdanniya Gosudarstven-naya Duma, 1994); Gosudarstvennaya Duma Federal'naya Sobraniya Rossiiskoi Federatsii, Vtorogo Sozyva (Moscow: Izdanniya Gosudarstvennaya Duma, 1996).

As one might expect, those ethnic groups without a designated homeland tended to do better in the PR election than in the single-member districts, particularly in 1993. At that time, Ukrainians, Belorussians, and Jews managed to elect twenty-three deputies in the PR election, 66 percent of the non-Russian deputies elected in the PR tier, but only thirteen deputies in single-member districts, which accounted for 31 percent of non-Russian winners in that tier. A smaller disparity existed in 1995, with Ukrainians, Belorussians, and Jews winning eighteen seats in the PR election (51 percent of all non-Russian winners in that tier) and sixteen seats in the single-member districts (38 percent). One must conclude that these groups managed to achieve substantial legislative representation because of their greater assimilation in the dominant culture rather than mobilization around ethnic distinctiveness.

This seems to be the key to electoral success for these minorities (particularly Ukrainians) in the SMD tier as well. Of the sixteen non-Russians elected in districts in Russian regions (oblasts and *krai*), 75 percent came from highly assimilated groups that did not have their own ethnic homelands, more than half of which were Slavs (Ukrainians or Belorussians). As expected, highly assimilated ethnic minorities made up a much smaller (but not trivial) proportion of the minority contingent of deputies elected from the ethnic republics. Twenty-seven percent (seven out of twenty-six) of non-Russians elected in ethnic republics and autonomous okrugs were from highly assimilated groups, and 13 percent (two out of sixteen) of non-Russians elected in majority-minority districts came from highly assimilated minority groups.

Representation of minorities with ethnic homelands was driven by a combination of institutional and demographic factors. Not surprisingly, non-Russians were most successful in districts with a non-Russian majority. But ethnic federalism also had an impact. In many non-Russian regions, minority candidates were electorally viable in districts with Russian majorities as well as majority-minority districts. Indeed, minority candidates were elected nearly four times as often in Russian majority districts located in ethnic regions than in Russian majority districts in general.

Ethnic federalism seemed to provide the greatest benefit to the smallest minorities, such as the Evenks, Mari, and Buryats. Larger groups, particularly those that did not command a majority as titular nationality of their region, gained less representation. This is quite evident in the experience of the largest non-Russian minority, the Tatars, which was the most underrepresented major ethnic group in the 1993 and 1995 elections. The failure of Tatars to be elected in numbers proportional to their share of the population, even in single-member districts in their own region, is particularly striking given that, besides Chechens, Tatars have been the most mobilized minority in Russia. In 1993, the December parliamentary election was invalidated in Tatarstan because a Tatar nationalist boycott kept participation well under the 25 percent threshold required to make the elections valid. Elections were eventually held again in March 1994, but only after Tatarstan's president personally sponsored them following the signing of a bilateral treaty between Tatarstan and Russia that established a preferred status for the republic in the Russian Federation.[56] Moreover, ethnicity plays a strong role in shaping political attitudes in the republic, with the republic's population polarized between Tatars who support various degrees of autonomy and separatism and Russians who demand that Tatarstan remain a constituent part of Russia.[57] Consequently, political elites have been able to effectively use a tacit threat of secession to wrench favorable terms from Moscow regarding its federal status.

Tatars have not translated this potential for ethnic mobilization into parliamentary representation in the State Duma, however. In the March 1994 by-elections only one Tatar managed to get elected in the five single-member district races held in the republic. Another Tatar was elected in Bashkortostan, the other republic with a large Tatar minority, but in a district where Russians were the predominant group.[58] Only two Tatars were elected in the PR tier of the 1993 election, compared with thirteen PR deputies for the next largest minority, Ukrainians, which had one million fewer members.

Tatar representation doubled in 1995, but remained well below the minority's proportion of the population. Tatars captured two out of five single-member district races within Tatarstan and captured two other SMD seats outside Tatarstan. By comparison, neighboring Bashkortostan had four Bashkirs elected in its six single-member district races in 1993, even though Bashkirs constitute a mere 22 percent of Bashkortostan's population, behind both Russians (39 percent) and Tatars (28 percent).[59]

Demography and ethnic relations combined to work against the electoral success of Tatars in both halves of Russia's mixed system. Being from a relatively small, distinct, and unassimilated minority has made Tatar candidates risky bets on PR party lists.[60] In the single-member district races, where ethnic mobilization may be an advantage, Tatars have been hurt by geographic dispersion and the vagaries of ethnic federalism. In general, small minorities benefit more from being the titular nationality of a region than large groups. Thus, even if Tatars won all of the single-member districts in Tatarstan, these five seats would still not constitute a proportion of the 225 SMD seats equal to the group's share of the population; conversely, just a single SMD seat greatly overrepresents small minorities like the Evenks. The geographic dispersion of Tatars simply exacerbates the problem by creating very few electoral districts with a critical mass of Tatars. Only 32 percent of the Tatars living in Russia reside in Tatarstan. Within Tatarstan, Tatars make up only 48.5 percent of the population, whereas Russians account for 43 percent. Tatars constitute a majority in only two of the five districts in their own republic. Of course, minority status has not stopped many other non-Russian groups from gaining representation in their own republics, so demographic composition of the republic cannot be the only explanation for the relatively low level of parliamentary representation for Tatars.

In a search for other factors to account for Tatar underrepresentation, one must not discount the role of elite interactions and rhetoric. The heightened nationalist activity in Tatarstan may actually have worked against parliamentary representation of Tatars by mobilizing ethnic Russians and other groups against them. By contrast, groups like the Bashkirs have de-emphasized ethnicity, given their minority status in their own homeland. In the process, less mobilized groups like the Bashkirs may have made themselves more electable by not antagonizing other ethnic groups.[61]

Ethnic Diversity and the Party System
The Russian experience also provides counterintuitive outcomes when one considers the impact of ethnic minorities on party system fragmentation. As scholarship has shown, ethnic diversity promotes party proliferation (once one controls for the effect of the electoral system) presumably because ethnicity provides another electoral cleavage around which parties can form. Once again, Russia's mixed electoral system offers an excellent laboratory to examine this assumption through a controlled comparison of PR and SMD electoral rules operating simultaneously in the same social context. If the combination of PR and ethnic diversity presents the most conducive conditions for party proliferation, then one would expect a positive relationship between ethnic diversity and the effective number of parties in the PR tier of Russia's mixed system but no such relationship in the SMD tier (see note 62 on calculation of ENEP). The impact of social heterogeneity and electoral systems on the number of parties or candidates will be examined through an OLS regression analysis of electoral results in two parliamentary elections and two presidential elections.

The dependent variable in the regression analyses was the effective number of parties or candidates competing in the designated region (single-member districts or regions). The effective number of parties measure developed by Laakso and Taagepera weights each party according to the proportion of votes or seats it receives.[62] For the PR elections, this measure was computed based on the vote for party lists; in the (parliamentary) SMD elections and the presidential elections, this measure was computed based on the vote for each candidate running in the designated region. Many candidates in Russian SMD elections have run as independents, making it necessary to focus on candidates rather than parties. In essence, each independent was treated as an individual party. For the regional analysis, the effective number of contestants was operationalized as the average effective number of electoral contestants for all districts within a given region except for the 2000 presidential election, which had only regional results available.

Urbanization and ethnic diversity, the two most common proxies for social heterogeneity in the literature, served as the two independent variables in the regression analyses. Urbanization (URBAN in table 4.3) was operationalized as the proportion of the district's or region's population living in urban areas.[63] Following conventional wisdom in the literature, I assumed that more urban districts would promote greater party proliferation.

Two slightly different measures were used for ethnic diversity. Information on the ethnic composition of electoral districts was limited to the percentage of Russians (and hence non-Russian minorities as an undifferentiated group) living in each district. This limitation on the data allowed only for a dichotomous distinction between Russians and non-Russians. Therefore, I used the proportion of minorities (MINPRO in table 4.3) in each electoral district as a proxy for ethnic diversity. The higher the proportion of non-Russians, the more diverse a district was assumed to be.[64] Of course, such a measure poses certain problems, such as the fact that it glosses over the potential diversity to be found within the minority community of a district. To compensate for these shortcomings, I augmented the district-level analysis with a regional examination of the same relationship using ethnicity data for the eighty-nine regions of Russia. Data from the 1989 Soviet census include data for all ethnic groups, which were used to construct a more accurate measure of ethnic diversity, the effective number of ethnic groups (ENETH in table 4.3),[65] albeit at a higher level of aggregation. In all instances, it was expected that electoral districts or regions with higher ethnic diversity would promote party fragmentation. The results are reported in table 4.3.

The findings for both the district-level and regional tests show that the presence of ethnic minorities tends to be associated with a lower rather

TABLE 4.3
OLS Multiple Regression Analysis of Impact of Ethnic Diversity and Urbanization on the Effective Number of Parties in Russian Elections

Independent Variables	1995 PR tier Coefficient estimates (std error)	1995 SMD tier Coefficient estimates (std error)	1999 PR tier Coefficient estimates (std error)	1999 SMD tier Coefficient estimates (std error)	1996 presidential election Coefficient estimates (std error)	2000 presidential election[a] Coefficient estimates (std error)
District-level Analysis						
URBAN	0.055 (0.009)***	0.016 (0.007)**	0.029 (0.004)***	0.019 (0.007)***	−0.001 (0.002)	N/A
MINPRO	−0.017 (0.009)*	−0.048 (0.008)***	−0.014 (0.005)***	−0.032 (0.007)***	−0.010 (0.002)***	N/A
Constant	4.122 (0.787)***	1.532 (0.657)**	2.354 (0.398)***	1.548 (0.628)***	2.689 (0.199)***	N/A
Adjusted R^2	0.212	0.220	0.267	0.155	0.079	N/A
Regional Analysis						
URBAN	0.047 (0.018)**	0.041 (0.012)***	0.031 (0.008)***	0.030 (0.012)**	0.803 (0.399)**	0.510 (0.223)**
ENETH	−0.969 (0.766)	−1.041 (0.493)**	−0.541 (0.344)*	−0.739 (0.501)*	−0.497 (0.161)***	−0.349 (0.091)***
Constant	7.439 (1.864)***	4.796 (1.233)***	4.105 (0.008)***	4.382 (1.218)***	3.628 (0.396)***	2.584 (0.222)***
Adjusted R^2	0.098	0.205	0.195	0.106	0.179	0.241

Sources: McFaul and Petrov, 1997; Russian Central Electoral Commission Web site, www.fci.ru.
* $p < .10$, ** $p < .05$, *** $p < .01$
Variables:
URBAN: percent urban
MINPRO: percent non-Russian minority
ENETH: effective number of ethnic groups
[a] *Regression tests were done only at the regional level for the 2000 presidential election because district-level data were not available at the time of writing.*

than higher effective number of parties. There was a statistically significant *negative* relationship between my two measures of ethnic diversity and party fragmentation for both the PR and SMD tiers of the parliamentary elections and for both the 1996 and 2000 presidential elections.[66] Urbanization, on the other hand, was positively correlated with party fragmentation as expected.

One can only speculate about the causes and implications of these findings since they are based on such a small number of elections. But one can begin to explain the constraining effect that ethnic diversity has on party fragmentation by highlighting three aspects of ethnic politics in Russia.

First, the ethnic identity of minority groups can serve as a powerful voting cue for minority voters in a fluid electoral context that leaves most other voters without a high degree of partisan identification.[67] This may have created more cohesive voting blocs within non-Russian regions of the country and thus less party fragmentation.

Second, non-Russian regions may have fewer parties because of elite control over the electoral process. Ethnic regions are some of the most controlled regions of the country. In a study of regional electoral patterns, McFaul and Petrov designated fifteen regions as "controlled," meaning they were lacking in strong opposition parties, fundamental rights of expression and assembly, and any genuine sense of electoral competition. All of these regions were non-Russian regions.[68]

Finally, this outcome may be due to the fact that major parties and candidates have enjoyed a higher degree of support in regions with concentrations of ethnic minorities than in the rest of the country. This dynamic is most clearly seen in support for Russian presidential incumbents Boris Yeltsin and Vladimir Putin. Marsh and Warhola found that non-Russian regions consistently produced higher voter turnout and greater support for Yeltsin in 1996 than Russian regions, with a vast majority of these non-Russian regions (twenty-seven out of thirty-one) giving Yeltsin a plurality of their votes.[69] These voting patterns were even more pronounced in the 2000 election. Non-Russian regions produced some of the highest voter turnouts in the country and were among the most supportive constituencies for Putin. Only Altai Republic failed to give Putin a plurality of its votes.[70] For ethnic diversity to promote party proliferation, one must assume that different ethnic groups support different parties. If an ethnic minority supports a major party or candidate and behaves as a more cohesive voting bloc than the majority population, however, ethnic diversity will constrain the number of parties rather than contribute to party proliferation.

Whatever the causes, these findings suggest that Russia presents a challenge to the conventional wisdom on the relationship between ethnic diversity and party system fragmentation. Further research using more disaggregated census data or individual-level survey data is necessary to disentangle the effects of ethnic identity and political machine politics on voting patterns in non-Russian regions.

Lithuania

Lithuania emerged from the collapsed Soviet empire as a relatively homogenous nation-state, especially compared with its immediate neighbors. The titular nationality comprises a substantially larger share of the population (83 percent) in Lithuania than in its Baltic neighbors Estonia and Latvia. Thus, it is hardly surprising that Lithuania was the only one of the three Baltic states to allow its minorities full citizenship and voting rights upon gaining independence. The size of the minority population alone makes the ethnic situation much more manageable than in Estonia and Latvia (or Ukraine) and more similar to moderately diverse countries such as Bulgaria, Slovakia, Romania, and Russia. Lithuania's minority population is dominated by two principal ethnic groups rather than one. Russians and Poles constitute nearly identical shares of the population— roughly 6 percent.[71] Both groups have significant homeland states neighboring Lithuania and were at one time the hegemonic people of the region, which overlays ethnic relations with a potentially complex set of postimperial overtones.

Research by Evans and Lipsmeyer shows that Lithuania's Russian and Polish minorities are better assimilated than many other ethnic groups in Eastern Europe. Russians and Poles in Lithuania are much more likely to speak Lithuanian and to marry Lithuanians than Russians in the other Baltic states, Hungarians in Slovakia or Romania, or Turks in Bulgaria.[72] This relative assimilation, along with the early incorporation of minorities in the Lithuanian polity (in stark contrast to its Baltic neighbors), has led to a relatively moderate degree of ethnic polarization among Eastern European states. Lithuania ranks fifth among thirteen Eastern European states in terms of ethnic polarization regarding support for minority rights, just behind Romania but significantly trailing the two other Baltic states and Slovakia.[73] In one survey Lithuania's Russian minority was more satisfied with democracy than the majority population.[74]

Other scholars have challenged this relatively sanguine assessment of interethnic relations in Lithuania. Clark argues that, although Russian-speakers have not reported greater economic hardships than ethnic Lithuanians, they tend to be much less optimistic about their economic prospects.[75] More important, Russian-speakers display less political loyalty toward the Lithuanian state, despite the fact that survey research provided little evidence of social discrimination against Russian-speakers at state and private institutions.[76] Russian-speakers were more than twice as likely as ethnic Lithuanians to see themselves as better off under Soviet rule than as part of the postcommunist Lithuanian state. Although this has not translated into a desire to reestablish the Soviet state (less than 10 percent of Russian-speakers agreed with a question referring to the desirability of a return to Soviet rule), it does suggest that the Russian-speaking minority has tenuous political attachments to the Lithuanian state.[77] Clark attributes these attitudes in part to the inability of Russian-speakers to effectively mobilize for representation in the Lithuanian legislature, the Seimas. According to Clark, geographic dispersion undermines the electoral prospects of Russian-speaking candidates in both the SMD portion of Lithuania's mixed electoral system (because of a lack of critical mass in most districts) and in the PR tier (because of a lack of communication and mobilization potential necessary for a viable ethnic Russian party).[78]

The Polish minority has been an even greater challenge to the Lithuanian state. The Polish-dominated Vilnius and Salcininkai regions in the southeastern corner of Lithuania were the subject of heated political battles over special rights of autonomy between the Polish community and the emerging Lithuanian state during the final years of the Soviet Union. Regional authorities under Polish leadership (with support from Soviet authorities) designated these regions as autonomous territories, which the national Lithuanian legislature promptly annulled. These same regional leaders voiced support for the putchists during the failed coup to reestablish Soviet control in August 1991. Immediately afterward, the regional governments were brought under direct rule by the national government.[79] This history has apparently left its scars. Survey research has demonstrated that Poles are less satisfied with democracy in Lithuania and less likely to feel represented in elections than both the Russian minority and the majority population.[80]

Ethnic Parties

Ethnic parties have played a greater role in Lithuanian politics than in Russia. Russian and Polish candidates have run predominantly under the banner of ethnic parties, although these parties have not enjoyed enough electoral success to consistently win a significant number of seats. In the first postcommunist election, in 1992, no party was explicitly devoted to representing the Russian-speaking community. A Russian party, the Union of Lithuanian Russians, did emerge in the following election, in 1996, but won less than 2 percent of the national PR vote. The party fared better in the 2000 election but only because it became part of a large left-of-center electoral coalition. The Polish party did not perform much better. The Union of Lithuanian Poles (later Electoral Action of Lithuanian Poles), which was founded in 1988, won less than 3 percent of the PR vote in each of the three postcommunist elections.

One might expect the Polish party to better mobilize its ethnic constituency, given the greater geographic concentration of Lithuanian Poles and the recent conflict over special territorial rights during Lithuania's drive for independence. But a number of demographic and political factors have undermined the success of ethnic parties in both communities.

First, both the Russian and Polish communities make up too small a proportion of the population (6 percent) to comfortably sustain a viable ethnic party, given the electoral system in place, specifically a PR tier with a 5-percent legal threshold. Originally, the electoral law was "friendlier" to ethnic minorities. In the 1992 election, the legal threshold was 4 percent, and a provision allowed minority parties to gain representation with only 2 percent of the PR vote. This provision provided the Union of Lithuanian Poles two PR seats. But in 1996 the legal threshold was raised to 5 percent, and the lower threshold for ethnic minority parties was removed.[81] The SMD tier did not provide many more electoral opportunities for ethnic parties. Territorial districts were drawn up by Lithuanian nationalists within the Sajudis party in power immediately after independence, who made clear their intention to create districts with Lithuanian majorities.[82] Thus, even under the most conducive conditions, mobilization for ethnically based parties would be difficult at best.

Second, internal divisions within both communities prevented both Russians and Poles from being cohesive voting blocs. This was particularly true for the Russian community, which Popovski argues was divided into several competing groups, the largest of which prioritized integration into Lithuanian society and thus rejected the idea of a Russian party.[83] The Polish community was more cohesive and culturally separated from the majority population than the Russian community, but cumulative linguistic and urban-rural cleavages divided the community.[84] Perhaps more important, political mobilization within the Polish community was undermined by a relatively low educational level and lack of an intelligentsia because of emigration. This meant that voter participation among Poles was lower than the rest of the population, in part because of both poor socioeconomic conditions and lack of effective political entrepreneurs capable of marshaling the latent discontent within this community.[85]

Minority Representation
Like Russia, Lithuania uses a mixed electoral system. Half of the 141 seats in the Seimas are elected through a party-list PR election and half are elected through single-member district elections. Parties must overcome a 5 percent legal threshold (7 percent for coalitions) to win seats in the PR tier. In the first two postcommunist elections, Lithuania utilized a two-round majority runoff system in its SMD tier. If no candidate won a majority of the votes cast, a runoff was to be conducted between the two top vote getters. This system was changed to a plurality election for the SMD seats in 2000.

The demographic context of PR and SMD elections in Lithuania has offered a mixed picture for minorities. Although the two major minority groups have large enough populations to conceivably field a PR party capable of overcoming the 5-percent legal threshold, such an enterprise would require very cohesive support for a single ethnic party within each community. Yet, the situation should have been more encouraging than that of minorities in Russia. At the very least, Lithuanian PR parties should have felt greater electoral pressure to field Russian and Polish candidates to capture the ethnic vote than Russian PR parties to field non-Russian candidates.

It is not possible to pinpoint the number of majority-minority districts in the seventy-one single-member districts that make up the SMD tier of the system, because SMD boundaries do not coincide with the boundaries of the smallest demographic subunits (municipalities) for which data on ethnicity from the latest census are available. But it is safe to say that neither Poles nor Russians occupy a majority or even plurality status in many single-member districts. Lithuanians make up a majority (more than 50 percent) in fifty-seven out of sixty municipalities and a super-majority (more than 70 percent) in fifty municipalities. Poles are a majority in only two municipalities and Russians are a majority in only one.[86] Extrapolating from these data, one can assume that minorities constitute a plurality in far fewer than 10 percent of Lithuania's seventy-one single-member districts.

Contrary to the Russian experience, the titular nationality has been overrepresented in the national legislature in Lithuania. Table 4.4 shows the ethnic breakdown of deputies to the Seimas elected in 1992, 1996, and 2000. With the exception of the election in 2000, the data portray a consistent picture of (ethnic) Lithuanian predominance in the Seimas.

Success of minority candidates in the SMD elections depended more on the ethnic context of the electoral district than party affiliation. In short, Russian and Polish SMD candidates tended to contest districts with

TABLE 4.4

Ethnic Composition of Deputies in the Lithuanian Seimas, 1992–2000

Nationality	1992 PR n = 69	1992 SMD n = 71	1996 PR n = 70	1996 SMD n = 67	2000 PR n = 70	2000 SMD n = 71
Lithuanian	65 (93%)	66 (93%)	67 (96%)	63 (94%)	62 (89%)	66 (93%)
Russian	1 (1%)	2 (3%)	0 (0%)	3 (5%)	6 (9%)	3 (4%)
Polish	3 (4%)	3 (4%)	2 (3%)	1 (2%)	2 (3%)	2 (3%)
Other	0 (0%)	0 (0%)	1 (1%)	0 (0%)	0 (0%)	0 (0%)

Sources: *Project on Political Transformation and the Electoral Process in Post-Communist Europe*, www.essex.ac.uk/elections.

a substantial concentration of their co-ethnics and performed best in districts dominated by the targeted minority community. Russian candidates were less tied to ethnic Russian or minority parties than Polish candidates. Although more than half of all Polish SMD candidates ran under the banner of the Polish party, less than a third of Russian candidates were affiliated with ethnic Russian parties. Most important, a lack of coordination seemed to exist among co-ethnic elites that potentially split the ethnic vote and arguably denied a minority candidate the chance to advance to the second-round runoff in the 1992 and 1996 elections. Russian and Polish candidates also competed with one another in certain districts, further undermining minority representation. As one might expect, in those districts with the highest concentration of Polish or Russian minorities virtually every candidate was a member of the dominant nationality of the region. But in some instances a single Russian or Polish candidate could have won election or at least advanced to a runoff, but multiple minority candidates split the vote.[87]

Patterns of minority candidates' party affiliation in the PR tier followed those of the SMD tier. Polish candidates were far more likely to run under the Polish party label, whereas Russian candidates were dispersed across a wider range of ethnic and nonethnic parties. It is difficult to determine whether these differences could be attributed to elite strategy or necessity. Surely both impulses were at work. Polish elites may have gravitated to the Polish party for strategic reasons of party list placement but also because no other party would take them as a result of the greater divisions between Lithuanians and Poles. Russian elites clearly made the strategic decision to join the A. Brazauskas Social Democratic Coalition but were able to make such a move because of their greater penetration of major parties on the left such as the Lithuanian Democratic Labor Party. Table 4.5 shows the distribution of Russian and Polish candidates among Lithuanian PR party lists.

Prior to the 2000 election, neither ethnic party mobilization nor co-optation within major nonethnic parties seemed to offer a viable route to legislative representation for Lithuania's minorities. Ethnic parties were the clearer failure since neither the Russian nor Polish parties ever managed to win more than 3 percent of the PR vote. A multiethnic minority party, the Alliance of National Minorities, did not fare any better and may have actually further split the ethnic vote in 1996. In the 1992 and 1996 elections, nomination by a nonethnic party did not provide much greater opportunities for election. Major parties on both the left and the right tended to shun Polish candidates. Russian candidates had greater success penetrating these parties, especially parties on the left. But this

TABLE 4.5

Russian and Polish Candidates on Lithuanian PR Party Lists, 1992–2000

	1992 Election		
Party (% of PR vote)	# of Russian Candidates	Party (% of PR vote)	# of Polish Candidates
Lith. Commonwealth (—)	8	Union of Lith. Poles (2)	20
Lith. Centre Mvt. (2.5)	2	Lith. Commonwealth (—)	3
Lith. SDP (6)	1	CDP/Prisoners/DP (—)	2
Union of Lith. Poles (2)	1	Lith. Dem. Labor Party (44)	1
Sajudis (21)	1	Lith. SDP (6)	1
Lith. Dem. Labor Party (44)	1	Total	27
Others	4		
Total	18		

	1996 Election		
Party (% of PR vote)	# of Russian Candidates	Party (% of PR vote)	# of Polish Candidates
Union of Lith. Russians (1.7)	21	Elect. Action of Lith. Poles (3)	19
Alliance of Nat'l Minorities (3)	13	Alliance of Nat'l Minorities (3)	4
Lith. Dem. Labor Party (10)	7	Lith. SDP (7)	2
Elect. Action of Lith. Poles (3)	7	Homeland Union (31)	1
Lith. Party of Economy (1.3)	6	Lith. Dem. Labor Party (10)	1
Lith. People's Party (—)	5	Lith. Women's Party (4)	1
Lith. Socialist Party (—)	5	Lith. Liberal Union (2)	1
Lith. SDP (7)	4	Union of Lith. Russians (1.7)	1
Lith. Centre Union (9)	2	Lith. Peasant's Party (1.7)	1
Lith. Women's Party (4)	2	Others	3
Republican Party (—)	2	Total	34
Others	4		
Total	78		

	2000 Election		
Party (% of PR vote)	# of Russian Candidates	Party (% of PR vote)	# of Polish Candidates
A. Brazauskas SD Coalition (31)	13	Elect. Action of Lith. Poles (2)	43
New Union (20)	5	New Union (20)	3
Lith. Liberal Union (17)	4	Lith. Liberal Union (17)	2
Elect. Action of Lith. Poles (2)	4	A. Brazauskas SD Coalition (31)	2
For Just Lithuania (1.5)	4	Lith. Centre Union (3)	1
Social Dem.-2000 (—)	3	Social Dem.-2000 (—)	1
Lith. Centre Union (3)	2	Others	3
Homeland Union (9)	1	Total	55
Others	2		
Total	38		

Source: Project on Political Transformation and the Electoral Post-Communist Europe, www.essex.ac.uk/elections.

did not translate into many seats in the first two elections because the number of Russian candidates remained small (and poorly placed) in relation to Lithuanian candidates. Of eighteen Russian candidates on party lists in 1992, only three were on lists that won PR seats and only one Russian PR candidate won election on the Lithuanian Social Democratic Party list. In 1996, the overall number of Russian candidates rose sharply to seventy-eight, but most were nominated by ethnic and other minor parties. Only nine Russian candidates were on lists that overcame the 5 percent barrier, and none of the nine won election.

In 2000, Russian candidates orchestrated something of a breakthrough by combining the two strategies. The Union of Lithuanian Russians joined the major leftist coalition, the A. Brazauskas Social Democratic Coalition, managing to gain significant representation on a list that won 31 percent of the PR vote. The A. Brazauskas Social Democratic Coalition fielded thirteen Russian PR candidates, of which four gained election. Russian candidates also maintained a presence in other major parties, resulting in two more Russian candidates winning election in the PR contest as members of centrist parties, the New Union and the Lithuanian Liberal Union. By contrast, the Electoral Action of Lithuanian Poles continued to be the primary vehicle for Polish politicians, and consequently Polish representation in the PR tier remained marginal.

Ethnic Diversity and the Party System

Data limitations prevented a direct examination of the impact of ethnic diversity on party fragmentation in parliamentary elections in Lithuania.[88] But electoral and census data did allow for an examination of the impact of ethnic diversity on party fragmentation in sixty towns and municipalities for Lithuania's 2000 presidential election. Table 4.6 shows the results of an OLS multiple regression analysis using the effective number of candidates as the dependent variable and the effective number of ethnic groups (ENETH) and population per square kilometer (URBAN) as independent variables.

Unlike in Russia, ethnic diversity in Lithuania tends to follow expectations and to promote the proliferation of electoral contestants. The effective number of ethnic groups was statistically significant and *positively* correlated with the effective number of presidential candidates in the first round of elections. Surprisingly, urbanization was negatively correlated with party fragmentation but was not statistically significant. Further tests (results not shown) showed a difference between the effect of Russian and Polish minorities on the number of parties. Both coefficients were positively correlated in multiple regression analyses (which also included

TABLE 4.6
OLS Multiple Regression Analysis of Impact of Ethnic Diversity and Urbanization on the Effective Number of Parties in Lithuania's 2000 Presidential Election

Independent Variables	Coefficient Estimates (std error)
ENETH	0.415
	(0.181)**
URBAN	-0.327
	(0.244)
Constant	4.871
	(0.234)***
Adjusted R^2	0.059

Sources: *Project on Political Transformation and the Electoral Process in Post-Communist Europe, www.essex.ac.uk/elections; Department of Statistics of Lithuania, 2002.*
** *p < .05,* *** *p < .01*
URBAN: Percent Urban
ENETH: Effective Number of Ethnic Groups

urbanization), but the proportion of Russians was statistically significant whereas the proportion of Poles was not.

Given that this is a study of only a single election, one can only speculate on the explanation and implication of these findings. Two explanations are most likely. First, minorities, specifically Russians, may increase the number of viable electoral presidential candidates by voting as a bloc for a minor candidate that the majority population does not support. Given the internal divisions within the Russian community, this is not very likely. Rather, Russians are likely to split their votes more widely than the rest of the population and thus contribute to party fragmentation. Thus, Lithuania actually runs counter to the Russian experience and the thrust of the underlying theory of cross-national studies. Minorities in Lithuania probably contribute to party fragmentation not by giving rise to ethnic parties but by being less cohesive as a voting bloc than the rest of the population.

Conclusion

The role of ethnic minorities in emerging party systems in new democracies has been a neglected topic in the literatures on ethnicity and democratization. The experience of postcommunist states offers some cause for cautious optimism regarding the ability of ethnically diverse societies to sustain competitive democratic politics. For the most part, postcommunist states have avoided the worst-case scenario in which parties representing ethnic minorities and ultranationalist parties of the majority dominate the political spectrum, grounding politics in exclusive and polarized identities. Ethnic parties have been a prominent part of the political landscape in many postcommunist states; but these parties have tended to play by the democratic rules of the game and have found a place for themselves in mainstream politics. Moreover, ethnic minorities have been incorporated into the polity through legislative representation in a variety of demographic and institutional contexts.

Given the wide variety in demography, institutions, history, and politics within the region, no two cases of postcommunist ethnic electoral politics will look the same. But the Russian and Lithuanian cases examined here do offer lessons that may be generalizable beyond their borders.

First, demographic factors strongly influence the viability of parties appealing exclusively to ethnic minorities. Under PR electoral rules, a minority group needs to be sufficiently larger than the legal threshold in order to sustain its own ethnic party. This is the case for Slovakia and Bulgaria, which contain minority populations dominated by a single group comprising at least 9 percent of the population. But the smaller Russian and Polish communities of Lithuania, comprising only 6 percent of the population, have failed to sustain viable ethnic parties in the face of a 5-percent legal threshold. The even smaller ethnic minorities of Russia never stood a chance of establishing ethnic parties. Romania seems to provide a counterexample here. Its Hungarian minority constitutes less than 7 percent of the Romanian population but has managed to support a very successful ethnic party in the UDMR. Granted, the legal threshold in Romania's first two postcommunist elections was only 3 percent.[89] Nonetheless, the success of the UDMR in Romania highlights the critical role of mobilization of voter turnout and a cohesive ethnic voting bloc. The relative failure of Polish and Russian parties in Lithuania can be blamed as much on the lack of effective mobilization (low voter turnout and internal divisions) as on the small size of the groups themselves.

The other chief demographic factor is geographic concentration, which, of course, increases the likelihood of minority candidates getting elected in districts with high concentrations of their co-ethnics. Such representation is not necessarily achieved through ethnic parties, as the experience of Russia demonstrates. Minority candidates running as independents and members of nonethnic parties fared quite well in single-member districts in ethnic regions and were also elected in relatively large numbers from the PR lists of major parties, none of which proclaimed a specific appeal to Russia's ethnic minorities.

Second, institutions play a vital role in the degree and manner in which ethnic minorities are represented. In PR elections, the legal threshold is the most important instrument for influencing representation. Thus, special provisions that lower the legal threshold for parties representing ethnic minorities can be a primary means for minorities to gain representation in parliament. When Lithuania removed the special 2 percent threshold for ethnic parties in 1996, it shut off one possible avenue for legislative representation of its minorities, particularly the Poles. Conversely, Romania's electoral law that provides an extraordinarily low threshold for ethnic parties has one of the largest and most diverse minority legislative contingents in Eastern Europe.[90]

But electoral laws are not the only institutional instruments affecting the electoral mobilization of minorities. In the Russian case, ethnic federalism was the most important institutional factor influencing ethnic representation. Russian minorities that had their own federal subunits (especially very small groups) had distinct advantages in the SMD races that enhanced their capacity for legislative representation beyond what one would expect based solely on geographic concentration.

Third, both the Russian and Lithuanian cases underscore how ethnic minorities can sometimes use assimilation with the majority population as an effective strategy for gaining representation. Ukrainians in Russia were extremely successful at gaining legislative representation in both PR and SMD electoral rules because of their relative assimilation into the Russian population; conversely, Russians in Lithuania gained significant PR representation only when they entered into a coalition with parties of the Lithuanian majority. Of course, this is a limited strategy strongly conditioned by demographic factors of group size and social distance. Larger groups such as the Hungarians in Romania and Slovakia or the Turks in Bulgaria have successfully opted to mobilize their own ethnic parties. This dynamic is important to note, however, in order to balance the emphasis on electoral mobilization through ethnic parties and to draw attention to alternative routes used by minorities to gain representation.

Finally, the Russian and Lithuanian cases demonstrate the different ways that ethnic minorities influence broad characteristics of the party system. The cross-national literature assumes that ethnic diversity increases party system fragmentation by increasing the number of electoral cleavages. But ethnic diversity constrained the number of parties under both PR and plurality rules as well as in presidential elections in Russia. Lithuania, on the other hand, followed the expected pattern of ethnic diversity increasing the number of parties, although probably for different reasons than the literature usually emphasizes. This is one area in which study of the postcommunist experience could fill a hole in the literature and provide a more nuanced theory of how ethnicity affects party systems.

The interrelationship between ethnicity and electoral politics is a complex, multifaceted phenomenon. By centering on specific aspects of this relationship, I have tried to identify certain patterns of ethnic mobilization in the electoral realm and their causes. This framework could be applied to other postcommunist states and beyond to begin to develop a more comprehensive understanding of the factors that produce the various patterns of electoral politics.

5

WHAT PROVOKES VIOLENT ETHNIC CONFLICT?

Political Choice in One African and Two Balkan Cases

DANIEL CHIROT

Since the collapse of European Communism in 1989, we have gone from unjustified wild optimism claiming that the world's ideological conflicts have been decided and that democratic capitalism will hold sway forever, to being shocked by genocidal ethnic wars in parts of the postcommunist world and Africa, and more recently by the religious wars that seem to be at the heart of increasing violence in the Middle East and in South and Southeast Asia. Yet even optimistic commentators, most famously Francis Fukuyama, always saw the dark cloud of "wars of the spirit" on the horizon, and knew perfectly well that a rational, perfectly liberal democratic system based only on enlightened self-interest was an impossibility.[1] Others, who were more realistic than the academics and policy makers who jumped on the bandwagon of self-congratulatory celebration of liberalism, understood from the start the dangers inherent in tribalism combined with the frustrations of all those people around the world who were going to feel left out by progress.[2]

From the start of the post-Cold War era, it has been obvious that one of the main sources of tension and possible war was ethnic conflict within state borders and cross-border irredentism. This was an old problem that somehow seemed to have been frozen by Cold War boundaries in Europe and even kept in check in many other parts of the world by the antagonistic but very real hegemony that the West and the Soviet Union imposed on their allies. Subsequently, we have seen that this tension is indeed something to worry about, especially if religious hostilities are added to ethnic ones. Ethno-religious conflict is far from being universal, however, even in areas that have had a history of it and still have difficult majority-minority relations. It behooves us, therefore, to study why some places have such conflicts, and others do not. The Balkans are a perfect laboratory for doing exactly that.

It may seem odd to devote a substantial part of a chapter on ethnic conflict in the Balkans to a long description of recent events in the West African country of Côte d'Ivoire. The reality, however, is that many of the tragic civil wars and other violent conflicts in Africa today bear some resemblance to the worst of the Balkan ethno-nationalist wars that occurred in the twentieth century. Such is the case not only in Côte d'Ivoire, but also in Liberia, Nigeria, Congo (Kinshasa and Brazzaville), Sudan, Uganda, Rwanda, Burundi, Mozambique, Angola, Ethiopia, Sierra Leone, and Chad. The Yugoslav wars of the 1990s, some of which remain just as unsettled as recently concluded African ones, bear a striking resemblance to African wars, and were it not for the fact that they were in Europe, they would have been called tribal wars. Africa and the Balkans, of course, have had very different histories, are at different levels of economic development, and are characterized by different cultures, so the fact that they still share some common outcomes tells us something about why it is possible to make some broad, comparative comments on ethnic conflict.

Not all Balkans countries have been involved in recent civil or international wars over issues of ethnicity and nationality. Romania and Bulgaria, the two Balkan cases I cover, have been remarkably peaceful since the fall of Communism, despite the fact that in the last decades of Communist rule both were ruled by regimes that were openly xenophobic, blamed ethnic minorities for many of their problems, and relied almost exclusively on extreme nationalism to buttress their collapsing legitimacy. Similarly, in Africa, not all countries are beset by ethnic and nationalist conflicts, though none of the ones who have mostly escaped so far are automatically immune in the future. How can we explain the absence of violent ethnic conflict when some seemingly similar cases do have conflict? Looking at contrasting cases in two parts of the world might offer a few ideas about how to do this. The more broadly comparative we can be, the more confident we will be in our conclusions.

Why Is Theorizing Violent Ethnic Conflict Difficult?

Many scenarios can lead to violent ethnic conflicts. Most of us believe that struggles for political power, for territorial control, and for economic goods are their most common causes. Coexisting communities that identify themselves and their competitors by some combination of cultural criteria (including habits, language, and religion) and an assumption of kinship, however distant, may live in relative harmony until competition for scarce resources becomes too serious to be resolved peacefully. Then these communities, generally labeled ethnic or religious groups (but sometimes nations or tribes), may resort to violence in order to get their way.

We know, however, that this kind of logic fails to cover many cases of ethnic conflict. It cannot explain why in so many cases competition between groups fails to produce violence; nor are such explanations of much use in specifying why some communities get defined as corporate bodies with distinct boundaries and others do not.

There are many examples of violence being directed against ethnic groups that only tenuously appear to be serious economic or political competitors. A good example is the attacks and general hostility toward Gypsies, or Roma, in Central and Eastern Europe. This reached genocidal proportions under Nazi rule and has resurfaced at a lesser but still serious level in most postcommunist countries. But the Roma pose no political or economic threat and control no valued resources. Rather, most of the hostility directed against them is caused by a profound disdain for their way of life, coupled with the perception that they engage in much petty crime. In other words, it is their culture, or popular notions about their culture, that provokes violence, not competition. As for the Nazi interpretation, Gypsies were deemed to be a mongrel race, and therefore racially polluted, but not dangerous in any economic or political sense, unlike the Jews, whom Hitler thought to be both dangerously powerful and racially polluting.[3]

On the other side of this question, it is possible to point to potentially divisive ethnic divisions that seem to stir very little trouble, despite significant disparities of wealth between majority and minority communities. For example, there is little anti-Sinicism in Thailand, where Sino-Thais have increasingly blended into the general population, despite some historical precedence for anti-Chinese sentiment and the Chinese's vastly disproportionate economic power.[4] In all of the sad history of ethnic disputes in the Balkans, there appear to be few instances of overt conflicts between ethnic majorities and the many dispersed Vlach groups. The Vlachs, as a matter of fact, never seem to have had a strong national identity and were not involved in the disputes over nationality and political control that developed in the nineteenth and twentieth century Balkans even though in some places they formed prominent shepherd and merchant communities.[5]

In part, this is a matter of timing. The absence of conflict at one time does not guarantee its absence later. Jews lived peacefully with Christian and Muslim neighbors for long periods of time, but not always. Tutsi and Hutu were not distinct ethnicities, but rather something more akin to status groups with differential prestige, and they intermarried, spoke the same language, and had the same religious traditions until some time in the colonial period when they became distinct, hostile ethnic groups.[6] It is difficult to predict which groups will establish semi-closed corporate identities and become involved in competitive conflicts with neighboring communities, and which will not.

Ethnicity and religions are often defined as being different, but that is probably misleading because religious communities can take on all the characteristics of ethnic ones: they may develop their own cultures, a sense of kinship reinforced by some measure of endogamy, and a group sense of solidarity against others. We think of Mormons as a religious community, but in some ways, in the United States they fit every definition of a distinct ethnic group except that their leaders decided in the 1860s to 1890s that it was far wiser to drop some of their most "un-American" habits (notably polygamy) and to define themselves as white, Protestant Americans, which is how they are generally viewed today. This case, not normally included in any ethnic comparisons, is a good example of how the leadership of a particular community tried, at first, to create a new ethnic group (originally, a separate nation in Utah), but then reversed course for practical reasons, and got the group defined as a "normal" religion.[7]

The same questions arise about violent conflict between religious groups as between those more narrowly defined as ethnic, and it is a mistake to be too strict about definitions in discussing ethnicity because of the fluidity of communal solidarities.

If pronounced religious or cultural antipathies, rigid boundaries between coexisting groups, or material competition always led to violence, ethnic conflict could be easily modeled. But since some combination of these may or may not cause violent conflict, depending on more particular, case-dependent variables, we are generally left with *post facto, ad hoc* explanations and theoretical controversies rather than with satisfactory predictions. The point is that purely objective group dynamics between competing communities do not sufficiently explain outcomes.

In recent years many of the best scholars studying ethno-religious conflict have stressed that violence is the exception, not the rule, and that it
requires a substantial effort by political entrepreneurs to provoke it. Thus,
Fearon and Laitin have contended that the overwhelming number of
potential ethnic conflicts never take place because it is rational for most
coexisting communities to resolve their differences peacefully.[8] Varshney
has shown that even well-defined religious communities that have had
a tradition of conflict, Hindus and Muslims in India, avoid violence if
local elites cooperate to maintain civil ties in politically dangerous times.[9]
Brubaker has stressed that being part of an "ethnic group," even if it has
been involved in conflict with another "group," is not a good predictor
of whether future conflicts will occur, because groups are not as bounded
as we think they might be, and ethnic dislikes often do not translate into
actual conflict unless specific competition for resources occurs between
collectivities rather than between individuals. In particular, he has found
that Hungarian-Romanian relations in Transylvania have remained largely
peaceful in postcommunist times despite efforts by some local politicians
to promote discord.[10] Brass, also working in India, has stressed the importance of ethnic entrepreneurs who deliberately provoke violence. Without
them, mass killings would not occur.[11] Oberschall's analysis of Croatian-
Serbian local relations in Yugoslavia at the start of the wars in the 1990s
demonstrated that these relations were often very peaceful; he found that
it required pressure from above and the introduction of violent threats
by provocateurs from outside communities to break up integrative civil
institutions that, left alone, would have maintained ethnic peace.[12]
Horowitz's encyclopedic review of about 150 cases of ethnic violence also
concludes that the authorities, both state or local politicians and police
forces, have to back violence for it to get very far. Small incidents may
occur spontaneously, but they sputter out quickly without organized help
from the powerful.[13]

On top of this, the vast literature on "imagined" or created memories
places the blame for conflicts on the enterprising intellectuals who fab-
ricate ethnic, religious, or national identities, or, at least, who reinterpret
them in conflictual ways. Scholars as different as Benedict Anderson and
Liah Greenfeld agree, as do most other contemporary students of nationalism, that intellectuals play the key role in redefining group identities,
and that these exercises have profound long-term consequences in determining how groups will get along.[14]

This partial scholarly consensus, that initiation of violence requires
deliberate action by key elites, not just a specific set of structural conditions, points to the missing element in most general theories of ethnic

conflict. Explanations such as those by Hardin, or Hechter, that elites who provoke nationalist or ethnic separatism do so because they perceive this to be in their self-interest, are certainly correct, though it remains unclear why some ethnic and religious provocateurs are successful and others not, or how, in fact, elites decide what is in their interest.[15] Structural situations are rarely obvious enough to enable analysts to predict the reaction of the mass of followers to particular kinds of leaders. This means that the quality of leadership counts, and that leaves us with the problem of analyzing small—sometimes very small—numbers of politically powerful actors. That is where most social science theories balk, because the behavior of a few key individuals who happen to be in power is almost impossible to model.

Another practical problem—theoretically less interesting, but important—affects the contemporary study of ethnic and communal religious conflicts. It is possible to appreciate an argument such as the one presented by Fearon and Laitin which shows that in Africa less than 1 percent of all potential ethnic conflicts take place, and ask, so what?[16] How does an Africanist or, better yet, someone working for an NGO trying to promote peaceful economic development and democratization in Africa use the impeccable logic that proves this point? The unfortunate fact is that over half of all African states have had serious ethnic wars since independence, and some of them have resulted in the deaths of millions. Côte d'Ivoire had only a few, minor outbreaks of interethnic violence before the late 1990s, and no civil war until 2002. Now it has both, and saying that for most of the time and between most groups there was no conflict until recently is of little help. Likewise, little value exists in the observation that the current war is hardly a war of all against all, but a matter of two large coalitions that have divided the country between north and south. Why was Côte d'Ivoire seemingly exempt from the general African pattern until the mid-1990s, and what changed? Can anything be done to reverse this tragedy?

The same question can be asked in Eastern Europe and the former Soviet Union. Here, in most cases, little violent ethnic, religious, or nationalist conflict has occurred since the collapse of Communism, but there have been enough very bad cases to bring some parts of this region, notably the Balkans, the Caucasus, and a few parts of Central Asia, to worldwide attention, and to create the impression that postcommunist states, like Africa and large parts of the Middle East and South Asia, are areas of endemic ethnic conflict.[17]

Journalistic and popular conceptions about these regions may be overly simplified, and exaggerate the prevalence of violence. But those

trying to deal with the actual consequences of violent conflict find themselves unable to learn much from general theories that downplay the
extent of violence and from analysts who correctly reject primordialist
explanations. The unfortunate fact is that once ethnic boundaries have
been essentialized and violence has occurred, those involved tend to interpret conflict as based on primordial distinctions, even if scholars can
point out that these are relatively recent fabrications.

All of this leads me to make some suggestions about what to look for
in order to explain and to predict whether violent ethnic conflict will take
place, and to base this on the brief examination of my three cases, Côte
d'Ivoire in West Africa and Romania and Bulgaria in the Balkans.

What Happened in Côte d'Ivoire?

Côte d'Ivoire, along with mainland Tanzania, was, until the 1990s, one of
the few multiethnic and multireligious African states to avoid overt ethnic
conflict. Unlike Tanzania, Côte d'Ivoire was also, at least into the 1980s,
an economic success story.[18] Rapid economic growth, internal peace, and
political stability were based on close cooperation with France, the former
colonial power, chief investor, aid donor, military guarantor, and cultural
model for the new, aspiring nation. Côte d'Ivoire became the world's
main cocoa exporter (about one-third of world production) and its third
largest coffee producer. Other tropical goods, including lumber, were also
exported, and some light industry based on these products was developed.
The resulting prosperity attracted large numbers of immigrants from
neighboring, much poorer countries, so that from 1950 to 2001, the population grew from about 2.6 million to 16 million, a sixfold increase. This
was even more than could have been expected by natural increase, despite
the high birthrates, and indeed, in the 2001 census some 5 million were
listed as non-Ivoiriens. Of these, 3.5 million were from Burkina Faso, and
1 million from Mali, both poor Sahelian lands. Another 70,000 came
from Nigeria, 50,000 were Lebanese, and over 20,000 were French (the
largest European population in sub-Saharan Africa outside South Africa
and, at least until recently, Zimbabwe).

As might be expected, a disproportionate share of the wealth was controlled by the French and Lebanese, but most of the agricultural exports
were raised by small to medium-sized African landowners in the southern
part of the country, and along with a substantial, growing African middle
class of civil servants and professionals, there was a rural middle class. This
rural class of small and medium landowners had formed the backbone of

the anticolonial movement in the late 1940s and early 1950s, and their leader, Félix Houphouët-Boigny, had been the country's dominant politician throughout late colonial times.

In 1960, at independence, Houphouët-Boigny became Côte d'Ivoire's first president, a post he occupied until his death at the official age of 87 (though he was rumored to be older than 90) in 1993.

The independence movement's origins in a class of landholders differed markedly from the origins of most African anticolonial movements. Rather than just being in the hands of a tiny, Western educated, largely socialist elite with shallow social roots, the Ivoirien political elite was formed in the struggle against French planters and colonial forced-labor laws from which the French drew much of their labor force. Once the battle against forced labor was won shortly after World War II, French planters could no longer compete with African farmers, and much of the anti-French animus dissipated. Houphouët, who had allied himself with the French left for tactical reasons, could then revert to his, and his political base's, more conservative instincts. By late colonial times, Houphouët had already become the effective ruler of the country, a powerful French deputy with influential ties in Paris, a frequent minister in Fourth Republic cabinets, and a moderate, politically stabilizing leader. As the one who had ended the hated forced-labor laws and stood up to the racism of French planters, effectively ending their rule, he was also widely popular. If it had not been for what was happening elsewhere in Africa, however, Côte d'Ivoire likely would not have sought independence. In a famous exchange between Houphouët and his neighbor, President Kwame Nkrumah of Ghana, Houphouët told Nkrumah that the path of complete cooperation with the old colonial power and a more conservative development policy would reap greater benefits than Nkrumah's socialism and radical break with colonialism. Given Ghana's subsequent history of coups and its precipitous economic decline from the 1960s to the 1980s, it was clear that Houphouët turned out to be right—up to a point. Despite economic reverses in the 1980s due to the fall in commodity prices and the gradual overvaluation of the French supported African Franc (CFA), Houphouët probably died convinced that his creation based on French-African political, economic, and cultural cooperation had led to the most stable, the richest, and the most harmonious new nation in West Africa, or even in all of sub-Saharan Africa. France fully reciprocated this feeling, considered Houphouët its most reliable African friend, and was proud of Côte d'Ivoire as its greatest neocolonial success.

Appearances, however, were deceptive, not only because Côte d'Ivoire remained too dependent on a few export commodities, but also because too much of its wealth was concentrated in relatively few European, Lebanese, and African elite hands. In addition, Houphouët's benign autocracy failed to create institutional continuity.

Houphouët, a Catholic from the south-central part of the country, always recognized the potential for ethno-religious conflict. Most of the country's sixty ethnic groups have their own language. The north is mostly animist (that is, many local, tribally based religions) and Muslim, and the south animist and Christian, but the division is far from neat; there are some northern Christians as well as southern Muslims. Many of the immigrants from outside the country and many of those who moved from the poorer north to the richer south were Muslims. As might be expected, among those who had been northern animists, moving to a new environment promoted conversions to Islam because the people most like them from the Sahel and northern Côte d'Ivoire who were not animists were Muslims. The same tendency toward increasing Christianization exists among southern animist migrants from West African coastal regions who move into cities or new rural areas. The country is now 38 percent Muslim, 32 percent Christian, and 15 percent animist, with the rest uncertain or claiming no religion. (Some individuals say that they are sometimes Christian and sometimes Muslim, though the devout in both religions do not accept this as good practice.)

For migrants from Burkina Faso and Mali who were either Muslim or likely to become Muslim, and who formed the large majority of non-Ivoirien immigrants, the boundaries between their countries and Côte d'Ivoire were nonexistent in colonial times, and barely meaningful in the early postcolonial period. Côte d'Ivoire needed more labor, and the migrants were welcomed in both rural and growing urban areas. There was plenty of land, work, and opportunity. However unevenly the prosperity was distributed, there was no question that more schooling, better health care, and in general better services were available than in the famine prone, desiccated Sahelian regions from which they emigrated. Furthermore, as might be expected, ethno-religious boundaries hardly coincided with internal French administrative divisions, so that migrants from these countries found many linguistically and religiously related Ivoiriens already in place when they arrived.

Houphouët's solution to potential ethnic problems was threefold. First, he constantly emphasized the fact that Côte d'Ivoire was a land of "*hospitalité authentique*" and that "the land belongs to those who cultivate" rather than to any traditional tribal community. Secondly, he made sure that he appointed important officials from all areas, not just from his own southern tribal group. One of his most prominent late appointments as prime minister was a northern Muslim, part of whose family had arrived in colonial times from Burkina Faso (then Upper Volta), Alassane Ouattara. Third, he promoted an Afro-French national identity that was nonreligious and strongly non-tribal.[19]

All of this fell apart in the 1990s for three reasons. First, by then economic growth had greatly slowed because of lower export prices and the overvalued currency, which Houphouët refused to change, as that would have damaged the urban and political elite's ability to import Western products. (France backed its old friend and devalued the CFA only 50 percent after his death.) Second, slow growth and a much larger population meant increasing competition for land and jobs that were no longer abundant. Third, France, going along with Western opinion and the wave of democratization sweeping the world, demanded that he allow free elections. Houphouët, with his immense prestige and control of a well-oiled political machine, easily won reelection in 1990 with over 80 percent of the vote in a reasonably fair election against the socialist Laurent Gbagbo, but after Houphouët's death, the situation changed.

Houphouët's successor, Henri Konan Bédié, lacked his prestige, and faced with his chief rival— former Prime Minister Alassane Ouattara, a popular northerner— he began to promote a new policy designed to keep himself and his largely Christian, southern political allies in power. In the 1995 presidential election Ouattara almost certainly would have won a fair election. Not only had northerners (including, of course, many who now lived in the more prosperous south and in the economic capital, Abidjan, as well as in other cities in the cocoa and coffee belts) become a majority because of the influx of migrants from northern countries, but the former socialist dissident, Gbagbo, had signed on to a tactical alliance with Ouattara to oppose Houphouët's old ruling party. Furthermore, Ouattara, as former prime minister and a respected former International Monetary Fund official, was recognized both locally and internationally as a competent leader. Bédié's response was to push through a new law excluding candidates who could not prove that they had four Ivoirien grandparents (later modified to both parents). This effectively disenfranchised the majority of the population, including Ouattara. Not only had there been much mixing among northerners and migrants, but also many people from northern ethnic groups lacked documented "proof" that their families had come entirely from within the old colonial borders of Côte d'Ivoire. Boundaries had been administratively convenient and sometimes shifting; consequently, many northerners were not even sure of how "Ivoirien" they might be, and this, of course, threatened their property as well as their civil rights. Subsequently, in fact, a significant number of land seizures occurred in the cocoa area as autochthonous people seized land long cultivated and presumably owned by migrants who were now being told that it had only been "loaned," sometimes for more than a generation.

With his chief opponent disqualified (and the French not saying much), Bédié was reelected to the presidency. In 1996 he supported a group of southern Baoulé intellectuals who created an official doctrine of "*Ivoirité*." Bédié, like Houphouët, was a Baoulé, and the Baoulé, mostly Christians, were the main landowners in the heart of the cocoa region as well as a traditionally relatively well educated group. (The Baoulé are Akan people, like the Ashanti in neighboring Ghana, also the most prosperous cocoa farmers in that country.) Being authentically "Ivoirien" was defined as being virtually Baoulé, or a member of one of the related, southern Christian peoples. Northerners and Muslims were "immigrants" and therefore, not Ivoiriens "*de souche*" (not of Ivoirien "stock").[20]

Côte d'Ivoire was now ready for an ethnic war as northerners, especially those who lived in the south, began to feel increasingly threatened, and southern politicians, led by the president and a small political and intellectual elite, pushed the new doctrine. In barely half a decade, the situation was transformed from one in which ethnicities and religions had coexisted fairly peacefully, into one in which they were now officially defined as having different citizenship rights. There was no history of widespread conflict, no prior legitimizing ethnic mythology analogous to that which, for example, had existed between Serbs and Croats before the Yugoslav wars, and no history of extreme, overt discrimination. There were cultural differences, and differential degrees of access to wealth, but these were less marked between Africans themselves than between Africans and the French and Lebanese minorities. There was political competition, but that, also, was fairly new, as it had remained remarkably inoperative during Houphouët's long, autocratic, but largely benign, rule. Houphouët's policy had been very similar to that of Julius Nyerere in mainland Tanzania, who also devalued tribal identities and languages in favor of a national, Swahili identity.[21] For Houphouët, the new identity was Ivoirien and French, and indeed, the proportion of French speakers in Côte d'Ivoire is over 50 percent and still growing. But with the coming of elections, and the realization that the southern elite would be unable to muster electoral majorities, all of this changed.

Absent free elections, or perhaps if Houphouët had had the wisdom to make Ouattara his designated successor, this might not have happened. Nor would it have occurred if Bédié had been willing to concede electoral defeat in 1995.

The story of how civil war began is almost anticlimactic and can be told briefly. Bédié's hold on power was weakened by the questionable legitimacy of his election, by the growing dissatisfaction of those of northern origin, and by the economy's failure to rebound. In December 1999, the army mutinied over issues of salary, and General Robert Gueï, a Yacouba from the western part of the country with ties to both southerners and northerners, took power. He promised to redress the problems raised by Bédié's doctrine of *"Ivoirité."* This did not happen. France insisted that elections be held, and in July 2000 soldiers again mutinied over their pay. Gueï kept control, but to build a popular base for the coming elections, he continued to pander to southern opinion and refused to end discrimination against northerners. In the election of October 2000, Ouattara was again declared ineligible, even though, again, he probably would have won a fair election. His party boycotted the election, which allowed the southern socialist, Gbagbo, to win. Gueï refused to give up power, but without French support, his rule collapsed, and with rioting in the streets of Abidjan against military rule, Gbagbo ascended to the presidency.

Gbagbo, as an old socialist foe of neocolonialism, got the immediate support of the French government, whose socialist prime minister, Lionel Jospin, prevailed on French President Jacques Chirac to accept the truncated election. Gbagbo had, indeed, won, though a majority of the electorate had abstained because their favorite candidate, Ouattara had been excluded. (The United States, however, did not recognize the election as legitimate.)

Gbagbo, now completely dependent on southern support, continued to exacerbate ethnic tensions, and added a strong religious element. His influential wife, Simone, is a born-again Christian and the Gbagbos interpreted the situation as a Christian-Muslim face-off, not simply as an ethnic or regional dispute.

Another attempted military coup occurred in January 2001, but the French prevailed on Gbagbo to try to create a coalition of the country's main political forces, including General Gueï, former President Bédié, and former Prime Minister Ouattara. In June 2002, the Ivoirien courts gave Ouattara a "certificate of citizenship," but it was too late. The southern political elite had already provoked deadly ethnic riots, with massacres of northerners in some of the slum districts of Abidjan, and ethnoreligious mistrust was high. Northerners, especially the Dioula (originally Muslim merchants from the north, but now a generalized name for Malinké Muslim northerners and migrants), were blamed for the country's economic woes. Although French socialists continued to celebrate the "democratic" ascension to power of their "comrade" Laurent Gbagbo, he had actually become completely dependent on a narrow and increasingly intolerant ethno-religious base.

On September 19, 2002, northern soldiers in the army, who were losing their jobs as Gbagbo was trying to create a religiously loyal army, mutinied. The mutiny was actually led by northern officers who had previously fled to Burkina Faso, and the Burkinabé government helped with logistical support. Gbagbo's police and loyal military units put down the rebellion in Abidjan, and death squads were let loose to eliminate political enemies. Gueï was murdered. He had probably promised the mutineers he would take their side, but was not informed of the date of the uprising, and so was taken unaware. Ouattara narrowly escaped a death squad by fleeing with his family to the German embassy, and then the French embassy, as his house in Abidjan's most fashionable quarter was burned to the ground. Though they failed in Abidjan and in most of the south, the mutineers were able to seize the north of the country and to establish themselves in Bouaké, from which they were able to control most of the north.

Both sides fell victim to ethno-religious massacres, with thousands of deaths. Over a million refugees fled to their home regions, or in some cases, to their countries of origin. Burkina Faso gave aid to the northern rebels.

Gueï's people, the Yacouba, have strong ethnic ties with groups in Liberia, and some of these Liberians as well as allied Sierra Leonese fighters came into the far west, where they established a kind of "free fire" zone controlled neither by the northern rebels nor by Gbagbo's government. They slaughtered and killed substantial numbers, mostly Guéré people linguistically related to President Gbagbo's Bété tribe. The Gbagbo government recruited other Liberians who were related to the Guéré, and they increased the level of violence as the Liberian civil war spilled over into Côte d'Ivoire. This continued well into mid-2003.

Very belatedly, the French realized that they had lost control of their most prized neocolony, and sent four thousand troops (later close to five thousand) to protect the government in the south from the northern and western rebels, and to maintain a truce line between the different zones. In January 2003 they forced all parties to sign a power-sharing agreement in France. This provoked anti-French rioting in Abidjan, where Gbagbo's police and military supporters feared that any power-sharing agreement would leave them exposed to reprisals for their murderous acts. (It is worth noting that what began the march to a genocide in Rwanda in 1994 was a 1993 United Nations brokered power-sharing agreement with the

Tutsi, which panicked the Hutu political elite, who feared loss of power and reprisals for their past murders.[22])

As of mid-2004, the French had failed to force through some sort of power-sharing agreement. The Gbagbo regime has systematically refused to adhere to the agreements signed in January 2003, has continued to operate death squads, and has engaged in occasional massacres of opponents and northerners living in Abidjan. The alliance Gbagbo had with Houphouët's old party and its Akan-speaking supporters has broken apart because of Gbagbo's increasing unwillingness to share the spoils of office, and the proposed elections of 2005 are unlikely to occur; if they do, they will certainly not be fair. On the other side, the rebel authorities have engaged in looting to sustain themselves, they have lost control over some of their local allies, and they have decided that unless Gbagbo is removed, there can be no solution. About 6,500 United Nations peacekeepers are supposed to be sent in, but they rely on French support and are not mandated to solve political problems. Nor are they capable of enforcing any but purely local truces. Even the French are recognizing that as long as the present leadership on all sides, particularly in the presidency, is in place, the prospects of resolving the situation are increasingly remote.[23]

Even if peace were restored, after thousands of deaths, after the population has been mobilized on ethno-religious grounds, and after neighboring states and tribal groups have become involved in Ivoirien politics, a return to the days of Houphouët are most unlikely. With both French and domestic confidence shaken, investments will be few, and there is little prospect for an economic revival. Whatever political twists and turns take place, Houphouët's dream of creating an Afro-French, modern, harmonious and prosperous nation is dead. As of this writing, one year after the start of the war, nothing is settled, and if it were not for French intervention, Côte d'Ivoire would be in the midst of an even bloodier, probably genocidal, ethnic and perhaps even religious civil war between northerners and southerners.[24]

These days, Ghana, once again, looks more promising, and the long dead Kwame Nkrumah, who was overthrown in 1966, is once again a national hero.[25]

Why Not in Romania and Bulgaria?

It is unnecessary to give little histories of Romania and Bulgaria in order to make some important points, as these are much better known in scholarly circles than that of Côte d'Ivoire.

After the fall of Communism it would have been entirely logical to expect ethnic violence directed against minorities. First, both countries have long-standing, historically deep ethnic animosities that have resulted in substantial amounts of killing. In late Communist times, the dictators, Nicolae Ceaușescu and Todor Zhivkov, both exacerbated old ethnic differences to try to shore up their own legitimacy by appealing to narrow nationalist sentiment. Secondly, after the fall of Communist regimes in 1989, both the Romanian and Bulgarian economies, which had been in gradual decline in the 1980s, fell sharply. Much of the population, especially older workers in state industries, retired people, and marginal rural populations that had subsisted on inefficient collective farms, was thrown into dire poverty. Third, in both countries, free elections took place almost immediately, and continued to be held regularly in the 1990s and early 2000s, so that political power actually shifted back and forth between contending parties. Sometimes the reformed old Communists were in power, and at other times more liberal forces took power. All sides had ample opportunities to try to mobilize political support by appealing to majority ethno-religious solidarity and to blame their countries' frustrations on the minorities, as happened in Yugoslavia in the late 1980s and early 1990s.

In Romanian and Bulgaria the large majority are ethnically Romanian or Bulgarian, and Eastern Orthodox Christians. The main minorities are mostly Protestant Hungarians in Romania (7 percent of the population), and mostly Muslim Turks in Bulgaria (10 percent of the population), though the situation is vastly complicated by the presence of small numbers of other ethnic groups and religions, and in Bulgaria, the presence of Turkish-speaking Christians and Bulgarian-speaking Muslims.[26]

In both countries, especially in Romania, some politicians tried to play on ethno-religious hostilities and tensions to gain support, but none of these were able to take power at the national level. There were a few—very few—killings based on ethnic hostilities (more Roma have been murdered in scattered incidents than either Hungarians in Romania or Turks or Muslims in Bulgaria), but no episodes of large-scale deadly ethnic riots, much less ethnic cleansings or forced displacement of any populations.[27]

Why not? One easy answer is that neither Hungarian politicians in Romania nor Turkish or Muslim ones in Bulgaria ever threatened to take power, whereas in Côte d'Ivoire a northern Muslim could have won the presidential election. On the other hand, where a rich history of ethnic conflict and prejudice exists, unscrupulous politicians have often scapegoated unpopular minorities.[28] That is essentially the situation that southern politicians created in Côte d'Ivoire, as there was never any prospect that even an electoral victory by Ouattara would have changed the essential power or economic structure. As a former IMF high official, Ouattara was firmly committed to continuing Houphouët's pro-market, conservative system.

Looking at how some politicians in, say, India (most notably the BJP that was in power until the 2004 elections) have used the Muslim minority as a scapegoat to win power shows that there is nothing unusual about doing this, and that it can lead to very deadly results.[29] In Côte d'Ivoire, ethnoreligious tensions had to be activated by political will. In Bulgaria and Romania, with tensions as old and as fresh as those in Yugoslavia and certainly more deeply rooted than in Côte d'Ivoire, no such thing happened.

A second answer could be that both Bulgaria and Romania have firmly established majority nationalism. These loyalties may not be ancient creations, as the mythologized roots of these nations in the Middle Ages or even earlier are largely fictitious, but they certainly date back at least to the second half of the nineteenth century.[30] In Côte d'Ivoire, there was at most a third of a century of nationalizing effort, not nearly long enough to create a solid sense of "*Ivoirité.*" The irony is that it is precisely now, in the midst of a bitter ethnic conflict, that real nationalism is developing in Côte d'Ivoire, but only among southern Christians. As many scholars have noted, nothing is quite as propitious to social boundary formation and communal solidarity as conflict with others.[31]

The fact that Bulgaria and Romania were already well established nation-states in the 1990s meant that at least some politicians believed that they needed to consider national needs—not just their own personal and party interests—when they weighed their actions. It appears unclear whether any of the major politicians in power who followed Houphouët took such national considerations seriously (except Ouattara, who refused to encourage his supporters to take up arms). That is one of the most common, and correct, interpretations of why Africa is so filled with deadly ethno-religious, regional, and clan conflicts. There are very few nationalists. Once the colonial powers had been thrown out, anticolonialism was not at all the same thing as binding nationalism.

The Yugoslav case is instructive, because the experience of the 1920s and 1930s, culminating in the terrible ethnic wars during World War II, destroyed incipient Yugoslav nationalism. This had to be rebuilt under Tito, and he had only a few more years than Houphouët—thirty-six for Tito (1944 to 1980), thirty-three for Houphouët (1960 to 1993). Both

Bulgaria and Romania had at least three to four generations to construct a sense of national solidarity, and in neither Romania nor Bulgaria was this broken by World War II.[32]

The benign postcommunist period should not, however, make us forget that both Romanian and Bulgarian nationalism originally was built on ethno-religious hostility and exclusion, in much the same way that a new southern Ivoirien national identity is now being created out of bitter internal warfare. Somewhat the same thing has happened to Muslim Bosnian national identity, shaped as it has been by the ethnic political disputes in the late Tito era and hardened in the 1990s by a deadly war.[33] Here, again, it is all a matter of timing, political choice, and the international situation.

From its start in the 1850s and 1860s, construction of Romanian nationalism by an insecure landowner elite whose own ethnic roots were heavily Greek rather than Romanian was based on anti-foreign and particularly anti-Semitic sentiment. Anti-Semitism remained at the heart of Romanian nationalism until the end of World War II. Most Romanian Jews were the descendants of immigrants from Habsburg and Russian lands who came to Romania during the spectacular growth of its export wheat economy in the nineteenth century (much like the Dioulas' migration south into Côte d'Ivoire in its agricultural export boom). The Jews became convenient targets of blame for all the new inequalities and disruptions that ensued from the development of a wheat-exporting economy. At the same time, Romanian nationalists promoted a racial conception of the nation, claiming that a unique mixture of "rational" Latin blood and "barbaric" Daco-Thracian energy distinguished them from neighboring Slavs and especially Magyars. Thus, Romanian nationalists viewed Hungarians (the political masters of Transylvania, claimed as the ancestral Romanian homeland) and Russia (the Slavic giant on Romania's borders) with suspicion and hostility, whereas Jews were simply parasitic interlopers. This constructed xenophobia was exacerbated after Word War I, when Romania expanded into Transylvania, took over some slices of Bulgaria, and annexed Bessarabia (roughly today's Moldovan Republic). This vastly increased the number of non-Romanian, non-orthodox minorities, and in the case of the new Hungarians, Germans, and large numbers of Jews in Transylvania, Bukovina, and Bessarabia, these new inhabitants were generally better educated and able to take advantage of the modern sectors of the economy. Romania, as has happened over and over again in backward new states, overproduced intellectuals trained for civil service jobs but not for economically productive ones, and these new intellectuals bitterly resented more successful "foreigners" in Romania. In the end, this led to the rise of fascism and to Romania's enthusiastic participation as Hitler's ally in World War II.[34]

Nicolae Ceauşescu, who ruled from 1965 to 1989, increasingly revived the old, right-wing ethno-nationalism of the prewar era, and by the end, was using anti-Hungarian and anti-Slavic—that is, mainly anti-Russian—sentiment as the main legitimizing ideology of his rule. There are almost no Jews left in Romania (half were killed during World War II, and most of the rest immigrated to Israel from 1945 to 1950), almost no Germans (half left after World War II, and most of the rest slowly left in the 1970s and 1980s), very few Slavs, and only tiny numbers of other minorities except for Roma and Hungarians. So after 1989 these latter two ethnicities might have become the targets for politicians trying to gain support from a population inculcated by generations of xenophobic, racist ideology.[35]

The Bulgarian story is different in details, but not in substance. Probably the first example of massive ethnic cleansing in modern European history took place in Bulgaria after the Russian army expelled the Ottomans in 1878. In order to insure a Christian, Slavic-speaking majority, the Russians encouraged outrages in Bulgaria that forced massive Muslim emigration and set off the series of massacres and counter massacres that eventually became widespread in the Balkans before World War I. Some Turkish historians even ascribe the Armenian genocide in 1915 to the Ottoman authorities' fear that a Russian victory in World War I would produce the same result in Eastern Anatolia. Bulgaria turned itself into a warlike, ultranationalistic little country that in its first few decades of independence was involved in wars with all of its neighbors. Jews were not targeted because there were relatively few of them, and unlike in Romania, they were well established Sephardim who were not particularly prominent as "foreign" entrepreneurs. But Turks, Muslims of all kinds, and Greeks were viewed with hostility, and Bulgarian claims to Macedonia made Serbs enemies as well.[36]

Bulgarian hypernationalism was as much a staple of official school history as similar doctrines were in Romania, Hungary, Serbia, Greece, and Turkey in the interwar years. Bulgarian nationalists claimed that nation and ethnicity were identical, that the pure descendants of Bulgar Huns and Slavic tribesmen had a right to occupy the territory held by the medieval Bulgar Empire, and that they had a uniquely valuable, unified, millennial cultural and religious tradition. Bulgaria then joined the Axis to occupy parts of Macedonia, Greece, and Romania during World War II. It turned over the Jews in its newly occupied regions, but resisted turning over any of its "own" Jews.[37]

Bulgaria's economic decline in late Communist times was not as pronounced as Romania's but it was severe enough in the 1980s to throw the regime's legitimacy into doubt. Todor Zhivkov's regime hit on a wonderful expedient: it revived warnings of a Turkish ethno-religious threat, supposedly caused by the higher Muslim birthrate, and initiated a violent anti-Turkish and anti-Muslim campaign. The Turkish minority population of about nine hundred thousand (out of nine million Bulgarians) was forced to change personal names to Slavic ones, and over three hundred thousand ethnic Turks were forced, or "encouraged," to emigrate. There was some resistance by Turkish villagers, and some were killed by Bulgarian troops. A Turkish activist in Germany told me hundreds were killed and an organized resistance was being prepared, but that is difficult to verify. In any case, some deaths did occur, thousands were arrested and sent to concentration camps, mass flight occurred, and tensions worsened until Zhivkov's overthrow in November 1989.[38]

Although Romanian and Bulgarian nationalism helped to stabilize these countries after the fall of Communism and to create a sense of national responsibility among its politicians, this very nationalism was built on ethno-religious conflict, cemented by frequent wars in the late nineteenth to mid-twentieth centuries, and the promotion of ethnic prejudice, xenophobia, and nationalist resentment of foreigners and minorities during the Communist period. So the strength of both examples of nationalism certainly cannot explain why the situation changed so dramatically in the 1990s, except that it did create a political elite with some concern for national rather than purely parochial interests.

It is easy to misunderstand the role played by a strong national identity. On one hand, much of the prevailing scholarship on nationalism tends to dislike it because such scholarship views the phenomenon as being promoted by self-serving elites and used as a justification for discriminatory and imperialist policies.[39] On the other hand, civic consciousness is seen as something positive, although civic consciousness means something very similar, a strong sense that the larger community is owed respect and loyalty. The confusion arises from the use of the term "civil society," especially in the context of Communist Eastern Europe, where that term came to mean social organizations that were independent of government control. Such "civil society" organizations played a major role in bringing down Communism, and it was therefore assumed that "civil society," or, by association, anything termed "civic," was necessarily liberal and benign.[40] This impression has been strengthened by the work of Robert Putnam.[41] All of this is complicated by the continuing debate about whether there are two kinds of nationalism, a "civic" (that is, liberal and tolerant) kind and an "ethnic" or "blood" (that is, ethno-centric, intolerant) kind.[42]

States that lack a legitimating nationalist identity are inherently fragile in the modern world. Discontent or even ordinary political competition can produce damaging splits because politicians will appeal to their ethnic, religious, or regional constituencies to secure their base of power. People will sense that they are unable to rely on the state to protect their interests, and will be amenable to such divisive appeals in times of crisis. On the other hand, a strong nationalism is more likely to hold together those who accept it. This hardly means that nationalism is always benign. Bulgaria and especially Romania developed their sense of nationalism *against* their own minorities, and persecuted them, often violently. Nor was this unique. All of the strong modern nation-states have had episodes of such persecution against those presumed to be ethnic outsiders, even France and the United States, two supposed paragons of "civic" nationalism.

Even civil society (that is, social organizations that operate indepen-dently of the government, but are broader than mere family institutions) may not be necessarily benign. As Reşat Kasaba has argued, Islamic soci-eties contain religious "civil society" institutions that may or may not be democratic, that may or may not preach tolerance, and that may or may not be conducive to the promotion of "civic" nationalism.[43]

In other words, to say that Romania and Bulgaria, unlike Côte d'Ivoire, benefited from a strong sense of nationalism that played some role in holding these countries together and giving their politicians a sense of responsibility for the national well-being is not to claim that this explains their benign postcommunist ethnic policies. There is little question that without a sense of nationalism political leaders seem to have little stake in acting for the good of any but their immediate constituents, but after all, Adolf Hitler also felt a sense of duty to the German nation. It was just that Jews, Roma, and others were excluded from that nation.

Thus, the lack of a genuine Yugoslav nationalism (as opposed to a Serbian or Croatian one) had something to do with the collapse of Yugoslavia, just as the lack of a strong sense of nationalism in Côte d'Ivoire has made its politicians more shortsighted than they might otherwise have been. But in both cases, enough of a base existed that more tolerant and farsighted leaders could have contributed to the continuing development of national unity rather than breaking their states apart. In Romania and Bulgaria, on the other hand, a stronger sense of national unity made it easier for political leaders to make the right choice, but that was not pre-ordained by any means, since the entire history of nationalism in these countries had been intolerant and often violently hostile to minorities.

The choices made by the postcommunist leaders in both countries illustrates this history.

During the early postcommunist period (1990–1996), under President Ion Iliescu, the ruling coalition, closely tied to former Communist elites, made tactical alliances with ultranationalists, but worked to prevent killings or overt hostility and tried to dampen Hungarian-Romania tensions. In some localities, most notably in the Transylvanian capital of Cluj, there were strong political forces dedicated to stirring up xenophobic violence against Hungarians, but without control of the means of violence and without central state support, this produced little more than inflammatory verbiage.

In 1996, with a weak economy and lagging political legitimacy, Iliescu and the old Communist elite faced elections likely to turn them out of power. They easily could have raised nationalistic fervor to try to counter this, especially since the small but well organized Hungarian minority allied itself with the liberal, anticommunist opposition. Why Iliescu rejected this alternative is unclear, because for him, at age 66, electoral defeat almost certainly meant the ignominious end of his career, and for his followers, it meant a loss of power and prestige. Some of those who know him say it was a deliberate choice on his part to eschew too close an identification with the forces of right-wing nationalism. Certainly, one factor was the realization that if Romania turned back to its prewar or late Communist xenophobia, it would alienate Europe and the United States. Romania's future now clearly rested on increasing ties to the West, to Western investment, and to Western aid. Whatever his personal inclinations, Iliescu certainly knew this, and a political victory achieved at the cost of ruining Romania's future was unacceptable to him. He lost the election and retired gracefully; the liberals took power in a parliamentary alliance with the Hungarian party.[44]

The reversal in Bulgaria was even more dramatic. A large proportion of the Turks expelled or induced to flee in the 1980s were allowed back in, a Turkish party was organized (despite the constitutional provision against ethnic parties), free elections were allowed, and the Turkish party, like the Hungarians in Romania, became a swing group bartering parliamentary support for favors. The Bulgarian government has made strong efforts to include ethnic minorities, including Roma, in Bulgaria's political life, and has gone out of its way through a series of power shifts to maintain ethno-religious tolerance.[45]

As in Romania, one of the reasons few major politicians promoted xenophobia was the fear that this would alienate Europe and the United

States. Bulgaria even went so far as to abandon claims to Macedonia, and to steer clear of the ethnic warfare and contentious politics of that little neighbor, just as Romania has stayed away from overt interference in neighboring Moldova. Ultranationalism and the persecution of minorities no longer play very well in Europe or the United States, as Slobodan Milošević discovered. Even without the threat of American military intervention, the economic and political consequences of reverting to past practices and antagonizing the European Union would be high, at least for small European states.[46]

We should not underestimate the personal choices made by a few powerful politicians such as Iliescu in Romania. Scarred by personal experiences with tyranny and the sinister consequences of ultranationalism, Bulgarian and most Romanian political elites have been willing to lose power rather than to provoke new disasters. No doubt, the example of Yugoslavia was sobering as well, because it became clear that Milošević's policies could only provoke national disasters.[47]

In fascinating interviews conducted by Vladimir Tismaneanu, Iliescu explained his view of the problem of ultranationalism and showed his awareness of Milošević's role in destroying Yugoslavia. In fact, he said that "the exacerbation of nationalism only explains a small part of the Yugoslav tragedy." Yugoslavia had more moderate leaders, Iliescu said, but in a "situation that was already tense, they could not resist the inflexible, hard line personality of Milošević." Iliescu recognizes that the Serbian leader was well educated and sophisticated, and that he should have known better, but his brutality and his harshness in dealing with other leaders led to an outcome that could have been avoided by wiser tactics. To be sure, as a political leader, Iliescu is bound to think that personalities of key players are important, but at least his statements show that he was aware of what Milošević's approach had wrought, and he was determined to avoid such errors.[48]

For Iliescu, his thoughtful decency paid off handsomely. In 2000 he was returned to office, a crowning success to his long Communist and postcommunist political career in which he has transformed himself from one of Ceaușescu's closest confidants into a liberal, tolerant, and grandfatherly leader of his nation. His main opponent was an ultranationalist, Corneliu Vadim Tudor, who tried to capitalize on anti-Semitism, anti-Hungarian, and anti-Gypsy feelings, but Iliescu won an overwhelming electoral victory by about 2 to 1.[49]

So why does Côte d'Ivoire or, for that matter, most of Africa lack such leadership?

Conclusion: Timing, the International Situation, and Leadership

There is little in the history of nationalism to make anyone optimistic. Depending on how one measures the process, it took at least five hundred years, from the mid-fifteenth to the mid-twentieth century, to establish more or less stable nation-states in Western Europe. The period was characterized by almost perpetual warfare, including vicious religious wars, numerous civil wars, and several bloody attempts by the Habsburgs, Napoleon, and Hitler to create pan-European empires. In the United States, it was certainly not until the end of a terrible civil war in 1865 that American nationalism could start to create a genuinely unified nation-state. In Central Europe and the Balkans, nation-state formation was equally bloody, and only since the end of World War II at best has the process started to produce reasonably stable nation-state structures north of the Balkans. In the former Yugoslavia and in some parts of the former Soviet Union, the process is still under way. Romania and Bulgaria are fortunate to be ahead of the Yugoslav and many former Soviet lands in this respect, but only in the past decade have their elites felt confident enough to stop using ethnic intolerance to fortify their cultural and political boundaries.

The generous behavior of Romanian and Bulgarian political elites can be attributed in part to the liberal behavior of a few individuals. But it is much more than that. It also reflects a shrewd assessment of the international situation. The exclusion of Serbia from international (that is, Western) respectability was a striking proof that the kinds of nasty nationalism practiced in the 1930s and early 1940s were no longer acceptable. In the late nineteenth and early twentieth centuries, such behavior had been congruent with the behavior of some of the great European powers themselves. But timing is everything. In the 1870s the great powers could overlook Romanian anti-Semitism; in fact, Russia was as bad. The big powers could use Bulgarian, Romanian, and, for that matter, Serbian and Greek nationalism in their own competition, and the international mores of that time could abet such nationalism. During Communist times, as long as the Soviet Union protected Communism in Eastern Europe, Romania and Bulgaria could stoke intolerance and ethnic prejudice to strengthen their regimes. Those times have passed, at least for the time being.[50]

Whether Romanians or Bulgarians are generally tolerant is not the real issue. Plenty of evidence indicates that anti-Gypsy sentiment remains high, and that many ethnic Romanians do not trust Hungarians or Jews. Yet, without political support from some powerful authority and the backing of a military or police force, ethnic conflict does not get very far, no matter how distrustful various communities may be of each other. Left to their own devices, they will, as Varshney and Laitin and Fearon have shown, be far more likely to find some way of controlling their disputes to maintain peace, and to vent their prejudices verbally. Over time, such prejudices can decrease as long as they are not fed by political support, but rather countered by official tolerance.

The Romanian and Bulgarian treatment of the Roma problem exemplifies this. In order to maintain the good will of the European Union, of the United States, and of many NGOs supported by the West, the various governments in both countries have gone out of their way to show tolerance and to create institutions to help their Roma populations. Without state support or major political backing, prejudice against Roma may occasionally be murderous, but incidents remain scattered and very small-scale. No ethnic cleansing, systematic massacres, or legal discrimination occurs. A Romanian worker for a local NGO once told me, "I don't know why you Americans think so well of those dishonest, filthy Gypsies, but we get all our money from you, so we have to think that way, too."[51]

Timing is the key in Côte d'Ivoire, and elsewhere in Africa, too. European and American pressure is less effective because in most cases extreme poverty leaves elites little choice but to fight for control of government power. There is no other way for them to maintain even middle-class lifestyles. Beyond this, they themselves do not view their states as nations. Rather, to establish national cultural boundaries will require conflicts that define who is in and who is out. Given that many cultural groups exist, and that some will inevitably fare better than others in economic competition, mobilizing one's own group against others is particularly easy. When a particular alliance of linguistically, religiously, or regionally based groups can seize state power, its leaders have every incentive to solidify their hold on the state by creating a kind of new nationalism— we, our tribe, our religion, are the state, and we must defend it against outsiders. That is, after all, what older nations once did, and the logic remains the same today.

This conclusion is not optimistic, because, in essence, it says that Bulgaria and Romania went through more than a century of war, ethnic cleansing, and violent, often murderous, prejudice before being stabilized. Unlike the situation in Yugoslavia, a modicum of political continuity during this period allowed a strong sense of nationhood to jell, however much it was based on fabricated and prejudicial history. If it will take this long for borders to be readjusted and for nationalism to become established in Africa states, we can expect another century of bloody ethnic and probably religious wars in that continent. Moreover, it is very unlikely that any Western power will play the same moderating rule there as the one the European Union, NATO, and the United States play in Bulgaria and Romania.[52]

When the French pressured Gbagbo to sign a power-sharing agreement, his followers let loose a wave of anti-French rioting rather than giving in. He continued this pattern in 2004.[53] That this has come close to destroying Côte d'Ivoire is of less concern to the Ivoirien leaders than preserving their own power, and they correctly assume that in such dire circumstances, France cannot easily retaliate, and international donors will continue to provide relief aid, if not development funding. In the long run, this may fatally compromise the country's long-term development prospects, but clearly, that is not the leaders' first concern.

There is an international system that defends state boundaries and pretends that all states are nations, but in Africa the system is as new and fragile as the situation was in the late nineteenth century Balkans. In Africa the system is probably disintegrating. In such circumstances, without direct European or American intervention, practically every state in Africa will follow the path already taken by the Congo-Kinshasa, and most recently by Côte d'Ivoire. Only exceptionally visionary, liberal political leaders could avoid this outcome, and Africa is likely to produce very few of these because that is not where political incentives lie.

In terms of national construction, Côte d'Ivoire is now where Romania and Bulgaria were in the mid- to late nineteenth century, and perhaps where France was during its wars of religion in the sixteenth century. We can be pleased that Romania and Bulgaria seem to have moved to a new stage, and we should hope that this change is permanent. It can be if Europe holds itself together, and if the European-American alliance remains an important source of aid and support for reasonably secure nations. For Africa to produce a significant number of more liberal and farsighted, ethnically tolerant leaders, more akin to Ion Iliescu than to Slobodan Milošević, Europe and the United States will have to become much more involved and to offer stronger inducements. Because that is unlikely, we are only at the beginning of a long and bloody period of ethnic warfare in Africa, the "Balkans" of the twenty-first century. The Houphouëts, Nyereres, and the Nelson Mandelas will be the exception.

Much of this conclusion can be misrepresented. I think the evidence presented in these cases clearly shows the importance of choices that leaders make; some political leaders are more or less benign, others more or less polarizing. By and large, social scientists do not believe in the importance of individuals, preferring instead to explain what happens in terms of larger social and economic forces.

My argument is not meant to imply that leaders are entirely independent actors, but that they play a role. Equally important, of course, is the historical stage at which a state finds itself and its international setting. It is far easier for an Ion Iliescu to be tolerant of Hungarian minority wishes, and to renounce anti-Semitism, than it was for his pre-World War II predecessors or their Bulgarian counterparts who ran a major risk of being assassinated for their moderation. Whatever problems his nation faces, it is no longer so insecure as to cause its elites to think that they might cease to exist if they do not close their borders to foreign and minority influences. Half of Romania's Jews were exterminated, and almost all of the rest fled from 1940 to 1950. Europe will not allow a Hungarian-Romanian war, and both Hungary and Romania care much more about being accepted in Europe than in reviving old border issues. The same is true of Bulgarian-Turkish relations, and of Bulgaria's old claims for territory now held by its neighbors.

Good leadership can make historical transitions easier and can use a state's international position more or less wisely; but what this means is that to promote peaceful ethnic relations an African leader needs to be exceptionally farsighted and benign, whereas a Balkan leader need only be reasonably aware of his or her environment. It would take far greater courage on Laurent Gbagbo's part to be a peacemaker in his country than it does for Ion Iliescu because the situation of the southern Ivoirien political and cultural elite is far more precarious than the situation of the equivalent Romanian classes.

Still, when all is said and done, leadership does matter, and we ignore its consequences at our peril.

6

MIGRATION AND ETHNIC POLITICS IN EASTERN EUROPE AND EURASIA

CHARLES KING

States and empires are both wary of movement. Modern states desire stable borders, safeguarded by competent guards checking on the comings and goings of their inhabitants. States and empires want some way of keeping undesirables out and of benefiting from the productive capacities of those who live there permanently or temporarily. They may also desire that their denizens become genuine citizens, feeling that they have a stake in the state, rather than simply being governed by it. Visas and passports accomplish the first thing, tax collectors the second, and elections the third. Empires, especially those that stretch over vast portions of contiguous territory, are similar in some respects, but the difficulty of fixing the bounds of their dominion is compounded by the very vastness of the imperial landscape and the loose political allegiances on which imperial power normally depends. Rival powers might threaten to pull away outlying territories or to persuade particular groups to shift their allegiance. Populations along the frontier might play the center against another patron, using their position on the periphery as a lever against the imperial capital.

Historically, states have worried about keeping people out; empires have more often worried about keeping them in. The distinction between the two kinds of problems can fade away, however, when empires are transforming themselves into modern states—when the structures of state

power remain weak, lines of authority uncertain, and the territorial boundaries of the new political entity disputed. That is the case today across
Eastern Europe and Eurasia, the former inner and outer empires of the
Soviet Union. The demographic changes of the 1990s—the movement
of people out of conflict regions, the "return" of ethnic groups to newly
created national homelands, the out-migration to neighboring states and
farther afield—may well have changed the population structure of the
region in as profound a way as the tragedy of Soviet collectivization in the
1930s, World War II, and the forced deportations of the 1940s and 1950s.[1]
The real effects of these changes are poorly understood, however. The
social and political outcomes of demographic change usually appear only
gradually, and with the exception of a few areas (such as job competition
among migrants and locals, for example, or conflict between refugees and
host populations) they are rarely of immediate concern to politicians. Still,
the postcommunist world provides a magnificent setting in which to study
the impact of population movements on social structures and political
behavior, particularly interethnic relations and ethnic politics.

The first section of this chapter briefly surveys the literature on migration, an interdisciplinary field that has grown considerably in the last
decade but which has found only limited representation in mainstream
comparative politics. It also gives an account of the current state of international migration in postcommunist Europe and Eurasia based on the
available data, which are admittedly imperfect.

The second section illustrates how a study of postcommunist migration
can speak to one of the core concerns of comparative politics: the functions of formal and informal institutions and their effects on political and
social behavior. There are, of course, many ethnic dimensions to international migration. People might move abroad because they feel dis-
criminated against in their home countries. They might become refugees
from ethnic conflict. They might use networks of co-ethnics to facilitate
migration. But getting to the heart of how ethnicity matters—and
doesn't—in international migration is difficult. This section presents two
case studies as a way of addressing this issue. One concerns the policies
of postcommunist states toward co-ethnic populations abroad; the second
addresses the international migration of sex workers. The cases deal with
two aspects of migration: the attempt by states to develop a legal regime
for dealing with co-ethnics abroad and an undesirable form of irregular
migration, the trafficking of women. The two cases also focus on different types of institutions, the formal ones that states create to regularize
relations with potential migrant groups and the informal ones that arise
among migrant populations themselves.

The third section elaborates on the case studies by arguing for the reducibility of ethnicity; that is, the examination of the term itself and the elucidation of the precise political processes that the term often masks. Exploring these processes in more detail can help bring international migration more squarely within the comparative politics subfield and, by extension, sort out the relationship between ethnicity, migration, and postcommunism.

International Migration, Comparative Politics, and Postcommunism

Over the past half century, much of the social scientific literature on migration has been dominated by debates about the economic or social causes of movement. Initially, theorists focused on the microeconomic rationality of potential migrants (such as the desire for higher wages) or the structural push-pull factors in sending and receiving countries (excess labor supply on the one hand and labor demand on the other). In the last few decades, the field has moved toward more nuanced interpretations—structural explanations that highlight the peculiar conditions of postindustrial economies, world systems theories, and the rise of global cities, among others.[2] The focus throughout, however, has been on understanding the basic cause of international migration as a phenomenon: why individuals and households choose to move across international frontiers.

That way of defining the basic subject of research has tended to treat the state only obliquely—as an intervening variable acting on underlying structural causes—or simply to ignore it altogether. In the rare instances in which state policies, institutions, and actors have come into the picture, the focus has normally been on explaining the development of immigration policy in receiving states; but that literature, in turn, has had to do mainly with the arcana of bureaucratic politics and international treaties, the negotiation of reciprocal agreements between states, and their execution through some of the lowest levels of a state's foreign policy bureaucracy. (It is not for nothing that the entry-level position in foreign embassies has long been the visa officer.) Good reason existed for all of this. Immigration issues are only intermittently matters of high politics; when they are, they frequently reduce to debates about whether immigration is good or bad, how many people should be "let in," and how to keep tabs on them once they have arrived—debates that are usually more important as matters of symbolic politics and political rhetoric than they are of actual policy making.

This research program began to change in the late 1980s and 1990s, largely in response to real-world changes in international migration. As in the past, high labor supply in the developing world coincided with high demand in the developed West (both because of, among other things, differential birthrates). But this natural push-pull scenario was now accompanied by the receiving countries' desire to confine immigrants to the labor market and to discourage their long-term settlement.[3] Wealthier countries sought to reap the productive benefits of labor immigration without shouldering the burdens of social integration.

In the same period, both intrastate and interstate migration increased in virtually every region of the world. New international arrangements, such as the North American Free Trade Agreement and the deepening commitment of EU states to coordinated immigration policies, placed migration questions at the forefront of state policy. As the 1990s progressed, the tightening of immigration and asylum laws in the global North was accompanied by an upsurge in illegal migration from the South, which in turn gave rise to anti-immigrant politicians and parties in Europe and North America. New armed conflicts in Europe and Eurasia, along with ongoing ones in sub-Saharan Africa and South and Southeast Asia, created new tides of refugees, while a growing norm of humanitarian intervention meant that external states were more likely to intervene to assist them. Most spectacularly, in the aftermath of 9/11, the lowly visa officer, both in the U.S. Foreign Service and in many other countries' diplomatic corps, was raised from bureaucratic obscurity and made the first line of defense against the influx of potential "terrorists."

By and large, however, the political science field has not kept up with such changes in the importance of migration as a political issue. The study of international migration is a relative newcomer to political science. Its natural home has long been in departments of sociology, anthropology, and demography. Where political science has drifted into migration issues, it has usually been in only two areas: the study of immigration as a security threat—one of the "soft security" concerns increasingly analyzed in the security studies subfield—or the study of the determinants of immigration policy in receiving states (for example, why some states adopt more liberal policies than others, and how these policies intersect with conceptions of citizenship).[4]

But there are clearly several areas in which the core interests of political scientists, particularly comparative politics specialists, intersect with the concerns of other social scientists who have long studied migration. Migration cuts to the heart of how politicians and citizens define the polity: who can and cannot be a member and how such questions are decided. It is a good rough measure of state capacity—the degree to which the state is capable of regulating movement in and out of its borders—and the policy area on which much else that the state does depends. It can play a role in electoral politics, by changing the structure of voting populations and by becoming a rhetorical resource for politicians. It can change the nature of debate in a variety of public policy arenas, from tax policy and the provision of social services to state-supported education and the status of minority languages.

Migration is also perhaps the preeminent example of the link between domestic politics and international relations, and in this area the potential for large-scale migration from the postcommunist world attracted attention in the early 1990s. Young people, especially in the former Soviet Union, seemed to evince a strong willingness to move abroad. Conflicts from Moldova to Azerbaijan to Tajikistan pushed people from their homes. The economic attractiveness of Western Europe and North America also seemed to be an irresistible magnet. In the first half of the decade, several scholars and policy analysts predicted a vast wave of migrants, both legal and illegal, from the former Communist world, a wave that would put an immediate strain on social systems in the target states and bleed off the productive potential of the postcommunist countries.[5]

Most of these fears turned out to be unfounded. By and large, observers overestimated the willingness of Eastern Europeans to move permanently and underestimated the power of restrictive immigration policies in Western Europe as a discouragement to migration. After an initial upsurge in the early 1990s, permanent emigration from the postcommunist world, especially from Central Europe to the EU, decreased as the decade continued.[6] In certain areas, however, population movements have been significant, and they have begun to have an impact on domestic politics and international relations in Eastern Europe and Eurasia.

International immigration has been of three major types, although these categories are, to some degree, overlapping.

Long-Term International Migration

The flow of permanent migrants out of postcommunist Europe and Eurasia rose rapidly in the late 1980s, peaked at all-time highs in most countries in the early 1990s, then fell off as the decade progressed (see table 6.1). In part, this pattern was the result of the exhaustion of pent-up demand for migration; however, it also reflected the gradual tightening of immigration laws in receiving countries. Considerable numbers of

TABLE 6.1
Migration Flows between Eastern Europe/Eurasia and the
West, 1980–1998 (Documented migration only)

Years	Emigration from Eastern Europe and Eurasia to the Developed West	Immigration to Eastern Europe and Eurasia from the Developed West
1980–1984	1,167,000	511,000
1985–1989	2,708,000	746,000
1990–1994	6,074,000	1,811,000
1995–1998	3,255,000	1,442,000

Source: Population Division, Department of Economic and Social Affairs, United Nations Secretariat, International Migration from Countries with Economies in Transition: 1980–1999 (New York: United Nations, 2002), 1.

migrants were able to take advantage of their special status as members of "unredeemed" ethnic minorities, such as Jews and German *Aussiedler*, who benefited from special laws facilitating immigration to Israel and Germany. Even for these privileged groups, however, permanent immigration declined throughout the decade.

Yet this general trend masked two other important developments. One was an increase in the flow of asylum seekers to Western Europe and North America in the late 1990s. As channels of regular migration narrowed, potential migrants found asylum laws an attractive, although uncertain, route to a new life in advanced democracies. The traditional first ports of call for migrants—Germany, Austria, Italy—had tightened their asylum policies already in the early part of the decade, and the flow of newcomers was redirected toward countries with more liberal regimes farther to the west, such as Britain and Canada. Evidence that migrants use asylum applications strategically—a backup route abroad if other forms of legal migration are closed off—comes from the simple fact that the level of political repression or the presence of armed conflict in the sending country has never been a clear predictor of the likely source of asylum applicants. Throughout the 1990s, the largest number of applicants in Western Europe came, predictably, from the former Yugoslavia, but the second-largest source was Romania, which experienced no significant social violence. Slovak asylum applications skyrocketed *after* the political demise of the authoritarian president, Vladimir Meciar. Moldovan applications increased *after* the end of the war in the secessionist Transnistria region.

Second, short-term labor migration accelerated in the 1990s. The mechanism seems to be the classic push-pull in sending and receiving states: surplus labor in the poorer postcommunist countries and labor shortages (at particular wage levels) in the richer postcommunist countries and in Western Europe. This form of movement can be either extremely short-term (a weekend) or rather longer (a year or more); it may, of course, be legal or illegal. Small-scale traders take advantage of multiple-entry visas and set up shop in border regions between wealthier and poorer countries, establishing sprawling weekend markets that are now almost universally known in Western and Eastern Europe alike as "Russian bazaars." Longer-term immigrants may gain work permits for legal employment. In the better-off postcommunist states, most of the legal labor migrants are from other parts of the postcommunist world. In the late 1990s, over 40 percent of work permits in the Czech Republic were granted to citizens of Ukraine, and nearly 50 percent of those in Hungary went to citizens of Romania.[7]

Forced Migration and Refugees

The wars of the Communist succession—in the former Yugoslavia and across the former Soviet Union—produced a wave of refugees and internally displaced persons (IDPs). The conflicts increased the number of asylum seekers in Western Europe and put pressure on overburdened governments that bordered the conflict zones. The cessation of violence in most of the conflicts by the mid-1990s led to a decrease in international migration from these zones, but in some instances IDPs were still in dire straits. In Azerbaijan some 570,000 IDPs remained without permanent resettlement after the end of fighting in the Nagorno-Karabakh conflict of 1994. In Georgia over 250,000 IDPs were in a similar predicament because of the continuing standoff over the status of the secessionist regions of Abkhazia and South Ossetia. Some half a million or more refugees have fled the wars in Chechnya. By the early 2000s, these problems had become the concern not so much of international relief agencies, which had largely wound down their operations in the postcommunist world, but rather of immigration bodies in particular states. The most savvy potential migrants were learning that IDP status could be parlayed into a reasonable case for asylum in the EU or North America.

Transit Migration and Postcommunist States as Destinations

An unexpected dimension of international migration in the region has been the rise of former Communist states as transit countries for migrants from farther afield; over time, some of these original transit migrants have even come to see the postcommunist countries as permanent destinations. Especially in the postcommunist north—Poland, Hungary, the Czech Republic, and the Baltic states—the relatively better economic conditions have made these countries attractive destinations for migrants from the postcommunist south, the Middle East, and East and Southeast Asia. Likewise, in Romania and the Balkans, the relatively lax border controls have made these countries attractive staging grounds for eventual illegal migration to the European Union. Throughout the region, loose visa and asylum laws encouraged immigration in the first half of the decade; however, as some countries began to alter their immigration policies in advance of their accession to the European Union, legal immigration began to fall off. In 2000 the Czech Republic instituted a visa regime covering migrants from most of the countries of the former Soviet Union. Estonia, Poland, Bulgaria, and Hungary have adopted similarly restrictive policies.[8] Those new restrictions were cemented with the enlargement of the EU to include eight former Communist states in May 2004. Unlike in the early years of the postcommunist transition, a clear migration barrier now cuts through the former Communist world itself.

Case Studies

Studying migration across Eastern Europe and Eurasia is not easy. Weak states find it difficult to collect data. Strong states have an incentive to falsify data in order to present their citizens as generally happy, prosperous, and disinclined to leave. Individuals have an incentive to misrepresent their preferences to migrate and generally to stay below the radar of state institutions, including census bureaus and border guards. In any setting, finding out why people move is difficult. A 2001 survey by the International Organization for Migration (IOM) found that over a quarter of irregular migrants transiting through Bosnia into the European Union were doing so because of political repression. Yet it is difficult to know to what extent this response may have been conditioned by simple farsightedness. Declaring political repression to a nosy IOM official might be the first step toward filing an asylum claim within an EU state.

More than in other areas of political life, migrants seek to avoid the state altogether. It is not surprising, therefore, that people who study them have likewise tended to leave the state out of their analyses. The following case studies present two examples of how states matter in international migration and how institutions—formal, government institutions and the informal ones that underlie all social order—intersect with ethnicity, sometimes in unexpected ways.

Kin-States, Migration, and Diaspora Laws

Almost every country in postcommunist Europe and Eurasia is defined, at least in part, as a national state, the political instantiation of a distinct, culturally defined nation's struggle for liberation. Yet all of the states that are so defined also have a portion of the nation located outside the national homeland, communities that were left out of the territorial changes that produced the countries' current boundaries.

Over the last decade, most of these imperfect nation-states have developed specific laws that define their relationship with the unredeemed portions of the national community; these laws might be termed "diaspora laws."[9] In broad terms, the co-ethnic group is described as part of the greater national community, with certain rights and privileges to be expected from the kin-state, whereas the kin-state itself is cast as the "guarantor" or "protector" of the cultural, spiritual, and administrative (and sometimes political) rights of the kin group abroad. An individual's nationality, as distinct from his citizenship, is thus considered to be a sufficient reason for a kin-state's interest in his well-being.

The laws differ, however, in the kin-state's level of engagement with the co-ethnic minority. The Romanian law (1998) established a special center under the education ministry to sponsor cultural and educational activities among Romanians abroad. The Russian law (1999) guarantees Russian "compatriots" (which includes potentially any former citizen of the Soviet Union) the state's support "in exercising their civil, political, social, economic and cultural rights, and in preserving their distinctive identity." Bulgaria's law (2001) grants ethnic Bulgarians abroad the "right of protection of the Bulgarian state," with no clear indication of what form such "protection" would actually take. These laws are not a uniquely postcommunist phenomenon, of course. Several other European states, including Germany, Italy, Austria, and Greece, have long had laws that either guarantee co-ethnics privileged immigration rights and access to social services in the kin-state, or seek to promote the cultural and economic development of co-ethnics abroad.[10] The separation of citizenship from ethnicity is not even a particularly European phenomenon. In the 1990s, one of the greatest innovations in Mexico's relationship with Mexican-Americans was the state's effort to separate its relations with "co-nationals," people with an affective connection to Mexico and Mexican culture, from "co-citizens," people with Mexican citizenship and, crucially, voting rights.[11]

That such legal regimes exist is not surprising. There is often considerable domestic pressure to reach out to co-ethnic populations abroad; especially in instances in which the co-ethnics are the subject of discriminatory policies in their host states, the kin-state is the natural spokesperson for the rights of the embattled minority. The real questions about such laws are not why they come about, but rather what their actual effects are: Do they promote or hinder immigration—or have no effect? Do they promote either disloyalty to the host state or, instead, a unique form of multilocal politics? Do such laws promote the kind of cultural "unmixing," in Rogers Brubaker's phrase, that has characterized the postcommunist world over the last decade or more? An answer to these questions may lie in the newest and most technically detailed diaspora law in the region, Hungary's Act on Hungarians Living in Neighboring Countries, the so-called Status Law.

The Status Law applies to ethnic Hungarian communities in six states around Hungary, but given the size of the minorities in Slovakia and Romania (9.7 percent of Slovakia's population, 6.7 percent of Romania's), these are the host states most directly affected. The special relationship between Hungary and co-ethnic minorities was mentioned in Hungary's bilateral treaties with its neighbors throughout the 1990s, but the Status Law, adopted by the Hungarian parliament in June 2001, aimed to codify that relationship: to set out what precisely the legal and administrative ties between the state and the minority would be, and what status members of the minority were to have if they entered Hungary. Except for Germany's long-standing law on the "return" of ethnic Germans, Hungary's is so far the most serious attempt in the region to specify what the practical relationship between a kin-state and an ethnic minority should be.

The reaction of the Slovak and Romanian governments to the new law was swift. Both complained that the law represented an attempt to interfere in the domestic politics of a foreign state. They also argued that it unfairly privileged some of their citizens over others solely on the basis of ethnic affiliation. That was a particular concern to Romania, which at the time was still on the European Union's list of countries whose citizens required visas to enter the Schengen area; Romania was the last of the twelve EU accession countries still under a visa requirement. (That policy was lifted in January 2002.) Both states appealed to international organizations such as the OSCE High Commissioner on National Minorities and the Council of Europe to issue statements condemning the new law as a violation of international norms on citizenship and territorial integrity. In October 2001, on Romania's request, the Council of Europe's Venice Commission produced an analysis of the law. The various sides in this dispute interpreted the report differently. The Romanians and Slovaks said the text condemned the law; the Hungarians said it supported it. But over the course of 2002, active diplomacy by Hungary and the recasting of several provisions in the law helped ease tensions, although plenty of problems remained.[12] An amended version of the law was finally adopted in June 2003.

It is easy to regard the Status Law, and indeed most of the other laws on co-ethnic populations abroad, as a simple attempt to reach out to a distinct group based on criteria of identity other than citizenship. At worst, such laws can even seem like violations of concepts of territorial integrity, as the Romanians and Slovaks argued, or perhaps like a form of "virtual nationalism."[13] But the fascinating thing about the Status Law is its implicit linkage of ethnicity and migration.

The Status Law should not be characterized primarily as an effort to craft a role for the kin-state in the life of "its" diaspora. That function, in fact, is usually covered by reciprocal clauses in interstate treaties of friendship and good-neighborliness (for example, Article 11 of the 1996 Romanian-Hungarian treaty). Rather, the Status Law concerns the relationship between a kin-state—or, more properly, simply the state—and noncitizens who enter the state through legal channels. The Status Law governs access to social services, work permits, and other aspects of short- and long-term migration for co-ethnic citizens of neighboring states once they reach Hungary. It does not, however, specifically ease permanent immigration or allow easy access to citizenship, as do classic "laws on return" such as those in Germany or Israel. Indeed, the Hungarian law has to do with the minority's "status" inside Hungary, not with Hungary's status among the co-ethnic community abroad.[14]

As a result, Hungary's law is primarily about the relationship between a kin-state and individuals, not about minority populations as collectivities. That distinction is important. The Status Law has nothing to say about communal governance in the host state or about group rights. It is silent on the question of cultural institutions abroad, such as responsibility for the maintenance of churches, schools, or clubs (something, again, usually covered in bilateral agreements).[15] It has nothing to say about the use of the minority's language in social interactions or in relations with government institutions. Although often criticized as promoting "group rights," the Status Law is quintessentially individual in its language and application.

Diaspora laws such as Hungary's are relatively new; most were passed only in the very late 1990s or early 2000s, although they build on a much longer tradition of similar legal regimes in Western Europe. So far, however, little evidence indicates that they have encouraged migration from kin-states to host states; that movement occurred mainly in the early 1990s, long before the diaspora laws were on the books. There is a reason for this: if Hungary's Status Law is representative of a general trend, diaspora laws are in fact the antithesis of "diaspora politics"—the effort by a kin-state to leverage its co-ethnic minority abroad to influence domestic politics in or international relations with the host state.[16] They are not simply the product of a kin-state's desire to "protect" members of the nation abroad. Rather, they respond to a need to regularize a relationship with the group deemed most likely to migrate from poorer areas to a relatively more privileged kin-state. Ethnic identity, in this instance, matters less as an impetus for policy making than as a convenient predictor of the most migration-prone group abroad.

Seeing diaspora laws such as Hungary's as simply an outgrowth of a government's desire for a privileged relationship with its co-ethnic community abroad rather misses the point. The special relationship emerges from a desire by states to control migration, not from their desire to encourage it (or, much less, from their desire to change territorial borders). The leveraging of diasporas turns out to be more about keeping people out than trying to "return" them to the homeland. It is not surprising, then, that one of the most energetic proponents of diaspora laws, Hungary, is also one of those states in Central Europe first in line to join the EU—countries that have been most concerned about the influx of potential migrants once the border of the EU, and of the common migration regime known as the Schengen area, shifts to the east.[17]

Brigid Fowler has argued that diaspora laws are an example of the rise of "fuzzy citizenship" in Europe, in which multilocal identities and multiple definitions of the polity can exist at the same time and for the same individual.[18] One wonders, however, if Hungary's law and others like it are rather more prosaic: an attempt to regularize the movement of potential migrant populations from neighboring states and to take advantage of their labor capacity, but to limit their full integration into the societies in which they move. That has been the pattern followed by most advanced postindustrial states since World War II, and it may be repeating itself in the postcommunist world. For all the rhetoric surrounding a kin-state's duty to defend the interests of "its" ethnic minority abroad, the most advanced of the diaspora laws—Hungary's—looks little different in real intent from the immigration policies pursued by other economically successful states.

At the moment, the content of diaspora laws is a mixed bag. Some of the laws are mainly declarative. Others combine policy toward co-ethnic populations with policy toward expatriate citizens. Still others deal mainly with the general support of the kin-state for the cultural development of the diaspora inside the host state. But Hungary's law may well be a sign of things to come throughout the region. Kin-states that find themselves the most attractive destinations for future migration—either because they will soon become members of the European Union or because they are simply better-off economically than most of their neighbors—may well follow Hungary's course: attempting to combine a special relationship with an ethnically defined diaspora with the desire to limit that diaspora's ability to participate fully in the polity.[19]

Sex-Workers and Social Networks

From the standpoint of research and policy, few subjects in the international migration field are more obviously important than the issue of trafficking in women.[20] Beginning in the late 1990s, an upsurge in interest in this phenomenon occurred, and a variety of states, multilateral institutions, and nongovernmental organizations began to develop policies and programs to address the problem. In 2000 the United States created an office to oversee policy on combating human trafficking, especially forced prostitution and the international commerce in sex workers. The office, housed within the Department of State, is now required by law to issue an annual "trafficking in persons" report and to survey the steps taken by the United States and other countries against trafficking, much like the annual reporting and certification processes in the "war on drugs" and the "global war on terrorism."[21]

Several countries and international organizations have adopted specific legislation on trafficking. The European Commission has developed programs to encourage judicial cooperation and has allocated funds for victim assistance. Various EU member states, most notably Ireland, now have a clear legal framework for prosecuting traffickers on their soil. Multilateral and nongovernmental organizations have also been extremely active in this field. The UN High Commissioner for Refugees has set up working groups on the problem. Human Rights Watch and other monitoring organizations have issued numerous reports. Specialized NGOs such as the Coalition Against Trafficking in Women and the Global Survival Network have provided forums that bring together organizations interested in women's rights, trafficking, sexual violence, and related themes.

It is not difficult to see why the issue of female trafficking has garnered particular attention. Women, and often young girls, are moved across international frontiers and are put into roles that are at best indentured servitude and at worst outright slavery. They are made to work in clubs and restaurants and are sometimes engaged in the pornography industry, all in addition to being expected to service paying clients and their (usually male) bosses. They are often prevented from making contact with their homes or families. Their passports or other identity documents are seized, making them wholly reliant on their traffickers in an otherwise alien environment.

The problem is not restricted to any particular region, and the reach of the coercive sex industry is genuinely global, with both short-distance migrations from poor villages to burgeoning cities in the developing world and long-distance journeys directly to Europe and North America. As one example, in 2001 police uncovered a trafficking scheme operated by a research assistant at the University of Texas at El Paso; the scheme brought women from Uzbekistan to work as nude dancers in the United States.[22] As with the drug trade, the precise dimensions of the business are difficult to gauge, and there are few reliable data on the scale of industry. Unlike the drug trade, however, estimates of the scale of the problem come from assisted returns, not from arrests, which makes gathering reliable information even more difficult. Traffickers and prostitutes are notoriously tough to apprehend, especially because prostitution is in some measure legal in many countries and because few countries have adequate legislation for prosecuting traffickers. The disparity between estimates and the real world of prosecution is evident in a revealing figure. The International Organization for Migration estimates that some seven hundred thousand women are trafficked globally each year, of which a sizable number—perhaps several hundred thousand—go to or through Eastern Europe. But in a September 2002 raid by several Eastern European law enforcement bodies, only 237 women and 293 suspected traffickers were arrested across the region.[23]

Beyond assessing the scope of the problem, another difficulty has been determining exactly why and how women enter the global sex industry in the first place. Given that there are many ways to move beyond borders—legal migration, nonsexual illegal migration, guest-worker status—how is it that such large numbers of women become involved in trafficking? In other words, is sexual trafficking purely a human rights concern, or does it intersect with the classic migration issue of "human smuggling," the illicit but (in theory) noncoercive and nonexploitive movement of people across borders?[24] Of course, in some instances, outright abduction is the simple answer. Yet this form of trafficking seems relatively rare compared with the much larger number of women who enter the system to some extent voluntarily—women who are themselves complicit in the illegal movement across frontiers, if not in the sexualized businesses in which they will eventually become engaged.[25]

In the postcommunist world, another problem has been understanding the significant disparities in the sources of trafficked women. An overwhelming number of women who make their way directly into the EU or into first-stage migration countries such as Bosnia or Albania come from a surprisingly small number of countries farther east, particularly Moldova, Romania, and Ukraine. In 2000, of the 652 trafficked women whom the IOM assisted in voluntarily returning to their countries of origin from Southeastern Europe (including Greece), 48 percent were from Moldova, 26 percent from Romania, and 12 percent from Ukraine.[26] Some parts of Eastern Europe and the former Soviet Union are barely on the trafficking map. The south Caucasus states and central Asia, for example, are a comparatively insignificant source of trafficked women (although the flow of women from these areas to the United Arab Emirates and Turkey does seem to be increasing). In addition, some countries that are extremely important as routes or as first-stage target destinations before entry into the EU—particularly Turkey and Bosnia— seem to be less important as sources of women.

There are two obvious answers to the questions about why women become involved and about the different levels of participation in trafficking in different states. First, it is often argued, women from the most economically depressed regions are the most willing to move abroad to earn money by whatever means; and second, women become involved in trafficking because they are tricked into doing so. Both answers have become part of the way in which the trafficking problem is generally conceptualized. As Michael Specter of the *New York Times* reported in 1998, "[S]elling naive and desperate young women into sexual bondage has become one of the fastest-growing criminal enterprises in the robust global economy."[27] (There is also a third explanation, of course. At a conference in Odessa, when I raised the question of why women from Ukraine are more frequently trafficked than, say, Georgians, the Ukrainian presidential advisor on women's issues—a woman, incidentally— responded, "It is because Ukrainian women are more beautiful." The subjective preferences of traffickers cannot be discounted, but this is almost certainly not of primary significance.)

None of these answers is adequate. In the first place, no clear correlation exists between economic deprivation and participation in trafficking. Women who end up in Western Europe or farther afield are, by and large, from the most economically depressed states in the former Soviet Union, measured according to general macroeconomic indicators. But within this group the depth of misery is no predictor of involvement in the interstate sex-worker industry. Moldova and Georgia, for example, are similar on several macroeconomic indicators, but the latter is far less important as a source country for trafficked women than the former. Moreover, women who become involved in the sex industry are by and large from cities, especially national capitals, where the effects of the economic crisis are generally more muted than in the countryside.[28] If economic factors were the primary source of differentiation in the industry, one would expect rural migrants to be most vulnerable.[29]

Second, arguments about economic misery and trickery as the primary motivations and means of sex-worker trafficking leave out what seems to be one of the most important players in the trafficking game: states. One of the major criticisms that human rights organizations have leveled at the annual U.S. State Department report on international trafficking has been the department's refusal to address corruption and state complicity in trafficking in many parts of the world.[30] Rather, the global trafficking industry is attributed to the specter of "organized crime" or, particularly in Eastern Europe, to an ill-defined "Russian mafia."[31] Trafficked women do not usually sneak across borders, however; they and their handlers are allowed to do so by state authorities. Sex workers in receiving states do not ply their trade clandestinely; they often work in licensed clubs as hostesses, waitresses, and dancers, even though local police authorities know that the clubs also function as illegal brothels. The lines of state complicity are in many cases very long, indeed. State-licensed travel agents book tickets on state-supported airlines. State-licensed taxi drivers shuttle women to and from airports. Receiving countries issue visas. Local police authorities turn a blind eye to, or actively benefit from, the sex industry itself.

The obvious arguments about the sources of international trafficking are problematic for a third reason: they overemphasize forced prostitution as the essence of international trafficking. The standard narrative about sex-worker migrants runs as follows. Young women answer an advertisement in a local newspaper that promises work abroad in the hospitality industry—as waitresses or hostesses, for instance—in glamorous and cosmopolitan settings in Western Europe or North America. Their passage abroad is arranged by the "businessmen" who sponsored the advertisements. Once at their destination, however, the women learn that the jobs turn out to require working as exotic dancers. The women are eventually forced into prostitution, usually on the pretext of paying back their handlers for the passage from their home countries.

This is the narrative that has largely defined the U.S. and, to a great degree, international responses to the trafficking issue. Congressional hearings on the matter have featured testimony by women who confirm that they were misled from the moment they first read of the possibility of work or marriage abroad in their local newspaper. But this narrative does not fit perfectly with the reality of trafficking as a general phenomenon. As interviews with trafficked women have confirmed, the vast majority of trafficked women are aware that they will be involved in some wing of the sex industry when they go abroad, at least as exotic dancers, perhaps even as prostitutes.[32] The clarity begins with the newspaper advertisement itself. In Russian-speaking areas, an advertisement for women *bez kompleksov*—with no complexes—is a clear signal that the employment involves some form of sex work. In many countries, a social stigma is attached to sexual labor, but that stigma also admits certain interpretations. In a survey of over a thousand women in Ukraine, the IOM found that all age groups agreed that "a job in the sex industry" was an unacceptable form of employment abroad; however, when asked if being a "dancer" or "stripper" was acceptable, all the women in the 15–17 age bracket answered yes.[33]

From a legal perspective, the real problem with international trafficking is not the sex. In most countries, sex work in one form or another, from pornography to prostitution, is a legal activity. Rather, the central issue is illegal servitude. Women typically are stripped of their passports and other identity papers; they are made to work without pay; and they are prevented from leaving their "employer" or returning home. It is because the reality of interstate trafficking comes up against the narrative of forced prostitution that human rights organizations sometimes even underemphasize women's own complicity. If one is trying to sell a U.S. senator on the importance of combating trafficking, it is clear which narrative is a better strategy: one that features an innocent woman taken from her home and forced to work as a sex slave abroad, or one that features a woman who is complicit in her own illegal migration but perhaps finds herself in over her head once she arrives abroad.[34]

Arguments about economic deprivation and narratives of trickery fail to consider the context in which trafficking occurs—the formal and informal institutions, some drawn along ethnic lines, that facilitate movement and, in part, account for differentiation in routes, rates, and ramifications of the phenomenon across the postcommunist world.

Weak States and the Geography of Movement

The passage of many first-stage migrants—that is, from one part of Eastern Europe to another, before movement into Turkey or the EU—often takes place through legal channels. Women simply board airplanes with tickets, passports, and visas in hand. In many instances, however, migration itself is illegal, effected clandestinely across a poorly guarded international frontier. The relative weakness of the border regime in any country is a reasonable indicator of the strength of human trafficking through it, and countries that have experienced separatist violence or have unrecognized secessionist regimes on their own territory are either sources of trafficked women or important transit zones: Moldova (host to the unrecognized Dnestr Moldovan Republic), Georgia (with the unrecognized republics of South Ossetia and Abkhazia), Bosnia (with its largely self-governing but non-sovereign Republika Srpska), Serbia-Montenegro (with the UN-administered Kosovo), and Macedonia (with the western region around Tetovo largely under local Albanian control). Of course, each of these states has an incentive to overemphasize state weakness as a facilitating condition for trafficking, largely because it absolves state institutions from any active role in the trafficking industry. But even if state institutions made a good-faith effort to combat the phenomenon, the very weakness of the institutions—including the basic inability of many states to control the territory that they claim as their own—would hinder their efforts.

Geography is also important here. For example, rivers account for some forty percent of the border between Bosnia and Croatia and Serbia-Montenegro; of the more than four hundred potential crossing points, only fifty-two are registered and regularly monitored.[35] The border between Georgia and Turkey is easily transgressed, by either land or sea. The border between Russia and Georgia, including via the two secessionist areas (Abkhazia and South Ossetia), is not adequately controlled. The distance between Albania and Italy across the strait of Otranto can be crossed in very short order, especially in high-speed boats used by traffickers and smugglers. Over the last decade, the assistance of the International Organization for Migration and the EU has been crucial in helping postcommunist countries improve and professionalize border crossings. For countries that still have preternaturally weak state structures, however, even the most incompetent traffickers are able to move people across the postcommunist world and even into the EU with relative ease.

Visa and Asylum Regimes

The visa and asylum regimes of postcommunist states and EU members are a critical dimension of the trafficking phenomenon. In most instances, postcommunist states (and Turkey) have relatively liberal visa regimes, especially countries that are not yet on the list of EU accession states. That means that first-stage migration from the former Soviet Union to Eastern Europe through legal channels is relatively easy. The jump from Eastern Europe to the EU can then be accomplished illegally through one of many trafficking networks in the Balkans or elsewhere, many of which use the routes previously outlined.

An estimated 400,000 to 500,000 migrants are smuggled into the EU each year, of which perhaps 50,000 arrive via Southeast Europe, principally through Bosnia and Albania.[36] Of these, a sizable number are trafficked women, many of whom enter first-stage migration countries legally. The numbers of transit migrants can be staggering. In 2000 just over 30,500 persons registered as "tourists" at Sarajevo International Airport from Iran, Turkey, India, Bangladesh, and China; only about 6,000 were recorded as having left.[37] Obviously, not all or even most of these people are trafficked women, but they are certainly among their number. The point is that traffickers can use even legal channels of transit migration or nonexploitive smuggling networks for the first-stage move from the former Soviet Union to Eastern Europe.

States and Ethnic Networks

In transit countries in particular, there is an informal economy of human trafficking that has little or nothing to do with the sex industry itself. The taxi driver who transports migrants from an airport to a land crossing, the travel agent who books a flight or arranges fictional hotel accommodation, and the peasant who may allow a migrant to stay in his house are all part of the informal economy of human trafficking.[38] These networks often have an ethnic dimension, however, and it is here that we might look for clues to the differential rates of participation in female trafficking and the routes that traffickers use. Conclusive data on this phenomenon are still lacking, but what evidence exists suggests intriguing hypotheses about ethnicity, social networks, and exploitive migration.

Traffickers move people because doing so is profitable. Profit derives from three major sources: first, fees levied on the trafficked women before they leave their home countries, ostensibly for setting up a job in the target country, providing transportation or other overhead expenses and initial outlays borne by the trafficker; second, revenue produced by the labor of the women themselves, as dancers in nightclubs or as prostitutes; and third, the sale of women to other traffickers. Of these, the first and third are largely supplementary to the second. Women are rarely able to provide much of an up-front fee, which is one of the reasons that traffickers are able to hold over them the cost of their transport to the target country and to insist that they pay it back through the sex industry. Likewise, the "price" of women in trafficker-to-trafficker transactions seems to be remarkably low: in Albania in 2000, the market price was supposedly a thousand dollars, and women would be sold only if they became too "difficult to handle"—that is, by repeatedly attempting to escape, refusing to work, or publicly disgracing their (usually male) bosses.[39]

Given the importance of women's labor as the primary source of profit, traffickers desire stable routes for moving women from east to west—that is, a stable network of relationships that will ensure that tickets can be purchased, visas granted (or forged), ground transportation made available, and the necessary state institutions circumvented (or co-opted) along the way. In many instances, these networks can be built on top of preexisting ethnic or regional connections. Such networks are sometimes given the catchall label "mafias," but they are usually very different from the extensive system of "private protection" provided by the classic Sicilian Mafia model.[40] Rather, they are simply informal groups of friends and family, often from the same ethnic group and the same town or village, who are then able to extend their primary relationships across international borders. These networks can also be self-reproducing. Significant numbers of recruiters—up to 70 percent in Ukraine, on one estimate—are women who return to their own towns or neighborhoods to recruit even further waves of women from the same ethnic group or region.[41]

These networks, which often extend all the way down to the city or neighborhood level of a woman's country of origin, provide the essential sanctioning mechanism that allows the trafficking system to work. When a trafficker says that a woman's family will suffer if she tries to escape or goes to the police, it is usually not an idle threat. A cell phone call can be sufficient to command an associate in the home city or village to carry it out. Indeed, without this mechanism, women would have little disincentive to attempt to escape from traffickers in the host country or, even easier, to confess to police when a brothel or nightclub is raided and the women taken into custody. Police and human rights groups, however, report that women are almost universally unwilling to testify against the men who have kept them in effective bondage. The very real ability of traffickers to sanction women—and their families back in the sending country—who do not comply with the system depends on the network itself. The sanction can also be a positive one. In Armenia, traffickers' agents will occasionally bring money to a woman's family and tell them that their daughter sent it from abroad. That scheme creates goodwill in local communities and also helps ensure a future supply of women prepared to use the traffickers' services if they decide to go abroad.[42]

In attempting to account for the variability of women who are trafficked and the regions they come from, researchers have traditionally looked mainly at classic push-pull factors: the depth of misery in the sending country or the desire for sex workers in the host country. But the relative strength of the social networks that facilitate movement has gone largely unexplored. An explanation may well lie in the broader structure of organized crime—which forms of illegal commerce are the most profitable, and what kind of networks facilitate which kinds of crime. In other words, it is not that Ukrainian women are more desperate or that social institutions in Ukraine are more lax (or, indeed, that Ukrainian women are more beautiful, as my Odessa interlocutor argued) that accounts for the differential levels of participation in international trafficking. Rather, it is the existence of a broad, interstate network of traffickers who, in the case of Ukraine, Moldova, and Romania, have found the business of moving people to be particularly lucrative, and those networks are in large part built on top of older linkages of ethnic group and regional provenance. Given other circumstances, members of the same network might be engaged in smuggling hazelnuts and copper wiring (as in Abkhazia) or Mercedes cars and heroin (as in South Ossetia). In some cases, however, the commodity is women.

Theorizing Ethnicity and Movement

The unifying theme of the two case studies is the degree to which institutions—both the formal ones of states and the informal ones of social networks—might trump ethnic identity as an explanation for particular migration policies and types of migration. As the first case study showed, what seems to be an "ethnic" phenomenon—the effort by states to reach out to co-ethnic, diaspora populations abroad—may in fact be another version of a state's attempt to limit new immigrants to particular labor markets. The second case study illustrated the ways in which ethnicity might matter less as an explanation for why and how immigrants move abroad—why, for example, members of particular ethnic groups seem more involved in female trafficking—than as a convenient label for the ability to sanction at a distance. In both cases, ethnicity is both less and more than it might appear. It is less in the sense that it rarely functions as an inscrutable form of "identity," working itself out in the lives and behaviors of individuals, much like the mysterious *Geist* of German idealist philosophers. It is more in the sense that it masks a variety of social networks of trust and mechanisms of sanction, all of which need to be investigated on their own terms.

Especially in instances in which ethnic allegiances are strongly felt, it is tempting to reify "ethnicity" as a catchall cause for complex social phenomena, from the relationship between kin-states and diasporas to the differential rates of participation in sexual trafficking. But without an understanding of the particular constraints on ethnicity, or the particular social institutions through which identity is channeled, one risks attributing far too much power to individual identity as a cause of such varied outcomes as ethnic conflict, ethnic separatism, migration, state collapse, and any other social ills afflicting states in the postcommunist world. Focusing on the ethnic dimensions of institutions, both formal and informal, can be one way of unraveling the many strands of ethnicity and seeing which are useful in explaining a particular dimension of international migration.

How might one begin to unravel these strands? In a recent survey of the state of comparative politics, David Laitin argued that there is an emerging consensus that the subfield's core methodology consists of three things: broad statistical research to identify overarching patterns, theory refinement based on deductive understandings of human behavior, and ground-level fieldwork to test hypotheses and to add nuance.[43] The third dimension of this method has been taken for granted by researchers on international migration; more than in most social science fields, immigration specialists have long assumed that a perfectly reasonable way of trying to understand why people behave as they do is simply to ask them. But the first two dimensions of Laitin's emerging consensus are rather more novel in this field, and employing them might speak not only to the relationship between ethnicity and movement but also to the relationship among the study of international migration, postcommunist studies, and comparative politics in general.

First, the systematic, statistical study of the ethnic dimensions of migration is only beginning. Numbers are notoriously difficult to acquire, largely because so much of international migration as a phenomenon takes place off the books, through extralegal channels. That is even more the case in instances in which there is a clear ethnic component to movement: when migrants are seeking to escape from a repressive government in a sending state, when they rely primarily on ethnic networks to circumvent state institutions, or when they have reason to believe that they would be targeted because of their ethnicity in the receiving state.

An important step, however, is to try to develop better ways of understanding broad patterns. The use of systematic surveys or structured interviews among immigrant or at-risk groups is one method, although as the experience of the postcommunist world in the 1990s illustrated, survey results can overstate the willingness of people to move abroad without taking into account their ability to move. Moreover, national-level data for many postcommunist countries are unlikely to be better in the foreseeable future than they are at present. Not only are data-collecting agencies weak (or even nonexistent), but also data on the flow and stock of people—on emigration, immigration, and total population—are usually highly politicized. Recent debates about the form and structure of censuses in the Russian Federation and elsewhere are ample testimony of the degree to which simply counting people coming in, leaving, and staying is not a purely academic enterprise.[44]

Second is the need to question the concept of ethnicity and to link up ethnic politics with deductive theorizing about human behavior. In much of the literature on ethnicity, we are often asked to make certain heroic assumptions about the determinants of political behavior. We are asked to assume that most people, most of the time, are willing to sacrifice a great deal for an imagined nation or ethnic group; that they will leave home or fight to the death for a perceived transgression to their national pride; or that they would rather suffer untold hardship than spend one more hour in the company of someone of an opposing ethnic group, now deemed to be an enemy. Only recently, however, have both scholars and journalists begun to question whether, in fact, there might be more to the story of ethnicity and politics than the mysterious workings of "identity."[45] That is surely the way forward in thinking about ethnicity and migration, as well.

For example, states are critical players in the migration game, but not always in obvious senses. State institutions make and implement migration policy and seek to remedy the uncontrolled movement of people across their borders; there is obviously no "migration policy" without the institutions that formulate it. But states are more than policy-making engines, responding to the desires of migrants who want to get in and the desires of domestic political actors who want to keep them out. As the two case studies have shown, states can actually end up influencing migration in ways that a simple reading of their policies on migration would not reveal.

If Hungary's Status Law is representative of an emerging trend, the laws on ethnic diasporas across Eastern Europe and the former Soviet Union may be a way of ensuring that the diasporas stay in their host states, not return permanently to their ostensible homelands. The rhetoric of nationalists can thus be misleading. As the Hungarian Status Law reveals, what was initially perceived by nationalists in both host states and kin-states as a genuine effort either to help the diaspora or to interfere in host state affairs actually turned out to be a way of limiting migration. Likewise, in the case of sex workers, the facilitating policies of some states—the relatively liberal visa regimes in transit states along the EU border, for example—can have an important impact on the routes via which traffickers move women into the EU.

Ethnicity matters in equally obvious ways, and much of the migration literature has been helpful in charting why particular groups might choose to migrate at particular times, the impact of ethnic migrants on ethnic relations in receiving states, the power of identity issues in providing a context for violence among migrant co-ethnics, and the complex relationship between sending and receiving states.[46] What has been less clear, however, has been the ethnic linkages and social networks that might lead migrants to move in the first place and then ease their passage once on the road, or the precise effects of state policy on the ethnic affiliations of potential migrant groups. Taking ethnicity seriously means attributing less to the imponderable power of "identity" and exploring the actual mechanisms through which ethnic affinity really matters—or does not.

In an important book on patterns of global migration, Paul Massey and others argue that theories of international migration must contain at least four elements: an account of the structural forces that promote emigration; an account of the forces that attract immigration; a microtheory of the motivations and goals of individual migrants; and a theory of the social and economic structures that link regions of out- and in-migration.[47] Most of the literature in the social sciences has focused on the first three of these areas. A greater appreciation of the institutional dimensions of migration can help flesh out the fourth element of Massey's comprehensive theory. I have dealt with only two factors that the post-communist cases can contribute to theory building in this regard, but there are many more. Eastern Europe and Eurasia are regions that, taken as a whole, have more weak states than strong ones. They have experienced periods of intense internal and interstate migration, and they now straddle the borders of a political entity, the EU, seeking to harmonize immigration policy among its existing members and accession countries.

They are regions in which migration is wrapped up in fundamental questions about state- and nation-building and about who is a legitimate citizen. They are regions in which these questions are still as thorny as they were in the immediate years after the collapse of Communism. There are thus few more propitious areas for exploring the mutual influences of the state, ethnicity, and movement.

7

NATIONAL MINORITIES IN POSTCOMMUNIST EUROPE

The Role of International Norms and European Integration

WILL KYMLICKA

Since 1989, we have witnessed a remarkable trend toward the internationalization of minority rights issues in the European context. A wide range of international institutions—including the Organization for Security and Cooperation in Europe (OSCE), the Council of Europe, the European Union, and NATO—is now actively involved in decision making about state-minority relations. These institutions formulate standards about how states should treat their minorities, monitor whether states are living up to these standards, and make recommendations about how to improve state-minority relations. They also offer a wide range of rewards for countries that comply with these international standards and recommendations, and impose penalties on countries that fail to do so. Although these norms are in principle supposed to apply to all European countries, West and East, the focus of these organizations has fallen almost exclusively on the postcommunist states of Central and Eastern Europe.

The precise details of how these various international organizations operate—their standards, monitoring functions, reporting procedures, and enforcement mechanisms—have been described elsewhere.[1] And though many of these institutions are still relatively new, they have made some attempts to evaluate the effectiveness of particular mechanisms in protecting minorities and preventing or reducing ethnic violence in postcommunist Europe.[2]

In this chapter, I step back and ask more general questions about this trend toward internationalizing minority rights. The very project of internationalizing minority rights implies that there are such things as "international norms" (or at least "European standards") regarding the rights of national minorities. In reality, however, there are important disagreements about the rights of national minorities, both within the Western democracies, and between Western and Eastern Europe. In particular, there are deep disagreements about whether national minorities have a right to territorial autonomy or self-government.

Given these disagreements, European organizations have tried to avoid appealing to such a right when formulating their international norms. Instead, they have relied heavily on two less controversial ideas: (1) the right to enjoy one's culture; and (2) the right to effective participation. European organizations have hoped that if these two rights are respected, there will be no need for, and no demand for, more controversial ideas of autonomy and self-government.

But the idea of self-government, though contested and resisted, cannot easily be avoided. It often reenters the debate through the back door, albeit in ad hoc ways. The result is various manifestations of confusion, ambiguity, and moral inconsistency in the application of international norms to postcommunist Europe. These ambiguities have short-term uses in deferring or papering over difficult issues, but the long-term prospects for the peaceful and democratic accommodation of minority nationalisms in postcommunist Europe require rethinking the nature and function of international norms of minority rights.

The Internationalization of Minority Rights in Postcommunist Europe

As Communism collapsed in Central and Eastern Europe in 1989, violent ethnic conflicts broke out. In retrospect, these violent conflicts have largely been confined to the Caucuses and the Balkans. But this was not clear at the time. In the early 1990s, many commentators feared that ethnic tensions would spiral out of control in wide swaths of postcommunist Europe. For example, predictions of civil war between the Slovak majority and Hungarian minority in Slovakia, or between the Estonian majority and Russian minority in Estonia, were not uncommon. Overly optimistic predictions about the rapid replacement of Communism with liberal democracy were supplanted with overly pessimistic predictions about the replacement of Communism with ethnic war.

Faced with these potentially dire trends, the Western democracies in the early 1990s felt they had to do something. And they decided, in effect, to "internationalize" the treatment of national minorities in postcommunist Europe. They declared, in the words of the OSCE in 1990, that the status and treatment of national minorities "are matters of legitimate international concern, and consequently do not constitute exclusively an internal affair of the respective State."

The international community often makes pious declarations of its concern for the rights and well-being of peoples around the world, without intending to do much about it. But in this case, the West backed up its words with actions. The most important and tangible action was the decision by the European Union and NATO in December 1991 to make minority rights one of the four criteria that candidate countries had to meet in order to become members of these organizations. Since most postcommunist countries viewed membership in the EU and NATO as pivotal to their future prosperity and security, any "recommendations" that the West might make regarding minority rights were taken very seriously. As a result, minority rights moved to the center of postcommunist political life, a core component of the process of "rejoining Europe."

With the decision in 1990–91 that the treatment of minorities in postcommunist Europe was a matter of legitimate international concern, the next step was to create institutional mechanisms that could monitor how postcommunist countries were treating their minorities. Since 1991, therefore, various international bodies have been created with the mandate of monitoring the treatment of minorities, and of recommending changes needed to live up to European standards of minority rights. A crucial step here was the formation of the Office of the High Commissioner on National Minorities of the OSCE (OSCE-HCNM) in 1993, linked to OSCE mission offices in several postcommunist countries. Another important step occurred at the Council of Europe, which set up advisory bodies and reporting mechanisms as part of its Framework Convention on the Protection of National Minorities (FCNM) in 1995. The European Union and NATO did not themselves create new monitoring bodies specifically focused on minority rights,[3] but they have made clear that they support the work of the OSCE-HCNM and the Council of Europe, and expect candidate countries to cooperate with them as a condition of accession.

In short, Western states have made a serious commitment to internationalizing minority rights, embedded not only in formal declarations but also in a dense web of European institutions. An interesting question is why and how this commitment emerged. After all, the EU had shown very little interest in the question of minority rights prior to 1989, and had deliberately avoided including any reference to minority rights in its own internal principles. Nor have Western countries traditionally shown much interest in protecting minorities elsewhere around the world. On the contrary, Western states have often propped up governments in Africa, Asia, or Latin America that were known to be oppressive to their minorities, even to the point of selling military equipment with the knowledge that it would be used against minority groups (for example, selling arms to Indonesia to suppress minorities in Aceh and East Timor, or to Guatemala to suppress the Maya). So why did the West suddenly become a champion of minorities in postcommunist Europe?

One factor was humanitarian concern to stop the suffering of minorities facing persecution, mob violence, and ethnic cleansing. But humanitarian concern is rarely enough, on its own, to mobilize Western governments. A more self-interested reason was the belief that escalating ethnic violence would generate large-scale refugee movements into Western Europe, as indeed happened from Kosovo and Bosnia. Also, ethnic civil wars often create pockets of lawlessness that become havens for the smuggling of arms and drugs, or for other forms of criminality and extremism.

Another reason, more diffuse, was the sense in the West that the ability of postcommunist countries to manage their ethnic diversity was a test of their overall political maturity, and hence of their readiness to "rejoin Europe." As the general secretary of the Council of Europe put it, respect for minorities is a fundamental measure of a country's "moral progress."[4] The ability of a country to get its deficits under 3 percent of GDP (one of the other accession criteria) may be important from an economic point of view, but does not tell us much about whether the country will "fit" into European traditions and institutions.[5]

In short, for a complex mixture of humanitarian, self-interested, and ideological reasons, minority rights have became "internationalized" in Europe. Acceptance of the international monitoring and enforcement of these norms has become a test of a country's readiness for Europe. Meeting international norms of minority rights is seen as proof that a country has left behind its "ancient ethnic hatreds" and "tribal nationalisms," and is able to join a "modern" liberal and cosmopolitan Europe.

Defining European Minority Rights Norms

Between 1990 and 1993, all of the major Western organizations reached a rapid consensus that the treatment of national minorities by postcommunist countries should be a matter of international concern, and that there should be international mechanisms to monitor a country's compliance with international norms of minority rights.

This approach had one glaring problem, however: it presupposed that there were "international norms" or "European standards" of minority rights for postcommunist countries to comply with. In reality, there were no such standards. There were no formal declarations or conventions enumerating the rights of national minorities. Indeed, the very term "national minority rights" or "rights of national minorities" was largely unknown in the West.

Western countries differ greatly in how they talk about accommodating diversity. For example, some countries (for example, France, Greece, Turkey) simply deny that they have "minorities."[6] Other countries acknowledge that they have "minorities," but differ about what sorts of groups this term applies to. In some countries (for example, the UK), the term "minorities" generally refers to postwar migrant groups, typically from the Caribbean or South Asia, not to the historic Welsh or Scottish groups. In other Western countries (as in most of postcommunist Europe), it is the opposite: the term "minorities" typically refers to historic groups (like the Slovenes in Austria), not to postwar migrants (like the Turks in Austria), who are instead described as "foreigners."

So the term "minority" has different connotations across the West. In any event, in none of these countries was there widespread reference to general principles about "the rights of national minorities." Consider debates about Scots in the UK, or about Catalans in Spain, or about Slovenes in Austria. These debates were not phrased in the form that:

> all national minorities have a right to X;
> Scots/Catalans/Slovenes are a national minority;
> therefore Scots/Catalans/Slovenes have a right to X.

Claims of particular national groups are not deduced from some broader principle or theory about what "national minorities" as a category have "rights" to. Instead, the rights of particular groups are debated in terms of historic settlements, built up over time, by which various accommodations have been reached between different communities.

In fact, the term "national minority" had no legal status or meaning in any Western country prior to the adoption of the Framework Convention in 1995. No legislation in any Western country specified which groups were "national minorities" and which rights flowed from having this status. No Western country had an "Office of National Minorities" or a "Law on National Minorities."

In short, there was no Western discourse of "the rights of national minorities" prior to 1990, either within particular countries or across Europe as a whole. If you asked citizens or elites in Western Europe what were "the rights of national minorities," you would probably get a blank stare. So the decision to internationalize state-minority relations through the articulation of "European standards of the rights of national minorities" was, in a sense, a remarkable decision. That Western governments wanted to "do something" about ethnic conflict in postcommunist Europe was not surprising, but it was surprising that they chose do so in an idiom or vocabulary that was essentially foreign to the Western experience. As Chandler notes, Western countries were determined to develop European standards as a way of monitoring postcommunist countries, but they "had no conception of how to apply such policies in relation to their own minorities."[7]

How then were these international norms constructed? Observers with a long memory recalled that this question had been tackled earlier, at the last major period of imperial breakdowns after World War I, resulting in the "minority protection scheme" of the League of Nations. A mini-industry has arisen examining that older plan and trying to learn lessons from it for contemporary European debates.[8]

But the minority protection plan of the League of Nations was particularistic, not generalized. It involved multilateral treaties guaranteeing particular rights for particular minorities in particular (defeated) countries, while leaving many other minorities unprotected. It did not attempt to articulate general standards or international norms that all national minorities would be able to claim. That indeed was one reason that the idea of minority rights fell out of favor and largely disappeared from the postwar international law context, replaced with a focus on "human rights."

The idea of minority rights did not entirely disappear from international law, however. It retained a foothold in some of the human rights declarations at the United Nations. In fact, two quite different provisions at the UN could be seen as laying a foundation for international norms on the rights of national minorities. The first provision, dating back to the very Charter of the United Nations, and reaffirmed in Article 1 of the 1966 International Covenant on Civil and Political Rights (ICCPR), states that all "peoples" have a right to "self-determination" by which they can "freely determine their political status." The second provision, found in Article 27 of the same Covenant, states that members of minorities have the right to "enjoy their own culture," "in community with the other members of their group."[9]

These two provisions have been part of international law since at least 1966, and have been invoked by minorities around the world. But neither of them, as articulated by the UN's ICCPR, is adequate for the context of national minorities in postcommunist Europe. To oversimplify, we can say that for most national minorities, Article 1 (as traditionally understood) is too strong, and Article 27 (as traditionally understood) is too weak. Most national minorities need something in-between, and recent developments in Europe regarding minority rights are precisely an attempt to codify certain standards in between Articles 1 and 27.

The right to self-determination in Article 1 is too strong, for it has traditionally been interpreted to include the right to form one's own state. Precisely for this reason, its scope has been drastically restricted in international law. It has been limited by what is called the "salt-water thesis." The only "peoples" who have a right to independence are those subject to colonization from overseas; national minorities within a territorially contiguous state do not have a right to independence. Hence internal minorities are not defined as separate "peoples" with their own right of self-determination, even if they have been subject to similar processes of territorial conquest and colonization as overseas colonies.

For those national minorities denied recognition as "peoples" under Article 1, the only other option was to appeal to Article 27. But this Article is too weak, for the right "to enjoy their own culture" has traditionally been understood to include only negative rights of noninterference, rather than positive rights to assistance, funding, autonomy, or official language status. In effect, it simply reaffirms that members of national minorities must be free to exercise their standard rights of freedom of speech, freedom of association, freedom of assembly, and freedom of conscience.

Needless to say, there is a vast space between Article 1 rights to an independent state and Article 27 rights to freedom of cultural expression and association. Indeed, almost all of the conflicts relating to national minorities in postcommunist Europe are about this middle area: for example, about the right to use a minority language in courts or local administration; the funding of minority schools, universities, and media; the extent of local or regional autonomy; the guaranteeing of political representation for minorities; the prohibition on settlement policies designed to swamp minorities in their historic homelands with settlers from the dominant group, and so on. These issues are an important source of ethnic conflict and political instability in postcommunist Europe. Yet international law, until recently, had virtually nothing to say about any of them.

As a result, national minorities have been vulnerable to serious injustice. Article 27 has helped protect certain civil rights relating to cultural expression. But it has not stopped states from rescinding funding for minority-language schools, or from abolishing traditional forms of local autonomy, or from encouraging settlers to swamp minority homelands. None of these policies, which can be catastrophic for national minorities, violate the rights to cultural expression and association protected in Article 27.[10]

For these and other reasons, it is widely recognized that we need a new conception of the rights of national minorities that can fill in the gap between Articles 1 and 27. We need a conception that accords national minorities substantive rights and protections (unlike Article 27), but that works within the framework of larger states (unlike Article 1). This was the task facing European organizations when developing "European standards of minority rights."

Despite a broad consensus that these standards should fill in the gap between Articles 1 and 27, disagreement occurred about where to start. To oversimplify, we can say that some actors wanted to start with Article 1's right to self-determination, but to weaken it to render it consistent with the territorial integrity of states. This leads us in the direction of various models of "internal self-determination." Other actors wanted to start with Article 27's right to enjoy one's culture, but then to strengthen it to provide substantive protections. To date, neither option has proven adequate.

The Right to Internal Self-Determination

Not surprisingly, most minority elites preferred to start with a (weakened) form of a right to self-determination. Throughout the early 1990s, many intellectuals and political organizations representing national minorities pushed for recognition of a right to internal self-determination, typically through some form of territorial autonomy (hereafter TA). And, for a brief period, from 1990 to 1993, there was some indication that this campaign might be successful. For example, the first statement by a European organization on minority rights after the collapse of Communism—the initial 1990 OSCE Copenhagen Declaration—went out of its way to endorse territorial autonomy (Article 35):

> The participating States note the efforts undertaken to protect and create conditions for the promotion of the ethnic, cultural, linguistic and religious identity of certain national minorities by establishing, as one of the possible means to achieve these aims, appropriate local or

autonomous administrations corresponding to the specific historical and territorial circumstances of such minorities and in accordance with the policies of the State concerned.

This paragraph does not recognize a "right" to TA, but recommends it as a good way of accommodating national minorities.

An even stronger endorsement of TA came in 1993, in Recommendation 1201 of the Council of Europe Parliamentary Assembly. It contained a clause (Article 11) stating that

> in the regions where they are a majority, the persons belonging to a national minority shall have the right to have at their disposal appropriate local or autonomous authorities or to have a special status, matching this specific historical and territorial situation and in accordance with the domestic legislation of the State.

Unlike the OSCE Copenhagen Declaration, this Recommendation recognized TA as a "right." Of course, parliamentary recommendations are just that: recommendations, not legally binding documents. But still this shows that in the early 1990s, there was movement in the direction of endorsing a general principle that justice required an effective mechanism for sharing power between the majority and national minorities, specifically mentioning TA as one such mechanism.

Many national minority organizations in postcommunist Europe viewed the passage of Recommendation 1201 as a great victory. Ethnic Hungarian organizations in particular viewed it as evidence that Europe would support their claims for TA in Slovakia, Romania, and Serbia. They assumed this Recommendation would play a central role in the Council of Europe's Framework Convention, which was being drafted at the same time, and that complying with this Recommendation would be required for candidate countries to join the EU.

This expectation was bolstered by the fact that internal self-determination for national minorities has clearly become the general trend within the West itself. The practice of territorial autonomy for sizable, territorially concentrated national minorities has become virtually universal in the West. Indeed, one of the most striking developments in ethnic relations in the Western democracies over the past century has been the trend toward creating political subunits in which national minorities form a local majority, and in which their language is recognized as an official language, at least within their self-governing region, and perhaps throughout the country as a whole. At the beginning of the twentieth century, only Switzerland and Canada had adopted this combination of territorial autonomy and official language status for substate national groups. Since then, however, virtually all Western democracies that contain sizable substate nationalist movements have moved in this direction. The list includes the adoption of autonomy for the Swedish-speaking Åland Islands in Finland after World War I; autonomy for South Tyrol in Italy, and for Puerto Rico in the United States, after World War II; federal autonomy for Catalonia and the Basque Country in Spain in the 1970s; for Flanders in Belgium in the 1980s; and most recently for Scotland and Wales in the 1990s.

If we restrict our focus to sizable and territorially concentrated national minorities, this trend is now essentially universal in the West. All groups over 250,000 that have demonstrated a desire for TA now have it in the West, as well as many smaller groups (such as the German minority in Belgium).[11] The largest group that has mobilized for autonomy without success is the Corsicans in France (175,000 people). But even here, legislation was recently adopted to accord autonomy to Corsica, and only a ruling of the Constitutional Court prevented its implementation. So France too, I think, will soon join the bandwagon.

Moreover, although the shift to territorial autonomy was originally controversial in each of the countries that adopted it, it has quickly become a deeply entrenched part of political life in these countries. That Spain or Belgium or Canada, for example, could revert to a unitary and monolingual state is inconceivable. And no one is campaigning for such a reversal. Indeed, no Western democracy that has adopted territorial autonomy and official bilingualism has reversed this decision. This is evidence that this model for accommodating sizable and concentrated national minorities has been very successful in terms of liberal-democratic values of peace, prosperity, individual rights, and democracy.[12]

In short, if there is such a thing as a "European standard" for dealing with mobilized national minorities, some form of internal autonomy would appear to be it. This is the model Western democracies today use to deal with the phenomenon of substate nationalist groups, and national minorities in postcommunist Europe have reason to hope that it will be established as a norm for their countries as well.

Of course, the fact that internal autonomy has become the norm in practice in the West does not mean that it can be codified as a general norm in international law. These Western practices were not debated in terms of general principles of "the rights of national minorities," and it is not clear how a norm of internal self-determination could be formulated in a generalized way. Yet this very issue was being debated in a closely related context of international law: namely, the rights of indigenous peoples. The UN's Draft Declaration on the Rights of Indigenous Peoples, submitted in 1993, has several articles affirming the principle of internal self-determination, including:

Article 3: Indigenous peoples have the right of self-determination. By virtue of that right, they freely determine their political status and freely pursue their economic, social, and cultural development.

Article 15: [Indigenous peoples] have the right to establish and control their educational systems and institutions providing education in their own languages, in a manner appropriate to their cultural methods of teaching and learning.

Article 26: Indigenous peoples have the right to own, develop, control, and use the lands and territories . . . which they have traditionally owned or otherwise occupied or used. This includes the right to the full recognition of their laws, traditions, and customs, land-tenure systems and institutions for the development and management of resources. . . .

Article 31: Indigenous peoples, as a specific form of exercising their right to self-determination, have the right to autonomy or self-government in matters relating to their internal affairs. . . .

Article 33: Indigenous peoples have the right to promote, develop, and maintain their institutional structures and their distinctive juridical customs, traditions, procedures and practices, in accordance with internationally recognized human rights standards.

This draft declaration is still a draft, and hence not binding international law.[13] But the basic idea that indigenous peoples have a right to internal self-determination is now widely endorsed throughout the international community, and is reflected in other recent international declarations on indigenous rights, including by the Organization of American States and the International Labour Organization.

This shows that there is no inherent reason that international law cannot accept the idea of internal self-determination. The status of national minorities in postcommunist Europe is not identical to that of indigenous peoples in the Americas or Asia. But there are some important similarities in both history and aspirations, and many of the standard arguments for recognizing a right of internal self-determination for indigenous peoples also apply to national minorities.[14]

So there were several reasons that national minorities in postcommunist states could reasonably hope that some form of internal self-government would be codified as part of the "European standards" for the treatment of national minorities. This approach is in fact the norm within Western Europe today, it has been recognized as a valid principle in international law with respect to indigenous peoples, and it was endorsed in important statements by European organizations, including the OSCE in 1990 and the Council of Europe Parliamentary Assembly in 1993.

As it turns out, however, the Assembly's Recommendation 1201 reflects the high-water mark of support for TA within European organizations. Since then, there has been a marked movement away from support for TA. The Framework Convention, adopted just two years after Recommendation 1201, avoided any reference to TA. Not only was TA not recognized as a "right," but it also was not even mentioned as a recommended practice. Nor has TA appeared in any subsequent declaration or recommendation of European organizations, such as the series of Hague, Oslo, and Lund recommendations adopted by the OSCE from 1996 to 1999,[15] or the new constitution of the European Union. And the European Commission for Democracy through Law has ruled that national minorities do not have rights of self-determination.[16] For all intents and purposes, ideas of internal self-determination have disappeared from the debate about "European standards" on minority rights.

There are a number of reasons for this. For one thing, the idea of autonomy faced intense opposition from postcommunist states. They feared that recognizing any idea of internal self-determination or minority autonomy would be destabilizing. Governments feared that granting TA to some groups would lead to problems of both "escalation" and "proliferation."[17] The escalation fear is that groups granted internal self-determination will then escalate their demands into full-blown secession. The proliferation fear is that if internal self-determination is offered to one highly vocal or mobilized group, then other groups, previously quiescent, will come out of the woodwork and demand their own autonomy.

Of course, the same two fears of escalation and proliferation were present in the West as well, and yet Western states have nonetheless proceeded with internal autonomy. Fears of escalation and proliferation have turned out to be exaggerated, at least in the Western context.[18] But these fears are exacerbated in many postcommunist countries by the fact that national minorities often share a common ethnic or national identity with a neighboring state, which they may therefore view as their "kin-state" or "mother country" (for example, ethnic Hungarian minorities in Slovakia vis-à-vis Hungary; ethnic Russian minorities in the Baltics vis-à-vis Russia). In such cases, the fear of escalation is not so much that minorities will become secessionist, but rather that they will become irredentist—that is, that they will serve as a fifth column, supporting efforts by their neighboring kin-state to take over part or all of the country.[19]

More generally, the very idea of recognizing minorities as "nations within," possessed of their own inherent rights to self-government, challenges the ideology of most postcommunist states. These states aspire to be seen as unified nation-states, premised on a singular conception of popular sovereignty, rather than as unions or federations of two or more peoples.[20]

For a variety of reasons, then, claims to internal self-determination have been bitterly resisted in postcommunist Europe. As the OSCE High Commissioner on National Minorities has noted, claims to TA meet "maximal resistance" from states in the region. Any attempt by Western organizations to push such models would therefore require maximum pressure, and would make relations between East and West much more conflictual and costly. Hence, in the High Commissioner's judgment, it is more "pragmatic" to focus on more modest forms of minority rights.[21]

Moreover, there was also strong opposition to the idea of entrenching a right to TA for minorities *in the West* and the idea that there would be international monitoring of how Western states treated their minorities. As we have seen, France, Greece, and Turkey have traditionally opposed the very idea of self-government rights for national minorities, and indeed deny the very existence of national minorities. And even those Western countries that accept the principle do not necessarily want *their* laws and policies regarding national minorities subject to international monitoring. This is true, for example, of Switzerland and the United States.[22] The treatment of national minorities in various Western countries remains a politically sensitive topic, and many countries do not want their majority-minority settlements, often the result of long and painful negotiation processes, reopened by international monitoring agencies. In short, although they were willing to insist that postcommunist states be monitored for their treatment of minorities, they do not want their own treatment of minorities examined.

Given these obstacles, it is not surprising that efforts to codify a right to autonomy or to internal self-determination for national minorities have failed.

The Right to Enjoy One's Culture

As support for recognizing a right to internal self-determination has dwindled, the obvious alternative has been to build instead on the principle underlying the ICCPR's Article 27—namely, the "right to enjoy one's culture." In many ways, the provisions of the Council of Europe's 1995 Framework Convention, and of the 1996–99 OSCE recommendations, can be understood in this way. They start from a right to enjoy one's culture, but seek to strengthen it, so as to entail certain positive rights and protections.[23] These positive rights include such things as public funding of minority elementary schools and of minority media, or the right to spell one's surname in accordance with one's own language. In contexts where minorities form a local majority, these rights might also include the right to bilingual street signs and the right to submit documents to public authorities in the minority language. All of these are said to enable the members of minorities to "enjoy their own culture, to profess and prac-tise their own religion, or to use their own language."[24]

Although stronger than the original Article 27, this approach is still rel-atively weak in the rights it accords to national minorities. In particular, it provides no recognition of self-government rights, and no guarantees of official language status. Nor does it guarantee that minorities can pursue higher education or professional accomplishment in their own language.

More generally, there is nothing in the Framework Convention or OSCE recommendations that challenges the desire of postcommunist states to be unitary nation-states, each with a single official language. States can fully respect these standards, and yet centralize power in such a way that all decisions are made in forums controlled by the dominant national group. They can also organize higher education, professional accreditation, and political offices so that members of minorities must either linguistically assimilate in order to achieve professional success and political power or migrate to their kin-state. (This is often referred to as the "decapitation" of minority groups: forcing potential elites from minor-ity communities to leave their communities to achieve higher education or professional success.) In short, these norms do not preclude state poli-cies aimed at the disempowering and decapitation of minorities.

From the perspective of minorities, therefore, and of many commen-tators, these documents smack of "paternalism and tokenism."[25] By con-trast, most postcommunist states are relieved about the general direction these norms are taking. Postcommunist states have expressed much less resistance to the 1995 Framework Convention and the 1996–99 OSCE recommendations than to earlier documents endorsing TA. The states grumble about the double standards in the way these norms are applied, but they do not contest their basic validity.[26] In this sense, the decision to base European standards on an updated version of the Article 27 right to enjoy one's culture has indeed proven more "pragmatic."

In another sense, however, this approach has proven quite ineffective. The original point of developing these norms was to deal with violent ethnic conflicts in postcommunist Europe, such as in Kosovo, Bosnia, Croatia, Macedonia, Georgia, Azerbaijan, Moldova, and Chechnya. None of these conflicts revolved around Article 27-type rights to enjoy one's culture. The violation of such rights was not the cause of violent conflict, and respect for such rights would not resolve the conflicts. The same is true about the other major cases in which European organizations feared potential violence, such as the Hungarian minorities in Romania and Slovakia, or the Russian minority in Ukraine.

In all of these cases, the issues in dispute are not covered by the FCNM or the OSCE recommendations. These are conflicts involving large, territorially concentrated groups who have manifested the capacity and the aspiration to govern themselves and to administer their own public institutions in their own language, and who typically have possessed some form of self-government and official language status in the past. They have mobilized for territorial autonomy, official language status, minority-language universities, and consociational power sharing. None of these groups would be satisfied with the meager rights guaranteed by the FCNM and OSCE recommendations.

The fact that these national minorities are not satisfied with these provisions is sometimes taken as evidence of the illiberalism of their political culture, or of the radicalism of their leadership. But no sizable politically mobilized national minority in the West would be satisfied either. No one can seriously suppose that national minorities in Catalonia, Flanders, Quebec, Bern, South Tyrol, the Åland Islands, or Puerto Rico would be satisfied simply with minority elementary schools but not mother-tongue universities, or bilingual street signs but not official language status, or local administration but not regional autonomy.

This is not to say that there are no contexts in postcommunist Europe in which current FCNM or OSCE norms would provide a realistic basis for state-minority relations. I think they will work well in those countries which are essentially ethnically homogenous—for example, where the dominant group forms 90–95 percent of the population—and where the remaining ethnic groups are small, dispersed, and already on the road to assimilation. This is the situation, for example, in the Czech Republic, Slovenia, and Hungary. None of the minorities in these countries are in fact capable of exercising regional autonomy, or of sustaining a high degree of institutional completeness (for example, of sustaining their own universities), and most already show high levels of linguistic assimilation. For these groups, the FCNM/OSCE norms provide all that they could ask

for. The norms allow such small and half-assimilated minorities to negotiate their integration into the dominant society with a certain amount of
dignity and security. In essence, the norms allow them to "die with their
boots on."[27] Similarly, the norms will likely be satisfactory to small, dispersed, and partly assimilated minorities in other postcommunist countries, such as the Vlachs in Macedonia, or the Armenians in Romania.

The problem, of course, is that these minorities were not (and are not)
the ones involved in serious ethnic conflict. The problem of ethnic
violence and potentially destabilizing ethnic conflict in postcommunist
Europe is almost exclusively confined to groups that are capable of exercising self-government and of sustaining their own public institutions,
and which therefore contest with the state for control over public institutions.[28] For these groups, the FCNM and OSCE norms are largely
irrelevant.

In the end, therefore, the new European standards are not very pragmatic after all. If the goal is to effectively deal with the problem of potentially destabilizing ethnic conflict, then we need norms that actually
address the source of these conflicts. And any norms that start from an
Article 27-style "right to enjoy one's culture" are unlikely to do that.[29]

A Retreat from Minority Rights?

It seems then that neither of the two approaches to building European standards of minority rights—whether based on a right to self-
determination or a right to enjoy culture—has succeeded in developing
meaningful and effective international norms. Even though self-
determination is being interpreted in a weakened form compared with
its original formulation in Article 1 of the ICCPR, it is still too strong for
many countries to accept. And even though the right to enjoy one's
culture is being interpreted in a strengthened form compared with its
original formulation in Article 27 of the ICCPR, it is still too weak to
actually resolve the sources of ethnic conflict.

If neither of these options is feasible and effective, what are the alter-
natives? One option is to abandon the idea of developing European
norms on minority rights. After all, the EU and NATO survived and flour-
ished for many years without paying any attention to minority rights.[30]
Why not reconsider the decision to make minority rights one of the foun-
dational values of the European order?

Indeed, one could argue that the original decision in the early 1990s
to develop such norms was based on a mistaken prediction about the like-

lihood that ethnic conflict would spiral out of control. It has since become clear that ethnic violence is a localized phenomenon in postcommunist Europe, and that the prospects for violence in countries like Slovakia or Estonia are virtually nil for the foreseeable future. So perhaps it is unnecessary to monitor whether these countries are treating their minorities in accordance with (so-called) European norms.

To be sure, Western observers might not like some of the policies that these countries would adopt if left to their own devices. But it is unlikely that these policies would lead to violence and instability. Some of these countries might experiment with heavy-handed assimilationist policies, but if so, these policies would almost certainly fail, and in the end a domestic consensus would emerge on a more liberal policy. This is precisely what happened in the West, and there is no reason to assume that it would not or could not happen in the East. Moreover, liberal policies are more likely to be perceived as legitimate, and hence to be stable, if they emerge from these sorts of domestic processes, rather than being imposed from without.

For these reasons, some commentators have suggested that we stop pressuring postcommunist countries to comply with international norms on minority rights.[31] This would not necessarily preclude all forms of Western intervention. After all, ethnic conflicts can undermine regional peace and stability. Violence, massive refugee flows, and arms smuggling can spill over into neighboring countries, and destabilize entire regions. The international community has a right to protect itself against such potentially destabilizing ethnic conflicts in postcommunist Europe.

Insofar as *security* is the real motivation for Western intervention, however, then presumably state-minority relations should be monitored, not for their compliance with international norms, but for their potential threats to regional peace and security. Monitoring should aim to identify those cases in which the status and treatment of minorities might lead to these sorts of spillover effects.

And indeed European organizations have been engaged in this sort of security monitoring. In addition to the monitoring of compliance with international norms, European organizations have been engaged in a parallel process of monitoring countries for their potential threats to regional security. This parallel process has largely been organized through the OSCE, including the Office of the High Commissioner on National Minorities. Indeed, the High Commissioner's mandate is explicitly defined as part of the OSCE's "security" basket, and his task is to provide early warnings about potential threats to security, and to make recommendations that would defuse these threats.[32] And behind the OSCE, of course, lies NATO, with its security mandate, and its power to intervene militarily if necessary, as we saw in Bosnia and Kosovo.

In short, we have two parallel processes of "internationalizing" state-minority relations: one process monitors postcommunist states for their compliance with general norms of minority rights (what we can call the "legal rights track"); and a second process monitors postcommunist states for their potential threats to regional stability (the "security track").[33]

The existence of this parallel security track means that even if compliance with international norms was no longer monitored, Western states could still intervene based on considerations of regional security where there are identifiable spillover risks. In fact, this security track has always been more important than the legal rights track in determining actual intervention in postcommunist states. The most important and well-known cases of Western intervention on minority issues in postcommunist states have worked through the security track. These interventions have been based on calculations about how to restore security, not on how to uphold universal norms such as the FCNM's.

Consider the way Western organizations have intervened in the major cases of ethnic violence in postcommunist Europe: for example, in Moldova, Georgia, Azerbaijan, Kosovo, Bosnia, and Macedonia. In each of these cases, Western organizations have pushed postcommunist states to go far beyond the requirements of the FCNM. They have pushed states to accept either some form of territorial autonomy (in Moldova, Georgia, Azerbaijan, Kosovo) and/or some form of consociational power sharing and official language status (in Macedonia and Bosnia).

In short, in the contexts where Western organizations really have faced destabilizing ethnic conflict, they have immediately recognized that the FCNM is of little use in resolving the conflicts, and that some form of power sharing is required. The precise form of this power sharing has been determined by a range of contextual factors, not the least of which has been the actual military balance of power among the contending factions. Since the motivation for Western intervention has been to protect regional security, the West's recommendations have had to be based on an accurate assessment of the actual threat potential raised by the various actors.

Since the security track has done much of the real work in enabling and guiding Western policies toward postcommunist Europe, why do we need the legal rights track? If, as I have argued, there is no feasible way to ground effective international norms of minority rights on either a right to self-determination or a right to enjoy culture, why not just give up on the idea of a legal rights track, while preserving the capacity to intervene in postcommunist Europe based on considerations of security?

I suspect that some leaders of Western organizations regret having established the legal rights track in 1990 and might now wish to retreat from it. But I doubt that this is possible. Ideas of minority rights have now become institutionalized at several levels in Europe, and would be difficult to dislodge.

Moreover, the security track may not work without an underlying legal rights track. On its own, the security track has a perverse tendency to reward state intransigence and minority belligerence. It gives the state an incentive to invent or to exaggerate rumors of kin-state manipulation of the minority, so as to reinforce the state's claim that the minority is disloyal and that extending minority rights would jeopardize the security of the state. It also gives the minority an incentive to threaten violence or simply to seize power, since this is the only way its grievances will reach the attention of the international organizations monitoring security threats. Merely being treated unjustly is not enough to get Western attention within the security track, unless it is backed up with a credible threat to be able to destabilize governments and regions.[34]

For example, consider the OSCE's approach to TA. As we have seen, after its initial recommendation of TA in 1990, the OSCE has shifted toward discouraging TA, and has counseled various minorities, including the Hungarians in Slovakia, to give up their autonomy claims. But the OSCE has supported autonomy in several other countries, including Ukraine (for Crimea), Moldova (for Gaugazia and Transnistria), Georgia (for Abkhazia and Ossetia), Azerbaijan (for Nagorno-Karabakh), and Serbia (for Kosovo). What explains this variation? The OSCE says that the latter cases are "exceptional" or "atypical,"[35] but the only way in which they appear to be exceptional is that minorities seized power illegally and extra-constitutionally, without the consent of the state.[36] Where minorities have seized power in this way, the state can revoke autonomy only by sending in the army and starting a civil war. For obvious reasons, the OSCE discourages this military option, and recommends instead that states negotiate autonomy with the minority and accept some form of federalism or consociationalism that provides after-the-fact legal recognition for the reality on the ground. Hence the HCNM advised that it would be dangerous for Ukraine to try to abolish the autonomy that Russians in Crimea (illegally) established.[37]

By contrast, wherever a minority has pursued TA through peaceful and democratic means, within the rule of law, the OSCE has opposed it, on the grounds that it would increase tensions. According to the HCNM, given the pervasive fears in postcommunist Europe about minority disloyalty and secession, any talk about creating new TA arrangements is bound to increase tensions, particularly if the minority claiming TA borders on a kin-state. Hence the HCNM's recommendation that Hungarians in Slovakia not push for TA, given Slovak fears about irredentism.[38]

In short, the security approach rewards intransigence on the part of both sides. If a minority seizes power, the OSCE rewards it by putting pressure on the state to accept an "exceptional" form of autonomy; if the majority refuses to even discuss autonomy proposals from a peaceful and law-abiding minority, the OSCE rewards the majority by putting pressure on the minority to be more "pragmatic." This is perverse from the point of view of justice, but it seems to be the inevitable logic of the security-based approach. From a security perspective, it may indeed be correct that granting TA to a law-abiding minority increases tensions, whereas supporting TA after it has been seized by a belligerent minority decreases tensions.

Insofar as this is the logic of the security approach, it has the paradoxical effect of undermining security. Long-term security requires that both states and minorities moderate their claims, accept democratic negotiations, and seek fair accommodations. In short, long-term security requires that state-minority relations be guided by some conception of justice and rights, not just by power politics. And this, of course, is what the legal rights track was supposed to be promoting, and why it must supplement the security track.

The Right to Effective Participation

We seem to be caught in a bind. European organizations have made an irreversible commitment to developing international legal norms regarding national minorities. But existing attempts to develop such norms have been either too strong (if based on norms of self-determination) or too weak (if based on a right to enjoy one's culture). Is there some third approach that can fill the gap between Articles 1 and 27, and that can provide a more principled guide for regulating the sort of claims that actually underlie the serious cases of ethnic conflict in postcommunist Europe?

One option is to invoke the principle that the members of national minorities have a right to "effective participation" in public affairs, particularly in matters affecting them. This idea of effective participation was already present in the original 1990 Copenhagen Declaration. Indeed, it was on the basis of this principle that the Declaration recommended TA. Minority autonomy was advocated as a good vehicle for achieving effective participation. More recent declarations have dropped the reference to internal autonomy, but retain the commitment to effective participation.[39] Indeed, references to effective participation are becoming more prominent. For example, it is the central topic of the most recent set of OSCE Recommendations (the Lund Recommendations on Effective Participation of National Minorities, adopted in 1999).

This idea of a right to effective participation is attractive for a number of reasons. For one thing, it sounds admirably democratic. Moreover, it avoids the tokenist connotations of a right to "enjoy one's culture." It recognizes that minorities want not only to speak their languages or to profess their religions in private life, but also to participate as equals in public life. A right to effective participation recognizes this political dimension of minority aspirations, while avoiding the "dangerous" and "radical" ideas of national self-determination.[40]

The main reason that effective participation has become so popular, however, is that it is vague, subject to multiple and conflicting interpretations, and so can be endorsed by people with very different conceptions of state-minority relations. In this sense, the apparent consensus on the importance of effective participation hides, or postpones, deep disagreements on what this actually means.

On the most minimal reading, the right to effective participation simply means that the members of national minorities should not face discrimination in the exercise of their standard political rights to vote, to engage in advocacy, and to run for office. This minimalist reading is invoked to push Estonia and Latvia to grant citizenship to their ethnic Russians, and to enable them to vote and to run for office even if they lack full fluency in the titular language.

On a somewhat more robust reading, effective participation requires not just that members of minorities can vote or run for office, but that they actually achieve some degree of *representation* in the legislature. This may not require that minorities be represented precisely in proportion to their share of the overall population, but serious underrepresentation would be viewed as a concern. This reading is invoked to prohibit attempts by states to gerrymander the boundaries of electoral districts so as to make it more difficult to elect minority representatives. It can also be invoked to prohibit attempts by states to revise the threshold needed for minority political parties to gain seats in proportional representation (PR) electoral systems.

In Poland, for example, the German minority regularly elects deputies to parliament because it is exempted from the usual 5 percent threshold rule. A similar policy benefits the Danish minority party in Germany. By contrast, Greece raised its electoral threshold precisely to prevent the possibility of Turkish MPs being elected.[41] This sort of manipulation might well be prohibited in the future.

But neither of these two readings—focusing on the nondiscriminatory exercise of political rights and equitable representation—gets to the heart of the problem in most cases of serious ethnic conflict. Even when minorities are able to participate without discrimination, and even when they are represented in rough proportion to their population, they may still be permanent losers in the democratic process. This is particularly true in contexts where the dominant group views the minority as potentially disloyal, and so votes as a bloc against any policies that empower minorities. (Consider the nearly universal opposition within Slovakia to autonomy for the Hungarian-dominant regions, or the opposition within Macedonia to recognizing Albanian as an official language). In these contexts, it may not matter whether minorities exercise their vote, or elect MPs in accordance with their numbers: they will still be outvoted by members of the dominant group. The eventual decision will be the same whether minorities participate in the decision or not.

Taken literally, the term "effective participation" would seem to preclude national minorities from being permanent political minorities. After all, "effective" participation implies that participation should have an effect—that is, that participation changes the outcome. The only way to ensure that participation by minorities is effective, in this sense, is to adopt rules that require some form of power sharing. This may take the form of internal autonomy or of consociational guarantees of a coalition government.

We can call this the maximalist reading of a "right to effective participation"—one that requires counter-majoritarian forms of federal or consociational power-sharing. This is obviously the interpretation that many minority organizations endorse. But most states, East and West, strongly resist it for the same reason that earlier references to internal self-determination were resisted (fears of escalation, proliferation, irredentism, and so on). Having blocked the move to codify a right to internal autonomy, states are not going to accept an interpretation of effective participation that provides a back door for autonomy. Agreement on a right to effective participation was possible precisely because it was seen as an alternative to, not a vehicle for, minority self-government. The interpretation of effective participation is therefore likely to remain focused at the level of nondiscrimination and equitable representation—that is, at a level that does not address the actual sources of ethnic conflict.

There is one potential exception to this generalization. European organizations may adopt a maximalist interpretation of effective participation *where forms of power sharing already exist.* It is widely recognized that attempts by states to abolish preexisting forms of minority autonomy are a recipe for disaster (for example, Kosovo, Nagorno-Karabakh, and Ossetia). European organizations would therefore like to find a basis in international law to prevent states from revoking preexisting forms of minority autonomy. The norm of effective participation is a plausible candidate: attempts to revoke preexisting autonomy regimes can be seen as deliberate attempts to disempower minorities, and hence a denial of their right to effective participation.

This idea that effective participation protects preexisting forms of autonomy and power sharing has been developed by some commentators,[42] and has implicitly been invoked by the OSCE itself, when justifying its recommendations for TA and consociationalism in countries like Georgia and Moldova. Although these power-sharing recommendations emerged out of the "security track," rather than from any reading of international legal norms, Western organizations have been keen to show that these recommendations were not just a case of rewarding belligerent minorities, and that there is a normative basis for their recommendations. The claim that abolishing preexisting forms of power sharing erodes effective participation provides a principled basis for their recommendations.

The difficulty, of course, is to explain why it is only *preexisting* forms of TA that protect effective participation. If TA is needed to ensure the effective participation of Abkhazians in Georgia, or Armenians in Azerbaijan, why is it not also needed for Hungarians in Slovakia or Albanians in Macedonia? If abolishing preexisting autonomy disempowers minorities, why are minorities whose claims to autonomy were never accepted also not disempowered? (Conversely, if power-sharing institutions are not needed to ensure the effective participation of the Hungarians in Slovakia, why are they needed for Armenians in Nagorno-Karabakh, or for Russians in Crimea?)

No principled basis seems to exist for privileging those minorities that acquired or seized autonomy at some point in the past. The differential treatment of minority claims to autonomy can be explained only as a concession to realpolitik. From a prudential point of view, it is simply much more dangerous to take away preexisting autonomy from minorities who have fought in the past to acquire it than to refuse to grant new autonomy to minorities who have not shown the willingness to use violence in their pursuit of autonomy.

In short, interpretations of "effective participation" that privilege preexisting autonomy suffer from the same flaw as the security track: that is, they reward belligerent minorities while penalizing peaceful and law-abiding minorities. Like the security track, the "effective participation" approach, as it is currently being developed, is calibrated to match the threat potential of the contending parties. Those minorities with a capacity and willingness to destabilize governments and regions can get serious forms of power sharing in the name of effective participation; those minorities who have renounced threats of violence do not.

This suggests that the "effective participation" approach replicates, rather than resolves, the problems we identified with the other approaches. If effective participation is interpreted maximally to entail power sharing, then it is too strong to be acceptable to states, and will be rejected for the same reason that the internal self-determination approach was rejected. If effective participation is interpreted minimally to cover only nondiscrimination and equitable representation, then it is too weak to actually resolve serious cases of ethnic conflict, and will be ineffective for the same reasons that the right to culture approach was ineffective. And if we examine how the idea of effective participation has actually been invoked in cases of conflict, we will see that, like the security track, it is based on power politics, not general principles.

We can make the same point another way. When we talk about effective participation, we need to ask: Participation in what? From the point of view of most postcommunist states, the members of national minorities should be able to effectively participate in the institutions of a unitary nation-state with a single official language. From the point of view of many minority organizations, the members of national minorities should be able to effectively participate in the institutions of a multilingual, multination federal or consociational state. These different conceptions of the nature of the state generate very different conceptions of what is required for effective participation within the state. Commentators sometimes write as if the principle of effective participation can be invoked to resolve these conflicts between states and minorities over the nature of the state, but in fact we need first to resolve the question of the nature of the state before we can apply the principle of effective participation. And to date, that basic conflict over the nature of the state has been resolved in postcommunist Europe by force, not principles. Where minorities have seized autonomy, effective participation is interpreted as supporting federal and/or consociational power sharing within a multilingual, multination state. Where minorities have not used force, effective participation is interpreted as requiring only nondiscriminatory participation and equitable representation within a unitary, monolingual state.

Advocates of the idea of effective participation suggest that it can provide a principled formula for resolving deep conflicts over the nature of the state. It seems to me, however, that the idea of effective participation presupposes that this issue has already been resolved, and is therefore either too strong (if it presupposes that states have accepted the idea of internal self-determination within a multination state) or too weak (if it presupposes that minorities have accepted the idea of a unitary and monolingual state).

Notwithstanding these limitations, it seems clear that European organizations now view the idea of effective participation as the most promising avenue for the ongoing development of international norms on minority rights. So we are almost certain to see new, and perhaps more successful, interpretations emerging in the future.[43]

Conclusion

Attempts to develop international norms of minority rights in Europe since 1990 have run into a series of dilemmas. Appeals to a right to internal self-determination have proven too controversial; appeals to a right to enjoy one's culture have proven too weak; and appeals to a right to effective participation have proven too vague to actually address any of the conflicts in postcommunist Europe that generated the call for the "internationalization" of minority issues.

This is not necessarily a bad thing. The initial impulse to develop these norms was an unduly pessimistic view about the likelihood of ethnic violence in postcommunist Europe. If violence is unlikely, then why not let countries come to their own settlements on ethnic issues at their own speed? After all, it took Western countries many decades to work out their current accommodations with national minorities, and some people would argue that the success of these accommodations is due to the fact that they were the result of gradual domestic negotiations, rather than being imposed through external pressure.

Actually, international pressure did play an important and beneficial role in several Western cases, although this is now often forgotten. For example, the autonomy arrangement for the Åland Islands was an externally determined solution under the League of Nations which has nonetheless worked very well. Germany's accession to NATO in 1955 was conditional on its working out a reciprocal minority rights agreement with Denmark which is now seen as a model of how kin-states can work constructively through bilateral relations to help minorities in neighboring states. In 1972 there was strong international pressure on Italy to accord autonomy to South Tyrol, which today is seen as a exemplar of successful accommodation. In all of these cases, a certain degree of international pressure was needed to initiate the settlements,[44] although these settlements have now become domestically self-sustaining (and indeed have often been enhanced or expanded as a result of domestic procedures).[45]

So it would be inaccurate to suggest that Western states have "naturally" or inevitably gravitated toward fair accommodation of national minorities without international pressure. In fact, some combination of international pressure and/or domestic violence was present at one point or another in most Western cases of autonomy.[46] Given this history, it seems naïve to assume that countries in Eastern and Central Europe will inevitably and peacefully move toward significant minority rights through their own domestic democratic processes. As in the West, some extra-parliamentary push—whether it is international pressure and/or domestic violence—may be needed for postcommunist countries to seriously consider federal or consociational power sharing. The goal of any international pressure, however, should be to start a process that becomes domestically self-sustaining (and, ideally, domestically self-improving).

In that sense, perhaps the international community should limit its role in postcommunist Europe to ensuring that there is the minimum level of respect for human rights and political freedom needed to create a democratic space for states and minorities to slowly work out their own accommodations. The increasing prominence of the idea of effective participation may reflect the belief that Western intervention should be aimed at creating the conditions for postcommunist societies to work out their own accounts of minority rights through peaceful and democratic deliberations, rather than seeking to impose some canonical set of internationally defined minority rights.

This may be the direction we are headed. And perhaps this is the most we can reasonably expect. Attempts to formulate general principles of international law to resolve deep conflicts over autonomy, power sharing, and language rights may simply be unrealistic.[47] Over time, we might hope and expect postcommunist countries to follow the Western trend toward multilingual, multinational states, but it is unnecessary, and perhaps counterproductive, to try to jump-start this process through the codification and imposition of international norms of substantive minority rights.

If this is indeed the direction we are headed, however, it is important that the minimal standards being demanded of postcommunist states be presented as precisely *minimum* standards. A serious problem is that many actors view the FCNM and other international norms not as a minimum floor from which minority rights should be domestically negotiated, but rather as a maximal ceiling beyond which minorities must not seek to go.

In fact, most postcommunist states make a concerted effort to present the FCNM and OSCE recommendations as the outside limits of legitimate minority mobilization. Any minority leader or organization that asks for something beyond what these documents provide is immediately labeled as a radical. These minimal international standards are not being treated as the preconditions needed to democratically negotiate the forms of power sharing and self-government appropriate to each country, but rather are viewed as eliminating the need to adopt, or even to debate, forms of power sharing and self-government. When minority organizations raise questions about substantive minority rights, postcommunist states respond, "We meet all international standards," as if that forecloses the question of how states should treat their minorities. The claim that "we meet all international standards" has in fact become a mantra among postcommunist states, taking the place of any substantive debate about how to actually respond to minority claims regarding powers, rights, and status.

Sadly, I believe that the international community is often complicit in this effort to treat international norms as a maximal ceiling rather than a minimal floor, and to stigmatize minority leaders who dare to ask for the sorts of substantive minority rights enjoyed by most sizable national minorities in the West.[48] If codifying substantive minority rights in international law proves impossible, we must at least be clear that the meager provisions currently codified in European instruments are the starting point for democratic debate, not the end point.

Conclusion

Roger D. Petersen

How can the course of postcommunist ethnic politics be best described? Many key issues are still at play. The balance between individual and collective rights has not yet been found. The question whether certain minorities will assimilate or maintain group rights and identities remains to be answered. In some states, ethnic parties have formed, whereas in others they are absent; levels in the institutionalization of ethnicity remain in flux. Ethnic violence has been absent in much of the region, but violence tore Yugoslavia to shreds and potentially explosive situations still simmer in Kosovo, Macedonia, Moldova, and the Caucasus. Leveled Grozny serves as a reminder of the worst possibilities. Newly created diasporas have experienced a wide range of outcomes. Serbs have been cleansed from Krajina, remain in tenuous enclaves in Kosovo, and maintain parallel structures of government in the Bosnian protectorate. The fate of the large Russian and Hungarian diasporas has been far different and, on the whole, far more encouraging. The same might even be said for the Roma.

So, after reading the preceding chapters, what can one generalize about this seemingly riotous field of variation? In a volume published in 1993, Ian Bremmer wrote: "Much as Gorbachev's calls for a new Soviet federation based upon a new set of integrative principles failed to deal with the distinctiveness of Soviet nationalities, *any* abstract prioritizing of the conflictual issues dividing nationalities, or between nation and state, would be misguided. Only a systematic consideration of individual nations may yield such an agenda. Different relationships weigh more heavily in different regions; different cleavages have varying effects upon political mobilization."[1] A dozen years later, one might see even less ability to generalize across the postcommunist world. How can we compare the Czech Republic with the poorer states of the former Soviet Union? Even within former Yugoslavia, Slovenia and Macedonia would appear to have very little in common today.

Yet, despite their present dissimilarities and obvious differences in their recent histories, the postcommunist states have at least two things in common which can form the basis for comparison and generalization. First, and most obvious, they were Communist. Thus, for each state the question of legacy of the old system is relevant. For the region as a whole, the preceding chapters provide a basis for generalizing about the situations in which this legacy was most and least powerful in determining the nature of ethnic politics. Second, all of these states have been operating in a unipolar world system and have had to come to terms with the overwhelming dominance of the West. Again, the work in this volume can be used to generalize about the ways Western influence and norms have changed, or failed to change, ethnic politics across this set of states.

Addressing these two issues requires that we also address a fundamental theoretical question. As Ron Suny pointed out in the Introduction to this volume, the dominant perspective on ethnicity in Western scholarship is constructivist. In this view, as Suny writes, identities and concepts of nation are "a product of human action and imagination—a historical product of the efforts of activists and intellectuals, artists and poets, warriors and statesmen." The contributors to this volume, to varying degrees, subscribe to this view. But although actors may construct and shape identities, they do not do so without constraints. Implicit in this collective body of work is a view about how much political actors within postcommunist societies are free to construct identities and how much their actions and decisions are bound by history and structure.

This conclusion thus asks three different but connected questions: Will the power of international norms and Western influence inevitably drive the postcommunist states toward convergence with Western Europe on ethnic and minority policy? To what extent will the legacy of Communism block or redirect these influences? Is the overall process exhibiting the malleability and agency that would be predicted by the constructivist approach to ethnic politics?

What Is the Influence of the West on Postcommunist Ethnic Politics?

The chapters in this volume illustrate a powerful Western influence on the development of ethnic politics in the postcommunist states of Eastern Europe, although probably less so for many of the remnants of the USSR.[2] On several important issues, many postcommunist states appear not only to adapt to Western sanctions and incentives, but also to be adopting certain Western norms.

David Laitin's contribution perhaps demonstrates this impact most clearly. Many of Estonia's nationalist political elites wished to undo the demographic effects of Soviet rule by disenfranchising the Russian minority and encouraging them to leave. By 2000, however, it had become evident that policy toward the Russian minority would have to change. Rather than inducing migration, Estonian policy transformed into "integration" in which adjustments in linguistic and cultural practices of all ethnic groups slowly led toward relatively harmonious coexistence, if not assimilation. Laitin attributes this change in policy to the strategic needs of the Pro Patria Party in electoral competition, the need for language rationalization, the continued presence of a large Russian minority, and the need to satisfy Europe. It is clear from Laitin's discussion that the last factor was a powerful constraint on action. As also discussed by Will Kymlicka, a host of Western European organizations pressured Eastern European states to conform to certain standards. In the Estonian case, the Organization for Security and Cooperation, the EU, and the Open Society Institute criticized the Estonian policies of the early 1990s and supported the changes that came later. As Laitin mentions, for some Estonian political elites, such as former President Lennart Meri, integration with Europe is as important as the national consolidation of Estonia itself.

In Laitin's chapter, the reader gets the impression that something more is happening than a simple response to Western sanctions and incentives. Laitin's terminology is revealing here. At one point he states, "The notion that the Russian-speaking population could not be ignored became a new common sense." Laitin's use of the term "common sense" harks back to his earlier work *Culture and Hegemony* in which, borrowing from Gramsci, he explains how certain concepts of identity become hegemonic. The notion of common sense is also close to that of a "norm." One ceases to calculate decisions when under the effects of either common sense or an internalized norm. Political elites in Estonia no longer devise strategies inducing migration but rather have simply accepted the fact that being part of Europe means having to tolerate and deal with minority populations, even ones tied to the Soviet Union and its demographic policies. In Estonia, the effect of these norms appears to have washed over both majority and minority populations. As Laitin points out, "It is now well-known that Estonian and Russian opinion has converged through the 1990s for most issues such as evaluation of democracy, independence of Estonia, and joining the EU."

Other contributors to the volume also point to the influence of the West and the possible development of norms of ethnic tolerance. Daniel Chirot emphasizes the ugly aspects of Romanian and Bulgarian nationalism, including Zhivkov's violent campaign against Bulgaria's Turks and Muslims in the last years of Communism. In both cases, the reversal of policy toward minorities has been dramatic. In Romania, Iliescu declined to foment antipathy against minorities although that option seemed available, and even politically desirable, in the mid-1990s. In Bulgaria, Turks have returned and not only participate in elections but also form a critical swing group. Perhaps most remarkably, efforts have even been made to provide political outlets to Roma. Again, these changes can be ascribed to a considerable extent to Western sanctions and incentives. The Serbs have provided an example of what happens to those who fail to play by Western rules. It is not coincidence that Milošević sits in The Hague while Ceaușescu's former right-hand man Iliescu has reconstructed himself as an enlightened liberal.

And of course, money and aid are important. Anyone who has traveled in Eastern Europe appreciates the insight of Chirot's quotation of a Romanian working for a local NGO: "I don't know why you Americans think so well of those dishonest, filthy Gypsies, but we get all our money from you, so we have to think that way, too." But still, "thinking that way" could become a habit, the basis of a norm of tolerance not historically part of the region. Moser finds that ethnic parties in postcommunist Europe tend to play by democratic rules. The clear desire of these parties to stay in the mainstream supports the notion that certain norms have developed, that some options are now simply out of bounds.

Are the postcommunist states destined to shape their ethnic politics toward conformance, and eventual convergence, with Western European policies and practice? Although Western influence is powerful, Kymlicka's chapter demonstrates that its overall effects are uneven and unpredictable. There are two major reasons that we should not expect smooth conformance with the West. First, Western theory and practice on ethnic and minority rights is filled with contradictions and incoherence. As Kymlicka explains, Western states, influenced by the events in Yugoslavia, came to believe that it was necessary to impose "international norms" or

"European standards" of minority rights across Eastern Europe. The only problem, Kymlicka argues, was that no such standards existed. There had been no coherent discourse on minority rights prior to 1990, and even the term "national minority" had no legal status prior to 1995. What did exist were Article 1 and Article 27 of the 1966 International Covenant on Civil and Political Rights. The former states that "peoples" have a right to self-determination, whereas the latter states that "members of minorities" possess rights to practice their culture. As Kymlicka summarizes: "Needless to say, there is a vast space between Article 1 rights to an independent state and Article 27 rights to freedom of cultural expression and association." During the last dozen years, attempts have been made to fill in this space. But Western thought and practice have failed to produce a coherent regime. In the West, almost every territorially concentrated ethnic group with more than 250,000 members that has sought territorially based autonomy has gained a variety of rights. Examples include not only Switzerland and Canada but also the Åland Islands in Finland, South Tyrol in Italy, Puerto Rico in the United States, Catalonia and the Basque Country in Spain, Flanders in Belgium, and Scotland and Wales in Great Britain. So, logically, the same norm of territorial autonomy should apply to Eastern Europe as well—except that the Yugoslav tragedy unfolded. After reconsideration, it became clear that the approach to self-determination would have to be handled differently in the East than in the West. The approach toward postcommunist states would be dominated by fear of escalating security threats (and, to pick up again on Charles King's chapter on migration, fear of refugee flows). It became common practice to pacify groups that mobilized for violence by promising territorial autonomy or even independence. On the other hand, other groups (those unable or unwilling to mobilize for violence) would be discouraged from seeking such autonomy and would be encouraged to settle for lesser forms of self-determination.

This lack of consistent application of principles leads to the second major reason that the East should not be expected to easily conform to a Western path. Minority groups in the East have proven to be good learners. They understand the weaknesses and contradictions in Western policy and often exploit them to their advantage. The West's practice provides incentives for groups to mobilize for violence in expectation that the West, dominated by security fears, will become more likely to consider demands for territorial autonomy or independence. The primary example here is perhaps Kosovo, where the insurgent Kosovo Liberation Army escalated violence in an effort to force the West's hand to intervene.[3] Kymlicka adds Moldova, Georgia, Azerbaijan, and Macedonia to the list of related cases.

Some cases—Estonia, for example—might witness a trend toward the steady inculcation of Western norms. In other cases, political entrepreneurs will be looking for opportunities and advantages to bend these norms to their own advantage, or to mobilize identities in ways that bend around such norms. In the end, Kymlicka concludes that the best the West might be able to do is to try to set minimum standards for treatment of minorities. Devising general principles of international law regarding minority rights might simply be impossible. Kymlicka advises us to lower our expectations in terms of finding a magic formula to regulate ethnic conflict in Eastern Europe. The same conclusion would seem to be even more applicable to the postcommunist states of the Caucasus and Central Asia.

What Is the Legacy of Communism on Postcommunist Ethnic Politics?

If the West and international community are only able to set minimal standards and to shape the broad contours of ethnic politics, might not the legacy of the Communist system fill in much of what remains? There are good reasons to believe that this legacy could leave powerful remnants able to shape and constrain the transformation of ethnic politics in the region. Above all, Communist political systems were geared to heighten the saliency of ethnic categorizations. Indeed, Communism, especially in its Soviet form, was a fantastic exercise in ethnic engineering.

The saliency of ethnicity can be seen in the very inception of the Soviet state. As Mark Beissinger pointed out in his chapter, the Soviet Union was the first multiethnic state to claim to be against imperialism. The Soviet state would "project itself as a postimperial form of power, a civic state that aimed to transcend national oppression in the name of class solidarity." In an attempt to gain allies in their struggle to build the Soviet state, the Bolsheviks created an ethnofederal entity built on ideas of self-determination that would differentiate the new state from the Tsarist and Hapsburg Empires.

Ethnically defined federal units formed a key part of this effort. In the Soviet Union, ethnically based units included union republics, autonomous republics, krais, and autonomous oblasts. At each level, the Soviets acted, in the words of Terry Martin, as an "affirmative action empire" that promoted local languages and indigenization of the local positions. Although the Soviets directed development from the center, and the system required knowledge of the Russian language to advance, the policy did work to create some support among sizable segments of minority populations, as Beissinger notes. On the other hand, the system often relied on ethnically based repression. As is well documented, violence and forced deportations were also an essential part of this system. In addition to earlier actions against Cossacks, from the mid-1930s to the mid-1950s, the Soviet Union forcibly moved Kurds, Turks, Koreans, Karachai, Chechen and Ingush, Balkars, Kalmyks, Crimean Tartars, Meskhetian Turks, and Germans, as well as tens of thousands of Lithuanians, Latvians, Estonians, and others.

Given this history of ethnic engineering, ethnically defined territories, ethnic deportations, and general ethnic salience, Soviet scholars and the population as a whole tended to view ethnicity in primordial terms. Valery Tishkov points out that even in the post-Soviet period, Russians scholars are loathe to abandon previous views of ethnicity. Tishkov points to the example of Yuri Semenov, who states, "[A]lthough there exists a notion of 'bread,' there also exists real bread which is eaten. And although there exists a notion of 'chair,' real chairs on which people sit also exist. Applied to scholarship, this means that although there exists . . . a notion of 'ethnos,' there are also real ethnoses, and the peoples exist, like Russians, English, Serbs, and Abkhazians."[4] When ethnic groups are seen to have the essential reality of bread or a chair, these groups become "givens" in the sense of primordialism described by Shils and Geertz.[5] The salience and repetitive use of the Communist-era ethnic categories could be expected to lead to their "freezing" and continued relevance and political use in the postcommunist period.

Combined with other economic and institutional legacies of the Communist era, the salience of ethnicity could be expected to lead to a series of negative outcomes. To take one example, it was logical to expect that scapegoating of minorities would be a prevalent feature of the postcommunist landscape. One quality of the old system was economic leveling.[6] In comparison with the West, this system exhibited a small difference between rich and poor. On the whole, the general population experienced low levels of social differentiation and enjoyed a measure of equality. The transition to capitalism in the wake of the collapse of Communism changed all of this. Economic differences were real and visible. Combined with the troubles accompanying transition, postcommunist states were ripe for ethnic scapegoating or violent action against minorities and immigrants.[7]

Some problems have occurred. In the eastern regions of Germany, fascist youths have attacked immigrants. Anti-Semitic acts have taken place and are a significant problem in several countries. On the whole, however, the record is quite mixed. As Daniel Chirot points out in his chapter, Bulgarian and Romanian tolerance is surprisingly high. It is noteworthy that the most important recent major conferences on anti-Semitism took place in France, not in Eastern Europe. Despite fears, the difference between East and West in terms of scapegoating is not remarkable.

On the other hand, the legacy of ethnofederal institutions has undoubtedly helped lead to separation and violence. It is not a coincidence that all of the units having Union Republic status (save the ambiguous and still evolving case of Montenegro) have become independent states. Union Republic status provided the mobilization capacity, ready boundaries, and level of international legitimacy necessary to claim independent statehood. The ambiguities of this system have also helped lead to war. Situations of mixed populations have created security dilemmas (Bosnia, for example)[8] and issues of unresolved political status (Nagorno-Karabakh, for example)[9] have led to violent efforts at redress. The creation of new states based on existing federal boundaries has also led to the reshaping of previous ethnic hierarchies and the creation of embittering status reversals.

Still, the effects of the Communist ethnofederal systems have not been completely negative.[10] These institutions did provide for a quick division of territory that has allowed for many peoples to fulfill their aspirations of statehood. Today, with a few exceptions, large regional majorities control their own political destinies, and in most cases, have agreed to stay out of the affairs of their neighbors (see King's chapter). Post-communist states in Eastern Europe and elsewhere have experienced considerable violence, but it is not clear how much of this violence can be directly attributed to the specific politics and institutions of Communism, rather than to the opportunities and problems that would be accompanied by the collapse of any political system.

The authors in this volume appear to be in general agreement that the legacy of the old system is not that strong. In fact, there is surprisingly little emphasis on the legacy of Communism at all, at least in terms of broad, sweeping forces that operate in a consistent manner across the entire region. To be sure, the authors point out influences of the Communist ethnopolitical legacy. But these influences operate in conjunction with more general variables.

The Barany and Moser chapters are perhaps the clearest examples. The most critical factors in Zoltan Barany's "mobilizational prerequisites" model are political opportunity, identity, leadership, and organizational capacity (the possibility of a single party or umbrella organization being able to coherently represent the group). In his overview of these factors, Barany illustrates his method with reference to McAdam, Kitschelt, Tarrow, and Horowitz—in other words, scholars who develop broad theories with general applicability. Moreover, Barany concludes that his own model should be applicable not only to postcommunist ethnic movements, and not only to ethnic movements, but also to social and political movements in a wide variety of contexts. East European postcommunist multiethnic states are thus seen largely as "normal" states that can be analyzed without taking into consideration specific historically based constraints. For example, Barany's explanation of the treatment of the Roma would seem to apply to the Roma in both Western and Eastern European contexts.

Robert Moser does set up his chapter with reference to specific features of the old system. In his introductory comments, Moser mentions that the breakdown of multinational empires in the region has heightened consciousness of ethnicity, and he discusses how Communist rule diminished civil society and leveled class structures. He finds that Russian federalism, a holdover from the old system, is a significant factor in influencing political behavior. Nonetheless, Moser finds that two variables unconnected to the Communist legacy—demographic concentration and differences in electoral institutions—explain much of the variation in the number of ethnic parties and diversity in representation. Like Barany, Moser ends his chapter by stressing the generalizability of his approach, stating that his "framework could be applied to other postcommunist states and beyond to begin to develop a more comprehensive understanding of the factors that produce the various patterns of ethnic electoral politics." Indeed, his framework seems appropriate for analyzing the role of ethnic groups in the emerging party systems of almost any new democracy.

On this score, Charles King's contribution aligns with Barany and Moser. King identifies general variables affecting migration and trafficking. The key insights concern the weakness of state institutions and the strength of ethnic networks. On migration, King finds that states pass laws as much to keep their ethnic kin out as to correct historical grievances. King does not concentrate on the presence of constraints based in past experience but rather on the general absence of constraints often found in a newly emerging state system. Like Moser, he believes that how this system will evolve has more to do with specific institutions rather than with general cultural and social features of the region.

In contrast, Daniel Chirot does base his analysis in the wide sweep of history. Chirot argues that Bulgaria and Romania may have avoided ethnic violence and pogroms in the postcommunist period in part because they possess firmly established forms of majority nationalism. Under the influence of this nationalism, elites are constrained to some extent to put the good of the nation ahead of the short-term gains that might be accomplished through ethnic violence and chauvinism. Chirot, however, traces the development of Bulgarian and Romanian nationalism back to at least the second half of the nineteenth century. It is a process going back well before the introduction of Communism and one that newly developing countries, such as those emerging in Africa, cannot hope to repeat in a few short decades. In fact, Chirot points out that Yugoslavia, in spite of its Communist program, failed to develop conflict-preventing nationalism because of its short lifespan, less than four decades.

In sum, the chapters here do not present much evidence that today's political actors are greatly constrained by the legacy of Communism. Perhaps Communism has a powerful legacy that simply does not show up in ethnic politics. There may be a Communist/Orthodox "civilization" that breeds preferences for the collective over the individual. There may be a general political apathy and lack of efficacy in the region. Maybe in some states there is a desire for a strong leader who can bring order, Putin being a possible example. Surely, the Communist past distorted and retarded the level of civil society. Nevertheless, the authors in this volume have not seen the necessity to raise these issues in the context of explaining variation in key ethnic phenomena.

The collective lack of concentration on the old system in this volume raises the question why previous ethnic policies have not had more resonance in a broad and consistent fashion. On this issue, Mark Beissinger's chapter suggests an answer. Unlike the Russian Empire, the Hapsburg Empire, and the Ottoman Empire, the Soviet Union became an "empire" in an age when sovereignty and self-determination were becoming established norms. As a result, the ethnic institutions of the new Soviet state could not make the same claims to dominance as those made in the previous century. The Soviet Union was, in Beissinger's words, "one of the first of a new form of empire whose crucial contributions to the history of empires were its denial of its imperial quality and its use of the very cornerstones of the modern nation-state system . . . as instruments of nonconsensual control over culturally distinct populations." As Beissinger points out, when ultimately "denuded as imperial," such states are subject to collapse. I would add that the inherent contradictions in the ethnic politics of such states undoubtedly diminish their postimperial legacy.

Ultimately, using self-determination as a form of nonconsensual control is contradictory. It is nearly impossible to maintain a system based on "national forms and socialist content." Vacuous statements about "brotherhood" and "unity" became tired and meaningless. Given these problems and inconsistencies, successor states were likely to discard most of the old system onto the trash heap of history and look for new institutions and norms elsewhere.

Ethnic Politics, the Postcommunist Era, and Constructivist Theory?

Constructivist theory is built on a few clear assumptions.[11] First, individuals are assumed to possess multiple identities—linguistic, religious, national, racial, regional, and so on. In other words, they possess identity repertoires. Second, individuals will identify along one cleavage in one situation and another cleavage in a different situation; they will act according to race in one set of circumstances and religion in another. Third, individuals choose specific identities in order to maximize a certain good—economic, political, or psychological. Fourth, political elites, knowing the distribution of identity repertoires in the general population, will strategically act to raise the salience of one type of identity over another in order to prevail in political struggles. Elites structure individual incentives so that one identity is made the basis of voting or violence rather than another. Elites can manipulate identities in order to form winning electoral coalitions, or they can use violence in order to force individuals to rally around one particular identity.

Constructivist theory rests on the idea that identities are chosen, by both elites and masses, to maximize certain preferences. It follows that in a situation of institutional fluidity, we are likely to see elites attempting to change the saliency of certain ethnic categories. Given new demographics and new political institutions, we should see elites stressing language over nationality, or religion over language, as the primary categories for identification. Correspondingly, we should see individuals switching their primary identifications to be on the winning side in elections, to gain better access to jobs, and so on. We should also see entirely new identities emerging. David Laitin's book *Identity in Formation: The Russian-Speaking Populations in the Near Abroad* is one of the best examples here. In that work, Laitin predicted the emergence of a new identity group that focused on language rather than a continued focus on nationality categories.[12]

If constructivist theory is overstated, then we should see individuals retain identities even if it means nonoptimal payouts on political or economic measures. In this case, psychological attachments to identity categories may be preventing fluidity in identity change. Along the lines of primordialism, identities take on a fundamental reality and cannot be easily thrown off or taken on.

Alternatively, the constructivist approach might be theoretically valid, but choice might be highly constrained by powerful historical or structural forces. These forces may reduce the number of identities in repertoires or they may line up language, religion, and nationality so tightly that these various identity categories cannot be separated from one another for purposes of political mobilization. In this case, elites might have little ability to significantly restructure incentives to induce identity switch at the mass level. Here, it would seem more appropriate to concentrate on the larger forces constraining choice rather than on the limited opportunities of individuals and elites.

So what do the chapters here indicate about these three possibilities? It may be an unsatisfying answer, but the jury seems to still be out. Laitin's chapter is evidence of the ambiguity here. Laitin is a foremost proponent of the constructivist approach. Even the title of his chapter, "Culture Shift in a Postcommunist State," highlights the dynamic aspects of identity. He discusses three political "games" that involve strategic choice as the dominant concept. Yet, he is forced to conclude, "The processes described in this chapter have a deterministic quality to them." In his view, "In sum, young Russian-speakers will have little choice but to accept the challenge of a dual integration process—into Estonia and into Europe." Although choice-based strategic action models help us understand underlying processes, it is these underlying processes that are doing the heavy lifting. The ability of elites to make choices to change the direction of culture shift seems limited.

Constructivists often criticize existing work on ethnicity as unselfconsciously taking ethnic group categories as givens, rather than justifying their use and being sensitive to the possibilities of change in ethnic identity. In this volume, the authors would appear to be guilty of this charge. The authors do usually analyze ethnic groups as givens. Barany finds it relatively unproblematic to discuss Macedonian Albanians and Roma; Moser analyzes Russians, Lithuanians, and Poles; Chirot talks about Romanians and Bulgarians. The fact is that most scholars working in the postcommunist region still feel comfortable using such categories. In my own present work on Kosovo, I feel perfectly comfortable describing a conflict between Serbs and Albanians. In fact, I feel that it would be a waste of effort to spend too much time on justifying the use of these categories. Even for the Serbs in Kosovo who can speak the Albanian language, a switch from "Serb" to "Albanian-speaker" as primary political identity is simply not in the works.

To be sure, identities across postcommunist states have changed and are changing, but it is legitimate to ask whether there is something about ethnic identity in the postcommunist states in general that limits present possibilities for identity change and retards the rate of ethnic demographic change.

Even accepting the premises of constructivist theory, we find that several elements of the history of the region may limit the fluidity of identity change. First, reductions have occurred in the number of identities in individual repertoires capable of being mobilized. Consider the major sources of cleavage in the region: language, nation, and religion. During the Communist period, religion atrophied in some cases to the point that it could no longer be a viable choice for political mobilization. In other cases, two of the three categories have become essentially synonymous. Orthodoxy defines Serb nationality, for example. In other cases, language and nationality are inseparable. In still other cases, all three categories seem to go together in one seamless package. The Lithuanian nation is nearly synonymous with Lithuanian-speaking and Catholicism. Although one can always point out exceptions in any case, the number of ethnic categories that can realistically mobilize a significant portion of the population is often very limited. In Africa, by way of contrast, the numbers of tribal, linguistic, and local affiliations are often quite numerous. In Dan Posner's forthcoming work on ethnic politics in Africa, he points out that Zambia has either thirty-nine or seventy tribes, depending on how you count them, as well as four major languages and the major religions.[13] In this situation, political entrepreneurs may have several choices in raising the salience of a given dimension in order to form a new type of winning coalition. In India, multitudinous linguistic, religious, regional, and caste identities provide numerous opportunities for the strategic construction of identity. In contrast, the number of categories available for mobilization in Eastern Europe today is usually more limited.

Furthermore, Communist politics and regional history have worked to limit the types of strategies available to both individuals and elites. Many republics witnessed a process of consolidation of power and ethnic homogenization in favor of the titular nationalities.[14] In some cases, this political process built on a demographic "unmixing" of peoples that occurred earlier, to use Brubaker's terminology.[15] The result has been one clearly dominant ethnic group facing off against minorities. In this situation, strategic decisions are limited. The major question is simply how the minorities will adapt to a subordinate status, and, as in the case of Estonia's Russians, this choice often seems largely determined in advance.

Finally, the use of force and violence in the region tends to harden ethnic boundaries. In much of the postcommunist world, schoolchildren learn the stories of when an "other" committed atrocities against "us."[16] Although it may be easy to mobilize victim-based identities for defense or violence, these identities may prove resistant to the types of combination and evolution envisioned by constructivist theory.

Still, many of the postcommunist states provide a laboratory for the study of identity change and the testing of constructivist hypotheses. In Ukraine, many who identify with the Ukrainian nation speak only Russian, and some who identify themselves as Russians are fluent in Ukrainian. What long-term evolution can we expect in this case? The Hungarian and Russian diasporas face crucial decisions regarding language and assimilation. Albanian-speakers are spread across Albania, Kosovo, Macedonia, southern Serbia, Montenegro, and Greece. Will a common Albanian identity emerge capable of generating a "greater Albania" movement? What is the difference between a Serb and a Montenegrin and is that difference worthy of another independent state? Could the term "Bosnian" ever be embraced by the majority of people who live in Bosnia? And what about the Ruthenians? In each of these cases, we can expect to find identity entrepreneurs at work. Whether and to what extent they can restructure incentives to shape the direction of identity shift in these cases is an open question.

Directions for Future Research

To appreciate the level of complexity in the ethnopolitics of postcommunist states, one need only survey the nature of variation in the empirically oriented chapters of this volume. In Zoltan Barany's study, Roma have been less able to mobilize than the Albanian community in Macedonia despite the assistance Roma have received from the international community and NGOs. In Charles King's work on trafficking, the majority of trafficked women appear to come from the three states of Moldova, Romania, and Ukraine, whereas other states in the region are "barely on the trafficking map." In Robert Moser's chapter, we see wide variation in the ability of ethnic groups to form and sustain parties, with significant differences even between the Poles and Russians in Lithuania. In David Laitin's work, integration of domestic cultures, linguistic assimilation, and integration into a common external framework are occurring simultaneously. In Daniel Chirot's view, the same leaders are capable of fostering both ethnic tolerance and ethnic hatred, depending on the setting and timing of their decisions. In every case, it is necessary to examine multiple variables working in conjunction in order to explain the outcome.

So, to return to the question at the beginning of this essay, what are social scientists supposed to do with this riotous variation? The chapters in this volume suggest directions for future research. First, if the contributions here are representative of current and future scholarship, work on postcommunist ethnicity will be conducted at different levels of analysis. Laitin studies the impact of individual choices of the general population. Barany examines the organizational and mobilization capacities of ethnic groups. King concentrates on the state and its institutions. Chirot's essay is an impassioned call to take into account the power of individual leaders to change the course of events. Beissinger's work in this volume is at the level of the international system. Given all of the work done at different levels of analysis, there is a need to examine the ways in which outcomes at one level affect outcomes at another level. For example, one could imagine working to integrate the insights of Barany and Laitin. Barany's definition of political mobilization is "the process by which a group goes from being a passive collection of individuals to an active participant in public life." Barany concentrates on group level characteristics such as opportunity, educational levels that breed leaders, and identity formation. Barany's work raises several interesting questions that might be answered through a closer look at micromechanisms. Some of these individual level mechanisms can be found in Laitin's tipping models. Focusing on these forces would help explain why individuals choose to end their passivity and take an active role in an ethnic group's political life. For instance, Barany illustrates how certain ethnic groups such as Roma lack organizational capacity because of excessive fragmentation in political representation. But what accounts for individuals in that group continuing to join a wide variety of seemingly ineffective institutions? Barany suggests some answers to this question, but there is room for systematic individual level work, perhaps employing game theory, to answer such questions more definitively. Likewise, King's chapter suggests directions for linking levels of analysis in this fashion. King outlines the influence of formal state level institutions and the role of informal ethnic networks, but rewarding work can be accomplished by more specifically establishing the link between the two. What are the ways in which changes in state capacity transform ethnic networks? What are the ways in which the continued success of informal ethnic networks in subverting and avoiding state sanctions change the way in which states evolve?

Second, Beissinger's and Chirot's chapters make a convincing case for cross-national comparison with countries outside the region. Although most comparative work will remain "most similar case design" by nature (as in both Barany's and Moser's chapters), extremely useful insights can be gained by designs approaching "most different design." Chirot constructs such a design by comparing African cases with Balkan cases. At various junctures in his chapter, Beissinger compares the discourse and claims-making about empire across a wide variety of cases. At the core of the study of postcommunist states is the issue of an empire (or at least a multinational entity) transforming itself into a set of modern states. The Soviet Union is not the only instance of this phenomenon, and lessons can surely be learned from other cases and from systematically comparing these cases.

Third, although the contributors here have not dwelled on the lasting effects of the old system, I find it hard to believe that we have a full understanding of Communism's legacy. Moser's chapter suggests several important aspects of this legacy in post-Soviet electoral politics. The nature of ethnic federalism is one example. The nature of continued elite control over the electoral process in the non-Russian regions of the Russian Federation is possibly another. The general high salience of ethnicity in the region is a third. Still, the shadow of the Soviet Union, and also Yugoslavia, is not fully understood.

Finally, Kymlicka's chapter points out the absolute necessity of studying international influences and norms on postcommunist ethnic policies in a globalizing world. His chapter shows both the importance of these forces and their indeterminacy.

I will end by quoting from Suny's Introduction: "The essays in this volume range from optimistic to pessimistic, but overall the impression they give is of no inevitable slide from difference to discrimination to conflict." Ethnic politics in postcommunist states will be influenced by the policies of the West, the legacies of Communism, and other historical and social forces, but the range of possibilities for the region remains wide. The politics of the region will remain complex. It is a good time to be a social scientist studying ethnic politics in postcommunist states because opportunities and challenges abound.

NOTES

Introduction

1. Ernest Gellner, *Nations and Nationalism* (Ithaca: Cornell University Press, 1983), 48–49; Ronald Grigor Suny, *The Revenge of the Past: Nationalism, Revolution, and the Collapse of the Soviet Union* (Stanford: Stanford University Press, 1993), 3–4. The latter term was suggested by my late friend Reginald Zelnik.

2. For a contrasting view, see Charles King, "Crisis in the Caucasus: A New Look at Russia's Chechen Impasse," *Foreign Affairs* 82:2 (2003): 138.

3. For a representative sample of works dealing with nations and nationalism, see Gellner, *Nations and Nationalism;* Eric J. Hobsbawm and Terence Ranger, eds., *The Invention of Tradition* (Cambridge: Cambridge University Press, 1985); Benedict Anderson, *Imagined Communities: Reflections on the Origins and Spread of Nationalism* (London: Verso, 1991); Rogers Brubaker, *Nationalism Reframed: Nationhood and the National Question in the New Europe* (Cambridge: Cambridge University Press, 1996); Partha Chatterjee, *Nationalist Thought and the Colonial World: A Derivative Discourse* (Minneapolis: University of Minnesota Press, 1993); Suny, *Revenge of the Past;* Geoff Eley and Ronald Grigor Suny, *Becoming National: A Reader* (New York: Oxford University Press, 1996); Ronald Grigor Suny and Michael D. Kennedy, eds., *Intellectuals and the Articulation of the Nation* (Ann Arbor: University of Michigan Press, 1999); and Michael Hechter, *Containing Nationalism* (Oxford: Oxford University Press, 2000). For various approaches to ethnic, civil, and nationalist conflict, see David D. Laitin, *Identity in Formation: The Russian-Speaking Populations in the Near Abroad* (Ithaca: Cornell University Press, 1998); Michael E. Brown, Owen R. Core, Sean M. Lynn-Jones, and Steven M. Miller, eds., *Nationalism and Ethnic Conflict* (Cambridge: MIT Press, 2001); Jeff Goodwin, James M. Jasper, and Francesca Polletta, eds., *Passionate Politics: Emotions and Social Movements* (Chicago: University of Chicago Press, 2001); E. J. Hobsbawm, *Nations and Nationalism Since 1780: Programme, Myth, Reality* (Cambridge: Cambridge University Press, 1992); Stuart J. Kaufman, *Modern Hatreds: The Symbolic Politics of Ethnic War* (Ithaca: Cornell University Press, 2001); and Roger D. Petersen, *Understanding Ethnic Violence: Fear, Hatred, and Resentment in Twentieth-Century Eastern Europe* (Cambridge: Cambridge University Press, 2002).

Chapter 1. Rethinking Empire

1. Terry Martin, *The Affirmative Action Empire: Nations and Nationalism in the Soviet Union, 1923–1939* (Ithaca: Cornell University Press, 2001), 19.

2. Dominic Lieven, *Empire: The Russian Empire and Its Rivals* (New Haven: Yale University Press, 2000), xvi. Throughout this chapter, I use the terms modern state and nation-state interchangeably, as all states today claim to represent "nations."

3. Lieven, *Empire*, 22. Even those non-historians who studied empires did so in an historical fashion. See S. N. Eisenstadt, *The Political Systems of Empires: The Rise and Fall of the Historical Bureaucratic Societies* (New York: Free Press, 1963); John Kautsky, *The Politics of Aristocratic Empires* (Chapel Hill: University of North Carolina Press, 1982); Michael Doyle, *Empires* (Ithaca: Cornell University Press, 1986).

4. John Connell and Robert Aldrich, "The Last Colonies: Failures of Decolonisation?" in Chris Dixon and Michael Hefferman, eds., *Colonialism and Development in the Contemporary World* (London: Mansell, 1991), 196–97.

5. See, for instance, Lieven, *Empire*; Karen Dawisha and Bruce Parrott, eds., *The End of Empire? The Transformation of the USSR in Comparative Perspective* (Armonk, N.Y.: M. E. Sharpe, 1997); Richard L. Rudolph and David F. Good, eds., *Nationalism and Empire: The Habsburg Empire and the Soviet Union* (New York: St. Martin's Press, 1992); Karen Barkey and Mark von Hagen, eds., *After Empire: Multi-Ethnic Societies and Nation-Building: The Soviet Union and the Russian, Ottoman, and Habsburg Empires* (Boulder, Colo.: Westview, 1997); Alexander J. Motyl, *Imperial Ends: The Decay, Collapse, and Revival of Empires* (New York: Columbia University Press, 2001). A number of the essays in the Barkey and von Hagen volume question whether the USSR deserves to be treated as an analytical unit analogous to Tsarist, Ottoman, and Habsburg empires.

6. Alexander J. Motyl, *Revolutions, Nations, Empires: Conceptual Limits and Theoretical Possibilities* (New York: Columbia University Press, 1999), 121–22.

7. Thomas J. Barfield, "The Shadow Empires: Imperial State Formation along the Chinese-Nomad Frontier," in Susan E. Alcock, Terrence N. D'Altroy, Kathleen D. Morrison, and Carla M. Sinopoli, eds., *Empires: Perspectives from Archeology and History* (Cambridge: Cambridge University Press, 2001), 33.

8. See William H. Sewell Jr., "Three Temporalities: Toward an Eventful Sociology," in Terrence J. McDonald, ed., *The Historic Turn in the Human Sciences* (Ann Arbor: University of Michigan Press, 1996), 245–80. This latter issue, known as Galton's problem, is a much more serious problem within social science than simply the study of empires. See John H. Goldthorpe, "Current Issues in Comparative Macrosociology: A Debate on Methodological Issues," in Grete Brochmann et al., eds., *Comparative Social Research*, vol. 16 (Greenwich, CT: JAI Press, 1997), 9–12.

9. The most obvious example is empire's disembodiment from the state by Michael Hardt and Antonio Negri to represent "the political subject that effectively regulates . . . global exchanges, the sovereign power that governs the world." Michael Hardt and Antonio Negri, *Empire* (Cambridge: Harvard University Press), xi.

10. Referring to the collapse of Soviet Union and Ethiopia, Miles Kahler, for instance, writes: "The last remaining multinational empires collapsed in the 1990s. . . . Although many contemporary multinational states oppress ethnic and linguistic minorities, none can be characterized as an empire." Miles Kahler, "Empires, Neo-Empires, and Political Change: The British and French Experience," in Dawisha and Parrott, *The End of Empire?*, 286.

11. This is a point made by both Charles Tilly and Eric Hobsbawm in Barkey and von Hagen, *After Empire*, 5, 13.

12. See David D. Laitin, "The National Uprisings in the Soviet Union," *World Politics* 44:1 (1991): 142–43.

13. Ronald Suny, "Ambiguous Categories: States, Empires, and Nations," *Post-Soviet Affairs* 11:2 (1995): 185–96.

14. Rogers Brubaker, *Nationalism Reframed: Nationhood and the National Question in the New Europe* (Cambridge: Cambridge University Press, 1996), 13–22.

15. Rogers Brubaker made this point at the conference at which this essay was first presented.

16. Class is another example of a category of practice that also can function as a category of analysis, particularly if we accept E. P. Thompson's point that class is a social and cultural formation, not an objective category unrelated to consciousness of the category itself.

17. In an earlier essay, I suggested the term "empire consciousness" as a way of describing this quality of being regarded as an empire, paralleling the notion of class consciousness. See Mark R. Beissinger, "Demise of an Empire-State: Identity, Legitimacy, and the Deconstruction of Soviet Politics," in M. Crawford Young, ed., *The Rising Tide of Cultural Pluralism* (Madison: University of Wisconsin Press, 1993), 93–115. According to the *Oxford English Dictionary*, in the eighteenth and nineteenth centuries one could find (though rarely) the word "imperialness" to refer to the imperial quality of a person or thing, though the word was also used as a humorous and mocking title.

18. Brubaker, *Nationalism Reframed*, 16.

19. I should note that empire as an outcome need not be confined to authoritarian states. Indeed, widely recognized, illegitimate control over multiple, culturally distinct populations within or beyond state boundaries has been characteristic of many democratic states, including the United States, France, and Britain. On the United States, see Francis Jennings, *The Creation of America: Through Revolution to Empire* (Cambridge: Cambridge University Press, 2000); J. G. A. Pocock, "States, Republics, and Empires: The American Founding in Early Modern Perspective," in Terence Ball and J. G. A. Pocock, eds., *Conceptual Change and the Constitution* (Lawrence: University of Kansas Press, 1988), 55–77.

20. See, for instance, Johan Galtung, "A Structural Theory of Imperialism," *Journal of Peace Research* 8:2 (1971): 81–117; Andre Gunther Frank, *Capitalism and Underdevelopment in Latin America* (New York: Monthly Review, 1967); Theotonio dos Santos, "The Structure of Dependence," in K. T. Fann and Donald C. Hodges, eds., *Readings in U.S. Imperialism* (Boston: P. Sargent, 1971), 225–36. Stephen Howe observes that "a consensus definition would be that an empire is a large political body which rules over territories outside its original borders. It has a central power or core territory—whose inhabitants usually continue to form the dominant ethnic or national group in the entire system—and an extensive periphery of dominated areas." Stephen Howe, *Empire: A Very Short Introduction* (Oxford: Oxford University Press, 2002), 14.

21. Doyle, *Empires*, 12, 30, 45–46.

22. As Bruce Parrott explains, "The advent of nationality as a key criterion of political differentiation and of nationalism as a potent instrument of political mobilization fundamentally altered the internal dynamics of empires. Partly in consequence, by the middle of the twentieth century the term was commonly used to denote a political structure in which one nation dominated others, often on the basis of an authoritar-

ian metropolitan state." Bruce Parrott, "Analyzing the Transformation of the Soviet Union in Comparative Perspective," in Dawisha and Parrott, *The End of Empire?*, 6.

23. The contemporary Kingdom of Saudi Arabia is one such example.

24. See, for instance, Aviel Roshwald, *Ethnic Nationalism and the Fall of Empires: Central Europe, the Middle East, and Russia, 1914–1923* (New York: Routledge, 2001).

25. See, for instance, the *Oxford English Dictionary* entries on "empire," which, for all definitions, contain no structural connotations whatsoever.

26. Howe, *Empire: A Very Short Introduction*, 13.

27. Richard Koebner and Helmut D. Schmidt, *Imperialism: The Story and Significance of a Political Word, 1840–1960* (Cambridge: Cambridge University Press, 1964), xxv.

28. Quoted in Richard Koebner, *Empire* (New York: Grosset & Dunlap, 1961), 295. J. G. A. Pocock notes that, to the American revolutionaries, the term "empire" was used to refer to any large political unit with complex structure and was used interchangeably with the words "confederacy" and "republic." Pocock, "States, Republics, and Empires," in Ball and Pocock, *Conceptual Change and the Constitution*, 67–69.

29. Mandate implied a temporary rule in anticipation of nationhood. Thus, the League's Covenant recognized that "certain communities formerly belonging to the Turkish Empire" had already "reached a stage of development where their existence as independent nations can be provisionally recognized subject to the rendering of administrative advice and assistance by a Mandatory until such time as they are able to stand alone." See http://www.yale.edu/lawweb/avalon/leagcov.htm.

30. Koebner and Schmidt, *Imperialism*, xiii and xxii. See also Hans Daalder, "Imperialism," in David Sills, ed., *International Encyclopedia of the Social Sciences*, vol. 7 (New York: Macmillan, 1968), 101–109.

31. Rupert Emerson, *From Empire to Nation: The Rise of Self-Assertion of Asian and African Peoples* (Cambridge: Harvard University Press, 1967).

32. Doyle, *Empires*, 36.

33. Ernest Gellner, *Nations and Nationalism* (Ithaca: Cornell University Press, 1983), 1.

34. Jack P. Greene, "Transatlantic Colonization and the Redefinition of Empire in the Early Modern Era," in Christine Daniels and Michael V. Kennedy, eds., *Negotiated Empires: Centers and Peripheries in the Americas, 1500–1820* (New York: Routledge, 2002), 268.

35. Ann Laura Stoler and Frederick Cooper, "Between Metropole and Colony: Rethinking a Research Agenda," in Frederick Cooper and Ann Laura Stoler, eds., *Tensions of Empire: Colonial Culture in a Bourgeois World* (Berkeley: University of California Press, 1997), 7, 22. See also John L. Comaroff, "Images of Empire, Contests of Conscience: Models of Colonial Domination in South Africa," *American Ethnologist* 16:4 (1989): 661–85.

36. Motyl, *Revolutions, Nations, Empires*, 117–18. The evidence Motyl provides is that for three years, from 1976 until 1979, when he was overthrown, Jean-Bedel Bokassa, the corrupt and demented military dictator of the Central African Republic, proclaimed his country the Central African Empire in an attempt to imitate his hero, Napoleon I. Motyl sees this as evidence that the way in which polities label themselves is irrelevant, since the Central African Empire's claim to be an empire was absurd. Yet, Bokassa's insanity can be interpreted to support precisely the contrary view: that no ruler who cares about legitimacy and the duration of rule would dare label his or her polity an empire in a postimperial world.

37. As Bourdieu noted, "The harder it is to exercise direct domination, and the more it is disapproved of, the more likely it is that gentle, disguised forms of domination will be seen as the only possible way of exercising domination and exploitation." Pierre Bourdieu, *The Logic of Practice* (Stanford: Stanford University Press, 1990), 128.

38. Lieven, *Empire*, x.

39. Martin, *The Affirmative Action Empire*, 19.

40. Though not a central element of this essay, the United States also played a significant role in developing the practice of using emerging norms of sovereignty and self-determination to solidify nonconsensual control. Despite engaging in openly imperial activities throughout the nineteenth and early twentieth centuries, the United States eventually repackaged its early revolutionary history as anticolonial in the twentieth century in response to the growth of anticolonial nationalism as a major political force in world affairs. Ultimately, as British historian Niall Ferguson has noted, America became "the empire that dare not speak its name." Quoted in the *New York Times*, April 30, 2003, A31.

41. In imitation of the Soviets, in the 1930s and 1940s Nazi Germany and the Japanese similarly created formally sovereign "puppet" states in Eastern Europe and China as ways of establishing control over territories under the cover of norms of state sovereignty.

42. Zbigniew Brzezinski, *The Soviet Bloc: Unity and Conflict* (Cambridge: Harvard University Press, 1967), 39.

43. Adam Ulam, *Expansion and Coexistence: Soviet Foreign Policy, 1917–1973* (New York: Praeger, 1974).

44. David A. Lake, "The Rise, Fall, and Future of the Russian Empire: A Theoretical Interpretation," in Dawisha and Parrott, *The End of Empire?*, 35. Actually, most examples of informal empires are not as hierarchical and centralized as was the Soviet sphere of influence in East Europe.

45. G. John Ikenberry and Charles A. Kupchan, "Socialization and Hegemonic Power," *International Organization* 44:3 (1990): 286.

46. David A. Lake, "The Rise, Fall, and Future of the Russian Empire," in Dawisha and Parrott, *The End of Empire?*, 58–59.

47. Mark R. Beissinger, *Nationalist Mobilization and the Collapse of the Soviet State: A Tidal Approach to the Study of Nationalism* (Cambridge: Cambridge University Press, 2002).

48. Ian Clark, "Another 'Double Movement': The Great Transformation after the Cold War?" in Michael Cox, Tim Dunne, and Ken Booth, eds., *Empires, Systems, and States: Great Transformations in International Politics* (Cambridge: Cambridge University Press, 2001), 250.

49. The other state bearing significant responsibility for this transformation is the United States, particularly in its unusual policy of colonialism in the name of self-determination in Panama, the Philippines, and elsewhere in the early twentieth century. But this subject lies beyond the scope of this essay.

50. Though its classifications have been disputed, the State Failure Project, set up at the request of Vice President Al Gore in 1994 and led by the CIA, along with a distinguished group of academics, identified 136 cases of state failure from 1955 through 2001, but only a handful of these (the USSR and Ethiopia, for example) were subject to charges of being empires. For the project's list of cases, see http://www.cidcm.umd.edu/inscr/stfail/.

51. Lieven, *Empire*, 330.

52. Terry Martin "The Soviet Union as Empire: Salvaging a Dubious Analytical Category," *Ab Imperio* 2 (2002): 103.

53. Of postcolonial states, Indonesia has been most frequently described as an empire, in significant part because its invasion of East Timor and the subsequent violent struggle that this engendered, which undermined much of the anticolonial aura surrounding the Indonesian state (though even here, Indonesia has largely avoided widespread recognition as empire, in contrast to the Soviet and post-Soviet Russian cases). Its archipelago structure also makes for greater structural clarity between center and periphery. See Nicholas D. Kristof, "Indonesia Struggles to Find New Reasons to Stay Intact," *New York Times*, May 24, 1998, A1; Slobodan Lekic, "50,000 Rally for Independence in Indonesia," *Boston Globe*, November 5, 1999, A29; Mark Landler, "In Indonesia, Rebel Leader Gains Forum for His Cause," *New York Times*, November 28, 1999, A7; Eric Margolis, "The Decline and Fall of the Javanese Empire," at http://www.foreigncorrespondent.com/archive/timor.html.

54. A good example of the latter are the charges leveled against the United States of engaging in "genetic imperialism" in 1995–1996 by patenting a blood cell line drawn from a remote Papua New Guinea tribe. See Charles J. Hanley, "Blood's Value Fades, as Does 'Genetic Colonialism' Charge," *Wisconsin State Journal*, September 22, 1996, 4A.

55. On post-Soviet Russia, see Mark R. Beissinger, "The Persisting Ambiguity of Empire," *Post-Soviet Affairs* 11:2 (1995): 149–84. On Ethiopia, see Ruth Iyob, *The Eritrean Struggle for Independence: Domination, Resistance, Nationalism, 1941–1993* (Cambridge: Cambridge University Press, 1995); Edmond J. Keller, *Revolutionary Ethiopia: From Empire to People's Republic* (Bloomington: Indiana University Press, 1988). Accusations that contemporary China is an empire are widespread among Tibetans, Uighurs, and Mongols. See Gardner Bovingdon, "The Not-So-Silent Majority: Uyghur Resistance to Han Rule in Xinjiang," *Modern China* 28:1 (2002): 39–78; Ross Terrill, *The New Chinese Empire* (New York: Basic Books, 2003). Until his arrest and sentence to death in 1999, Abdullah Ocalan, the leader of the Kurdish Workers' Party (PKK), frequently made reference, in the language of Marxism-Leninism, to "Turkish colonialism," and the 1995 program of the party said the end to "Turkish colonialism" in Kurdistan was the main task of the party. Among Basques, ETA also has described itself fighting against "Spanish imperialism," with a heavy emphasis on Marxist-Leninist categories of analysis. On accusations that the United States has become an empire in the wake of the Bush administration's unilateralism and willingness to wield force around the globe to shape an international order to its liking, despite the administration's denial of imperial intent, description of pre-emptive war as self-defense, and deployment of a discourse of liberation and sovereignty to describe its actions, see Michael Ignatieff, "The American Empire: The Burden," *New York Times Magazine*, January 5, 2003, 22–27, 50–54. On current Azerbaijani accusations against Iran as an empire, see "Ethnic Azeris Urged to Fight for Independence in Iran," *Turan News Agency*, May 30, 1998, in *FBIS Daily Report (Central Eurasia)*, June 1, 1998; Brenda Shafer, *Borders and Brethren: Iran and the Challenge of Azerbaijani Identity* (Cambridge: MIT Press, 2002).

56. Interview with Putin in *Bratislava Narodna Obroda*, March 7, 2000, in *FBIS*, March 8, 2000.

57. Charles King, "Crisis in the Caucasus: A New Look at Russia's Chechen Impasse," *Foreign Affairs* 82:2 (2003): 138.

58. Beissinger, *Nationalist Mobilization and the Collapse of the Soviet State*, 263–267.

59. *Current Digest of Post-Soviet Press* 46:52 (1994): 7.

60. See Anatol Lieven, *Chechnya: Tombstone of Russian Power* (New Haven: Yale University Press, 1998). For more recent Chechen views, see the website of the Ministry of Foreign Affairs of the Chechen Republic of Ichkeria, at http://www.chechnya-mfa.info/.

61. Quoted in *New York Times Magazine*, March 19, 2000, 65.

62. *Chechnya Weekly* 4:4 (Jamestown Foundation), February 13, 2003; *Chechnya Weekly* 4:10, March 27, 2003.

63. *Ekspress khronika*, November 12, 1991, 2.

64. See, for example, Douglas W. Blum, ed., *Russia's Future: Consolidation or Disintegration?* (Boulder. Colo.: Westview, 1994).

65. See, for instance, *RFE/RL Bashkir-Tatar Report*, October 9, 2002.

66. Susan B. Glasser, "In a Russian Republic, ABCs Are Test of Power," *Washington Post*, April 16, 2001, A1.

67. For several excellent studies recognizing how the "stigma of empire" continues to color relations between the post-Soviet states, see Rawi Abdelal, *National Purpose in the World Economy: Post-Soviet States in Comparative Perspective* (Ithaca: Cornell University Press, 2001); Andrew Wilson, *The Ukrainians: Unexpected Nation* (New Haven: Yale University Press, 2000); Catherine Wanner, *Burden of Dreams: History and Identity in Post-Soviet Ukraine* (University Park: Pennsylvania State University Press, 1998); Graham Smith et al., *Nation-Building in the Post-Soviet Borderlands: The Politics of National Identities* (Cambridge: Cambridge University Press, 1998).

68. *Interfax*, December 15, 1999, in *FBIS*, December 15, 1999.

69. *Izvestiia*, October 27, 1999, 1.

70. *Interfax*, March 22, 1998, in *FBIS*, March 22, 1998; *RFE/RL Newsline*, August 31, 1999.

71. *Kommersant-Daily*, March 9, 2000, 11.

72. *RFE/RL Newsline*, September 22, 2003.

73. How widespread this discourse is remains unclear, though a public opinion poll conducted in 1999 discovered that 32 percent of the population of Russia agreed with the statement that the historical mission of Russia is to unite nations into a union that must become the successor to the Russian Empire and the USSR. *Novye izvestiia*, November 1, 1999, 1.

74. *Rossiiskaia gazeta*, December 4, 1999, in *FBIS*, December 4, 1999, 2.

75. Andrei Savel'ev, "Priglashenie k razgovoru," and Andrei Kol'ev, "Imperiia—sud'ba Rossii," in A. N. Savel'ev, ed., *Neizbezhnost' imperii* (Moscow: Intellekt, 1996), 3 and 81.

76. Igor' Yadykin, "My—imperiia-osvoboditel'," *Krasnaia zvezda*, March 20, 1999.

77. Quoted in Alexander Zevelev, "Russia-Belarus Union: A Step in the Right Direction," *Russia Journal*, March 3, 2000.

78. Ignatieff, "The American Empire: The Burden," 22.

79. Sebastian Mallaby, "The Reluctant Imperialist," *Foreign Affairs* 81:2 (2002): 2. For other statements to this effect, see James Chace, "Imperial America and the Common Interest," *World Policy Journal* 19:1 (2002): 1–9; Andrew J. Bacevich, *American Empire: The Realities and Consequences of U.S. Diplomacy* (Cambridge: Harvard University Press, 2002); Andrew J. Bacevich, ed., *The Imperial Tense: Prospects and Problems of the American Empire* (Chicago: Ivan R. Dee, 2003); Chalmers Johnson, *Blowback: The*

Costs and Consequences of American Empire (New York: Metropolitan Books, 2000); and the special issue of *National Interest* (spring 2003) devoted to America as an empire.

80. Quoted in *New York Times*, April 30, 2003, A31.

81. Max Boot, "American Imperialism? No Need to Run Away from Label," *USA Today*, May 6, 2003, A15.

Chapter 2. Culture Shift in a Postcommunist State

An earlier version of this essay, framed somewhat differently, was published as "Three Models of Integration and the Estonian/Russian Reality," *Journal of Baltic Studies* 34:2 (2003): 197–222. In addition to those acknowledged in that version, Rogers Brubaker and Robert Moser offered comments that help sharpen arguments for this revised version.

1. The most balanced account of the issue remains that of Paul Kolstoe, *Russians in the Former Soviet Republics* (Bloomington: Indiana University Press, 1995), in which he reports (290) that "many observers regard the new Russian diaspora as a threat to political stability in the former Soviet Union."

2. In this chapter, use of the term "Russian" refers to the non-Estonian population in Estonia. The term is interchangeable with "Russian-Estonians."

3. Here—as in much of my research—I focus on language and the medium of instruction in schooling as an indicator of culture. Since language repertoires influence social contacts, parental choices on schooling had long-term cultural implications. Whom their children would marry, and the cultural milieu that would be central to those children's future, would be heavily influenced by the choice of language medium for early education.

4. Not all titulars claimed fluency in their ancestral languages. In Tatarstan, 25% of the Tatars claimed no fluency in the Tatar language; in Estonia, the figure was the lowest in the union, at 0.8%. There was some trilingualism in the Soviet Union. In Tatarstan nearly 7% of the minority Bashkirs claimed fluency in Russian, Tatar, and Bashkir; in Bashkortostan, 23% of the Bashkirs and 16% of the Tatars claimed fluency in those three languages. However, these are special cases. For a discussion of the equilibrium and the data for these special cases, see David Laitin, "What Is a Language Community?" in *American Journal of Political Science* 44:1 (2000): 142–55.

5. The choices by Russians and titulars in regard to culture were best-guess calculations about coordinating with all members of their groups, because the success of any strategy was dependent on the strategies of others in a similar situation. Choice models are therefore most telling in times of disequilibrium, when calculation about others' likely behaviors is a crucial consideration in one's own choices. Thus, cultural strategy becomes manifest under conditions of rapid social and political change.

6. These were the trends as identified in my *Identity in Formation: The Russian-speaking Populations in the Near Abroad* (Ithaca: Cornell University Press, 1998). The fieldwork for that book was completed in 1994.

7. For this perspective, see Toivo U. Raun's distinguished *Estonia and the Estonians* (Stanford: Hoover Institution Press, 1987). For an Estonian scholar who rejects this primordialist approach to national culture, see Rein Taagepera, *Estonia: Return to Independence* (Boulder, Colo.: Westview Press, 1993). For data that show a mild but stable Estonian/Russian polarization, see Geoffrey Evans, "Ethnic Schism and the Consoli-

dation of Post-Communist Democracies: The Case of Estonia," *Communist and Post-Communist Studies* 31:1 (1998): 57–74.

8. An excellent theoretical introduction is that of R. A. Schermerhorn, *Comparative Ethnic Relations* (Chicago: University of Chicago Press, 1970).

9. Ernest Gellner, *Thought and Change* (Chicago: University of Chicago Press, 1964), chap. 7.

10. Abram de Swaan, *In Care of the State* (Oxford: Oxford University Press, 1989); David Laitin, "Language Games," *Comparative Politics* 20:3 (April 1988): 289–302.

11. Eugen Weber, *Peasants into Frenchmen* (Stanford: Stanford University Press, 1976).

12. Many studies, such as Geoffrey Evans and Christine Lipsmeyer, "The Democratic Experience in Divided Societies: The Baltic States in Comparative Perspective," *Journal of Baltic Studies* 32:4 (2001): 379–401, take evidence of discontent (about democracy) by the minority as evidence of a "hard-line nature of ethnic relations in Estonia" (394). They discount the possibility that what they call an "ethnic gap" (391) gives incentives for ambitious members of the minority group to "pass." My point will be that hard-line relations and assimilation are not alternative realities, but can be part of the same social reality.

13. The most comprehensive treatment of the internal political dynamics of this period in regard to the integration issue is that by Vello Pettai and Klara Hallik, "Understanding Processes of Ethnic Control: Segmentation, Dependency and Co-optation in Post-Communist Estonia," *Nations and Nationalism* 8:4 (2002): 505–29.

14. S. Smirnov, *Molodezh Estonii*, March 8, 1999.

15. For this essay, I examined all articles on the nationality issue that appeared in four newspapers (two in Estonian and two in Russian) during the first three days of each month, from January 1999 (the beginning of the integration program) through April 2002. This gave me a broad and random selection of articles for analysis that went into the narratives presented here. I did not perform quantitative content analyses of this dataset, though such work is being carried on at the Integration Foundation of Estonia. For a sophisticated use of content analysis of the Russian and Estonian newspaper reports on issues of integration, see Külliki Korts and Ragne Kõuts, "Media as the Open Forum of Integration," in Marju Lauristin and Raivo Vetik, eds., *Integration of Estonian Society* (Tallinn: Integration Foundation, 2000), 49–54. At the time of preparation of this book, data from this continuing media monitoring were not available for the period following the initiation of the integration program. I therefore constructed my own smaller dataset that is insufficient for statistical analysis. I believe, however, that I have captured the essence of the political debate. In the future, the Integration Foundation's dataset on media reports, after statistical analysis of content, should serve as a corrective to my interpretations herein.

16. Baltic News Service, *Estoniya*, April 1, 2002.

17. Open Society Institute, "Minority Protection in Estonia," 2001.

18. *Molodezh Estonii*, December 2, 2000.

19. *Eesti Päevaleht*, March 2, 2000.

20. *Molodezh Estonii*, January 2, 2000.

21. Maxim Rogalski, *Estoniya*, February 4, 2001.

22. *Molodezh Estonii*, February 2, 2000.

23. Aleksandr Erek, *Molodezh Estonii*, February 3, 2001.

24. Svetlana Loginova, *Molodezh Estonii*, January 6, 2001.

25. Yevgeny Kapov, *Estoniya*, February 6, 2001.

26. T. A., *Molodezh Estonii*, February 7, 2001.

27. *Eesti Päevaleht*, May 2, 2002.

28. *Molodezh Estonii*, May 2, 2002.

29. Open Society Institute, "Minority Protection in Estonia," *Monitoring the EU Accession Process*, 2001.

30. Granted, there are many grounds based on liberal political theory that would point to deficiencies in Estonia's treatment of Russians living in Estonia. See, for example, Will Kymlicka, "Estonia's Integration Policies in a Comparative Perspective," in *Estonia's Integration Landscape: From Apathy to Harmony* (Tallinn: Jaan Tõnissoni Instituut, 2000), 29–57. But although Estonia had been asked to meet the Copenhagen criteria for the protection of minorities in order to be accepted as a member of the European Union, several members of the Union do not themselves meet these criteria. Quite hypocritically, by EU law, Copenhagen criteria do not apply to EU members. On within-EU violations, see Open Society Institute, *Monitoring the EU Accession Process: Minority Protection*, vol. II, *Case Studies in Selected Member States* (Budapest, 2002), esp. 18–19. Although I endorse criticisms of Estonia's minority-rights record, I still claim with confidence that its record is not an outlier by all-European standards.

31. Veronika Maandi, *Molodezh Estonii*, February 4, 2001.

32. *Molodezh Estonii*, February 8, 2002.

33. Maxim Volkov, *Estoniya*, May 2, 2002.

34. Galina Smolina, *Molodezh Estonii*, February 9, 2002.

35. Sergei Ivanov, *Molodezh Estonii*, March 1, 2002.

36. Evgeni Kapov, *Estoniya*, October 3, 2001.

37. Yana Mayevskaya, *Molodezh Estonii*, August 2, 2001.

38. Yana Mayevskaya, *Molodezh Estonii*, October 1, 2001.

39. "Integratsiya," *Õhtuleht*, May 3, 2000.

40. Author interview, October 25, 2002.

41. Anneli Ammas, *Eesti Päevaleht*.

42. Rein Sikk, *Eesti Päevaleht*, October 2, 1999.

43. *Õhtuleht*, April 3, 2000.

44. Jüri Kõre, *Eesti Päevaleht*. That non-Estonians who speak Estonian earn higher wages is confirmed in Marje Pavelson and Mai Luuk,"Non-Estonians on the Labor Market: A Change in the Economic Model and Difference in Social Capital," 69–98, in Marju Lauristin and Mati Heidmets, eds., *The Challenge of the Minority*, VERA 2001.

45. David Laitin, "The Cultural Identities of a European State," *Politics and Society* 25:3 (1997): 277–302.

46. Readers may object and ask if language and other cultural repertoires are sufficient to grasp deeper cultural differences. I address this objection in David D. Laitin, "Culture and National Identity: 'The East' and European Integration," *West European Politics* 25:2 (2002): 74–77.

47. See Marika Kirch and Aksel Kirch, "Change of National Identity," *Institute for European Studies*, 10 July 2001. For some data that show polarized views between Russians and Estonians in Estonia, see Geoffrey Evans, "Ethnic Schism and the Consolidation of Post-Communist Democracies: The Case of Estonia," *Communist and Post-Communist Studies* 31:1 (1998): 57–74; and Evans and Lipsmeyer, "The Democratic Experience," 2001. Many of their questions focus on issues such as whether the respondent believes that "everyone has an influence on elections" or has "satisfaction

with democracy" (Evans and Lipsmeyer, "The Democratic Experience," 387–88). Because most Russians are not citizens of Estonia, their negative answers reflect not cultural distance but rather political outrage. On the differences in nationality on the issue of Yugoslavia, see *Eesti Päevaleht*, April 3, 1999.

48. Mart Helme, *Eesti Päevaleht*, February 1, 2002.

49. Lauri Vahtre, *Õhtuleht*, April 2, 2002.

50. *Eesti Päevaleht*, October 2, 2000.

51. The immensely popular artist (and footballer) Jüri Homenja sings with Estonian and English lyrics, but is said to come from a Ukrainian Russian-speaking background.

52. *Molodezh Estonii*, October 1, 2001.

53. David D. Laitin, *Identity in Formation: The Russian-Speaking Populations in the Near Abroad* (Ithaca: Cornell University Press, 1998).

54. *Molodezh Estonii*, March 10, 2000.

55. V. Andreev, *Molodezh Estonii*, February 1, 2002.

56. Rein Sikk, *Eesti Päevaleht*, September 1, 1999.

57. Ivo Proos, a sociologist at a National Library conference sponsored by the Round Table on "Estonian System of Education and National Minorities." Aleksandr Erek, "Lullaby or Requiem for Integrant," *Molodezh Eestonii*, April 2, 2001.

58. For details on the survey, see the note that precedes the tables.

59. See Marju Lauristin and Mati Heidmets, eds., *The Challenge of the Russian Minority*, part V, "Media and Minority" (Tartu: Tartu University Press, 2002).

60. Ivo Proos, "Significance of Estonian Language in Integration of Non-Estonians," in *Estonia's Integration Landscape: From Apathy to Harmony* (Tallinn: Jaan Tõnissoni Instituut, 2000), 129.

61. *Integration in Estonian Society 2000–2007*, State Programme, Approved by the Government of Estonia on March 14, 2000 (Tallinn), 24.

62. Marge Pavelson and Triin Vihalemm, "The Russian Child in the Estonian Language School," in Marju Lauristin and Mati Heidmets, eds., *The Challenge of the Russian Minority* (Tartu: Tartu University Press, 2002), 275.

63. Laitin, *Identity in Formation*, 130–32.

64. Aleksandr Erek, *Molodezh Estonii*, February 3, 2001.

65. Airi Selgmäe, *Eesti Päevaleht*, March 2, 2000.

66. Alexander Shegedin, *Estoniya*, January 8, 2000.

67. Raivo Vetik, " 'Elite versus People'? Euroscepticism in Estonia," *Cambridge Review of International Affairs* 16:2 (2003): 257–71.

68. For the distinction between self-enforcing and self-reinforcing equilibria and an application to Estonia, see Avner Greif and David Laitin, "A Theory of Endogenous Institutional Change," in *American Political Science Review* 98:4 (2004).

69. *Molodezh Estonii*, March 8, 1999.

70. *Postimes* editorial cited in *Molodezh Estonii*, March 8, 1999.

71. Eero Laidre, *Õhtuleht*, February 3, 1999.

72. *Molodezh Estonii*, January 2, 2000.

73. Valeria Jakobson provided critical translations for me of the Russian and Estonian press, as reported here and elsewhere in this chapter.

74. *Molodezh Estonii*, January 2, 2000.

75. M. Petrov, *Molodezh Estonii*, March 5, 2000.

76. S. Smirnov, *Molodezh Estonii*, March 8, 1999.

77. M. Petrov, *Molodezh Estonii*, January 2, 2000.

78. Alexander Shegedin, *Estoniya*, January 8, 2000.

79. *Eesti Päevaleht*, August 1, 2001.

80. *Estoniya*, October 3, 2001.

81. Priit Hõbemägi, *Eesti Päevaleht.*

82. Reported by Jüri Pino in *Õhtuleht*, December 3, 2001.

83. In my *Identity in Formation*, I wrote of a mutual expectation of nonviolence, which amounted to a "security community" (chap. 12).

84. Katrin Saks, *Õhtuleht*, October 2, 2001.

85. I discuss national revivals in *Identity in Formation*, 26–28. In my "National Revivals and Violence," *European Journal of Sociology* 36 (spring 1995): 3–43, I show how these revivals, which are a response to integration, induce both intra-nationality and inter-nationality violence.

86. On a more dynamic approach to game theory, see Greif and Laitin, "A Theory."

Chapter 3. Ethnic Mobilization in the Postcommunist Context

1. Susan Olzak, "Contemporary Ethnic Mobilization," *Annual Review of Sociology* 9 (1983): 355. See also Ted Robert Gurr, *Peoples versus States: Minorities at Risk in the New Century* (Washington, D.C.: United States Peace Institute Press, 2000), 74–75.

2. Charles Tilly, *From Mobilization to Revolution* (New York: Random House, 1978), 69.

3. J. P. Nettl, *Political Mobilization: A Sociological Analysis of Methods and Concepts* (New York: Basic Books, 1967), 32–33.

4. Michael Lipsky, "Protest as Political Resource," *American Political Science Review* 62:4 (1968): 1144–58.

5. Ted Robert Gurr, *Minorities at Risk: A Global View of Ethnopolitical Conflicts* (Washington, D.C.: U.S. Institute of Peace, 1993), 123.

6. See C. G. Pickvance, "Where Have Urban Movements Gone?" in Costis Hadjimichalis and David Sadler, eds., *Europe at the Margins: New Mosaics of Inequality* (Chichester, England: John Wiley & Sons, 1995), 212; and Jack Snyder, *From Voting to Violence: Democratization and Nationalist Conflict* (New York: W. W. Norton, 2000), 51.

7. See, for instance, William Julius Wilson, *When Work Disappears: The World of the New Urban Poor* (New York: Knopf, 1996).

8. See, for instance, Stephen Mennell, "The Formation of We-Images: A Process Theory," in Craig Calhoun, ed., *Social Theory and the Politics of Identity* (Cambridge, Mass.: Blackwell, 1994), 183.

9. See, for instance, Beatrice Drury, "Ethnic Mobilization: Some Theoretical Considerations," in John Rex and Beatrice Drury, eds., *Ethnic Mobilization in a Multicultural Europe* (Aldershot, England: Avebury, 1994), 15. She conceptualizes ethnic mobilization as a four-stage process.

10. See David A. Lake and Donald Rothchild, "Spreading Fear: The Genesis of Transnational Ethnic Conflict," in Lake and Rothchild, eds., *The International Spread of Ethnic Conflict* (Princeton: Princeton University Press, 1998), 31.

11. See Charles C. Ragin, "Ethnic Political Mobilization: The Welsh Case," *American Sociological Review* 44:4 (1979): 620–22; and Susan Olzak, "Contemporary Ethnic Mobilization," *Annual Review of Sociology* 9 (1983): 355–63.

12. See, for instance, Seymour Martin Lipset and Stein Rokkan, *Party Systems and Voter Alignments* (New York: Free Press, 1967), esp. 1–64; Juan J. Linz, "Early State Building and Late Peripheral Nationalisms against the State: The Case of Spain," in S. N. Eisenstadt and Stein Rokkan, eds., *Building States and Nations* (Beverly Hills, Calif.: Sage, 1973), 32–116; and Harold Isaacs, *Idols of the Tribe: Group Identity and Political Change* (New York: Harper & Row, 1975).

13. See Ernest Gellner, *Thought and Change* (Chicago: University of Chicago Press, 1969), 147–78; Michael Hechter, *Internal Colonialism: The Celtic Fringe in British National Development, 1536–1966* (Berkeley: University of California Press, 1975); and Francois Nielsen, "Toward a Theory of Ethnic Solidarity in Modern Societies," *American Sociological Review* 50:2 (1985): 133–49.

14. See, for instance, Pierre van den Berghe, *Race and Racism: A Comparative Perspective* (New York: Wiley, 1967); Fredrik Barth, ed., *Ethnic Groups and Boundaries* (Boston: Allen & Unwin, 1970); Michael T. Hannan, "The Dynamics of Ethnic Boundaries in Modern States," in John W. Meyer and Michael T. Hannan, eds., *National Development and the World System* (Chicago: University of Chicago Press, 1979), 253–75; Joane Nagel and Susan Olzak, "Ethnic Mobilization in New and Old States: An Extension of the Competition Model," *Social Problems* 30:2 (December 1982): 127–43; and Juan Diez Medrano, "The Effects of Ethnic Segregation and Ethnic Competition on Political Mobilization in the Basque Country, 1988," *American Sociological Review* 59:6 (1994): 873–89.

15. Rasma Karklins, *Ethnopolitics and Transition to Democracy: The Collapse of the USSR and Latvia* (Baltimore: Johns Hopkins University Press, 1994).

16. See, for instance, Rex and Drury, *Ethnic Mobilization in a Multicultural Europe.*

17. See Jan E. Leighley, *Strength in Numbers? The Political Mobilization of Racial and Ethnic Minorities* (Princeton: Princeton University Press, 2001).

18. See Snyder, *From Voting to Violence*, 315.

19. This discussion is based on Zoltan Barany, "Ethnic Mobilization without Prerequisites," *World Politics* 54:3 (2002): 277–307.

20. See, for instance, Doug McAdam, John McCarthy, and Mayer Zald, eds., *Comparative Perspectives of Social Movements* (New York: Cambridge University Press, 1996).

21. Sidney Tarrow, "Social Movements in Contentious Politics," *American Political Science Review* 90:4 (1996): 880.

22. Joseph Rothschild, *Ethnopolitics: A Conceptual Framework* (New York: Columbia University Press, 1981), 60.

23. Anya Peterson Smith, *Ethnic Identity: Strategies of Diversity* (Bloomington: Indiana University Press, 1982), 1.

24. Max Weber, *Economy and Society: An Outline of Interpretive Sociology* (Berkeley: University of California Press, 1978), 390.

25. The almost palpable surge of "Macedonianness" during the intensive attempts by Greece to isolate and damage the new Macedonian state emerging from the ashes of Yugoslavia in the early 1990s is an instructive example of how ethnic identity is strengthened in the face of adversity. See Lucano Bozzo and Carlo Simon-Belli, eds., *Macedonia: La Nazione che Non C'è* (Milan: Franco Agneli, 2000).

26. Paul Brass, *Ethnicity and Nationalism* (New Delhi: Sage, 1991), 25–30.

27. John Breuilly, *Nationalism and the State* (Chicago: University of Chicago Press, 1993), 19.

28. Cynthia Enloe, *Ethnic Conflict and Political Development* (Boston: Little, Brown & Co., 1973), 160.

29. See Donald Horowitz, *Ethnic Groups in Conflict* (Berkeley: University of California Press, 1985), 291–97.

30. Brass, *Ethnicity and Nationalism*, 49.

31. Hanspeter Kriesi et al., *New Social Movements in Western Europe: A Comparative Perspective* (Minneapolis: University of Minnesota Press, 1995), 53.

32. Milton Esman, *Ethnic Politics* (Ithaca: Cornell University Press, 1994), 34.

33. Enloe, *Ethnic Conflict and Political Development*, 183.

34. See Norman Cohn, *The Pursuit of Millennium* (New York: Oxford University Press, 1970).

35. See, for instance, Murray Edelman, *The Symbolic Uses of Politics* (Urbana: University of Illinois Press, 1985), and Ulf Hedetoft, ed., *Political Symbols, Symbolic Politics* (Brookfield, Vt.: Ashgate, 1998).

36. See Eric Hobsbawm and Terence Ranger, eds., *The Invention of Tradition* (Cambridge: Cambridge University Press, 1983).

37. For brief discussions, see Stoyan Pribichevich, *Macedonia: Its People and History* (University Park: Pennsylvania State University Press, 1982), 174–78; Elez Biberaj, *Albania: A Socialist Maverick* (Boulder, Colo.: Westview Press, 1990), 110–26; and Hugh Poulton, *Who Are the Macedonians?* (Bloomington: Indiana University Press, 1995), 182–91.

38. Rogers Brubaker, *Nationalism Reframed: Nationhood and the National Question in the New Europe* (New York: Cambridge University Press, 1996), 103.

39. Both Macedonian censuses have been very controversial, with persistent (and quite plausible) Albanian charges that census figures underreport the size of their community. See, for instance, Ulrich Büchsenschütz, "Macedonian Census Results Spark Controversy," *RFE/RL Balkan Report*, December 12, 2003. As may be gleaned from the census data, Albanians have high birthrates (actually, the highest of among all European ethnic groups; Roma have the second highest rate).

40. See the discussion by Loring M. Danforth, *The Macedonian Conflict: Ethnic Nationalism in a Transnational World* (Princeton: Princeton University Press, 1995), 144–45.

41. Biberaj, *Albania*, 10.

42. On this point see Barbara Jelavich, *History of the Balkans: Twentieth Century* (New York: Cambridge University Press, 1983), 90–91; and David I. Kertzer and Dominique Arel, "Censuses, Identity Formation, and the Struggle for Political Power," in Kertzer and Arel, eds., *Census and Identity: The Politics of Race, Ethnicity, and Language in National Censuses* (New York: Cambridge University Press, 2002), 21–22.

43. The solidarity was far stronger than, for example, between Hungarians in Hungary proper and in Slovakia or Transylvania. See László Kürti, *The Remote Borderland: Transylvania in the Hungarian Imagination* (Albany: SUNY Press, 2001).

44. See Hugh Poulton, *The Balkans: Minorities and States in Conflict* (London: Minority Rights Group, 1993), 83.

45. Poulton, *The Balkans*, 86. For more on this fascinating phenomenon, see Edith Durham, *High Albania* (London: Edward Arnold, 1909).

46. For a collection of these, see Robert Elsie, *Dictionary of Albanian Religion, Mythology, and Folk Culture* (London: Hurst, 2001). For insightful analyses of the impact of these myths on Albanian identity, see Stephanie Schwandner-Sievers and Bernd J.

Fischer, eds., *Albanian Identities: Myth and History* (Bloomington: Indiana University Press, 2002).

47. On these issues, see Stavro Skendi, *Albanian Political Thought and Revolutionary Activity, 1881–1912* (Munich: Druck Max Schick, 1954); Stavro Skendi, *The Albanian National Awakening, 1878–1912* (Princeton: Princeton University Press, 1967); Peter Bartl, *Die Albanische Muslime zur Zeit der Nationalen Unabhängigkeitsbewegung (1878–1912)* (Wiesbaden: Otto Harrassowitz, 1968); Bernd J. Fischer, "Albanian Nationalism in the Twentieth Century," in Peter F. Sugar, ed., *Eastern European Nationalism in the Twentieth Century* (Washington, D.C.: University Press of America, 1995), 21–54; and Nathalie Clayer, *L'Albanie, pays des derviches: Les ordres mystiques musulmans en Albanie à l'époque post-ottomane (1912–1967)* (Wiesbaden: Otto Harrassowitz, 1990).

48. Biberaj, *Albania*, 128.

49. Poulton, *The Balkans*, 85.

50. See Duncan M. Perry, "Destiny on Hold: Macedonia and the Dangers of Ethnic Discord," *Current History* 97:617 (1998): 124.

51. Sabrina P. Ramet, *Balkan Babel: The Disintegration of Yugoslavia from the Death of Tito to the Fall of Milosovic* (Boulder, Colo.: Westview Press, 2002), 189.

52. Kyril Drezov, "Bulgaria and Macedonia: Voluntary Dependence on External Actors," in Jan Zielonka and Alex Pravda, eds., *Democratic Consolidation in Eastern Europe*, vol. 2: *International and Transnational Factors* (Oxford: Oxford University Press, 2001), 418.

53. See, for instance, Farimah Daftary, "Testing Macedonia," European Centre for Minority Issues (Flensburg, Germany), ECMI Brief #4 (May 2001); and Ulrich Schneckener, "Developing and Applying EU Crisis Management: Test Case Macedonia," ECMI Working Paper #14 (January 2002).

54. *RFE/RL Newsline*, September 16, 2002.

55. Duncan M. Perry, "The Republic of Macedonia: Finding Its Way," in Karen Dawisha and Bruce Parrott, eds., *Politics, Power, and the Struggle for Democracy in South-East Europe* (New York: Cambridge University Press, 1997), 239.

56. Duncan M. Perry, "Macedonia: Melting Pot or Meltdown?" *Current History* 100:649 (November 2001): 364. See also "Xhaferi: Difficult to Gain Rights through Politics," Makfax Independent News Agency (Skopje), 30 December 2002.

57. *East European Constitutional Review* 10:2/3 (2001): 30.

58. See Robert Hislope, "Organized Crime in a Disorganized State: How Corruption Contributed to Macedonia's Mini-War," *Problems of Post-Communism* 49:3 (2002): 33–41.

59. On the importance of information flow in ethnic mobilization, see Stuart Hill, Donald Rothchild, and Colin Cameron, "Tactical Information and the Diffusion of Peaceful Protests," in Lake and Rothchild, *The International Spread of Ethnic Conflict*, 65–67.

60. This, of course, was a sensitive issue for majority Macedonians, whose own national emblems, adopted only in 1991, were hotly contested by Greece and later had to be changed. See Ulrich Büchsenschütz, "Macedonia and the National Flag Question," *RFE/RL Balkan Report*, February 20, 2004.

61. Ramet, *Balkan Babel*, 189. See also Poulton's different figures in *The Balkans*, 220.

62. See Ulf Brunnbauer, "The Implementation of the Ohrid Agreement," *Journal of Ethnopolitics and Minority Issues in Europe* 1 (2002) (www.ecmi.de); Brenda Pearson, "Putting Peace into Practice: Can Macedonia's New Government Meet the Challenge?" *Special Report #96, U.S. Institute of Peace*, November 2002; and Ulrich Büchsenschütz,

"Macedonia's Leaders Review Peace Plan and Security," *RFE/RL Balkan Report*, February 21, 2003.

63. *RFE/RL Newsline*, November 19, 2002, based on an article in *Utrinski vesnik* (Skopje) of the same day. Actually, the new body replaces the ten-member parliamentary Commission for Inter-Ethnic Relations in which Albanians had only two seats in contrast to six occupied by ethnic Macedonians. Author's interview with Elizabeta Georgieva, head of the Human Rights and Minorities Department, Ministry of Foreign Affairs (Skopje, November 23, 1999).

64. See *RFE/RL Newsline*, July 10, 2001, and October 31, 2001; and Zoltan Barany, *The East European Gypsies: Regime Change, Marginality, and Ethnopolitics* (New York: Cambridge University Press, 2001), 160–61.

65. Author's interview with Agnes Horváthová, head of secretariat, Slovak Helsinki Commission (Bratislava, September 8, 1999).

66. Slawomir Kapralski, "Identity Building and the Holocaust: Roma Political Nationalism," *Nationalities Papers* 25:2 (1997): 273.

67. See, for instance, *Romové v České republice* (Prague: Socioklub, 1999), 540–41.

68. Romani activist Ian F. Hancock, cited by Isabel Fonseca, *Bury Me Standing* (New York: Knopf, 1995), 296.

69. Author's interview with Klára Orgovánová, a program director at the Open Society Foundation (Bratislava, September 7, 1999).

70. See Samuel P. Huntington, *Political Order in Changing Societies* (New Haven: Yale University Press, 1968), 12–24.

71. See Barany, *The East European Gypsies*, 207.

72. Interviews with Gheorghe Raducanu, member of Parliament and of the Council of National Minorities, and a leader of the *Partida Romilor* (Bucharest, March 14, 1995), and Emilija Simoska, director of the Center for Ethnic Relations at the Institute for Sociological, Political, and Juridical Research (Skopje, November 23, 1999).

73. A 1998 research project on the Romanian Roma directed by Catalin and Elena Zamfir found that only 7.3 percent read newspapers "often" and 56 percent "never" (unpublished manuscript, University of Bucharest, 1999).

74. See Andrzej Mirga and Lech Mróz, *Cyganie: Odmienność i nietolerancja* (Warsaw: Wydawnictwo Naukowe PWN, 1994), 31–32.

75. Interviews with Emilija Simoska and Mirjana Najcevska (Skopje, November 23, 1999). See also Zoltan Barany, "The Roma in Macedonia: Ethnic Politics and the Marginal Condition in a Balkan State," *Ethnic and Racial Studies* 18:3 (1995): 515–31.

76. "Roma voksok ötezerért," *Magyar Nemzet*, 11 June 2004.

77. See "Iliescut támogatják a romák," *Szabadság* (Cluj), 25 October 1999; and the protocol's text published in the PR's newspaper, *Asul de trefla* 80 (1999), 17–19.

78. Author's interview with Nicolae Paun, president of Partida Romilor (Bucharest, November 5, 1999).

79. Gábor Havas, Gábor Kertesi, and István Kemény, "The Statistics of Deprivation: The Roma in Hungary," *The Hungarian Quarterly* 36:138 (1995): 80.

80. Author's interviews with Nicoleta Bitu of Romani Center for Social Intervention and Studies (CRISS) (Bucharest, May 23, 1996), and Géza Ötvös, head of the Wassdas Foundation (Cluj, October 26, 1999).

81. "Gypsies Miss Out as Eastern Europe's Democratic Caravan Hits the Road," *The Guardian*, 21 June 1990; "A Parlamentbe készül a Magyarországi Cigánypárt," *Népszabadság*, 15 June 1992; "Cigányvoksok," *Magyar Narancs*, 23 September 1993.

82. *Political Participation and the Roma in Hungary and Slovakia* (Princeton, N.J.: Project on Ethnic Relations, 1999), 5.

83. Author's interviews with János Báthory, the deputy chairman of the Office for National and Ethnic Minorities (Budapest, June 9, 1994); Gheorghe Raducanu (Bucharest, March 14, 1995); András Bíró, president of the Autonómia Foundation (Budapest, July 26, 1996); and Ivan Gabal of Gabal Analysis and Consulting (Prague, August 24, 1999).

84. *The Legislative and Institutional Framework for the National Minorities of Romania* (Bucharest: Romanian Institute for Human Rights, 1994), 100; and author's interview with Dan Oprescu, head of the National Office for the Roma, Department for the Protection of National Minorities, Government of Romania (Bucharest, November 2, 1999).

85. Author's interview with Petar Atanasov, secretary of the National Council on Ethnic and Demographic Issues at the Council of Ministers (Sofia, November 15, 1999).

86. Romani politicians and activists have compiled a long record of appealing to international organizations like the United Nations, the OSCE, and the EU, seeking remedies for their problems. See, for instance, Ian F. Hancock, "The East European Roots of Romani Nationalism," *Nationalities Papers* 19:3 (1991): 261–65; and Barany, *The East European Gypsies*, 256–67.

Chapter 4. Ethnicity, Elections, and Party Systems

1. Alvin Rabushka and Kenneth A. Shepsle, *Politics in Plural Societies: A Theory of Democratic Instability* (Columbus, Ohio: Charles E. Merrill, 1972); Dankwart Rustow, "Transitions to Democracy: Toward a Dynamic Model," *Comparative Politics* 2 (1970): 337–64; Juan Linz and Alfred Stepan, *Problems of Democratic Transition and Consolidation* (Baltimore: Johns Hopkins University Press, 1996).

2. Arend Lijphart, *Democracy in Plural Societies* (New Haven: Yale University Press, 1977); Donald Horowitz, *A Democratic South Africa?* (Berkeley: University of California Press, 1991); Richard Hislope, "Ethnic Conflict and the Generosity Moment," *Journal of Democracy* 9 (1998): 140–53; Ben Reilly and Andrew Reynolds, *Electoral Systems and Conflict in Divided Societies* (Washington, D.C.: National Academy Press, 1999); Ashutosh Varshney, "Ethnic Conflict and Civil Society: India and Beyond," *World Politics* 53 (2001): 362–98; M. Steven Fish and Robin S. Brooks, "Does Diversity Hurt Democracy?" *Journal of Democracy* 15 (2004): 154–66.

3. Donald L. Horowitz, *Ethnic Groups in Conflict* (Berkeley: University of California Press, 1985).

4. Jack Snyder, *From Voting to Violence: Democratization and Nationalist Conflict* (New York: Norton, 2000).

5. Rogers Brubaker, "Nationalizing States in the Old 'New Europe'—and the New," *Ethnic and Racial Studies* 19 (1996): 411–37; Ian Bremmer, "The Politics of Ethnicity: Russians in the New Ukraine," *Europe-Asia Studies* 46 (1994): 261–84.

6. Valerie Bunce and Maria Csanadi, "Uncertainty in the Transition: Post-Communism in Hungary," *East European Politics and Society* 7 (1993): 240–75; Geoffrey Evans and Stephen Whitefield, "Identifying Bases of Party Competition in Eastern Europe," *British Journal of Political Science* 23 (1993): 521–48.

7. Robert G. Moser, *Unexpected Outcomes: Electoral Systems, Political Parties, and Representation in Russia* (Pittsburgh: University of Pittsburgh Press, 2001).

8. Saul Newman, "Nationalism in Postindustrial Societies: Why States Still Matter," *Comparative Politics* 32 (2000): 21–41.

9. Horowitz, *Ethnic Groups in Conflict*, 291.

10. Ibid., 293.

11. Ibid., 83–85.

12. Ibid., 83–89.

13. Lijphart, *Democracy in Plural Societies*.

14. Horowitz, *Ethnic Groups in Conflict*; Horowitz, *A Democratic South Africa?*; Ben Reilly, "Electoral Systems for Divided Societies," *Journal of Democracy* 13 (2002): 156–70.

15. Indeed, Horowitz argues that a wholly nonethnic party system in an ethnically divided state is very rare although he does cite the Philippines as an example. Horowitz, *Ethnic Groups in Conflict*, 302.

16. Andrew Reynolds, "Constitutional Engineering in Southern Africa," *Journal of Democracy* 6 (1995): 86–99; Katherine Tate, "The Political Representation of Blacks in Congress: Does Race Matter?" *Legislative Studies Quarterly* 26 (2001): 488–92. There is also a continuing debate regarding whether maximizing minority representation in the legislature actually increases the substantive representation of minority interests. In the U.S. case, Cameron, Epstein, and O'Halloran have argued that maximizing the number of minority representatives does not necessarily maximize the substantive representation of minority interests. For different sides of this debate see also Lublin, 1999, and Epstein and O'Halloran, 1999. Charles Cameron, David Epstein, and Sharyn O'Halloran, "Do Majority-Minority Districts Maximize Substantive Black Representation in Congress?" *American Political Science Review* 90 (1996): 794–823; David Lublin, "Racial Redistricting and African-American Representation: A Critique of 'Do Majority-Minority Districts Maximize Substantive Black Representation in Congress?'" *American Political Science Review* 93 (1999): 183–86; David Epstein and Sharyn O'Halloran, "A Social Science Approach to Race, Redistricting, and Representation," *American Political Science Review* 93 (1999): 187–91.

17. Joel Barkan, "Elections in Agrarian Societies," *Journal of Democracy* 6 (1995): 106–16.

18. George A. Persons, "Electing Minorities and Women to Congress," in *Electoral Systems in the United States: Their Impact on Women and Minorities*, ed. Wilma Rule and Joseph Zimmerman (Westport, Ct.: Greenwood Press, 1992), 20.

19. Bernard Grofman and Lisa Handley, "Preconditions for Black and Hispanic Congressional Success," in *Electoral Systems in the United States: Their Impact on Women and Minorities*, ed. Wilma Rule and Joseph Zimmerman (Westport, Ct.: Greenwood Press, 1992), 38–39.

20. Reynolds, "Constitutional Engineering in Southern Africa," 86–99.

21. Rein Taagepera, "Beating the Law of Minority Attrition," in *Electoral Systems in the United States: Their Impact on Women and Minorities*, ed. Wilma Rule and Joseph Zimmerman (Westport, Ct.: Greenwood Press, 1992), 237. See also Reynolds, "Constitutional Engineering in Southern Africa," 86–99, and Andrew Reynolds, "The Case for Proportionality," *Journal of Democracy* 6 (1995): 117–24.

22. Gary Cox, *Making Votes Count* (Cambridge: Cambridge University Press, 1997); Peter C. Ordeshook and Olga V. Shvetsova, "Ethnic Heterogeneity, District Magnitude, and the Number of Parties," *American Journal of Political Science* 38 (1994): 100–23.

23. See Seymour M. Lipset and Stein Rokkan, *Party Systems and Voter Alignments: Cross-National Perspectives* (New York: Free Press, 1967).

24. Cox, *Making Votes Count*, 215; Ordeshook and Shvetsova, "Ethnic Heterogeneity," 111.

25. Mark P. Jones, "Racial Heterogeneity and the Effective Number of Candidates in Majority Runoff Elections: Evidence from Louisiana," *Electoral Studies* 16 (1997): 349–58.

26. Evans and Whitefield, "Identifying Bases of Party Competition in Eastern Europe."

27. Geoffrey Evans and Christine S. Lipsmeyer, "The Democratic Experience in Divided Societies: The Baltic States in Comparative Perspective," *The Journal of Baltic Studies* 32 (2001): 379–401; Lowell W. Barrington, "Examining Rival Theories of Demographic Influences on Political Support: The Power of Regional, Ethnic, and Linguistic Divisions in Ukraine," *European Journal of Political Research* 41 (2002): 455–91; Sarah Birch, "Interpreting the Regional Effect in Ukrainian Politics," *Europe-Asia Studies* 52 (2000): 1017–41; Vicki L. Hesli, William M. Reissinger, and Arthur H. Miller, "Political Party Development in Divided Societies: The Case of Ukraine," *Electoral Studies* 17 (1998): 235–56; Bremmer, "Politics of Ethnicity," 261–84; J. Fitzmaurice, "The Slovak Election of September 1994," *Electoral Studies* 14 (1995): 203–6; Herbert Kitschelt, D. Dimitrov, A. Kanev, "The Structuring of the Vote in Postcommunist Party Systems: The Bulgarian Example," *European Journal of Political Research* 27 (1995): 143–60; Paul Kolsto and B. Tsilevich, "Patterns of Nation-Building and Political Integration in a Bifurcated Postcommunist State: Ethnic Aspects of Parliamentary Elections in Latvia," *East European Politics and Societies* 11 (1997): 366–91; Marcus Harper, "Economic Voting in Postcommunist Eastern Europe," *Comparative Political Studies* 33 (2000): 1191–1227.

28. Timothy Colton, *Transitional Citizens: Voters and What Influences Them in the New Russia* (Cambridge: Harvard University Press, 2000); William L. Miller, Stephen White, and Paul Heywood, "Political Values Underlying Partisan Cleavages in Former Communist Countries," *Electoral Studies* 17 (1998): 197–216.

29. Hesli, Reissinger, and Miller, "Political Party Development in Divided Societies," 197–216; Barrington, "Examining Rival Theories," 455–91.

30. Narcisa Medianu, "Analysing Political Exchanges between Minority and Majority Leaders in Romania," *The Global Review of Ethnopolitics* 1 (2002): 28–41.

31. Zsuzsa Csergo, "Beyond Ethnic Division: Majority-Minority Debate about the Postcommunist State in Romania and Slovakia," *East European Politics and Society* 16 (2002): 1–29; Marina Popescu, "The Parliamentary and Presidential Elections in Romania," *Electoral Studies* 22 (2003): 325–35.

32. Karen Dawisha and Stephen Deets, "Political Learning in Postcommunist Elections" (paper presented at annual meeting of American Political Science Association, San Francisco, 2001). See also Michael Minkenberg, "The Radical Right in Postsocialist Central and Eastern Europe: Comparative Observations and Interpretation," *East European Politics and Societies* 16 (2002): 335–63.

33. Miller, White, Heywood, "Political Values Underlying Partisan Cleavages," 197–216.

34. Ciprian-Calin Alionescu, "Parliamentary Representation of Minorities in Romania," unpublished manuscript.

35. Moser, *Unexpected Outcomes*.

36. Johanna Birnir, "Party System Stabilization in New Democracies: The Effect of Ethnic Heterogeneity on Volatility of Electoral Preferences" (PhD diss., University of California, Los Angeles, 2001).

37. See V. Pettai, "The Games of Ethnopolitics in Latvia," *Post-Soviet Affairs* 12 (1996): 40–50; Jeff Chinn and Lise A. Truex, "The Question of Citizenship in the Baltics," *Journal of Democracy* 7 (1996): 133–47; Geoffrey Evans and Arianna Need, "Explaining Ethnic Polarization over Attitudes towards Minority Rights in Eastern Europe: A Multilevel Analysis," *Social Science Research* 31 (2002): 653–80.

38. Alionescu, "Parliamentary Representation of Minorities in Romania."

39. Sometimes electoral laws explicitly designed to produce a certain outcome have ironic effects. Bulgaria's constitution forbids parties that are explicitly devoted to representing ethnic minorities. But the Turkish party the Movement for Rights and Freedoms was formed before the constitution was enacted and was deemed a multiethnic party by the courts despite its strongly Turkish orientation. Therefore, the law has provided the ethnic party a virtual monopoly on the Turk constituency by hindering the formation of competing Turkish parties despite a PR system that would promote such party proliferation. John T. Ishiyama, "The Movement for Rights and Freedoms in Bulgaria," in *Ethnopolitics in the New Europe*, ed. John T. Ishiyama and Marijke Breuning (Boulder, Colo.: Lynne Rienner, 1998); V. Vassilev Rossen, "Post-Communist Bulgaria's Ethnopolitics," *The Global Review of Ethnopolitics* 1 (2001): 37–53.

40. Evans and Need, "Explaining Ethnic Polarization," 662.

41. Ishiyama, "The Movement for Rights and Freedoms in Bulgaria"; Csergo, "Beyond Ethnic Division"; Rossen, "Post-Communist Bulgaria's Ethnopolitics"; G. Karasimeonov, "Parliamentary Elections of 1994 and the Development of the Bulgarian Party System," *Party Politics* 1 (1995): 579–87.

42. Csergo, "Beyond Ethnic Division."

43. Rossen, "Post-Communist Bulgaria's Ethnopolitics"; Karasimeonov, "Parliamentary Elections of 1994 and the Development of the Bulgarian Party System."

44. Christopher Marsh and James W. Warhola, "Ethnicity, Ethno-territoriality, and the Political Geography of Putin's Electoral Support," *Post-Soviet Geography and Economics* 42 (2001): 1–14.

45. Chauncy Harris, "The New Russian Minorities: A Statistical Overview," *Post-Soviet Geography* 34 (1993): 577.

46. Ibid., 570.

47. In 1990 and 1991 the Russian Congress of People's Deputies elevated sixteen autonomous republics of the Russian Soviet Federated Socialist Republic (RSFSR) to "constituent republics" and elevated the status of four autonomous oblasts (Adigei, Gornii Altai, Karachaevo-Cherkassia, Khakassia) to republican status. In 1992 the Chechen-Ingush Republic was split in two, making the twenty-one republics that currently exist. John Ishiyama, "The Russian Proto-parties and the National Republics," *Communist and Post-Communist Studies* 29 (1996): 397.

48. These figures were calculated from table 3 in Harris, "The New Russian Minorities," 553.

49. Harris, "The New Russian Minorities," 571.

50. See Philip G. Roeder, "Soviet Federalism and Ethnic Mobilization," *World Politics* 43 (1991): 196–232; Daniel S. Treisman, "Russia's Ethnic Revival: The Separatist Activism of Regional Leaders in a Postcommunist Order," *World Politics* 49 (1997): 212–49.

51. See Robert G. Moser, "Sverdlovsk: Mixed Results in a Hotbed of Regional Autonomy," in *Growing Pains: Russian Democracy and the 1993 Elections*, ed. Timothy Colton and Jerry Hough (Washington, D.C.: Brookings Institution, 1998).

52. This section draws heavily from Moser, *Unexpected Outcomes*, chap. 5.

53. These observations are based on data from Michael McFaul and Nikolai Petrov, eds., *Political Almanac of Russia* (Moscow: Carnegie Endowment for International Peace, 1998), 668–71.

54. Data on the ethnicity of deputies from the 1999 and 2003 election were not available at the time of writing. The representation/populations ratio is calculated by dividing an ethnic group's percentage of legislative representatives by its percentage of the population. A ratio of one indicates parity between an ethnic group's population and legislative representation. Ratios under one indicate underrepresentation, and ratios over one indicate overrepresentation. Adapted from Wilma Rule and Pippa Norris, "Anglo and Minority Women's Underrepresentation: Is the Electoral System the Culprit?" in *Electoral Systems in the United States: Their Impact on Women and Minorities*, ed. Wilma Rule and Joseph Zimmerman (Westport, Ct.: Greenwood Press, 1992).

55. Persons, "Electing Minorities and Women to Congress."

56. Pauline Jones Luong, "Tatarstan: Elite Bargaining and Ethnic Separatism," in *Growing Pains: Russian Democracy and the 1993 Elections*, ed. Timothy Colton and Jerry Hough (Washington, D.C.: Brookings Institution, 1998), 656.

57. Luong found that Tatars were three times more likely to support the right of self-determination and secession within the Russian Federation than Russians living in Tatarstan. Luong, "Tatarstan: Elite Bargaining and Ethnic Separatism," 646.

58. Henry Hale, "Bashkortostan: The Logic of Ethnic Machine Politics and Democratic Consolidation," in *Growing Pains: Russian Democracy and the 1993 Elections*, ed. Timothy Colton and Jerry Hough (Washington, D.C.: Brookings Institution, 1998), 621–22.

59. See Hale, "Bashkortostan."

60. The sharp increase in Tatar PR deputies in 1995 would partially contravene this assertion. However, compared with the success of Ukrainians in the PR tier, this performance still falls far short of what may be expected given the relatively large numbers of Tatars within the minority population.

61. Hale argues that ethnicity played a secondary role in voting patterns in single-member districts in Bashkortostan, being outweighed by the influence of powerful state and socioeconomic interests, particularly agrarian interests. Candidates tended to avoid overtly ethnic appeals, and voters tended to vote according to other voting cues. The only SMD contest in which ethnicity played a major role in Bashkortostan was in the one district where Russians made up a majority. In this district a Russian won with a campaign protesting republican sovereignty and aimed at disgruntled Russians. Hale, "Bashkortostan," 619–20.

62. The effective number of parties index is calculated by squaring the proportion of the vote or seat shares of each party, adding these together, then dividing 1 by this total:

$$N_v = 1 / \sum \left(v_i^2 \right) \text{ or } N_s = 1 / \sum \left(s_i^2 \right).$$

Maarku Laakso and Rein Taagepera, "Effective Number of Parties: A Measure with Application to West Europe," *Comparative Political Studies* 12 (1979): 3–27.

63. Information on urbanization and ethnic composition of electoral districts was found in McFaul and Petrov, *Political Almanac of Russia*. These data for Russian regions

were taken from the 1989 census and found at the Norwegian Institute of International Affairs (NUPI) Web site, www.nupi.no.

64. Of course, this is not a completely accurate assumption. After a certain threshold (50%), the proportion of the minority population is actually inversely related to ethnic diversity. A district in which 90% of the population is non-Russian can hardly be defined as ethnically diverse in the sense of being comprised of individuals from different ethnic groups. This problem is mitigated by the fact that Russian districts tended to be very homogenous (90% Russian and higher), whereas non-Russian districts virtually never had a population that was less than 30% Russian.

65. The effective number of ethnic groups was calculated in the same way the effective number of parties or candidates was calculated, weighting each ethnic group by its proportion of the population.

66. Only the 1995 PR election failed to have a statistically significant relationship.

67. For a similar argument regarding other postcommunist states, see Birnir, "Party System Stabilization in New Democracies."

68. In a separate test on only the ethnic regions (results not shown), I included a dichotomous variable for controlled regions along with ethnic diversity and urbanization. This variable was negatively correlated with party fragmentation and statistically significant. The coefficient for ethnic diversity remained negative and statistically significant, whereas urbanization was positive but not statistically significant. These results suggest that both ethnic identity and elite control play a role in the lower level of party fragmentation found in ethnic regions.

69. Christopher Marsh and James W. Warhola, "Ethnicity, Modernization, and Regime Support in Russia's Regions Under Yeltsin," *Nationalism and Ethnic Politics* 6 (2000): 23–47.

70. Marsh and Warhola, "Ethnicity, Ethno-territoriality, and the Political Geography of Putin's Electoral Support."

71. It should be noted that the Russian population in Lithuania has dropped significantly since the collapse of the Soviet Union. The Russian population in Lithuania has experienced a 36 percent drop since the 1989 census, declining from over 9 percent of the population in 1989 to 6 percent in 2001. Belorussians and Ukrainians have witnessed similar declines. Poles have largely retained their numbers within Lithuania. Department of Statistics, *Population by Sex, Age, Ethnicity and Religion* (Vilnius: Department of Statistics to the Government of Lithuania, 2002), 13.

72. Evans and Lipsmeyer, "The Democratic Experience in Divided Societies," 352.

73. Evans and Need, "Explaining Ethnic Polarization," 662.

74. Evans and Lipsmeyer, "The Democratic Experience in Divided Societies," 389.

75. Terry Clark, "Primordial and Minority Pressures in Lithuania," *Studies in Public Policy* 285 (Glasgow: Centre for the Study of Public Policy, 1997): 7–9.

76. This is based on responses to survey questions on the fairness of treatment at various state and private institutions. Only one institution, the social security agency, registered a statistically significant difference between the ethnic groups. But Russian-speakers reported *better* treatment than ethnic Lithuanians. Clark, "Primordial and Minority Pressures in Lithuania," 14.

77. Clark, "Primordial and Minority Pressures in Lithuania," 10.

78. Ibid., 3.

79. Anatol Lieven, *The Baltic Revolution* (New Haven: Yale University Press, 1993), 168–73; Vesna Popovski, *National Minorities and Citizenship Rights in Lithuania, 1988–93* (Basingstoke: Palgrave, 2000), 131–34.

80. Evans and Lipsmeyer, "The Democratic Experience in Divided Societies," 387–89.

81. Algos Krupavicius, "The Lithuanian Parliamentary Elections of 1996," *Electoral Studies* 16 (1997): 544–45.

82. Lieven, *The Baltic Revolution*, 169.

83. Popovski, *National Minorities and Citizenship Rights in Lithuania*, 84–89.

84. Ibid., 111–18.

85. Ibid., 110–11.

86. Department of Statistics, *Population by Sex, Age, Ethnicity and Religion.*

87. For example, in the 1996 election District 10 had five Russian candidates who split nearly 30 percent of the vote, allowing a Polish candidate with only 15 percent of the first-round vote into the runoff with another Polish candidate. In the 2000 election, District 18 had two Polish candidates who split over 26 percent of the vote between them, allowing a Lithuanian candidate to win with 18 percent of the vote.

88. Neither data on the ethnic breakdown of single-member districts nor electoral results for PR or SMD parliamentary races aggregated in demographic regions used in the latest census were available.

89. Alionescu, "Parliamentary Representation of Minorities in Romania."

90. Another institutional device for achieving minority representation is reserved seats, a system that guarantees representation for designated minorities. Depending on how it is designed, this mechanism tends to de-emphasize the role of party mobilization of minorities, as witnessed in Croatia, where independents have dominated elections to its five seats reserved for ethnic minorities. Alionescu, "Parliamentary Representation of Minorities in Romania."

Chapter 5. What Provokes Violent Ethnic Conflict?

1. Francis Fukuyama, *The End of History and the Last Man* (New York: Free Press, 1992), 322–39.

2. Ken Jowitt, *New World Disorder* (Berkeley: University of California Press, 1992), 249–331.

3. The definitive work on the Gypsy situation in Eastern Europe is Zoltan Barany, *The East European Gypsies* (Cambridge: Cambridge University Press, 2002). See also Angus Fraser, *The Gypsies* (Oxford: Blackwell, 1995).

4. Daniel Chirot and Anthony Reid, eds., *Essential Outsiders: Chinese and Jews in the Modern Transformation of Southeast Asia* (Seattle: University of Washington Press, 1997), especially the essays by Chirot, Reid, Kasian Tejapira, Gary Hamilton and Tony Waters, and Linda Lim and Peter Gosling.

5. The Vlachs are not even mentioned in two key books on Balkan nationalism, Peter Sugar and Ivo Lederer, eds., *Nationalism in Eastern Europe* (Seattle: University of Washington Press, 1969), and Misha Glenny, *The Balkans* (New York: Viking, 2000), though they are cited as a despised shepherd people in Rebecca West's famous *Black Lamb and Grey Falcon* (Harmondsworth: Penguin, 1982, originally published in 1941), 20, 102, 599, 655, 657. They were also a significant linguistic minority in many parts of the Balkans, including Greek Macedonia. On this last point, see Anastasia Karakasidou, *Fields of Wheat, Hills of Blood* (Chicago: University of Chicago Press, 1997), 50–55, 142, 156. They figure prominently in Loring Danforth's *The Macedonian Conflict*

(Princeton: Princeton University Press, 1995). See also John Lampe and Marvin Jackson, *Balkan Economic History, 1550–1950* (Bloomington: Indiana University Press, 1982), 44–45.

6. Mark Cohen, *Under Crescent and Cross* (Princeton: Princeton University Press, 1994); Gérard Prunier, *The Rwanda Crisis* (New York: Columbia University Press, 1997).

7. Lawrence Wright, "Lives of the Saints," *New Yorker*, January 21, 2002, 40–57.

8. James Fearon and David Laitin, "Explaining Interethnic Cooperation," *American Political Science Review* 90:4 (1996): 715–35.

9. Ashutosh Varshney, *Ethnic Conflict and Civil Life: Hindus and Muslims in India* (New Haven: Yale University Press, 2002).

10. Rogers Brubaker, *Nationalism Reframed: Nationhood and the National Question in the New Europe* (Cambridge: Cambridge University Press, 1996), 156–61, and "Ethnicity without Groups," *Archives Européennes de Sociologie* 43:2 (2002): 163–89.

11. Paul Brass, "The Partition of India and Retributive Genocide in the Punjab, 1946–47," *Journal of Genocide Studies* 5:1 (2003): 71–101, and "The Gujarat Pogrom of 2002," *Items & Issues* (Social Science Research Council) 4:1 (2002/03): 1, 5–9.

12. Anthony Oberschall, "From Ethnic Cooperation to Violence and War in Yugoslavia," in Daniel Chirot and Martin Seligman, eds., *Ethnopolitical Warfare* (Washington, D.C.: American Psychological Association, 2001), 119–50.

13. Donald Horowitz, *The Deadly Ethnic Riot* (Berkeley: University of California Press, 2001).

14. Benedict Anderson, *Imagined Communities: Reflections on the Origin and Spread of Nationalism.* (London: Verso, 1991); Liah Greenfeld, *Nationalism: Five Roads to Modernity* (Cambridge: Harvard University Press, 1992).

15. Russell Hardin, *One for All: The Logic of Group Conflict* (Princeton: Princeton University Press, 1995); Michael Hechter, *Containing Nationalism* (Oxford: Oxford University Press, 2000).

16. Fearon and Laitin, "Explaining Interethnic Cooperation," 716–17.

17. One trait that links Africa to Yugoslavia and the most violent areas of the former Soviet Union is "state breakdown." A recent volume explores the common causes of such political failures in the former USSR and Africa. See Mark Beissinger and Crawford Young, eds., *Beyond State Crisis?* (Washington: Woodrow Wilson Center, 2002).

18. On Tanzania, see Aili Mari Tripp and Crawford Young, "The Accommodation of Cultural Diversity in Tanzania," in Chirot and Seligman, *Ethnopolitical Warfare*, 259–74.

19. On the economic history of contemporary Côte d'Ivoire, see J. C. Berthélemy and F. Bourguignon, *Growth and Crisis in Côte d'Ivoire* (Washington: World Bank, 1996); and Robin Alpine and James Pickett, *Agriculture, Liberalisation and Economic Growth in Ghana and Côte d'Ivoire* (Paris: OECD, 1993). On the political history to the early days of independence, see Aristide Zolberg, *One-party Government in the Ivory Coast* (Princeton: Princeton University Press, 1969). In his work on ethnic conflict in Africa, Donald Rothchild cites Houphouët's deft management of Côte d'Ivoire's problems in *Managing Ethnic Conflict in Africa* (Washington: Brookings Institution Press, 1997), 14–15.

20. Much of this story is discussed in the Human Rights Watch report, *The New Racism: The Political Manipulation of Ethnicity in Côte d'Ivoire* (New York: Human Rights Watch, 2001). Ongoing discussions of the political situation can be found in *Le Monde*, particularly pieces by its African reporter Stephen Smith. A good summary article of his is "La crise ivoirienne, un condensé des caractéristiques de tout un continent," *Le Monde*, February 20, 2003.

21. Tripp and Young, "The Accommodation of Cultural Diversity in Tanzania," 269, 272–73.

22. Prunier, *The Rwanda Crisis*, 192–213.

23. Stephen Smith and Jean-Pierre Tuquoi, "Le pouvoir ivoirien commet des exactions et défie la France," *Le Monde*, May 5, 2004; Stephen Smith, "La France et l'ONU impuissantes face à la crise en Côte d'Ivoire," *Le Monde*, June 4, 2004; Agence France Presse and Reuters, "Côte d'Ivoire: le processus de paix menacé par le limogeage de trois ministres de l'opposition," *Le Monde*, May 25, 2004.

24. Much of the material for this section of the chapter comes from interviews I conducted with about 150 people, from government officials to community leaders in both the government and rebel parts of the country in April and May 2003. See Daniel Chirot, "Proposals for Future CARE programs in Côte d'Ivoire" (Atlanta: CARE International, 2003). Further interviews were conducted in the far west, near the Liberian border, as well as in the central region of Bouaké in February and March 2004. See Daniel Chirot, "Suggestions for Reconstruction, Reinsertion, and Rehabilitation Projects to be Financed by the World Bank in Côte d'Ivoire" (Atlanta: CARE International, 2003). See also U.S. Congress, House Committee on International Relations: Subcommittee on Africa, *Prospects for Peace in the Ivory Coast* (Washington, D.C.: U.S. Government Printing Office, February 12, 2003). In *Le Monde* see Alexandre Jacquens, "La rébellion ivoirienne s'est installée à Bouaké," March 8, 2003, and Stephen Smith, "Un coup de force contre la Côte d'Ivoire aurait été déjoué, samedi, à Paris," September 1, 2003. The economy was already not in good shape before all of this. See *Country Report on Côte d'Ivoire* (London: EIU [*The Economist*], 2001).

25. On Ghana's long road to recovery from the disasters of Kwame Nkrumah's rule, and that of his various civilian and military successors, see Jeffrey Herbst, *The Politics of Reform in Ghana, 1982–1991* (Berkeley: University of California Press, 1993).

26. The major recent articles about the peaceful reality of ethnic relations in Romania and Bulgaria are Narcisa Medianu, "Analysing Political Exchanges between Minority and Majority Leaders in Romania," and Lilia Petkova, "The Ethnic Turks in Bulgaria: Social Integration and Impact on Bulgarian-Turkish Relations, 1947–2000," both in *The Global Review of Ethnopolitics* 1:4 (2002): 28–41 and 42–59.

27. In a fascinating essay on postcommunist Romania, the Romanian historian Dragoş Petrescu tries to show that Romania has been unable to democratize since the fall of Communism because its national mythology is so rooted in ethnic xenophobia. What is so useful is that he gives an excellent synopsis of all the reasons for despair; but of course, the facts do not bear him out as Romania has had regular elections, it has gone a long way toward de-socializing its economy, and it is both free and stable. (Dragoş Petrescu, "Can Democracy Work in Southeastern Europe?" in Balázs Trencsényi, Dragoş Petrescu, Cristina Petrescu, Constantin Iordachi, and Zoltán Kántor, eds., *Nation-Building and Contested Identities: Romanian & Hungarian Case Studies* (Budapest: Regio, 2001, and Iaşi: Polirom, 2001), 275–301. Petrescu cites Bulgaria as being similar to Romania, but again, the facts belie the analysis, even though the reasons given for pessimism are convincing. This reinforces the unexpectedness of the peaceful reality.

28. Former dissidents who are distraught about the failure of postcommunist countries to become ideal, prosperous, liberal states frequently express fears of a return to xenophobia. Thus, for example, Zhelyu Zhelev expresses disquiet about antiliberalism and the call to ethnic particularism in Bulgaria, whereas the reality has been that

despite poverty, corruption, and popular disgust with politics, anti-Turkish or Muslim sentiment has not played a major political role, and Bulgaria, like Romania, is firmly committed to an essentially liberal, Western kind of government. It also has been stable and has held regular elections. Zhelyu Zhelev, "Is Communism Returning?" in Vladimir Tismaneanu, *The Revolutions of 1989* (London: Routledge, 1999), 258–62.

29. On the origins and ideology of the BJP (Bharatiya Janata Party), see Paul Brass, *Theft of an Idol* (Princeton: Princeton University Press, 1997).

30. The classic, if somewhat old-fashioned, treatment of the rise of nationalism in these countries remains Marin Pundeff, "Bulgarian Nationalism," and Stephen Fischer-Galati, "Romanian Nationalism," both in Sugar and Lederer, *Nationalism in Eastern Europe*, 93–165 and 373–95.

31. Ken Jowitt, "Ethnicity: Nice, Nasty, and Nihilistic," in Chirot and Seligman, *Ethnopolitical Warfare*, 27–36. In an unpublished paper written to prepare for his United Nations fact-finding mission to Côte d'Ivoire, René Lemarchand cited one of the leading ideologues of "*Ivoirité*," Nimakey Koffi: "The collective 'we' must be distinguished from 'them'." Lemarchand describes how "we" came to mean just southern Christians. René Lemarchand, "The Venomous Flowers of Ivoirité," (2003). This is the beginning of a movement that is, after all, reminiscent of such early nationalistic expression of exclusivity and hostility to "them" as characterized mid-nineteenth century Romanian nationalism. See Katherine Verdery, *National Ideology under Socialism* (Berkeley: University of California Press, 1991), 36–40.

32. It is unnecessary to go over the well-known story of what happened to Yugoslavia. For the background of how nationalism had barely one generation to get established as southern pan-Slavism before World War II, how it was shattered, and how Tito tried to re-create it based on a new mythology of partisan resistance to fascism, see Aleksa Djilas, *The Contested Country* (Cambridge: Harvard University Press, 1991).

33. Glenny, *The Balkans*, 586–87, 644.

34. William Oldson, *A Providential Anti-Semitism: Nationalism and Polity in Nineteenth Century Romania* (Philadelphia: American Philosophical Society, 1991); Irina Livezeanu, *Cultural Politics in Greater Romania* (Ithaca: Cornell University Press, 1995); Leon Volovici, *Nationalist Ideology and Antisemitism* (Oxford: Pergamon, 1991). See also the wonderful quotes from Romanian nationalist writers on Romanian ethnicity and culture in Verdery, *National Ideology*, 38–49.

35. Verdery, *National Ideology*, esp. 98–134 and 167–214. On the fate of Romania's Jews, see Radu Ioanid, *The Holocaust in Romania* (Chicago: Ivan R. Dee, 2000). On how Romanian and Bulgarian Communists tried to whip up xenophobic resentments, see Vladimir Tismaneanu, *Reinventing Politics* (New York: Free Press, 1992), 228.

36. Glenny, *The Balkans*, 135–248, excellently traces the incredibly complex series of murderous wars, outrages, conspiracies, and diplomatic maneuverings that occurred in this part of the Balkans between 1878 and 1914. On the history of Turks (or Muslims called Turks) in Bulgaria, see Kemal Karpat, ed., *The Turks of Bulgaria* (Istanbul: Isis, 1990). Karpat himself believes that what happened in Bulgaria was a precedent for the genocide of Armenians in 1915, though of course that is contrary to Armenian historians' accounts. On the background of the "Macedonian Question," which was the source of the some of the worst international terrorism and tension in Europe in the early twentieth century, see Fikret Adanır, *Die makedonische Frage* (Wiesbaden: F. Steiner, 1979).

37. Richard Crampton, *A Concise History of Bulgaria* (Cambridge: Cambridge University Press, 1997), 171–83.

38. Petkova, "The Ethnic Turks in Bulgaria," 45–49; Crampton, *A Concise History*, 210.

39. Eric J. Hobsbawm's *Nations and Nationalism Since 1780* (Cambridge: Cambridge University Press, 1990) is most noteworthy in this respect, but there are many others who agree. See also Benedict Anderson's *Imagined Communities*, 83–111.

40. See, for example, Jean L. Cohen and Andrew Arato, *Civil Society and Political Theory* (Cambridge: MIT Press, 1992).

41. Most notably his work on Italy, *Making Democracy Work: Civic Tradition in Modern Italy* (Princeton: Princeton University Press, 1993).

42. As Anthony Smith has pointed out, this distinction has been exaggerated. *Nationalism* (Cambridge: Polity Press, 2001), 41–42.

43. Reşat Kasaba, "Cohabitation? Islamic and Secular Groups in Modern Turkey," in Robert Hefner, ed., *Democratic Civility* (New Brunswick: Transaction Publishers, 1998), 265–84.

44. The Project on Ethnic Relations (PER) specifically ascribes the accommodation reached between the various Romanian parties in power and the Hungarian party to good will and avoidance of conflict among top leaders. See PER, *Political Will: Romania's Path to Ethnic Accommodation* (Princeton: PER, 2001). Interviews I conducted with some of Iliescu's advisors in 2000 confirmed this.

45. In an analysis of Bulgaria's 2001 elections, Zoltan Barany agrees that Bulgaria has been the most exemplary of Balkan states with respect to its stability, tolerance, and democratic practices, even though he does not approve of the results of that particular election. Zoltan Barany, "Bulgaria's Royal Elections," *Journal of Democracy* 13:2 (2002): 141–55.

46. Project on Ethnic Relations, *The Bulgarian Ethnic Experience* (Princeton: PER, 2001). That the European Union's influence was important with respect to continuing economic reform as well as to maintaining democracy and an accommodating social policy is emphasized by Elena Iankova in *Eastern European Capitalism in the Making* (Cambridge: Cambridge University Press, 2002), 18–19.

47. This is based on my interview with some of his close election campaign aides in 2000.

48. Ion Iliescu and Vladimir Tismaneanu, *Marele şoc Din Finalul Unui Secolul Scurt: Ion Iliescu în dialog cu Vladimir Tismaneanu* (Bucharest: Editura Enciclopedică), 267, 386–87.

49. Tudor's unsavory background as Ceauşescu's court poet and then as an anti-Semitic, anti-Hungarian, and anti-Western xenophobe is discussed in Vladimir Tismaneanu's *Fantasies of Salvation* (Princeton: Princeton University Press, 1998), 41, 53, 78, 102, 108. On the 2000 election, see Elizabeth Pond, "Romania: Better Late Than Never," *Washington Quarterly* 24:2 (2001): 35–43; Alina Mungiu Pippidi, "The Return of Populism—the 2000 Romanian Election," *Government and Opposition* 36:2 (2001): 230–52. The liberal intellectuals in Romania and their friends abroad have always disliked Iliescu and his allies because in the early 1970s Iliescu was close to Ceauşescu, many of those around him were Communists, and he did not always behave like a perfect liberal. See, for example, Alina Mungiu [Pippidi], *Românii După'89* (Bucharest: Humanitas, 1995), and her rather gloomy (but, as it turned out, wrong) predictions about the fate of Romanian democracy.

50. The importance of the international setting for shaping or at least tolerating Romania's nationalist xenophobia in the past is discussed in Daniel Chirot, "Who Influ-

enced Whom? Xenophobic Nationalism in Germany and Romania," in Roland Schönfeld, ed., *Deutschland und Südosteuropa* (Munich: Südosteuropa-Gesellschaft, Band 58, 1997), 37–57.

51. Barany, *The East European Gypsies*, 267–81, discusses the international dimensions. See also Project on Ethnic Relations, *Roma and the Question of Self-Determination* (Princeton: PER, 2002).

52. One need only look at Romanian Prime Minister Adrian Năstase's speeches and press statements to see how crucial European and American support is thought to be to appreciate the strong moderating influence this perception exercises. Adrian Năstase, *NATO Enlargement: Romania and the Southern Dimension of the Alliance* (Bucharest: Monitorul Oficial, 2002).

53. Stephen Smith, "Côte d'Ivoire: Laurent Gbagbo mobilise la rue contre la France 'néocoloniale'," *Le Monde*, February 18, 2003; Stephen Smith and Jean-Pierre Tuquoi, "Le pouvoir ivoirien commet des exactions et défie la France."

Chapter 6. Migration and Ethnic Politics

Thanks to Adam Tolnay for research assistance; to Zoltan Barany, Rogers Brubaker, Rob Moser, and two anonymous referees for comments on an earlier draft; and to David Landau for helpful conversations.

1. Tim Heleniak, "The Changing Nationality Composition of the Central Asian and Transcaucasian States," *Post-Soviet Geography and Economics* 38:6 (1997): 357–78. On Russia, see Harley Balzer, "Human Capital and Russian Security in the 21st Century," in Andrew Kuchins, ed., *Russia after the Fall* (Washington: Carnegie Endowment for International Peace, 2002), 163–84.

2. See Douglas S. Massey et al., *Worlds in Motion: Understanding International Migration at the End of the Millennium* (Oxford: Clarendon Press, 1998), 17–59.

3. Massey et al., *Worlds in Motion*, 7.

4. For examples of the literatures in these areas, see Michael S. Teitelbaum, "The Population Threat," *Foreign Affairs* 71:5 (1992): 63–78; Myron Weiner, *The Global Migration Crisis: Challenge to States and to Human Rights* (New York: HarperCollins, 1995); Barry R. Posen, "Military Responses to Refugee Disasters," *International Security* 21:1 (1996): 72–111; C. Haerpfer, C. Milosinski, and C. Wallace, "New and Old Security Issues in Post-Communist Europe: An 11-Nation Study," *Europe-Asia Studies* 51:6 (1999): 989–1011; Rogers Brubaker, *Citizenship and Nationhood in France and Germany* (Cambridge: Harvard University Press, 1992); Jeannette Money, *Fences and Neighbors: The Political Geography of Immigration Control* (Ithaca: Cornell University Press, 1999); Christian Joppke, *Immigration and the Nation-State: The United States, Germany, and Great Britain* (Oxford: Oxford University Press, 2000); Stephen John Steadman and Fred Tanner, eds., *Refugee Manipulation: War, Politics, and the Abuse of Human Suffering* (Washington: Brookings Institution Press, 2003).

5. See F. Stephen Larrabee, "Down and Out in Warsaw and Budapest: Eastern Europe and East-West Migration," *International Security* 16:4 (1992): 5–33; special issue of *International Migration Review* 26:2 (1992); and Jeremy R. Azrael, Patricia A. Brukoff, and Vladimir D. Shkolnikov, "Prospective Migration and Emigration from the Former USSR: A Conference Report," *Slavic Review* 51:2 (1992): 323–31, which contains both

more and less sanguine assessments about the emigration potential of former Communist countries.

6. Claire Wallace and Dariusz Stola, "Introduction: Patterns of Migration in Central Europe," in Claire Wallace and Dariusz Stola, eds., *Patterns of Migration in Central Europe* (New York: Palgrave, 2001), 18.

7. Wallace and Stola, "Introduction," 32.

8. Population Division, Department of Economic and Social Affairs, United Nations Secretariat, *International Migration from Countries with Economies in Transition: 1980–1999* (New York: United Nations, 2002), 21.

9. Terminology is a problem here. Some laws, such as Russia's, are known as "compatriot laws" and include relationships with citizens and co-ethnic non-citizens under the same legal regime. Others, such as Romania's and Bulgaria's, explicitly apply only to co-ethnic noncitizens abroad. Still others, such as Italy's, concern residents of a former portion of the nation-state's territory that now lies in another country. I refer to all of these laws as "diaspora laws," with the proviso that there are many different types beneath this rubric. Rogers Brubaker first called attention to the politics of imperfect nation-states after Communism in the essays collected in his *Nationalism Reframed: Nationhood and the National Question in the New Europe* (Cambridge: Cambridge University Press, 1996).

10. The texts of these laws and those of other states may be found in the appendix to European Commission for Democracy Through Law, *The Protection of National Minorities by Their Kin-State* (Strasbourg: Council of Europe Publishing, 2002).

11. For a discussion of diaspora issues in a comparative light, see Charles King and Neil J. Melvin, "Diaspora Politics: Ethnic Linkages, Foreign Policy, and Security in Eurasia," *International Security* 24:3 (1999/2000): 108–38.

12. For an analysis of the Romanian and Slovak reactions, see David Adam Landau, "Identity, Institutions, and International Relations: The European Union and Hungary's Minority Abroad," unpublished paper, Georgetown University, 2003.

13. Zsuzsa Csergo and James M. Goldgeier, "Virtual Nationalism," *Foreign Policy* 125 (September–October 2001): 76–77.

14. Landau, "Identity," 54.

15. Nongovernmental organizations abroad can apply to the Hungarian government for funds for certain cultural activities deemed "beneficial to the preservation of national identity" (*Act on Hungarians Living in Neighboring Countries*, chap. 2, sec. 5). The law also allows the Hungarian government to engage in the "establishment, operation and development of higher education institutions" in neighboring states (chap. 2, sec. 14). But nothing in the law would indicate that this is meant to be different, say, from the Greek government's funding a chair of Hellenic studies in the United States.

16. King and Melvin, "Diaspora Politics," 113–16.

17. Territory is also important here. The most nationalist politicians in Hungary were particularly unwilling to see ethnic Hungarians in Slovakia and Romania move to Hungary precisely because the lands that they now inhabit were once part of the Hungarian state. Allowing unrestricted immigration would have reduced the Hungarian component of these territories' populations.

18. Brigid Fowler, "Fuzzing Citizenship, Nationalising Political Space: A Framework for Interpreting the Hungarian 'Status Law' as a New Form of Kin-State Policy in

Central and Eastern Europe," working paper 40/02, Centre for Russian and East European Studies, University of Birmingham (2002).

19. The immediate test case for this proposition is Romania's relationship with Moldova. In the early 1990s, Romania enthusiastically reached out to the Moldovan state, with its majority Romanian-speaking population, and allowed virtually unrestricted movement across the international border. In time, however, further restrictions were put in place as Romania's relationship with the EU improved. Once Romania becomes an EU member, perhaps in 2007, the country might well be expected to follow the Hungarian line: making special provision for Moldovans to work in Romania but discouraging long-term migration.

20. The International Organization for Migration distinguishes "alien smuggling" from "trafficking." The former is defined simply as the facilitation of an illegal crossing of an international border. The latter is alien smuggling plus the violation of the human rights of migrants.

21. The 2003 trafficking report is available at www.state.gov/g/tip/rls/tiprpt/2003/.

22. "Russian Husband and Wife Arrested on Federal Indictment Charging Alien Smuggling for Profit and Money Laundering," press release, U.S. Attorney's Office for the Western District of Texas, August 17, 2001.

23. David Binder, "In Europe, Sex Slavery Is Thriving Despite Raids," *New York Times*, October 20, 2002, A10. A subsequent multinational raid, in September 2003, netted 693 victims and 831 suspected traffickers. (The fact that raids seem to be held each year in the same month may account for the relatively low figures.) In the 2003 operation, only about 10 percent of the trafficked women accepted assistance from the International Organization for Migration. David Binder, "12 Nations in Southeast Europe Pursue Traffickers in Sex Trade," *New York Times*, October 19, 2003, A6.

24. Khalid Koser, "The Smuggling of Asylum Seekers into Western Europe: Contradictions, Conundrums, and Dilemmas," in David Kyle and Rey Koslowski, eds., *Global Human Smuggling: Comparative Perspectives* (Baltimore: Johns Hopkins University Press, 2001), 59. As many tragic cases have revealed, however, human smuggling is rarely nonexploitive.

25. There is an important distinction between the ideal-types of "migrant exporting schemes" and "slave importing operations." Women may initially believe they are getting involved in the former—that is, a system for moving them abroad in contravention of immigration restrictions—but end up falling into the latter. "As with many cons, it is the victim's own complicity in a relatively minor crime (illegal border crossing) that leads to the final snare of the confidence scheme." David Kyle and John Dale, "Smuggling the State Back In: Agents of Human Smuggling Reconsidered," in Kyle and Koslowski, *Global Human Smuggling*, 33–34.

26. "New IOM Figures on the Global Scale of Trafficking," *Trafficking in Migrants Quarterly Bulletin* (April 2001): 4.

27. Michael Specter, "Traffickers' New Cargo: Naïve Slavic Women," *New York Times*, January 11, 1998, A1.

28. "New IOM Figures," 5.

29. On urban-rural disparities, see *Trafficking in Women and Children from the Republic of Armenia: A Study* (Geneva: IOM, 2001), 20–21.

30. "U.S. State Department Trafficking Report a 'Mixed Bag'," Human Rights

Watch press release, July 12, 2001; "U.S. State Department Trafficking Report Missing Key Data," Human Rights Watch press release, June 6, 2002.

31. See, for example, Stephen Handelman, *Comrade Criminal: Russia's New Mafiya* (New Haven: Yale University Press, 1995). For less sanguine assessments, see James O. Finckenauer and Elin Waring, "Russian Émigré Crime in the United States: Organized Crime or Crime That Is Organized?" *Transnational Organized Crime* 2: 2–3 (1996): 139–55; and Federico Varese, *The Russian Mafia: Private Protection in a New Market Economy* (Oxford: Oxford University Press, 2001).

32. Author's confidential communications with researcher in women's rights division, Human Rights Watch, Washington, D.C.

33. "Slavic Women Trafficked into Slavery," *Trafficking in Migrants Quarterly Bulletin,* June 1998.

34. Interestingly, the same dual narratives are to be found in nineteenth-century arguments about "white slavery" in the Ottoman Empire. For some antislavery activists in Western Europe, the key issue was the rapacious Turk who stole women from their upland homes in the Caucasus mountains and took them across the Black Sea to the seraglio. When travelers encountered these women, however, many seemed only too willing to be "sold" to the Ottomans—a sure route to economic and social advancement. See Ehud R. Toledano, *The Ottoman Slave Trade and Its Suppression, 1840–1890* (Princeton: Princeton University Press, 1982), and Y. Hakan Erdem, *Slavery in the Ottoman Empire and Its Demise, 1800–1909* (New York: St. Martin's Press, 1996).

35. Lejla Mavris, "Human Smugglers and Social Networks: Transit Migration through the States of the Former Yugoslavia," New Issues in Refugee Research Working Paper No. 72, UNHCR (December 2002), 2.

36. Mavris, "Human Smugglers," 5.

37. Mavris, "Human Smugglers," 6; and Human Rights Watch, *Hopes Betrayed: Trafficking of Women and Girls to Post-Conflict Bosnia and Herzegovina for Forced Prostitution* (New York: Human Rights Watch, 2002).

38. Mavris, "Human Smugglers," 3.

39. Author's interview with Joseph Limprecht, U.S. ambassador to Albania, Tirana, July 20, 2000.

40. Diego Gambetta, *The Sicilian Mafia: The Business of Private Protection* (Cambridge: Harvard University Press, 1993).

41. Donna M. Hughes, "The 'Natasha' Trade: The Transnational Shadow Market of Trafficking in Women," *Journal of International Affairs* 53:2 (2000): 6.

42. *Trafficking in Women and Children from the Republic of Armenia: A Study* (Geneva: IOM, 2001), 24.

43. David D. Laitin, "Comparative Politics: The State of the Discipline," in Ira Katznelson and Helen V. Milner, eds., *Political Science: The State of the Discipline* (New York: W. W. Norton, 2002), 630–59.

44. See David I. Kertzer and Dominique Arel, eds., *Census and Identity: The Politics of Race, Ethnicity, and Language in National Censuses* (Cambridge: Cambridge University Press, 2001).

45. For representative examples, from different theoretical perspectives, see Roger Petersen, *Understanding Ethnic Violence: Fear, Hatred, Resentment in Twentieth-Century Eastern Europe* (Cambridge: Cambridge University Press, 2002); Mark Beissinger, *Nationalist Mobilization and the Collapse of the Soviet State* (Cambridge: Cambridge University Press, 2002); Ashutosh Varshney, *Ethnic Conflict and Civic Life: Hindus and*

Muslims in India (New Haven: Yale University Press, 2003); Kanchan Chandra, *Why Ethnic Parties Succeed: Patronage and Ethnic Headcounts in India* (Cambridge: Cambridge University Press, 2004).

46. For a catalogue of these dimensions, see Milica Bookman, *Ethnic Groups in Motion: Economic Competition and Migration in Multiethnic States* (London: Frank Cass, 2002).

47. Massey et al., *Worlds in Motion*, 281.

Chapter 7. National Minorities in Postcommunist Europe

1. See Gaetano Pentassuglia, "The EU and the Protection of Minorities: The Case of Eastern Europe," *European Journal of International Law* 12:1 (2001): 3–38; Gaetano Pentassuglia, *Minorities in International Law* (Strasbourg: Council of Europe Publishing, 2003); Minority Rights Group, *The Framework Convention for the Protection of National Minorities: A Guide* (London: Minority Rights Group, 1999).

2. John Packer, "The OSCE and International Guarantees of Local Self-Government," in *Local Self-Government, Territorial Integrity, and Protection of Minorities* (Strasbourg: European Commission for Democracy Through Law, Council of Europe Publishing, 1996), 250–72; John Packer, "Making International Law Matter in Preventing Ethnic Conflicts," *New York University Journal of International Law and Politics* 32:3 (2000): 715–24; Jonathan Cohen, *Conflict Prevention Instruments in the Organization for Security and Cooperation in Europe* (The Hague: Netherlands Institute of International Relations, 1998); Gudmundur Alfredsson and Danilo Turk, "International Mechanisms for the Monitoring and Protection of Minority Rights: Their Advantages, Disadvantages and Interrelationships," in Arie Bloed, ed., *Monitoring Human Rights in Europe: Comparing International Procedures and Mechanisms* (Norwell: Kluwer, 1993), 169–86; Kinga Gal, *Bilateral Agreements in Central and Eastern Europe: A New Inter-State Framework for Minority Protection* (Flensburg: European Centre for Minority Issues, working paper #4, 1999); Rob Zaagman, *Conflict Prevention in the Baltic States: The OSCE High Commissioner on National Minorities in Estonia, Latvia and Lithuania* (Flensburg: ECMI Monograph #1, European Centre for Minority Issues, 1999); Arie Bloed and P. Van Dijk, eds., *Protection of Minority Rights through Bilateral Treaties* (The Hague: Kluwer, 1999).

3. The EU did set up the European Monitoring Centre on Racism and Xenophobia in 1997, but it has focused primarily on immigrant groups (rather than national minorities), and primarily on member states in the West, not postcommunist Europe.

4. Quoted in Adam Burgess, "Critical Reflections on the Return of National Minority Rights to East/West European Affairs," in Karl Cordell, ed., *Ethnicity and Democratisation in the New Europe* (London: Routledge, 1999), 49–60.

5. The case of Greece was perhaps a warning here. Greece has the formal trappings of a liberal democracy with a market economy, and would seem therefore to be a good fit for the EU. But in fact, most Western European countries are exasperated by the way the often xenophobic and illiberal political culture of Greece has jeopardized various EU projects, and no one in the EU wanted to admit a dozen countries that would act in the same way. The poor record on minority rights in Greece is often seen as a symbol or indicator of its overall political culture.

6. Rachel Brett, "The Human Dimension of the CSCE and the CSCE Response to Minorities," in M. R. Lucas, ed., *The CSCE in the 1990s: Constructing European Security*

and Cooperation (Baden-Baden: Nomos Verlagsgesellschaft, 1993), 157–58. For a detailed discussion of the way various countries try to deny the existence of minorities, see Panayote Elias Dimitras, *Recognition of Minorities in Europe: Protecting Rights and Dignity* (London: Minority Rights Group, 2004).

7. David Chandler, "The OSCE and the Internationalisation of National Minority Rights," in Karl Cordell, ed., *Ethnicity and Democratisation in the New Europe* (London: Routledge, 1999), 66.

8. See Michael Burns, "Disturbed Spirits: Minority Rights and the New World Orders, 1919 and the 1990s," in S. F. Wells and P. Bailey-Smith, eds., *New European Orders: 1919 and 1991* (Washington: Woodrow Wilson Center Press, 1996); Mark Cornwall, "Minority Rights and Wrongs in Eastern Europe in the Twentieth Century," *The Historian* 50 (1996): 16–20; Alan Sharp, "The Genie That Would Not Go Back into the Bottle: National Self-Determination and the Legacy of the First World War and the Peace Settlement", in S. Dunn and T. G. Fraser, eds., *Europe and Ethnicity: The First World War and Contemporary Ethnic Conflict* (London: Routledge, 1996).

9. Article 1: "All peoples have the right of self-determination. By virtue of that right they freely determine their political status and freely pursue their economic, social and cultural development." Article 27: "In those States in which ethnic, religious or linguistic minorities exist, persons belonging to such minorities shall not be denied the right, in community with the other members of their group, to enjoy their own culture, to profess and practise their own religion, or to use their own language."

10. For a more detailed elaboration of the way that traditional human rights principles fail to protect national minorities from grave injustice, see my *Politics in the Vernacular: Nationalism, Multiculturalism and Citizenship* (Oxford: Oxford University Press, 2001), chap. 4. The Helsinki CSCE Decisions stated that states "will refrain from resettling and condemn all attempts, by the threat or use of force, to resettle persons with the aim of changing the ethnic composition of areas within their territories" (Helsinki Decisions 1992: VI 23 and 27). But prohibitions on resettling people (that is, ethnic cleansing) do not preclude deliberate state settlement policies—that is, providing financial incentives (such as free land or lower taxes) to people who move into a minority's homeland.

11. My focus here is on groups that demonstrate a desire for TA, as reflected for example in consistently high levels of support for politicians or political parties that campaign for TA. We can call these "mobilized" national minorities, since their members have demonstrated consistent support for typically nationalist goals of autonomy and official language rights. The emergence of such mobilized national minorities is of course the result of political contestation. National minorities do not enter the world with a fully formed nationalist consciousness; they are constructed by ethnic entrepreneurs and ethnic elites who seek to persuade enough of their members that it makes sense to mobilize politically as a national minority for national goals. In some cases these attempts to generate a nationalist consciousness among the members of a minority have failed. One case in Western Europe is the Frisians in the Netherlands. From a historical viewpoint, they have as much claim to be a distinct "nation" as any other ethnonational group in Europe. Yet attempts by Frisian elites to persuade people of Frisian descent or people living in historic Friesland that they should support nationalist political objectives have repeatedly failed. This is of course fully acceptable from a liberal point of view. National minorities may have a *right* to mobilize for territorial autonomy, but they certainly have no *duty* to do so. Whether claims for territorial auton-

omy are advanced should be determined by the wishes of the group's members, through free democratic debate and contestation.

My focus here is on how European states deal with those groups that have demonstrated a desire for territorial autonomy—that is, in which nationalist political leaders have succeeded in a free and democratic debate in gaining the support of a majority of the members of the group. I am not assuming that such nationalist constructions will (or should) succeed. Their success has to be explained, not simply taken as a given, just as the failure of the nationalists in Friesland has to be explained, rather than taken as somehow normal or natural. My project in this chapter is not to explain the success or failure of particular acts of nationalist construction, but rather to explore how states should respond to the cases of successful mobilization, in which the members of national minority groups have shown consistently high levels of support for nationalist objectives. These cases are the "problem" to which European organizations have been seeking a solution through the adoption of international norms of minority rights.

12. For a defense of this claim, see my "Justice and Security in the Accommodation of Minority Nationalism," in Alain Dieckhoff, ed., *The Politics of Belonging: Nationalism, Liberalism and Pluralism* (New York: Lexington, 2004), 127–54.

13. S. James Anaya, *Indigenous Peoples in International Law* (Oxford: Oxford University Press, 1996).

14. Indeed, the most influential commentator on the international law on indigenous rights accepts that other national groups should also be able to claim rights to internal self-determination (Anaya, *Indigenous Peoples*). For a detailed discussion of the similarities and differences between indigenous peoples and national minorities, see my *Politics in the Vernacular*, chap. 6. It is worth noting that organizations representing one national minority in Eastern Europe—namely, the Crimean Tatars—have explicitly defined themselves as an "indigenous people" for the purposes of international law.

15. Hague Recommendations on Education Rights of National Minorities (1996); Oslo Recommendations on Linguistic Rights of National Minorities (1998); Lund Recommendations on Effective Participation of National Minorities (1999).

16. European Commission for Democracy through Law, *Opinion of the Venice Commission on the Interpretation of Article 11 of the draft protocol to the European Convention on Human Rights appended to Recommendation 1201* (Strasbourg: Council of Europe, 1996).

17. Claus Offe, "'Homogeneity' and Constitutional Democracy: Coping with Identity Conflicts with Group Rights," *Journal of Political Philosophy* 6:2 (1998): 113–41; Claus Offe, "Political Liberalism, Group Rights and the Politics of Fear and Trust," *Studies in East European Thought* 53:3 (2001): 167–82.

18. I dispute Offe's claim that escalation and proliferation are inherent dangers of TA in "The Impact of Group Rights on Fear and Trust: A Response to Offe," *Hagar: International Social Science Review* 3:1 (2002): 19–36.

19. This is one of the factors that contribute to the general "securitization" of state-minority relations in postcommunist Europe (discussed further in my "Justice and Security"). It is interesting that even when national minorities in the West are linked by ethnicity to a neighboring state, they do not today raise fears of disloyalty or security. The French in Switzerland or Belgium are not seen as a fifth column for France; the Flemish are not seen as a fifth column for the Netherlands. Even the Germans in Belgium, who have historically collaborated with Germany's aggression against

Belgium, are no longer viewed that way. This is testament to the extraordinary success of the EU and NATO in "desecuritizing" ethnic relations in Western Europe.

20. This is particularly true of those countries, like Romania or Turkey, influenced by the French Jacobin tradition.

21. Max van der Stoel, *Peace and Stability through Human and Minority Rights: Speeches by the OSCE High Commissioner on National Minorities* (Baden-Baden: Nomos Verlagsgesellschaft, 1999), 111.

22. Chandler, "OSCE," 66–68; Stuart Ford, "OSCE National Minority Rights in the United States: The Limits of Conflict Resolution," *Suffolk Transnational Law Review* 23:1 (1999): 49.

23. A similar approach was under way at the United Nations. The UN's 1992 Declaration on the Rights of Persons Belonging to National or Ethnic, Religious and Linguistic Minorities was similarly an attempt to expand and strengthen Article 27.

24. 1966 International Covenant on Civil and Political Rights (ICCPR), Art. 27.

25. Steven Wheatley, "Minority Rights and Political Accommodation in the 'New' Europe," *European Law Review* 22 supplement (1997): 40. For example, although these norms often allow minorities to submit documents to public authorities in their language, the norms do not require that the minorities get an answer in their own language.

26. Postcommunist countries believe they are much more closely monitored for compliance with these norms than Western countries such as France or Greece, and that they are criticized for engaging in practices that occur unnoted in the West (Steven Ratner, "Does International Law Matter in Preventing Ethnic Conflicts?" *New York University Journal of International Law and Politics* 32:3 (2000): 591–698; Cohen, *Conflict Prevention*).

27. I take the phrase from Ina Druviete ("Linguistic Human Rights in the Baltic States," *International Journal of the Sociology of Language* 127 (1997): 161–85), although she was describing the attitude of the Soviet Union to minority languages.

28. One possible exception to this generalization is the Roma. Some commentators speculate that issues relating to the Roma could become sources of violence and instability, even though the Roma have not shown an interest in territorial autonomy or in creating their own separate public institutions. European organizations are therefore devoting much time and effort to examining state policies toward the Roma. But the current FCNM/OSCE norms were not intended to deal with the situation of the Roma. Indeed, the OSCE has recently recommended the adoption of a separate Romani Rights Charter.

29. There is no conceptual or philosophical reason that a right to enjoy one's culture cannot be interpreted in such a robust way as to support claims to territorial autonomy or official language status. This is precisely what various "liberal nationalist" political theorists have done in their writings. The idea of a right to culture is invoked by writers like Yael Tamir and Joseph Raz as the basis for their defense of a right to national self-determination (Yael Tamir, *Liberal Nationalism* [Princeton: Princeton University Press, 1993]; Avishai Margalit and Joseph Raz, "National Self-Determination," *Journal of Philosophy* 87:9 [1990]: 439–61). But, politically speaking, there is no chance that such a "nationalist" reading of a right to culture will be adopted in international law. As we have seen, the whole idea underlying the Article 27 right to enjoy one's culture was to provide an alternative to the Article 1 right of national self-determination.

30. Prior to 1989, the EU tacitly allowed Greece to persecute its minorities, and NATO allowed Turkey to persecute its minorities (Judy Batt and J. Amato, "Minority Rights and EU Enlargement to the East" [Florence: European University Institute, RSC Policy Paper #98/5, 1998]).

31. When Western governments were deciding whether to intervene in Kosovo, an American columnist famously said, "[G]ive war a chance." War is bad, he said, but it is important for both sides to learn the hard way that they cannot defeat the other, and so accept the need to sit down and negotiate a compromise. A more modest version of the same idea is defended by Adam Burgess. He says we should "give assimilation a chance" (Burgess, "Critical Reflections"). Assimilationist policies in post-communist Europe might be unpleasant, and might fail, but it is important for states (and dominant groups) to learn the limits of their capacities, and the strength of minority resistance, and so accept the necessity of coming to some settlement with their minorities.

32. Martin Estebanez, "The High Commissioner on National Minorities: Development of the Mandate," in Michael Bothe et al., eds., *The OSCE in the Maintenance of Peace and Security* (The Hague: Kluwer, 1997): 123–65; van der Stoel, *Peace and Stability*.

33. For a more detailed discussion of these two tracks, see Will Kymlicka and Magda Opalski, eds. *Can Liberal Pluralism Be Exported? Western Political Theory and Ethnic Relations in Eastern Europe* (Oxford: Oxford University Press, 2001), 369–86.

34. Chandler, "OSCE," 68; cf. "Minorities should not be confronted with the situation that the international community will only respond to their concerns if there is a conflict. Such an approach could easily backfire and generate more conflicts than it resolves. An objective, impartial and non-selective approach to minorities, involving the application of minority standards across the board, must therefore remain a crucial part" (Alfredsson and Turk, "International Mechanisms," 176–77).

35. Zaagman, *Conflict Prevention, 253n84.*

36. In all of these cases except Crimea, the minority seized power through an armed uprising. In the case of Crimea, the Ukrainian state barely existed on Crimean territory, and so the Russians did not have to take up arms to overthrow the existing state structure. They simply held an illegal referendum on autonomy and then started governing themselves.

37. Van der Stoel, *Peace and Stability*, 26; John Packer, "Autonomy within the OSCE: The Case of Crimea," in Markku Suksi, ed., *Autonomy: Applications and Implications* (The Hague: Kluwer, 1998), 295–316.

38. Van der Stoel, *Peace and Stability*, 25.

39. "The participating States will respect the right of persons belonging to national minorities to effective participation in public affairs, including participation in the affairs relating to the protection and promotion of the identity of such minorities" (OSCE Copenhagen Declaration, 1990, Article 35). "The Parties shall create the conditions necessary for the effective participation of persons belonging to national minorities in cultural, social and economic life and in public affairs, in particular those affecting them" (FCNM, 1995, Article 15).

40. Walter Kemp, "Applying the Nationality Principle: Handle with Care," *Journal on Ethnopolitics and Minority Issues in Europe* 4 (2002).

41. Minority Rights Group, *World Report on Minorities* (London: Minority Rights Group, 1997), 157.

42. Annelies Verstichel argues that the Advisory Committee examining conformity with the FCNM has implicitly adopted a non-retrogression clause regarding autonomy ("Elaborating a Catalogue of Best Practices of Effective Participation of National Minorities," *European Yearbook of Minorities Issues* 2002:3). Similarly, Sian Lewis-Anthony argues that the jurisprudence regarding Article 3 of the First Protocol of the European Convention of Human Rights can be extrapolated to protect existing forms of autonomy ("Autonomy and the Council of Europe—With Special Reference to the Application of Article 3 of the First Protocol of the European Convention on Human Rights," in Markku Suksi, ed., *Autonomy: Applications and Implications* [The Hague: Kluwer, 1998], 317–42). At a more philosophical level, Allen Buchanan has argued that there should be international protections for existing forms of TA, but denies that there should be norms supporting claims for TA by groups that do not yet have it (*Justice, Legitimacy and Self-Determination* [Oxford: Oxford University Press, 2004]).

43. For a more optimistic view of the potential of the right to effective participation to overcome this impasse, see Verstichel, "Elaborating a Catalogue"; and Marc Weller's report "Filling the Frame: 5th Anniversary of the Entry into Force of the Framework Convention for the Protection of National Minorities" (Strasbourg: Council of Europe, 30–31 October 2003).

44. Conversely, several commentators argue that some of the more intractable conflicts in the West, such as those in Northern Ireland and Cyprus, cannot be resolved by purely domestic procedures and negotiations, and that the international community needs to play a more active role. See the essays in Michael Keating and John McGarry, eds., *Minority Nationalism and the Changing International Order* (Oxford: Oxford University Press, 2001).

45. For a discussion of some of the factors that have helped make these settlements domestically self-sustaining and self-enhancing, see my "Canadian Multiculturalism in Historical and Comparative Perspective," *Constitutional Forum* 13:1 (2003): 1–8.

46. The role of violence is obvious in Northern Ireland, the Basque Country, Cyprus, and Corsica, but there were also low-level acts of violence in Quebec and South Tyrol (for example, bombings of state property like mailboxes or energy pylons). The knowledge that some members of the minority were willing to resort to violence undoubtedly concentrated the mind of the state. As Stephen Deets puts it, "Across Europe, autonomy came out of specific historical and political contexts, and it is far easier to discuss the political calculations and the desire to quell bombing campaigns that went into autonomy decisions than it is to point to a clear acceptance of principles of justice for minorities" ("Liberal Pluralism: Does the West Have Any to Export?" *Journal on Ethnopolitics and Minority Issues in Europe* 4 [2002]).

47. Yet the case of indigenous peoples shows what can be achieved on these issues through international law where there is a political commitment to do so.

48. Or so I argue in *Can Liberal Pluralism Be Exported?*

Conclusion

1. Ian Bremmer, "Preface," in Ian Bremmer and Ray Taras, eds., *Nations and Politics in the Soviet Successor States* (Cambridge: Cambridge University Press, 1993), xxiii.

2. The chapters in the volume concentrate on the European postcommunist states rather than on the Caucasus or Central Asia. Unless otherwise noted, here the term

Eastern Europe will not include the latter regions. Russia is a problematic case, of course. Also, at the time of final revision of this conclusion (September 2004), Putin was reorganizing center-periphery relations in the wake of the Beslan massacre. Whether Russia will be taking a much different path from that of the rest of the Eastern European states is a vital question, but beyond the scope of this Conclusion. More broadly, whether the term "Eastern Europe" should lump together Russia, Moldova, Ukraine, and Belarus with the states of the Balkans, the Baltic region, and Central Europe is another difficult issue, which this Conclusion may help address.

3. Alan Kuperman is doing some of the best work on the Kosovo case and the issue in general. See "Tragic Challenges and the Moral Hazard of Humanitarian Intervention: How and Why Ethnic Groups Provoke Genocidal Retaliation," unpublished dissertation (Cambridge, MA: MIT, 2002).

4. Valery Tishkov, *Ethnicity, Nationalism, and Conflict in and after the Soviet Union: The Mind Aflame* (London: Sage Publications, 1997), 5. Tishkov is quoting Yuri Semenov, "E'tnologia i Gnoseologia" (Ethnology and Gnoseology), *Etnograficheskoe Obozrenie*, no. 6 (November–December 1992): 3–20.

5. See Clifford Geertz, *The Interpretation of Cultures* (New York: Basic Books, 1973), and Edward Shils, "Primordial, Personal, Sacred, and Civil Ties," *British Journal of Sociology* 8 (2) 1957: 130–45, for classic statements of the primordial treatment of ethnic groups.

6. For a broad discussion of the legacy of Communism, see Zoltan Barany and Ivan Volgyes, eds., *The Legacies of Communism in Eastern Europe* (Baltimore: Johns Hopkins University Press, 1995).

7. The key feature here is the rapid and visible change in economic fortunes in the postcommunist era. The relationship between economic leveling and ethnic awareness may be more complex. It seems plausible to hypothesize that economic leveling, by reducing one form of group awareness, heightens the likelihood that other forms of identity, such as ethnicity, may become the focus of social comparison (see chapter 4 for more on economic leveling). As the anonymous reviewer of this Conclusion pointed out, in some cases there may be a two-stage process in which economic leveling in the Communist period sharpened ethnic awareness, and economic disparities in the postcommunist period may transform this awareness into antagonism.

8. The most concise treatment of the security dilemma in ethnic wars is Barry Posen, "The Security Dilemma and Ethnic Conflict," *Survival* 35 (1) spring 1993: 27–47.

9. See Monica Toft, *The Geography of Ethnic Violence: Identity, Interests, and the Indivisibility of Territory* (Princeton: Princeton University Press, 2003).

10. For a discussion of the various effects of these institutions, see Valerie Bunce, *Subversive Institutions: The Design and Destruction of Socialism and the State* (Cambridge: Cambridge University Press, 1999).

11. The assumptions listed have been clearly articulated in a collective project entitled "Collective Approaches to Ethnic Groups" led by Kanchan Chandra at the Massachusetts Institute of Technology. Many who would consider themselves constructivists would of course disagree with some of these assumptions.

12. David D. Laitin, *Identity in Formation: The Russian-Speaking Populations in the Near Abroad* (Ithaca: Cornell University Press, 1998).

13. Daniel Posner, *Institutions and Ethnic Politics in Africa*, forthcoming, Cambridge University Press.

14. This process was especially pronounced in Yugoslavia. For example, Sabrina Ramet felt comfortable in describing politics among the federal units in Yugoslavia in terms of balance of power relations usually reserved for the analysis of independent states in the international system. See Sabrina Ramet, *Nationalism and Federalism in Yugoslavia, 1962–1991* (Bloomington: Indiana University Press, 1992).

15. See Rogers Brubaker, *Nationalism Reframed: Nationhood and the National Question in the New Europe* (Cambridge: Cambridge University Press, 1996).

16. Steve Van Evera has discussed the effects of literacy and violence in hardening identities in "Primordialism Lives!" *Newsletter of the Organized Section in Comparative Politics of the American Political Science Association* 12 (1) winter 2001: 20–22.

CONTRIBUTORS

Zoltan Barany is the Frank C. Erwin Jr. Centennial Professor of Government at the University of Texas. His recent books are *The Future of NATO Expansion* (2003), *The East European Gypsies: Regime Change, Marginality, and Ethnopolitics* (2002), and, as co-editor, *Russian Politics: Challenges of Democratization* (2001) and *Dilemmas of Transition: The Hungarian Experience* (1999).

Mark R. Beissinger is the Glenn B. and Cleone Orr Hawkins Professor of Political Science at the University of Wisconsin, Madison. Among his books are the multiple-award-winning *Nationalist Mobilization and the Collapse of the Soviet State* (2002), *Scientific Management, Socialist Discipline, and Soviet Power* (1988), and, as co-editor, *Beyond State Crisis? Postcolonial Africa and Post-Soviet Eurasia Compared* (2002).

Daniel Chirot is Professor of Sociology and International Studies at the University of Washington. His recent books include *Modern Tyrants: The Power and Prevalence of Evil in Our Age* (1996), *How Societies Change* (1994), and, as co-editor, *Ethnopolitical Warfare: Causes, Consequences, and Possible Solutions* (2001) and *Essential Outsiders: Chinese and Jews in the Modern Transformation of Southeast Asia and Central Europe* (1997).

Charles King is Chair of the Faculty and Ion Ratiu Associate Professor in the School of Foreign Service at Georgetown University, with a joint appointment in the Department of Government. His books include *The Black Sea: A History* (2004) and *The Moldovans* (2000).

Will Kymlicka holds the Canada Research Chair in Political Philosophy at Queen's University in Kingston, Ontario. His many books include *Contemporary Political Philosophy* (2002), *Politics in the Vernacular: Nationalism, Multiculturalism, and Citizenship* (2001), *Multicultural Citizenship: A Liberal Theory of Minority Rights* (1995), *Liberalism, Community, and Culture* (1989), and, as co-editor, *Language Rights and Political Theory* (2003) and *Can*

Liberal Pluralism Be Exported? Western Political Theory and Ethnic Relations in Eastern Europe (2001).

David D. Laitin is the James T. Watkins IV and Elise V. Watkins Professor of Political Science at Stanford University. His books include the award-winning *Identity in Formation: The Russian-Speaking Populations in the Near Abroad* (1998), *Language Repertoires and State Construction in Africa* (1992), and *Hegemony and Culture: The Politics of Religious Change among the Yoruba* (1986).

Robert G. Moser is Associate Professor of Government at the University of Texas. He is the author of *Unexpected Outcomes: Electoral Systems, Political Parties, and Representation in Russia* (2001) and the co-editor of *Russian Politics: Challenges of Democratization* (2001).

Roger D. Petersen is Associate Professor of Political Science at the Massachusetts Institute of Technology. He is the author of *Understanding Ethnic Violence* (2002) and *Resistance and Rebellion: Lessons from Eastern Europe* (2001) and the co-editor of *Critical Comparisons in Politics and Culture* (1999).

Ronald Grigor Suny is Professor of Political Science and History at the University of Chicago. Among his many books are *The Soviet Experiment: Russia, the Soviet Union, and the Successor States* (1998), *The Revenge of the Past: Nationalism, Revolution, and the Collapse of the Soviet Union* (1993), and, as co-editor, *A State of Nations: Empire and Nation-Making in the Age of Lenin and Stalin* (2001) and *Intellectuals and the Articulation of the Nation* (1999).

INDEX

DATE DUE

GAYLORD			PRINTED IN U.S.A.